Pelican Books

The Mind

Anthony Smith, science journalist and writer, was born
in 1926. He was educated at the Dragon School, Oxford,
and at Blundell's School, Devon; he graduated in
Zoology at Balliol College, Oxford, in 1951. As a
journalist, he has worked on the *Manchester Guardian*,
first in 1953 and then again in 1956, and also on *Drum* in
Africa. He joined the *Daily Telegraph* as science
correspondent in 1957 and left in 1963 to write *The Body*
(Penguin, 1970). A Scientific Fellow of the Zoological
Society, he is also the author of *Blind White Fish in
Persia* (1953), *Sea Never Dry* (1958), *High Street Africa*
(1961), *Throw Out Two Hands* (1963), *The Seasons*
(1970; Pelican edition 1973), *The Dangerous Sort* (1970),
Mato Grosso (1971), *Beside the Seaside* (1972), *Good
Beach Guide* (with Jill Southam, 1973; Penguin edition
also 1973), *The Human Pedigree* (1975), *Animals on
View* (1977), *Wilderness* (1978), *A Persian Quarter
Century* (1979), *A Sideways Look* (1983) and *Smith and
Son* (1984). *The Body*, first published in 1968, has been
translated into thirteen languages. Anthony Smith, who
is married, with a son and two daughters, likes to travel,
and enjoys lighter-than-air flying in his spare time.

The Mind

Anthony Smith

PENGUIN BOOKS

Penguin Books Ltd, Harmondsworth, Middlesex, England
Viking Penguin Inc., 40 West 23rd Street, New York, New York 10010, U.S.A.
Penguin Books Australia Ltd, Ringwood, Victoria, Australia
Penguin Books Canada Ltd, 2801 John Street, Markham, Ontario, Canada L3R 1B4
Penguin Books (N.Z.) Ltd, 182–190 Wairau Road, Auckland 10, New Zealand

First published by Hodder and Stoughton Ltd 1984
First published in the United States of America by the Viking Press 1984
Published in Pelican Books 1985

Made and printed in Great Britain by
Cox and Wyman Ltd, Reading
Typeset in Times

Everything should be made as simple as possible, but not simpler – Albert Einstein

Tell me, I'll forget. Show me, I may remember. But involve me and I'll understand – Chinese proverb

Foreword

A man will turn over half a library to make one book
— Samuel Johnson

There is my truth; now tell me yours
— Friedrich Nietzsche

There are problems in writing a book on general science. The precision and qualification of scientific writing have to be translated into accurate but more digestible generalisation. Similarly, scientific words, however definite in their definitions, can obscure if their meaning is unfamiliar. Olfaction is smell, and smell is preferable, but anosmia is being without a sense of smell and has no other easy word. So too, again and again in this book. The strange terms cannot be avoided, and should not always be avoided, but a plethora of them can clog most disconcertingly.

So too can units of measurement, if not generally known. Is 30 centimetres more widely understood – yet – than a foot? Is 37°C a more familiar unit than 98°F, or is it best to mention only human body heat? And what of 10^9? Is that 1,000,000,000 or a thousand million, the population of China (which it is) or twenty times the British total (which it also is) or just 10^9 without need for more embellishment? I have used no rules but have made use of that other yardstick which changes every rule as seems preferable at the time. One millimetre can look better, and read better, than one twenty-fifth of an inch. A thousand paces can be preferred to a thousand yards or somewhat fewer metres. And cycles are preferable to hertz (almost) any day. The irregularities may irritate, but were paved with good intentions.

There is a logic both to the chapter order in this book and to its five parts, but certain words and explanations have to wait, so to speak, until their proper time. For example, left-handedness may first be mentioned in Evolution and reappear in other chapters, but it cannot be detailed properly except under Dominance where the brain's method of dealing with its two demanding halves is described. The Index should act as guide in this respect, with the entry involving most pages (and in bold type) referring to the major description in the text. Cross-references are also frequent, partly to link up with the fullest description and to help those who may wish to skip about and find their own reading order.

Besides, I have no idea which chapters will be read first, and, therefore, when terms like axon, neuron, synapse, dominance or dementia will be first encountered. (A previous book, *The Body*, always fell open at Puberty when adolescents picked it up.) I do not know where this volume will first be read – by youngsters, oldsters, or whoever. Consequently, as the words have to be understood if they are to be used at all, some sort of mini-definition is often necessary. This may be repetitive, but the habit is hopefully preferable to its alternative, which is defining everything once only and expecting that explanation to be encountered in its due and proper place. Often, to lessen the blow of repeated definitions, they are put in parentheses or between dashes to help to speed the flow. Such bracketings are also used where extra information may be helpful (an author's name, a place, another kind of measurement) but is not vital to the value of the phrase.

The Mind is unashamedly biological. Mankind did not spring, fully-fashioned, into the arena, but is one more product of the animal kingdom. Therefore, what happened to human ancestors, and what happens neurologically in animals, are likely to relate to the human condition. *Homo sapiens* is unlike every other species, but human nerve cells are seemingly identical to those in every other kind of nervous system. Humans are part of biology. Therefore, biology is, when and where need be, an integral part of this book.

Textbooks frequently keep the brain and its nervous system entirely within one compartment, with nothing at all about neurology seeping into any other chapter. An alternate strategy is to make such seepage happen everywhere, because the nervous system influences, controls, or is influenced by every other system. This book attempts to blend the two approaches. Everything is seen, so to speak, from the brain's point of view. Evolution was, therefore, a matter largely of change to the brain. Growth is brain growth, and comparative anatomy is the differences between nervous systems in the animal kingdom. Similarly vision is not so much what the eye does, but what the brain does with information from the eye. There are many kinds of physical abnormality, but only some affect the brain. There is plenty of damage to the body as a whole, but only some of it assaults the nervous system – palsy, stroke, schizophrenia, head injury, Parkinsonism, migraine, and so forth. Detailing everything from the brain's point of view means a wide range of interest. This book is large and wide, and so it should be.

Scientific papers are always peppered with references, full credit being given to every author, and to the title, and the journal, and its volume and page number. The facts are important, of course, but not in a work of general science. In the main I have identified only certain statements, if particularly novel, exciting, revolutionary, well-phrased, or bizarre, and then usually with one name. Or, on occasion, a place of origin. Or, just occasionally, a bit of both. I like to give credit but prefer a fluent text. If any of these prejudices, mannerisms and preferences fail to make more sense out of the subject matter I apologise here and now for the irritation they will surely cause.

Contents

INTRODUCTION   xv

PART I

1. EVOLUTION   2
    Brain size and capability / Growth / Primitive man /
    Origin of speech / The hand / Dexterity / Cultural
    evolution

2. ANIMAL ANATOMY   19
    Ascaris and *Aplysia* / Other invertebrates / Amphioxus /
    Fish / Amphibia / Reptiles / Birds / Mammals / *Homo
    sapiens*

3. GROWTH   30
    Embryology in general / Human foetal development /
    Neural calendar (before birth) / Prematurity / Reflexes /
    The skull / Growth after birth / Neural calendar (part
    II) / Brain damage / Head size, brain size

PART II

4. ANATOMY   58
    History / Naming of parts / Cerebral hemispheres / The
    lobes / The ventricles / Meninges / Cranial nerves /
    Spinal nerves / The plexuses / Blood supply

5. THE AUTONOMIC   85
    Sympathetic and parasympathetic / Plexuses / Adrenals /
    Pituitary / Thyroid / Hypothalamus

6. PHYSIOLOGY   95
    The neuron / Impulses / Conduction time / Synapse /
    Neuro-transmitters / Brain waves / Feedback /
    Blood–brain barrier

PART III

7. DOMINANCE   110
    Symmetry and asymmetry / Right side, left side /
    Dominant hemisphere / Split-brain / Hemispherectomy /
    Left hand, right hand / Left-sided speech / Digital
    dexterity

8. CONSCIOUSNESS   127
    Definition / Unconsciousness / Concussion / Stupor /
    Coma / Sleep / Active and normal / Dreams / Hypnosis /
    Convulsion / Epilepsy

9. ABILITY   146
    Learning / Intelligence / IQ / Speech / Language /
    Reading / Music

10. MEMORY   164
    Definition / Understanding of memory / Theories /
    Short term, long term / Amnesia / Retrograde,
    post-traumatic / The mnemonists

11. SENSES   175
    Seeing / Hearing / Smelling / Tasting / Touching / Hot,
    cold, pressure / Proprioception / Pain / Phantom limbs /
    Enkephalins and endorphins

PART IV

12. ABNORMAL ABILITY   204
    Genius / Precociousness / Prodigy / Norbert Wiener /
    Education / Mental deficiency / Mental institutions /
    Causes of retardation

13. MALFORMATION   222
    Neural tube defects / Spina bifida / Anencephaly /
    Hydrocephalus / Hydrancephalics / Down's syndrome /
    Huntington's chorea

Contents

14. DAMAGE 240
Definition / Cerebral palsy / Paraplegia / Head injury /
Phineas Gage and Co. / War wounds / Lyova Zasetsky /
Boxing / Other sports / Headache / Migraine /
Self-damage / Depression / Schizophrenia /
Parkinsonism / Stroke / Tumour

PART V

15. THE OLD BRAIN 282
Deterioration / Senility / Senile dementia / Other
ageing illness / Brain death / The new criteria /
Transplantation needs / Lawful death / Future ruling

16. POSTSCRIPT 308
Neurology in general / Early lobotomy / Modern
psychosurgery / Electroconvulsive therapy / Alcohol /
Drugs / Computers / Finale

INDEX 323

Introduction

An instrument has been developed in advance of the needs
of its possessor
                                        – Alfred Russel Wallace

It is, so say humans, the most important thing in the world, but it
looks as interesting as intestines, and indeed was frequently drawn
formerly as if intestinal, a tube from start to finish. Our forefathers
were more intrigued by the pulsing heart, the moody spleen, the
colour-changing liver, the wandering and peristaltic gut. Even
urine, in their opinion, held more excitement than the brain.
Modern anatomy books tend to follow suit, placing 'the nervous
system' anywhere but first among their chapter headings. They
might almost be echoing Aristotle who thought it a cooling system,
with the mucus of a runny nose proving this activity. Indeed some
modern medical texts, seemingly determined to banish all possible
interest, are forthrightly modest when confronted by the ultimate
endeavour of neuroanatomy: 'The brain is that part of the nervous
system enclosed by the skull.' We, who are equipped with this
evolutionary miracle, do likewise in our fashion and are, in general, about as good at naming its parts as in pinpointing mountains on
the moon. Yet the brain has made us. It is not our guts or liver that
has created *sapiens*. It is not our ordinary heart or our standard
lungs that have given us the power to make books, write music, or
destroy all life on planet Earth. It is the human brain.
However, its appearance does not excite. Externally there is
nothing to suggest ability of any kind, let alone the highest form of
intelligence, of thought and memory, of the rational and irrational
yet devised in the hurly-burly of evolution. It does not seem to be
what it is; but that is not its only paradox. A minute injury to the
brain can produce crippling effects, such as blindness, but a
crowbar can pass through it with only modest alterations to personality. (A recent Boston victim of this mishap walked away from
hospital 'with a slight limp'.) The human brain is neither the largest
among animals (those of elephants are four times larger while the
sperm whale's is six times human size), nor is it the largest by
comparison with body-size (many monkeys double our proportion). It consists of the same parts arranged in a similar manner as
in all vertebrate brains, yet is incomparably superior. The largest

apes have brains about half the size of those of men and yet, in human terms, all apes are imbeciles. Conversely some people have brains twice the size of other people's brains, and are not more intelligent. Indeed the largest human brains are often owned by idiots.

It is not even known why we are so clever, and why the brain reached its current size more than a hundred thousand years ago. Most of us do not tap the potential of our incredible brain power. Most of our ancestors, in hunter-gatherer communities several thousand generations before now, probably made even fewer demands upon their similarly-sized central nervous systems. And yet our modern brain evolved from them. Our powers, that have shaped computers, put footprints on the moon, and given us the wit to examine where even wisdom comes from, were created by natural selection for primitives who could hammer flint and stone, chase animals, find fruits and be little more than clever apes. They could speak, probably, but so can almost all of us, both the brilliant and the dullards of our community. Moreover, there are no hints as yet, in biopsy or autopsy, if someone's brain is a good example of its kind or not.

Mind Somehow or other in the past, and at some time or other, a nervous system became a mindful system. This world we know was initially lifeless and mindless. Life arose some four thousand million years ago, and later came mind; but, as Sir Karl Popper has written, we have not 'the slightest idea on which evolutionary level mind emerges'. Professor Steven Rose has posed the same kind of question: 'At what evolutionary stage does recognisable brain-controlled behaviour develop in an organism, and when does consciousness arise?' The condition of mind is not some curious extra, tacked on to distinguish man from all the animals, as was formerly believed. Without consciousness – of a kind – there cannot be conscious choices. Many animals use both kinds of behavioural programme, those that are closed (instinctive) and those that are open (choice). Evolution can operate through either of them, but the prime advantage of the latter course is that actual trial and error can be preceded by imagined trial and error. Is the unpleasant anticipation (work, pain, loss, etc.) greater or less than the pleasant anticipation (food, sex, warmth, etc.)? We each possess what the author John Hillaby called a skull projectionist, always ready to screen for our eyes only a short one-reeler that forecasts or retells a particular happening.

What we do not know, and cannot know, is whether we are just more intelligent than the animals or operating on quite a different plane. Are we self-conscious when they are not? Do we have a style of mind that they do not, and do we have soul when they have nothing of the kind? We do not consider that our stomachs are on a higher level, or our blood, or any other part of us. Of course cows can digest grass when we cannot, and dolphins can swim ten times faster than we do, but this is only a variation of the basic theme, or so we say. When it comes to the brain, to our particular lump of neural tissue, neither the largest nor biggest in proportion, we do frequently assume it to be not just an extension of other lumps but something quite unique. It has a soul, we say, and this makes a difference between the animals and us.

In the past the soul/mind was said to be located in the heart, in the ventricles (of the brain), in the pineal gland, in the stomach, in the blood, in the corpus callosum (between the hemispheres) and in the medulla spinalis (below the base of the brain). The most famous enthusiasts for each were Aristotle, Galen, Descartes, von Helmont, Harvey, Willis, Prochaska, and Pflüger. Part of the old confusion, and of the continuing philosophical discussion on the subject of mind, is that differing languages do not have equivalent words. In English there are three distinct nouns: mind, soul, spirit. In French there are not; mind is missing and Descartes himself used '*l'esprit*' to cover this meaning. (My French dictionary gives '*esprit, intelligence, tête*' as translations for the English 'mind'.) The Russian language is also without 'mind', which led to considerable misunderstanding between Charles Sherrington and Ivan Pavlov. To overcome this problem the Russian word *ym*, previously used for mind in Pavlov's laboratories, was dropped and replaced by 'higher nervous activity'.

This term has been welcomed by most neurologists. It frees them from eternal argument about the relationship between body and mind, eternal because many believe the argument to be insoluble. The soul is an abstraction and the brain is an organ. To speak of the mind is to blend the two. If mind means conscious self that need only be a function of the brain, something achieved in evolution, of advantage to the individual or the species. If, on the other hand, mind is equivalent to soul, a thing over and above the physics and chemistry of a brain that can exist without a body, a lot of people will not believe in it, preferring to stick to earthly laws. No wonder, faced with such opposing meanings, that Pavlov preferred to speak of higher nervous activity. *Ym* and mind were shelved.

And then dusted off to be the title of this book. Plainly an apologia or explanation is necessary. I think the best answer lies in our language. Words are always more than their dictionary definitions. They work in contexts, vary with time, and change according both to the user and the one they are used upon. To speak of someone's brain (or even of their brains, being uncertain if singular or plural) is to tell of their cleverness – or lack of it, of the organ in their cranium, the functional head of their nervous system. The word is mainly anatomical, conjuring up lobes, gyri, sulci, synapses. What it does not do, in my opinion, is to make us think as immediately of dreams, speech, depression, left-handedness, headache, alcohol, anaesthesia, music, dyslexia, thirst, phantom pain, taste – to name a ranging few. To my mind (and not to my brain) such words, symptoms, events are more likely to arise as thought if Mind is used instead of Brain. Mind is more embracing, encompassing both brain and brain's activity. Of the two words it is the bigger, or so I believe. Therefore this book is *The Mind* rather than *The Brain*. I think everything the brain does, and is, and might become is of interest, and I wanted the book to range as widely as possible. Pavlov might have preferred 'higher nervous activity' but I settled for *The Mind*.

A further point of introduction, basic or naive, is that we have only our brain with which to puzzle out our mind. Or rather we have just part of it, our conscious intellect, with which to understand the whole of it. This point, most fundamental, cannot be made about anything else. The greatest field of biological research for the future is the human brain, as Sir Macfarlane Burnet phrased it, and as most of us would readily concur. The strangeness is that the human brain itself is both the means and end of this endeavour. The brain must find out what it is.

No better time has ever existed for that finding out. Neurology is advancing faster than ever before. There was the age of physics, as atoms were first split and awesome nuclear power revealed itself. Then came molecular biology, spurred on by the model of DNA. And now neurology is having its form of heyday. The 1970s will seem like dark ages when this current decade comes to its end. Even those not working in the field of brain research concede this point. Those involved in it are delighted to be working in such a subject at such a time.

There is a personal addendum to this general statement. When I had finished writing *The Body* in the late 1960s it was almost inevitable that I should think of its corollary, the mind. Indeed, had I not experienced this thought myself, others would have been – and were – quick to suggest it for me. I began to collect relevant information, but in lacklustre fashion. The facts were exciting, but did not glow. However, as the 1970s advanced, and as the various files began to swell, the whole mood of the subject changed. So many issues suddenly bubbled to the surface, the brain-death controversy, psychosurgery, the new drugs. The brain's own drugs, the enkephalins and endorphins, abruptly emerged, as if from nowhere. Vision was no longer a matter of what the eyes did, but of what the brain did with impulses from the eyes. The hydrocephalics, seemingly damaged to no avail, started acquiring university degrees, and upset most applecarts in the process. Neurology *had* arrived, or had entered a phase never known before. *The Mind* was, therefore, written without delay, or rather in the three busy years from first research to final word.

The human brain *is* finding out what it is, faster than ever before. However, it began a very long time ago. It did not even start with the earliest kinds of men. Its roots go back to the fishes, and of course they too evolved from simpler forms. As with all good stories it is best to begin at the beginning and Evolution is therefore Chapter 1. The human brain has to be seen in its historical perspective, not least by all the human brains who are descendants from the past.

PART ONE

This first part, embracing evolution, animal anatomy, and growth, both sets the scene and introduces human inheritance. When each individual first has the wit to realise he or she possesses a brain, the organ is then complete, a piece of the past, a relative of every other brain, and a thing entirely and uniquely our own. These first three chapters provide the background to that event. Some general statements, about size, weight and capability, act as further introduction.

1. Evolution

Brain size and capability / Growth / Primitive man / Origin of speech / The hand / Dexterity / Cultural evolution

It is the only example of evolution providing a species with an organ which it does not know how to use; a luxury organ, which will take its owner thousands of years to learn to put to proper use – if it ever does

– Arthur Koestler

Anaxagorus indeed asserts that it is his possession of hands that makes man the most intelligent of the animals; but surely the reasonable point of view is that it is because he is the most intelligent animal that he has got hands

– Aristotle, *De partibus animalium*, IV X

The human brain consists of ten to fifteen thousand million nerve cells. (The anatomy books are always more precise, each opting for fourteen or eleven or fifteen billion as if its choice is the true and unassailable figure.) If that kind of number is bewildering, being three times as many as there are human brains alive on this planet, the number of synapses (nerve cell connections) is a thousand times more so, there being about one hundred million million of them, or more than the total number of humans who have ever lived since we acquired this fantastic brain in full measure those thousand centuries ago. Coupled with the nerve cells, supporting and nourishing them, are the glial cells whose number is on a par with the nerve cells that they sustain. By way of comparison, appreciating that such figures can put normal minds in turmoil, the clever little honey bee has about seven thousand nerve cells.

The whole human brain weighs some three pounds in the male and about 10 per cent less in females (or 1,400 grams as against 1,250 grams). This disproportion can seem unfair to women but their brains are relatively bigger, being 2½ per cent of total body weight as against 2 per cent for men. The three-pound weight makes our brain among the lightest of our organs, being very much less than muscle (42 per cent of the total weight for males, 36 per cent for females), much less than the combined total for the 206 bones of the human skeleton, less than the twenty-plus square feet of skin, less than the twenty-eight feet of intestine, less than the eleven pounds or so of blood, and just less than the four pounds of liver. However, it weighs more than the heart (which is one pound), the kidneys (a mere five ounces each), the spleen (six ounces), the pancreas (three ounces), and the lungs (two and a half pounds). A foetus, with its relatively huge head plus brain and its small everything else, is arguably a more accurate representation of *Homo sapiens*, but that big head wanes proportionately as the child grows wiser. There is undoubted paradox about our most remarkable property, all three pounds of it.

There is also conflict over its abilities. On the one hand, and for many a normal day, a particular brain may exhibit precious little intelligence. Its owner may eat what has been set before him, walk to a bus stop, reach work, perform the same repetitive task, return home, eat again and sleep. An animal could do the same. On the other hand there is the musician Hans von Bülow travelling by train from Hamburg to Berlin, reading Stanford's *Irish Symphony*, previously unknown to him, and then conducting it that evening without a score. Some musicians prefer reading a piece of music to hearing the work, claiming that the experience is without the blemishes of an actual performance. Wolfgang Mozart confided that a whole new composition would suddenly arise in his mind. At convenient moments he would translate this entire fabric of rhythm, melody, harmony, counterpoint and tone into the written symbols of a score. For those who have trouble with a telephone number or with a name to fit a face, it is even problematical contemplating the gap between us and them, the normal and the genius. Someone once asked A. C. Aitken, professor at Edinburgh University, to make 4 divided by 47 into a decimal. After four seconds he started and gave another digit every three-quarters of a second: 'point 0851063828787234042553314'. He stopped (after twenty-four seconds), discussed the problem for one minute, and then restarted: '191489' – five-second pause – '361702127659574468. Now that's the repeating point. It starts again with 085. So if that's forty-six places, I'm right.' To many of us such a man is from another planet, particularly in his final comment.

The bizarre fact is that the brains of von Bülow, Mozart and Aitken were inherited from a long line of hunter-gatherers. Why on earth, or even how on earth, did a brain system evolve that could remember symphonies or perform advanced mental arithmetic when its palaeolithic requirements were assuredly less demanding? And why, as the second major conundrum, did the process stop at least 100,000 years ago? Only since then, via population increase, larger and more settled communities, division of labour and a subjugation of nature, has the brain of man begun to realise its potential. Yet it is a prehistoric brain, there being no detectable difference (so far as can be judged from fossils) between then and now, theirs and ours, extremely primitive and very modern man.

The solar system is vast, incomprehensible to most of us, and staggering in its distances, and to mention it in the same breath as our three pounds of brain is apparently to relate like with unlike, a thing colossal with a thing minute. But the bracketing together is fairer than might be imagined. The dimensions that astronomers talk about, and seem to understand, have their parallel in the numbers that neuroanatomists relate, almost in passing, as if these too are understood. Already mentioned are the fifteen billion nerve cells, which is also the numeric total (more or less) of stars in our galaxy. Also mentioned are the synapses, a thousandfold greater, and therefore as plentiful as the stars of a thousand galaxies. Astronomers do use such figures, being more aware than most of the thousands of millions of light years existing between us and the furthest parts of the known universe; but there must be a limit even to their comprehension.

The human brain, I suspect, can confound them, not in its neurons but in the range of its possibilities. Nerve cells are the basic units, but their synapses create a framework for interconnections, for a variety of ways in which one nerve cell may be linked with another, and for that other to be connected with others yet again. The figure of possible connections within our modern brain is as good as infinite. It is certainly larger than the number of atoms presumed to exist in the entire universe and no one, I warrant, can begin to grapple with that thought. Somehow or other a bipedal, fairly hairless, hunting, scavenging ape did acquire this incredible possession and then handed it on to us. Why it did no one knows, or can even surmise. 'I haven't the foggiest notion,' replied Richard Leakey, anthropologist and skilful finder of early hominids, when asked why or how such a swelling of brain power could have occurred among early, primitive, and scattered tribes of men.

Growth   The speed of that swelling was considerable. From about five hundred cubic centimetres – and therefore comparable in size with gorilla brains – it leaped to the human size of fourteen hundred cubic centimetres in about three million years. Assuming the brain cells of earliest man to be as compressed as in a modern brain this means that some nine billion cells were added during those years, or approximately one hundred and fifty thousand per generation. That seems like a big increase for every single leap from parent to offspring, particularly when it is remembered that many invertebrates, all quite astute, have far less than that number, but in size it is not very large. In the brain there are about ten million cells in every cubic centimetre, and therefore that generation gap of one hundred and fifty thousand occupies a sixtieth of one cubic centimetre or just fifteen cubic millimetres. Such an increment is modest if viewed simply as bulk, and many another animal has increased its body size by much more than that per generation, the weight increase being only 0.015 grams or one two-thousandth of an ounce.

If elephants had only achieved their seven-ton weight from their, say, one-ton ancestors at this increment of 0.015 grams a generation it would have taken about four hundred million generations, or roughly eight thousand million years. However, it is tempting to regard brain-tissue weight-gain as more problematical in evolution than elephant weight-gain. The brain-gain seems more so because brains are of more significance – at least from our *sapiens* point of view – than mere bulk, a thicker skin or larger trunk. It is easier to be impressed with a tripling of nerve cells in three million years.

The brain growth seems less remarkable if thought of solely in terms of cell division. To achieve 15,000 million nerve cells it is necessary to have just 33 doublings of the parent cell. To achieve half that number only 32 doublings are necessary. In this light the difference between primitive and modern man seems less marked – scarcely more than one extra doubling in three million years. As the adult complement of brain cells is made during the first three months of pregnancy the 33 divisions therefore take place at an average rate of about one every three days. Bacteria double their number every twenty minutes or so, and the foetal brain increase is therefore not particularly rapid. In fact it is equivalent to all sorts of other increases going on in the embryonic human at the same time: liver growth, skin growth and so on. Brain growth just seems more remarkable, particularly when it is brought down to the level of brain cells. To possess 15,000 million neurons at the end of three months' gestational activity means growing them at the rate of 2,000 a second. Knowing that many small animals lead quite complex lives with that number of nerve cells, it is arguable that we should be far more intelligent than is actually the case; but it is obviously wrong to compare insect ability, however complex and admirable, with human capability. We are not equivalent to seven million insects. We just happen to have as many brain cells as they possess.

These paragraphs of figures, with so many noughts in them, may confuse rather than enlighten. Their purpose was to show that the acquisition of our three-pound brain is full of contradiction. It was a tremendous increase; yet would have been of little note had it occurred with some other kind of tissue. The three pounds are only beginning to achieve their potential for a very few people in modern times; yet they were developed for all our ancestors in relatively simple times. The brain's cells and synapses are merely numerous; the quantity of interconnections is about as infinite as anything we know. The brain's size is plainly crucial; and yet those individuals with twice the brain of others are none the wiser for it. Its growth was undoubtedly critical for the emergence of *Homo sapiens*, and for the development of this species; yet its size was probably curtailed by the practical demands of a relatively minor portion of anatomy, namely the elasticity at birth of the pelvic canal. It was easy for evolution to permit a steady growing of the foetal head; but birth must have been an increasing problem. Teleologically speaking, it was a good time for the mammals to introduce live birth in place of the egg birth that had ruled, more or less, since life began; but viviparity meant, in time, a limitation to head size. (Even so, we now have a brain more than suited to our needs. Perhaps it will teach us one day how to tap its real potential.)

Primitive man   Human beings are an amalgam from the past. Our first vertebrate ancestors, the fish, passed on to us a single heart, a pair of eyes, fore and hind limbs, three semi-circular canals, teeth, a liver, a pancreas, a spleen, two kidneys, ribs, a thyroid, a spinal cord in a vertebral column, a bony skull *and* a brain of five distinct parts. From the amphibia, successors to the fish, we received our inner ears, tympanic membranes, two auricles in the heart, two lungs, upper and lower divisions to four limbs, finger and foot bones, two scapulas, two clavicles *and* a fore-brain that is not just a simple olfactory lobe. From the reptiles, descendants of amphibia, we acquired a metanephros (a different style of kidney), a ureter, alveoli in our lungs, an amniotic membrane, *and* a more dominant fore-brain than had ever been before. With the arrival of the mammals came other features, such as hair, a lens able to change its focal length, three bony ossicles in the ear, warm-bloodedness, two ventricles in the heart, milk glands, the placenta, a single vagina *and* a stratified cortex of the ever-enlargening fore-brain. From the primates, our simian ancestors, we received forward-facing eyes, a single uterus, the human style of teeth, freely-mobile arms, hands, a long period of development *and* a much more convoluted brain than had ever been seen before.

The final inheritance, from whichever apes gave rise to ape-men and then to men, was an upright stance, a bowl-shaped pelvis, a flatter thorax (both resulting from uprightness), feet to walk upon, larger legs, relatively early birth (because the new walking pelvis had a less convenient birth canal), a more upright head *and* a greatly swollen brain. Although restricted by the birth canal, but made possible by a lengthy period of development after birth and by a vertical vertebral column that could more easily support a larger head, the brain of the men-apes and ape-men did steadily increase and resulted in the most complex and able nervous system in the entire animal kingdom.

However, the biggest leap forward in neural development occurred at the very beginning of vertebrate history when the basic pattern was laid down. Like the arch in architecture, or steam in industry, the advance in fish over every earlier nervous arrangement was crucial. The fact that the fish fore-brain, first devoted entirely to the sense of smell, became largely redundant when this sense waned in its importance later in evolution was equally critical. So too was the placing of the fore-brain, for its position at the front meant that expansion of its bulk was less likely to be disruptive. There is such a sense of logic in the brain's development from fish to amphibia to reptile to mammal to primate to ape to man that it appears preordained. But evolution occurred, as Julian Huxley phrased it, with no more purpose than rain falling from the sky. The fact that the human brain arrived, by accident as it were, need not detract one iota from our amazement at its capabilities. Its unplanned arrival is all the more astonishing. Finally, we did not so much eat the fruit of the tree of knowledge as descend from that tree, become bipedal, release our fore-limbs for other activities, and acquire a brain to reap the reward of standing upright.

Many species have enlarged this or that organ, or part of an organ, or system of organs. The orang-utan's arms are extremely lengthy. The gorilla's bulk, notably in the male, is outstanding. The giant elk possessed, until recent extinction, the largest antlers there have ever been, and the blue whale is the biggest animal that has existed. Mankind's enlargement is modest by comparison – just another pound or two of one particular organ – but the growth was of neural tissue. The result of this particular increase, however small by comparison and small in weight, has been to give our species tremendous power. We can, should we so mismanage things, even destroy all life on the planet that gave us birth.

This small, important enlargement of tissue was nothing like so speedy as was believed even twenty years ago. The few pieces of the jigsaw then indicated that everything of consequence had happened within the past 500,000 years. Following many finds in Africa, the timescale is now thought to have been more leisurely. It would appear that man, gorilla and chimpanzee had a common ancestor about four and a half million years ago. Within a million years from that date, as proved by footprints found by Mary Leakey at Laetoli (fifty kilometres south of the famous Olduvai Gorge in Tanzania), man's ancestors were fully bipedal. Walking on two legs preceded every other human attribute, manual dexterity, tool-making and expansion of the brain.

The individuals that first walked upright were probably no more intelligent than today's anthropoid apes. 'Behaviour doesn't fossilise,' as anthropologist Richard Leakey said; nor does practically everything that we would dearly love to know. The only clue to hominid intelligence lies in artefacts and cranial capacity. Nothing man-made has survived from the very beginning of mankind's upright existence; no implements and no fire-places. The cranial capacity then was ape-sized, roughly five hundred cubic centimetres (or one-third of the modern size, or one pint).

The actual fossil picture has much improved recently owing to the plethora of discoveries from Africa in general and East Africa in particular. In the mid-1960s only about forty pieces of hominid fossil had been found in East Africa. By 1970 the number was nearer one hundred, and by the end of the 1970s nearer seven hundred. Coupled with the findings from southern Africa the grand total of African hominid remains now exceeds one thousand. Consequently it is no longer a fact, as at the start of this century, that each new find creates yet another rearrangement of human evolution. There is still dispute, of course, as one thousand pieces of jigsaw by no means complete the picture of four and a half million years, and principal disagreement ranges round the Australopithecines (or southern apes). Did they coexist with the true ancestors of mankind and then die out, or were they an integral part of the hominid evolution? The argument can only be resolved when many more jigsaw pieces are found. If Australopithecines were a separate species the hominid line began long ago, perhaps four and a half million years or as much as seven million. If Australopithecines were our ancestors, retaining as they do so many ape-like qualities along with their human features, the true hominid line is probably no more than three million years old. The controversy is likely to rage for many years to come, for the human story always generates much heat.

However, whether over three million years, seven million or some other span, an ape-like and ape-sized brain did become transformed. A chimpanzee's brain is 400 cubic centimetres, a gorilla's is 500 cubic centimetres and the earliest Australopithe-cine brains were about 450 cubic centimetres. *Australopithecus robustus* (as against *gracilis*) had a 500 cubic centimetre brain. The first tool-maker and handyman, *Homo habilis*, had a 750 cubic centimetre brain and he was succeeded one and a half million years ago by *Homo erectus*, also tool-maker, but fire-user and possessor of a 900–1,100 cubic centimetre brain. Then, as another leap forward, came the Neanderthal men, heavy-boned, big, and occa-sional buriers of their dead. Their brains – at 1,500 cubic cen-timetres – were even larger than the average brains of today. So *Homo neanderthalensis* may indeed have been slightly more intelli-gent (who knows?), but the size of a brain is not the only factor. There is also the degree of convolution, which can sometimes be detected in the fossil material, and the neural organisation of the brain itself, which cannot even be detected in a living brain. There is also the conundrum of some modern human brains being twice the size of others without appreciable difference in intelli-gence.

Man-made tools first appeared about three million years ago. They were crude, being little more than pebbles with a flake or two knocked off to give a cutting edge. Thousands of generations were to pass before these acquired any degree of artistry, eventually becoming the superb flints of neolithic people. Mankind's evolu-tion is often said to be explosive, but the overall speed of advance in tool-making is not flattering. We can only judge from what has survived, and all wooden objects have vanished, but the slow progress of man's technological advance is as surprising and con-trary as the steady growth of his mental faculties. He acquired a bigger and bigger brain but left behind scant evidence that he was using or had need of it. The active history of *Homo sapiens* only began some thirty thousand years ago, but his brain had advanced to the *sapiens* level, at least in size, tens of thousands of years beforehand. Quite abruptly it then came into its own, with artistry, carvings, paintings and major advances in cultural evolution. More technological advance happened in the subsequent 20,000 years than had occurred in the previous two million. And, of course, everything that has happened since the neolithic revolution and the dawn of history – the past 10,000 years – makes every advance that occurred beforehand quite insignificant.

The overriding fact, never to be forgotten, is that our near antecedents have all been similarly equipped mentally. So far as is known, simple hunter-gatherer, early cave-man, cave artist, neolithic agriculturalist, Sumerian scribe, and modern office com-muter have all possessed the self-same brain. It is only cultural inheritance that has made them into us. This occurred, as Julian Huxley put it, when 'Man added tradition to heredity'.

Origin of speech   All higher animals communicate, but none in a manner that approaches mankind's ability. To have alarm calls, grunting signals, pleasure sounds and individual noises is not the same as human language (or rather as language, for there is no other kind). 'Speech alone has rendered man human,' said the German eighteenth-century theologian G. Herder. And it rendered simple the inheritance of tradition and culture.

What is not known to the slightest degree is when speech began. Anatomically (via tongue, larynx and palate) it was possible for hundreds of thousands of years. Neurologically it has been possible for a similar time, insofar as large and suitable lobes have been present in the brain. Opinions about the timing of speech origin vary from very recent (Aurignacian) to most ancient (when *Homo* began), and there are two main arguments.

The first, which considers language to be old, argues that mankind and speech have evolved together. The big brain, the unique art of talking and the advantages of refined intercommunication have all advanced in unison. The more the brain developed, in size and organisation, the more speech could be developed. And the more this happened the closer man advanced to his unparalleled status among the species of the world. To speak is to be human: therefore humans began when they began to speak.

The second argument, placing its origin in palaeolithic times, is based upon the suddenness of mankind's cultural evolution. For about one hundred thousand generations little happened, save that man and his brain grew larger. Then, abruptly, and about a thousand generations ago, mankind leaped ahead, proved itself distinct from the animals, made technological advances undreamed of formerly, and was undoubtedly *sapiens*. If this stride had been possible earlier why did it not happen earlier? If speech had occurred in some ancient era why did everything else wait until so recently? What caused the triggering of our talents?

Both theories are attractive. And both are subject to various other unknowns. What kind of pressure was exerted upon the early hominid that acted via selection upon his brain? And what sort of force goaded his ability to communicate? Man versus man would have provided a spur, but there is no evidence that mankind was outstandingly belligerent just as there is none that he was peaceable. Or rather such evidence as does exist – opened Australopithecine skulls, for example – is used by both sides. Either the victims were battered brutally or their brains were relished for their spiritual properties. The only certainty is that we shall never know.

It is also not known whether the advent of speech occurred slowly, much like some child's development but spread over tens of thousands of years, or whether it was precipitate. Animals can register moods, intentions, reactions, but only broadly. They cannot call a tree a tree. That advance, of giving things names, and adjectives to go with them, probably preceded grammar, but this crucial step in language could not have been far behind. Or perhaps there was a different order of events, but names to adjectives to grammar is the progression that infants prefer, going from dog to good dog to give me good dog. Infant development may be the best guide as well as the only guide to speech development. (Speech is unlikely to have happened as one famous infant, allegedly, made it happen. Thomas Carlyle's very first exclamation 'What ails wee Jock?' was to a fellow one-year-old.)

One more possibility is that humans developed signs to a re- markable degree before language became developed. We can convey even today a great deal of information merely by facial and bodily expression. It has been calculated that more different signs exist than there are words in the largest of dictionaries. Sir Richard Paget, 1869–1955, decided that mankind could make 700,000 gestures. This is generally thought to be an exaggeration; but, even if a hundredfold too many, the number is still impressive. There are 550,000 words listed in the most verbose dictionaries. As the bulk of us get by on far fewer – about four thousand – we can also think the dictionary is another exaggeration, and perhaps Paget is correct. In simple societies, and at the more depressed end of complex societies, speech may involve no more than four hundred words. The number of twitchings, grimaces, shrugs, sneers, eye- brow-liftings, lip-curlings, snarls, smirks, head-shakings, finger- movements and so on – some of which are extremely precise, and almost audible – could easily be in excess of four hundred for such people, or for all of us. Gestures convey mood and reaction, as in animal communication, rather than detailed facts, and perhaps – according to this argument – the explosive evolution of *Homo sapiens* only occurred when signs gave way to words.

Ernst Heckel, the German scientist, once postulated *Pithecan- thropus alalus* as our ancestor, the speechless ape-man. He did not carry on this thought and name us *Homo vocalis* as perhaps he should have done. Speech does not make us wiser, but it was a fantastic boost to our cultural evolution, only bettered when words could also be written down as script.

The hand In the absence of any other proof, the 'thumb alone would convince me of God's existence', said Isaac Newton. In which case the monkeys, with their opposable first digits, should have been no less convincing, and one wonders if the great mathematician ever saw a monkey or, if he did, reflected upon its dexterity; but he is right in his way. The hand is an exceedingly remarkable device. Current argument is less concerned with proof of deity than with the chicken-and-egg debate whether the hand of *Homo* permitted/encouraged/created the brain of man or if his steadily improving brain remorselessly improved manual dexterity. Every other kind of primate is neither so intelligent nor so able with its hands. The two abilities, to use a very human phrase, go hand in hand.

The human fore-limb arrangement is, in biological terms, both primitive and advanced. One upper arm bone (humerus), two lower arm bones (radius, ulna), a wrist (of eight bones in two rows), five palm bones (metacarpals), and five digits (each of three phalanges, save for the two-phalange thumb) is undoubtedly a primitive arrangement. Amphibians, for example, could regard their own pentadactyl system and not feel greatly humbled by the five-digit arrangement of the highest mammals, of apes and men. But many another mammal has greatly distorted and advanced that ancient system: all the ungulates run on just two digits while the horses run on one.

However, the human fore-limb is also advanced in many simple, subtle ways. It is still pentadactyl at its extremity but is not really comparable with the amphibian system, first evolved back in the Palaeozoic and which led to the later limbs. During the whole of the Tertiary, and for a period of some fifty million years, the monkey stock became increasingly adept at an arboreal existence. From tree-living lemur ancestors the tree-living monkeys further developed a most agile fore-limb. Both the scapula (shoulder-blade) and the clavicle (collarbone) were retained to give considerable motility to the upper arm (carnivores and ungulates have lost their clavicles). The elbow and wrist were also developed to permit a wide range of movements; and how many other animals can reach/scratch every single inch of their bodies with their fore-limbs?

Newton's thumb is a major asset but many other primates do have such an opposable digit. However, they cannot use their paws as humans do their hands for there are two crucial distinctions. The first is that the hand has two grips which can be exercised simultaneously. A ball, for instance, can be held tightly in the palm while some other object can be picked up delicately (or powerfully) by the thumb and the first two fingers. This double dexterity is believed to be of more use than mere opposability. The second and equally critical advance is the direct neural link between the fore-brain and the hand via the pyramidal tract. A chimpanzee's hand, for example, is not so well endowed neurologically and therefore its abilities are ham-fisted in comparison with the hand of a man. Watch a pianist at work. Know that the most skilled can strike ten times a second with a single forefinger. Observe an artist who can fashion a likeness not just of the human face but, irrefutably, of one human face in particular. A chimpanzee, for all its excellence, comes nowhere in this league.

The ape hand exists, but not the human brain to guide it. Nevertheless, it can be used to pick fruit, tear leaves, climb, eat, drink, groom, throw rocks, scratch, fight, build nests, use tools of a kind and even poke straws into ants' nests. Presumably the hand of early man was similarly able. As such activities encompass everything, or so one assumes, that he had to do, it is easy to wonder about the selection pressure adding to his dexterity. Unfortunately no hand bones have been discovered between the onset of *Homo habilis* (the 'handyman' of one and three-quarter million years ago) and the existence of Neanderthal man just 50,000 years ago. The question remains (and possibly for ever): did the human brain evolve partly to help the human hand or did the human hand advance in skill as the inevitable result of an advancing brain?

Great play has been made over the recent discovery that other primates fashion (or adapt) tools and then use them. So far thirteen different examples of tool-using have been observed in the chimpanzees alone. This facility has overturned a long-standing classification. Benjamin Franklin was among the first to define man as a 'tool-making animal'. After the chimpanzee observation anthropologist Louis Leakey said, 'We must either re-define tool-making or re-define man.'

In the end it is primarily tool-making that has been altered to exclude tool-modifying, the chimpanzee activity. Plainly there is little difference between knocking a flint or two from a pebble, as *Homo* did repetitively for well over a million years, and stripping the leaves from a twig to create a better ant-extractor. But the definition of man has also shifted. Formerly it was brain-size alone that mattered, with 'Keith's Rubicon' (after palaeontologist Sir Arthur Keith) being used as the touchstone for humanness. Man the tool-maker then ruled, for definition, but the chimpanzees' skills were upsetting, and the more modern tendency is to define by speech and language. Although undoubtedly unique to man neither of these fossilise, despite some clever work in detecting convolution imprints and possible speech areas within fossil crania. Therefore it is not possible to say when speech began and, as a consequence, when man began.

Dexterity is easier to date. After the pebble-tools had reigned for about sixty thousand generations – which is a kind of proof that mankind's intelligence, ingenuity, inventiveness and dexterity were all still at a modest level – the first hand-axes were made. The oldest are from Africa, fashioned 1,500,000 years ago, or 75,000 generations before now. Ingenuity elsewhere was still at a low ebb, for nothing of the sort has been found in Europe older than 400,000 years, and nothing in Britain older than 250,000 years. This proliferation of a good idea was snail-like rather than explosive, the adjective so frequently applied to human advance.

The slow pace of technological progress continued even after the hand-axe had been invented. Presumably wooden tools were being manufactured simultaneously, for a hand capable of fashioning a spear-head from flint or obsidian was unlikely to rest with that single achievement. It was presumably busy in other areas, perhaps making skins, traps, bows, houses and all manner of artefacts that have not and could not survive. Advancement was nevertheless slow, by every modern standard, however busy those hands. There were more than seventy thousand generations between the arrival of hand-axes and the onset of the upper palaeolithic industries, the cultures called Chatelperonian, Aurignacian, Cravettian and Magdalenian (in that order). By then artistry had arrived, making use of bone, antler, ivory, wood *and* flint and stone. Between then and now is just 2,000 generations, and the long period of technological stagnation was over; modern times had arrived. From then on change accelerated dramatically. The hand and brain were to work together as never before.

It is vexing that the fossil record of early man is so inadequate. With a thousand bits and pieces found from the 250,000 million humans who lived in the past five million years, assuming a million alive at any one time and twenty years per generation, the jigsaw is only of pathetic fragments here and there. Practically all of the story is conjecture. How advanced were those *habilis* brains? And their hands? When, to within a million years, did speech (the anatomy) and language (the grammar) evolve? Why was there such stagnation? Or, conversely, why was there technical advancement? (The aborigines reached Australia, possibly in more than one wave, some forty thousand years ago. As their brains, hands, eyes, language and needs are similar to those of other men elsewhere it is intriguing that there were only forty different man-made objects in their entire repertoire when European man arrived. There are even indications, notably in Tasmania, that fewer artefacts were being made as the millennia passed by in Australasia.)

Work in areas other than pure palaeontology does not provide answers to these queries. 'The more we know about communication (in apes and monkeys),' Jane Lancaster has written, 'the less these systems seem to help in our understanding of human language.' Humans of today find speech so useful that it is easy to forget how well the animals communicate. 'It is difficult to believe,' said J. S. Weiner, 'that cooperative hunting could be performed or skilled tool-making taught without language.' John Napier, considerable expert on hands, disagrees: 'Early man could still have cooperated without language.' He suggests that speech 'probably' was developed between the Australopithecines and *Homo erectus* 'when the capacity of the brain almost doubled, from 508 to 974 cubic centimetres'. As for hands, if they took a similar leap forward in tune with the brain's expansion, there is nothing to show for it. Presumably, because the chances of bones becoming fossilised are so slim, and the chances of those fossils being found are slimmer still, we will never acquire a neat lineage of human remains to demonstrate precisely just when brains became able (significantly better than those of apes), when hands became capable (similarly ahead of those of chimpanzees) and when speech was developed (putting communication on quite a different plane to the grunts and grimaces of our anthropoid relations).

There is even a theory that hands were initially more crucial for communication than in making things. It is a nice theory, and doubly nice when it permits me to quote the lyricism of John Bulwer, who wrote in 1644:

> The moving and significant extension of the Hand is knowne to be so absolutely pertinent to speech, that we together with a speech expect the due motion of the Hand to explaine, direct, enforce, apply, apparrell, and to beautifie the words men utter, which would prove naked, unless the cloathing Hands does neatly move to adorn and hide their nakedness, with their comely and ministeriall parts of speech.

Relationship between hands and the mind is more obvious, but even this association has an unobvious side to it. Charlotte Wolff, living in Poland before the Nazi invasion, was the foremost protagonist of the idea that hands could serve in the diagnosis of disease. The old arts of cheiromancy (fortune-telling by the hand)

and cheirognomy (palmistry) should not, she argued, be ignored in modern times. Just as astrology led to astronomy, alchemy to chemistry, and occultism to psychology, the study of hands must not be disregarded by modern medicine. Indeed there are strange links recognised, among them:

Down's syndrome, which can generally be observed in abnormal palm prints.

Malfunctioning pituitary, also detectable in the hand.

Psychosis, often accompanied by a cyanotic colour and typical hand postures.

Certain circulatory and pulmonary diseases, which may partner 'drumstick' deformity of fingers and 'watch-glass' nails.

Cancer, which can show in the growth of fingernails.

Professor Harold Cummins, of Tulane University, was the first (in 1936) to show that both palm and fingerprints were useful in medicine. Of prime importance was Down's syndrome (or mongolism, or trisomy 21 – see p. 233) which is partnered by a tendency for fewer whorls, arches and radial loops than in normal fingertips. Mongols are more likely to have such loops on their ring, or fourth, fingertips than are normal people, who usually have them on their index finger. They are also more likely to possess the so-called simian crease on the palm, a horizontal and singular line from side to side of the region nearest to the fingers. Some 80 per cent of mongols have this peculiarity but only 7 per cent of normal people, and the normal usually possess it on just one palm.

Palmists are also interested in personality. The Society for the Study of Physiological Patterns claims that certain kinds of individual can be linked with loops, whorls and arches on various fingertips. (A loop – the most frequent – is either radial – facing the thumb – or ulnar – facing the little finger. A whorl is the most distinctive, being composed of concentric circles. An arch is either tented – coming to a sharper point – or more rounded.) To have a loop on the thumb is allegedly to combine objectiveness with adaptability. If on the index finger, the adaptability is combined with initiative. On the second finger, where it is usually ulnar, the loop indicates a philosophical and flexible nature. On the third, or ring finger, where it is again usually ulnar, it shows artistic interest, and on the fourth, little or pinky, it shows humour and responsiveness. According to the Society a whorl on all fingers suggests criminal tendencies while a tented arch on all fingers means rebelliousness. A loop, it seems, is the best sort of shape to have, being a general sign of adaptability.

It is easy to mock such character assessment, and to lump the work with, for example, similar pronouncements once made by the phrenologists; but it is as well to remember two points. The first is that F. J. Gall's pioneering work, in which he affirmed that certain brain areas presided over certain characteristics, preceded by almost a century Broca's discovery, and then Wernicke's, that certain areas *did* control various characteristics. The second point is that Down's mental deficiency *is* partnered by distinctive eye-folds, a distinctive build and a no less distinctive printing on the palm. If one mental abnormality shows up in the hand it is more than possible that others do so. After all, somehow or other, the brain and the hand did evolve together. A defect in one may be partnered by an abnormality in the other. In 1934 Julian Huxley wrote: 'In man alone is the hand perfectly coordinated with the brain. A baby uses his hands very like a monkey, but as the brain develops quickly, he is soon able to make them do his will.' A concluding thought is that, save for a very few who are equal-handed, we apply most of our ingenuity using our brain and one hand. Try making anything with the non-dominant hand and the result has about as much artistry as a primitive *habilis* pebble-tool. Our better hand operates with quite a different order of compe-tence; in fact equivalent to the difference between a pebble-chopper and a delicate, neolithic, sharp-pointed arrow-head. Perhaps it was dominant handedness that was the crucial step to capable handiness, rather than handiness leading on to handed-ness.

Cultural evolution

It has been said against the African Negroes that they never produced a scientist; but what kind of scientist would he be who had no weights and measures, no clock or calendar, and no means of recording his observations and experiments? And if it be asked why the Negroes did not invent these things, the answer is that neither did any European . . .

Thus Lord Raglan, putting into perspective the presumption, certainly among Europeans, either that their ancestors created these things or, if they inexplicably failed to do so, some successor would surely have done so, and invented the wheel, the ruler, the telescope or any other simple device. However, inventions do not come that fast. Mankind is a skilled adapter rather than inventor. The balloon, for example, could have flown centuries before it first took to the air in 1783; the materials had been available long

17

beforehand. Gliders could have flown well before the end of the nineteenth century when the first practical steps were taken.

More important than mere inventiveness is the mood or climate of the time. The reason, continued Lord Raglan, why neither Africa nor Europe created those things was because 'the rare and perhaps unique conditions which made their invention possible were absent.' Mesopotamia several times in its history possessed those conditions. So did Renaissance Italy. And so did England when its time came. It had not always been so. 'Do not obtain your slaves from Britain, because they are so stupid and so utterly incapable of being taught that they are not fit to form part of the household of Athens,' recorded Cicero a millennium and a half before Britain embarked upon making slaves of much of the world while creating the biggest empire of them all.

The slow technical progress of *Homo* in the early years must mean that he was either extremely incapable of acquiring information and expertise or equally incapable of passing on what he had learned to his descendants. When those days were over, when knowledge could be both acquired and passed on, the acceleration was virtually inevitable. (Australian aborigines and the Tasmanians are more responsible than most for the qualification.) The remarkable fact is that this union of acquisition and inheritance only happened to any marked degree long after mankind had acquired his modern size of brain. That is the dominant conundrum of our evolution. We acquired the wit to initiate science, and ultimately to exterminate ourselves, by hunting and gathering, much as the apes do, but we were somehow different. In the past many species have become extinct owing to the excessive, and somewhat inexplicable, phylogenetic enlargement of some organ. In mankind's case the exceedingly developed, and no more comprehensible, fore-brain may also be the means of our extermination. Unlike every other huge increase, such as bulk or antler size, the human brain is not only able to destroy its own species but every other kind as well.

2. Animal Anatomy

Ascaris and *Aplysia* / Other invertebrates / Amphioxus / Fish / Amphibia / Reptiles / Birds / Mammals / *Homo sapiens*

> The longer you can look back the further you can look forward
> — Winston Churchill (in 1944 addressing the Royal College of Physicians)

The fact of there being 15,000 million nerve cells in the human brain can be daunting to all of us, but baffling to scientists. No wonder, therefore, that many researchers have concentrated upon species neurologically less well endowed. The intestinal parasitic worm *Ascaris*, for example, has precisely 162 cells in its brain, never more and never less. (This fact, discovered by German biologist Richard Goldschmidt in 1912, was disregarded for many years, a kind of proof of its importance.) *Ascaris* leads an uncomplicated life, but nevertheless can learn, does possess memory, and acts on information received. Its mental abilities are modest compared with *Homo sapiens* but, proportionately, it does extremely well with its 162 against our 15,000 million.

The honey bee, much admired for industry, is cleverer than *Ascaris* and even receives a nod or two of admiration from us, being able to perform certain tasks that we cannot. Its nervous system possesses about seven thousand neurons (ours is therefore two million times more privileged) and yet the bee can:

carry out a complex set of duties in the hive – comb-making, capping, feeding, cleaning, ventilating, repairing, sealing;
smell, particularly with regard to other bees, friendly or unfriendly;
estimate the sun's angle, within 2–3°;
detect colour, from ultra violet to yellow;
know the time of day, to within thirty minutes of the actual time;
estimate the weight of pollen being carried;
steer a course, taking note of sky illumination, landmarks, smells en route;

estimate distance travelled;

regurgitate food in correct part of the hive;

measure frequency of dance movements, and therefore know/ learn the distance of a food supply;

correlate between angle of sun, or brightest part of the sky, and direction of the vertical when the dance is performed on a vertical comb (probably achieved using antennae weight);

compensate for detours in flight, i.e. give true distance of honey source even though true, direct flight (possibly) never achieved;

recognise characteristic sounds emitted by other bees;

and recognise and attack an enemy.

All of this is achieved with a brain of 0.74 cubic millimetres. (Queens have slightly smaller brains – 0.71 cubic millimetres – than workers but those of drones are considerably larger – 1.175 cubic millimetres – mainly due to large optic lobes probably concerned with locating the queen on her mating flight.) Some of the bee's achievements, such as those concerned with navigation and passing on this information, would be particularly difficult even for humans. Moreover, in their short life of a few weeks, bees twice have to drop one set of activities and perform another, as they switch from nursing to building to foraging. All of this is achieved with the number of nerve cells which the human foetus manufactures in about the time that it takes an adult to say *Apis mellifora*.

Although modestly equipped from our swollen standpoint, the bee has far too big a nervous complex for many kinds of scientific study. Hence interest in the nematode worm *Ascaris*. Its 162 nerve cells not only make a manageable total, but they are ranged about its body in an even more manageable fashion, mainly in nervous bundles or ganglia. The total cell count is created from:

Subdorsal papillary ganglia	7 of 2 cells each:	14
Subventral papillary ganglia	7 of 2 cells each:	14
Lateral papillary ganglia	4 of 2 cells each:	8
Amphidial ganglia	11 of 2 cells each:	22
Internal lateral ganglia	11 of 2 cells each:	22
External lateral ganglia	13 of 2 cells each:	26
Circum-enteric nerve ring		4
Dorsal ganglion		2
Subdorsal ganglia	2 of 2 cells each:	4
Ventral ganglion		33
Retrovesiculum ganglion		13
		162

In *Ascaris*, apart from this precise number creating the central nervous system, there are a further ninety-two cells within the tail structure and enteric system that form a peripheral network. The grand total of 254, and always 254, has a pleasing simplicity to it, particularly for anyone who has previously been trying to unravel the human nervous system. The work with worms does not seek to contrast mankind with this simple animal. Plainly the two types of central nervous system are poles apart, with the intellectual capabilities of both species existing on quite different levels. Instead the work attempts to discover similarities in the two systems, and these certainly exist. Primarily, there do not seem to be any basic differences in function, chemistry or structure between the neurons and synapses of man and those of *Ascaris* or of many other invertebrates, such as molluscs. Therefore, facts discovered about nervous control in, say, the snail can have wider significance and may, at best, be relevant to us.

For example, the beating of the human heart is regulated by several thousand nerve cells, or neurons. This one simple activity is modulated by the inhibitory action of very many neurons in the vagus nerve *and* by the excitatory action of very many more neurons in the accelerator nerve. The large marine snail *Aplysia* also has a spontaneously beating heart. It too is similarly modulated by both inhibitory and excitatory neurons, but there are just four of them and not several thousand. Two cells stimulate its heart, with only one being important, and two slow it down. There are three further cells that control the constriction of the blood vessels, adjusting blood pressure. Blood-flow is therefore organised by just seven cells; but the system is even better than that. Ever since some work on crayfish (in 1938) it has been known that certain command cells exist which can organise a complete behavioural sequence. It is now known that the heart of *Aplysia* has such a cell. By its action alone, and via the six other neurons involved, it is responsible for increased blood-flow. Instead of worrying about the several thousand control cells in the human heart interest can be narrowed down to just one cell, or even as many as seven, to understand how a similar organ goes about the same activity of pumping more (or less) blood about a body. The snails, and others, have been most informative about their nervous systems, and therefore ours as well.

Other invertebrates A nervous system regulates, and it initiates, and on these two in particular learning can be imposed. Nevertheless it is difficult to say at what level in the animal kingdom such a system first appears. Protozoa, the single-celled animals, often have well-controlled cilia, can retreat from unpleasantness, advance upon food, dodge obstructions, and generally behave much like higher animals, but the scientific consensus is that they do not have nervous systems. Moving upwards in the kingdom the porifera, or sponges, are multi-celled but still extremely simple. They have no true sensory cells or nerve cells and their responses to external stimuli do not demand any specialised conducting arrangement. Therefore they too, it is thought, do not possess a nervous system.

That is no longer correct for the coelenterates, the simplest of animals with a single-body cavity (or enteron). What they possess by way of a nervous system is not fundamentally different, either in its structural or functional elements, from those of higher animals. Consequently it is considered that they have the simplest true nervous system. Even the speed of impulse transmission is commendable for such lowly forms of creation, being six inches a second in the stem of *Tubularia*, eight inches a second for polyp retraction in *Tubipora*, and twenty inches a second for the swimming beat of the jellyfish *Aurelia*.

Travelling up the animal kingdom to reach the platyhelminthes, the lowest group of bilaterally symmetrical multi-cellular animals, there is a well-developed central nervous system. This consists of a distinct brain plus a set of longitudinal nerve cords. Considering the size of the average flatworm the brain is not inconsiderable being, for example, 700 mu × 1,300 mu (or roughly one square millimetre) in a twenty-millimetre (almost one inch) *Notoplana*. If such a brain (or foremost ganglion) is removed, the animal survives but is slowed down. It travels less speedily, reacts to food less swiftly, sees less well, and is generally less adept than it used to be.

Perhaps the word brain should be defined, as it may be felt these primitive animals cannot possess an organ with such a prestigious name. To borrow from a book on invertebrate nervous systems, a brain is

> the enlarged and specialised rostralmost (nearest the front end) or highest ganglion of the central nervous system. It is not necessarily the largest nervous mass, but if the ganglion is not distinctive enough in size or differentiation or if it is too far from a distinct head, the term brain is not used.

In other words, as any schoolboy might define it, it is the large lump of nervous tissue at the front or head end. This is true for man, the worm and every creature in between. They are all equipped with brains.

The nemertines, which are mainly marine worms, represent another advance. There is a distinct brain but, instead of a set of longitudinal cords running backwards from it, there are only two. The removal of this brain leads to a definite disarray of the ciliary beating system and to the animal's sense of direction. Nematodes, or round worms, such as the already mentioned *Ascaris*, have a less distinct brain than the nemertines but their central nervous system, with its various ganglia, is most precise. No single ganglion has a preponderance of each animal's nerve cells but the various ganglia throughout the body serve in place of a concentrated brain.

Moving on again, and to the Annelids (worms with ringed segments), these have a pair of supra-oesophageal ganglia, tantamount to a brain, as well as a ladder-like arrangement of other ganglia running down the length of the body, one pair to every segment. Unlike the vertebrates, but like all the arthropods (the most multitudinous animals on Earth), this longitudinal column is paired rather than single and ventral rather than dorsal. The lowly earthworm, *Lumbricus*, is not lowly neurologically, at least when compared with the much-studied snail *Aplysia* (162 cells) or with the nematode *Ascaris* (254 cells). At hatching the earthworm has 6,000 nerve cells, a number which rises to 10,000 when it is mature four months later. Such a large number means that the earthworm's system has not been extensively studied, its cells being sixtyfold those of *Aplysia*, and it might at this stage be wondered who has counted such things. It is not, after all, the easiest, most exciting, or most rewarding kind of work. Quite the most prolific counter, to whom credit should be given and whose name appears over and over again in books on invertebrate neurology, was F. Ogawa who seemed to spend every minute of her time in the 1930s adding up these cells.

The greater number of earthworm nerve cells (over, say, the coelenterates) is partnered by greater ability. The worm's lateral giant fibres can conduct impulses at seven to fifteen metres a second while its median fibres can conduct at fifteen to forty-five metres a second. This is, at maximum, one hundred and forty feet a second, or about one hundred miles an hour, and among the fastest conducting times of all invertebrates. Nerves of the jellyfish *Aurelia*, by comparison, can conduct at twenty inches a second or one mile an hour. There are also many so-called sense cell clusters in the worm – 686 per square millimetre (and again it is easy to be astonished at the counting). However, its brain, formed by those two supra-oesophageal ganglia, does not possess the status of a vertebrate brain. If it is cut out the worm's abilities are lessened rather than curtailed. It then feeds and burrows slower and more awkwardly. It holds its head high, and is restless. It will even fall off an edge rather than avoid it. Nevertheless, such de-brained worms can still right themselves, enter into coitus, and learn a way through mazes.

The arthropods, namely invertebrates with segmented bodies and jointed limbs, are a mixed group neurologically. Spiders have fewer nerve cells than insects, and insects fewer than crustaceans. In the most endowed arthropods there are 100,000 nerve cells, which is the number that the human foetus grows in a minute. The general arthropod central nervous system is certainly complex, and more so than the systems of the lowest invertebrates, but many reflex actions are unimpaired by the arthropod brain's removal. For instance, crickets and cockroaches can still walk normally afterwards. They may still clean their legs, but these are sometimes bitten at the same time because they are unrecognised. The type of arthropod brain is determined by the creature's lifestyle. The odonata, or dragonflies, have brains dominated by large optic centres which occupy some 80 per cent of the space. The lepidoptera, or butterflies and moths, are also extremely visual and only modestly involved in scent. So their optic and olfactory lobes occupy 80 per cent and 2.3 per cent of the space respectively.

Sense organs in insects are extremely varied, there being statocysts, leg hairs and antennae as well as the more ordinary light and sound detectors. The number of cells in each sensory organ is also varied, ranging from one to several hundred. Some of the lepidopteran tympanic organs have two to three neurons, others hundreds. The lower figures indicate the unimportance of sound for that species. Odour is often far more critical, particularly for male moths that can detect the scent of females more than a mile away. (It must be a matter of inches for humans unless artificial scent aids are being employed in which case the distance leaps up – to several feet.) In ants the corpora pedunculata (in effect their brains) are relatively largest in the workers, intermediate in queens, and smallest in the males. The soldier ants have much bigger heads but, even so, smaller pedunculata than the ordinary workers. Soldier termites have half the brain size of the worker castes. One huge advantage of arthropods for scientists is that anything can be done – eyes removed, nerves severed, brains excised – by way of experiment.

Whatever their nervous arrangement the arthropods are undoubtedly a successful group. So too is the one above them, the mollusca. There are more living mollusc species – 104,000 – than there are living kinds of vertebrate, from fishes right up to man. There is great variation in mollusc size but there is also great disparity in brain size relative to total body weight. A small snail of 8.5 grams (0.33 of an ounce) has a brain 0.015 per cent of its body weight. A snail twelve times larger doubles its proportion of brain. An octopus of 300 grams (about ten ounces) has a brain 0.1 per cent of its body weight, and octopus ability reflects this proportionate increase. Loligo, a visual squid, betters even the octopus because its brain is 0.35 per cent of its weight (as against 2 per cent for humans, and 4 per cent for some monkeys). With such creatures the optic lobes are predominant, being much larger (2.68 times in loligo) than the rest of the brain. Some are even more disproportionate, such as the squid *Pyroteuthis*. Its optic lobes are four times the size of the remainder of its brain.

The attraction of the invertebrates for neurologists is their neural simplicity. Not every advanced feature of higher nervous systems is represented among them, but it is being increasingly realised that the basic aspects of all nervous systems can be found in the activities of just a few invertebrate neurons. In other words, human beings learn and remember in a most bewildering fashion, but many simple animals learn and remember in similar fashion with far less equipment. Rather than millions of neurons (or nerve cells) there may be half a dozen doing the same job. We shall fully understand a snail like *Aplysia* long before we understand humans, but the snail will help us along the path, just as the invertebrates lay along the path to higher evolution.

The invertebrates possess nerves and brains in a seemingly haphazard fashion. The line of evolutionary development is unclear, mainly because there are so many lines. With the arrival of the vertebrates there is an apparent sense of purpose, as the fish lead to the amphibia, the amphibia to the reptiles, and the reptiles to birds and mammals. There is a gradual development of the heart, of locomotion, of the skeleton, and the same logical progression is no less plain with the central nervous system.

Amphioxus is a marine creature beloved by zoologists because it is a living indication of a probable vertebrate ancestor. It is a chordate, which means that – at some stage – it possesses a notochord. This skeletal rod running the length of the back behind the nerve cord is a precursor of the vertebrate's vertebral column just as the *Amphioxus* nerve cord is a forerunner of the vertebrate's spinal cord. Even though it is an animal extremely primitive by all vertebrate yardsticks there is not only a dorsal nerve but an anterior brain divided into three parts – fore, mid and hind. A three-week-old human embryo has something of the appearance of

Amphioxus, the similarities being arguably greater than the dissimilarities.

Slightly less primitive are the cyclostomes, such as lampreys. They have no jaws but are fish-like in the adult form and *Amphioxus*-like when larvae. They are regarded as the next rung on the ladder, and their brains support this supposition. In a lamprey there are both olfactory bulbs and cerebral hemispheres projecting forward from the fore-brain, the first steps that will lead, eventually, to the swollen hemispheres of the human cerebrum. Both pairs of swellings are solely concerned with the sense of smell, and there is no thickening to the roof of the cerebral hemispheres, so crucial in creating the all-important cortex of the higher vertebrates. In lampreys the hind-brain and the nearby cerebellum do most of the brain's work. The days of the fore-brain are, so to speak, still ahead of us.

The bony fishes – teleosts – are the most numerous fish, both as individuals and species. They live in a wide variety of conditions but, despite this proliferation and a considerable distortion of fish-brain and fish-shape, everything is variation upon a theme. All fish, whatever their form, are emphatically fish, and their brains only alter within a stereotype. Sometimes the olfactory bulbs are considerably ahead of the main brain, connecting with it by lengthy stalks (as in the carp), and sometimes they closely abut the brain (as in the sturgeon), but the brain itself is similar. It is possible, to some degree, to gain an opinion of a fish's lifestyle by an examination of its central nervous system. The cerebellum, for instance, varies in size with the muscular activity of the fish species, being small in the frequently sluggish and often parasitic cyclostomes but large in the ever-swimming, ever-searching sharks.

With amphibia, the next stage up from fish, there is no dramatic alteration to the brain, at least nothing compared with the revolution of moving from the water on to land. Control of the body is still effected aft, so to speak, of the fore-brain, and the cerebral hemispheres are still mainly concerned with the sense of smell. A frog can continue almost normally if these hemispheres are removed. Nevertheless, they do show signs of their coming importance in vertebrate evolution. Both the top and bottom of the hemispheres have started to become correlation centres and, although not yet vital to a frog's existence, do represent a strategic advance, however much amphibian behaviour is little different from that of fish.

Intellectually a reptile may not seem much forward of an amphibian, but the reptile brain is markedly different, notably in its cerebellum and the cerebral hemispheres. The cerebellum is much larger, although nothing like so large as in birds and mammals, and the reptilian cerebral hemispheres have become yet more differentiated, following on from the process initiated in the amphibians. However, as reptiles led both to birds and to mammals, the reptile fore-brain evolved in two distinct directions. The first, with large (basal) lobes in the side wall of each hemisphere, led to the birds; and the second, with thinner cerebral walls and a more complex cortex, led to the mammals. Turtles confuse this clarity by possessing a bit of both lines of development, the turtles being the most general of all reptiles. The most specific are the alligators and crocodiles with very large basal lobes which place them clearly on the bird side of reptilian evolution. That the reptile brain is an advance upon the amphibian arrangement, and the amphibian is an advance on the fish, does not mean that the reptile brain can bewilder the fish anatomist. It is still, most blatantly, along the basic vertebrate design. Its medulla oblongata, cerebellum, mid-brain, and cerebral hemispheres are all easily identifiable and distinct. From the brain point of view a reptile is just an advanced form of fish.

A reptilian peculiarity is that both *Sphenodon*, a primitive member of the group, and the lizards possess a third visual organ on the top of their heads. This needs explanation. All vertebrates possess a pair of out-growths from the roof of the fore-brain, and one of these – usually the right-sided protrusion – forms the pineal organ. The fact that this structure is variously called pineal eye, pineal body, pineal organ, and pineal gland reflects correctly its changing form and role throughout vertebrate evolution. In the elasmobranchs, such as sharks and rays, there is a pineal body but it no longer resembles an eye, as it does in the lizards. In almost all higher fishes the pineal is missing. It is present in amphibia, and in some of them it possesses sensory cells. In birds and mammals it is also present, but with them it neither has sense cells nor resembles an eye. However, as it exists in all reptiles except crocodiles, has the structure of an eye in *Sphenodon* and the lizards, and reappears after a fashion in birds and mammals, this odd assortment of facts about one structure raises more questions than it answers. Is it a primitive organ, first developed in the earliest of vertebrates and retained (partly) ever since? Or is there a repeated need during vertebrate evolution for some sort of median eye/organ that is wholly or partly satisfied, wholly in the lizards, partly among amphibia, and quite differently among birds and mammals? There is no answer – as yet.

The bird brain is not on the true line that leads to man, but demands a mention. It is still much like a reptile's but is most conspicuously different in its cerebral hemispheres. At the back of the brain the optic lobes and cerebellum are also enlarged, as befits a creature which is both active and sees well. In fact the cerebellum projects so far forwards and the cerebral hemispheres so far back that they meet, virtually obscuring the mid-brain. The old visible simplicity of the fish design is therefore vanishing. The mammals also have enlarged cerebral hemispheres but the cause of such enlargement is very different between mammals and birds. In birds it is the basal nuclei (or corpus striatum) that is the swollen structure; in mammals it is the cortex. In fact the bird hemispheric swelling is at the expense of its cortex. How a bird's corpus striatum is organised – which part does what – is not known, but birds – unlike mammals – can still live if their cerebral hemispheres are removed. They can fly, run and peck without them, but cannot pair, build nests or care for their young. (The chicken running about with its head off is a short-lived event. The subtler surgery of removing just the hemispheres can leave the birds alive for a year or more.)

The mammalian brain has, as its most marked difference over the reptiles, a huge development of its cerebral hemispheres. These tend not only to eclipse the rest of the brain visually but make it easy to forget that other important changes have also taken place. For example, the mammalian cerebellum is much bigger and more complex than in other vertebrates, partly because mammalian locomotion is so much more complicated. The mid-brain has, in contrast, lost much of its former role, with its visual and auditory tasks being taken over largely by the cerebral hemispheres. Least altered is the medulla oblongata, if only because its traditional vertebrate roles are still carried on, those of respiration, blood flow and the basic physiological control of the body.

The fore-brain is not composed of just the cerebral hemispheres, and that part of it known as the diencephalon has certainly changed from the reptile model in many ways, but these alterations are overshadowed by the most dramatic difference of all between mammals and lower vertebrates, namely the increase in size and function of the cerebral hemispheres. As a result of their dominance in the mammals they control almost every activity with only involuntary actions being (largely) beyond their control. In the hemispheres are localised areas, dealing specifically with senses and muscles, and the so-called silent areas. To stimulate these artificially evokes no particular response, but much of the frontal lobes, with the proportion being greatest in the highest mammals, is formed of this silent zone.

'The evolution of the cerebral hemispheres is the most spectacular story in comparative anatomy,' wrote Alfred S. Romer, of Harvard, doyen of vertebrate textbook writers. And so it is, even if possessors of these hemispheres are expressing this opinion. The creation of a rhino's skin, an elephant's tusk, or a blue whale's bulk is also impressive; the brain's development is just more remarkable. It is not so much brain mass that is spectacular but the level and degree of organisation within it. A tusk, however awesome, is not more exciting than a single tooth. Its mass can be weighed and measured, and that is that. The internal complexity of the human brain is much more exciting and is still, for the main part, little understood. Some of the pathways, links, and areas are now quite well mapped, but the silent zones are least explored. Within them lies most of mankind's wisdom, imagination, forethought, compassion, and very distinctive lust for life, art, thought, invention and despair.

And somehow all of that arose from the elementary nerve network of the coelenterates, the more advanced ganglia of the later invertebrates, the crucial blueprint of the chordate brain, and its steady development through the fishes, amphibia, reptiles and mammals to man. There is such a logic to the story that it does seem preordained, like evolution with a purpose, a destination destined from the very start. If this is believable, or even arguable, the presumption must follow that every other end-point is equally determined, whether elephantine tusk or blue-whale bulk. In the context of creation every development has its own fascination, but it is inevitable that we should be particularly astonished by our own most remarkable characteristic. No other creature has a brain such as we have. An elephant brain is three to four times bigger, a whale's can be over six times heavier, but no other nervous system – so far as we, with ours, can judge – has the complexity, ability and ingenuity of the human brain. No wonder we agree with Romer that it provides the 'most spectacular story'. In fact we can go further and say there is nothing else like it in the universe. Somewhere out there must be better brains, but we have not found them yet (and they, we presume, have not found us). Until that day dawns the brain of *Homo sapiens* is quite the most extraordinary development of all.

3. Growth

Embryology in general / Human foetal development / Neural calendar (before birth) / Prematurity / Reflexes / The skull / Growth after birth / Neural calendar (part II) / Brain damage / Head size, brain size

> I must have a prodigious quantity of mind: it takes me as much as a week sometimes to make it up
> – Mark Twain

> What seems so puzzling is how the proper assembly of the parts endows the instrument with the extraordinary properties that reside in the brain
> – Stephen W. Kuffler and John G. Nicholls in
> *From Neuron to Brain* (1976)

Embryology 'No developing tissue has received so much attention as developing nervous tissue.' This statement, frequently reiterated, might make us believe that the process is now fully understood. In one sense it *is* understood. It is known when and where the first embryonic cells form the basis of all nervous tissue, when this becomes tubular, and where this fundamental central nervous system grows to form brain, spinal cord and nervous network. In another sense – and the more intriguing of the two – the how and why of all this when and where is still (almost) as unknown as it has always been. Scientists talk of breakthroughs, fresh insights, and leaps forward, but the solid knowledge so far accumulated is, by any real yardstick, extremely modest. This is so despite the fact that we are fascinated by the nervous system, including its development, and the further fact that it conveniently performs its earliest development most accessibly near the surface of the embryo.

The general statements are easy, and they sprinkle opening paragraphs. 'All of embryonic development is a feat of precision engineering, and none more than the development of the nervous system.' 'How nerves combine to produce behaviour may be broken down into two parts: how nerve circuits work, and how these circuits come to be appropriately wired during development.' 'The overall pattern of wiring – which nerve cells are connected to which – is found to be remarkably constant from one animal to the next, whereas the details of the wiring – the specific number and anatomical location of the connections – are quite variable.' 'The fascination of the embryo is that it controls its own development. It can ultimately behave as it does because it laid down its nerves in the manner that it did.' Each embryo knows where and when and what to do from the start.

Following conception the first few cell divisions show no sign of a nervous system. Nevertheless it appears early. Either before or just after gastrulation has ended, namely the process whereby the three primitive layers are first established – ectoderm, mesoderm, endoderm – there is a neural plate. This precursor of neural tissue is formed from ectoderm, the embryo's outermost layer, as is reasonable because senses, nerves and the outside world are all associated. The cells of this plate change from being cube-shaped into column-shaped, and this morphological change is accompanied by biochemical change as certain enzymes become concentrated in the neuro-ectoderm.

To begin with, and aware of the shifting biochemistry, researchers looked for some controlling chemical. The facts discovered turned out to be more complex; so they searched instead for interaction between several substances. They learned that ectoderm does not just develop on its own but is influenced by the mesoderm, its neighbouring embryonic layer. So filters were experimentally inserted to determine what passed from one layer to the other, but without great success. The principal difficulty lay in the lack of certainty about the kind of object being sought. Was it a chemical or some other stimulus? (Even damaging the ectoderm can cause it to become 'neuralised'.)

At all events certain cells are differentiated to form the neural plate. The whole of development is essentially a process of differentiation and this, put another way round, is a matter of increasing restriction. To begin with, in theory, all cells have a similar potential: they can each be progenitors of every kind of cell in the body. As differentiation proceeds their possibilities are reduced, first into primitive layer, then systems arising from that layer, and finally a particular part of that particular system. The one hundred and twenty-five thousand or so cells of the neural plate are no longer omnipotent. They are neural ectoderm, restricted to create some part of the nervous system. Which part and why is another enigma.

After its formation the neural plate becomes a thickened region of the ectoderm. It is still external and, as we all know, the eventual nervous system lies internally. This process starts when the neural plate becomes a neural tube. In the bony fishes (teleosts) this happens after the plate has sunk inwards as a double fold, with a tube resulting from this in-folding. In all other vertebrates the same end result of a tube is formed by the neural plate rolling upwards at its edges until these meet centrally. It seems that some microfilaments appear within the cells, then contract and cause the rolling up. Once the tube has been formed it too begins to differentiate, thickening its walls, particularly at the head (brain) end. Most of the swelling is due, initially, to a proliferation of cells through cell division, but the multiplying does not last long. In the chick it (almost) ceases after eight and a half days of incubation. Even in humans, so much better endowed neurologically than any chicken, it stops after four months or so of foetal life. The human is then less than an ounce in weight and the eight-and-a-half-day chick is also of a diminutive size. With both species the massive changes thereafter in nerve-cell tissue are largely due to increase in size and shape of the individual cells. (As there is no more replication the subsequent alterations in size and shape are due to cell migration and degeneration.)

After differentiation comes determination. Differentiation occurs as cells, such as the neural tube, become distinguished from their neighbours. They become quite different tissue and, although apparently identical to neighbouring cells in the earliest stages, their fate is distinct. A nerve cell next to a bone cell is not half-bone, half-nerve: it is one thing or the other. However, in the earliest stages and when differentiation is occurring, it is possible for cells to be manipulated – by an experimenter. Neural tissue can become other kinds of tissue if suitably transposed. Later, however manipulated, it can only become different kinds of nervous tissue. Later still, whatever the experimenter does, it can only become the kind of nervous tissue it is by then fated to be. It has become fully determined.

Somehow – an enormous word – the various cells fulfil their destiny. The anterior swelling of the neural tube becomes the brain, and its hollow centre at that end becomes the ventricles. The neural crest, a group of cells nipped off in the formation of the neural tube (and lying between it and the outside skin), is the basis of a wide variety of nervous components, such as spinal and cranial ganglia. Somehow – and the word is still no smaller – axons grow out from central nerve cells and find their way to (almost) every portion of the developing body, from big toe to little finger. At its conclusion the nervous system is the most highly patterned tissue, to use the embryologist's phrase, in the body. If its differentiation, determination and development could be understood, every other tissue formation in the body would be plain sailing by comparison.

Blood vessels, for example, are also a complex network, but there is not the same degree of specificity in the circulatory system. Each arteriole must be connected to the heart and each vein must also lead to that central organ, but with nerves there is no such broad outline. Each axon leaving the eye, for example, must connect with an exact target cell in the brain. The wiring of arteries is more like a country's water system: there must be such a ramifying network, with small and big pipes reaching everywhere. The wiring of nerves is more akin to the telephone. Each number links each house only with one precise portion of the central exchange.

For over a century neuroscientists have been enquiring about this detailed precision. The problem has been approached from both ends of the animal kingdom, from the simple creatures with simple systems to the advanced forms whose nervous network is most complex, intriguing, exciting and problematical. Both have their protagonists. For example, embryologist Ruth Bellairs advocates study of the more complicated organisms:

> In the past, many developmental biologists have regarded the simplest biological systems as being the most worthwhile ones to study. It seems unlikely, however, that the general principles to be derived from the study of development in simple organisms will help us greatly in understanding the details of how the complex patterns in the nervous system arise.

At the other end of the scale are embryologists William G. Quinn and James L. Gould recommending study of a single-celled creature: 'Paramecium is the one system where electrophysiology, membrane chemistry and genetics can all be directly applied to find out what a conductance channel looks like and how it opens and closes.' Presumably – to an outsider at least – no single strategy is best. Scientific solutions rarely come from a single approach to a multiple problem, but certainly it will be experimental animals, either big or very small, that will give the answers to explain just how each proto-human manages to make its extraordinary nervous system from the single fertilised egg that starts the story.

Human foetal development   Many mammals, such as rodents, are born three or four weeks after conception. The human infant traditionally spends 266 days in the uterus (or 38 weeks, or 8.75 months). This is more time than, for instance, monkeys, sheep, pigs, goats, lions, dogs and all smaller animals, but less than horses, cattle, llamas, badgers, camels and elephants. However, a human neonate is still most inept at the end of its time in the womb (unlike horses, cattle, camels and elephants), being incapable of survival without considerable assistance, and it must also live for many years before reaching sexual, physical and mental maturity – in that order. Such leisurely progress after birth might suggest that development in the uterus has also been laggardly, but not so. In fact, with the body in general and the nervous system in particular, almost everything proceeds with considerable speed. It is only growth that is slow. The nervous system starts to form by the time the mother is having the first twinges of suspicion that she may be pregnant. Abortions are often made to occur at the end of the third month. The foetus is then still very small but its brain, for example, is relatively large, well-rounded and shaped in its general outline much like an adult's brain. At that stage the product of conception is undoubtedly human, and no more so than in its nervous endowment.

To chart this progress a calendar of happenings is most convenient. Although conceptions can occur on any date, and with remarkable irrelevance to the seasons (when compared with almost all other mammals), this particular calendar will start for convenience on January 1 and in a non-leap year. It will emphasise quite how speedily, and in how few days and weeks, a human's nervous system comes into being.

Neural calendar (before birth)

Day 1½ (Jan. 2)	First division of fertilised cell. 2-cell stage.
Day 2 (Jan. 2)	Second division. 4-cell stage.
Day 3 (Jan. 3)	Cells reach total of 16 or 32. (The divisions are still synchronised.)
Day 4 (Jan. 4)	Ball of 60–70 cells. (Division no longer synchronised.)
Day 5 (Jan. 5)	Embryo enters uterus from Fallopian tube. Ball becomes hollow with a mass of cells at one end.
Day 6–9 (Jan. 6–9)	The several hundred cells attach to uterus wall and start differentiating into 2, then 3 layers. Embryo 1/100th of an inch long.
Day 10–13 (Jan. 10–13)	Embryo becomes plate-shaped and embedded in uterine wall. Size doubles every day. Primitive streak formed, a bulge in the ectoderm that is the first indication of an axis

and that a vertebrate is developing. It is the line along which spinal cord will develop. (The mother is still unaware of her condition, not yet having missed her period.)

Day 14–17
(Jan. 14–17)

Considerable differentiation, with embryonic cells forming not just embryo but yolk sac, umbilical cord, placenta, amnion. (Bleeding may occur now, resulting from increased blood-flow to implantation site, and may be confused with menstruation.)

Day 18
(Jan. 18)

Nervous system starts to form, and next 10 days often called neurula stage as so much developmental emphasis is upon this system. Both eyes and ears faintly detectable. (Mathematical mothers aware now that menstruation is late but confirmation of pregnancy comes later.)

Day 20
(Jan. 20)

Neural tube now formed along the length of the primitive streak. This primordial nervous system is composed of neuroblasts (or primitive neurons).

End of 3rd week
(Jan. 21)

Brain end of neural tube more swollen than the rest. Distinct hind-brain, mid-brain and fore-brain, with the fore-brain beginning to arch over ventrally. (Forthright mothers now make appointment to check on pregnancy.)

End of 4th week
(Jan. 28)

The head is the largest part of the embryonic body, and nervous system so arched over at brain end that its shape is akin to a walking stick. Embryo ¼ inch long, weight less than 1 gram. (Mother given confirmation of her state. Morning sickness often additional proof.)

5th week
(Feb. 4)

Brain growth paramount, although other organs developing rapidly. Heart has been pumping since 25th day. Finger outlines appear on 33rd day. External ears take shape. Embryo ½ inch long. (Some call it foetus by this stage mainly because of slight resemblance to human form. Others delay change of name until 9th week when resemblance more obvious. Mother has generally called it 'baby' from the start.)

6th week (Feb. 11)	Brain begins to lose walking-stick simplicity. A downward kink appears between mid-brain and hind-brain, and the fore-brain (having bent backwards) begins to enlarge at its forward end. By now brain is in 5 parts rather than 3, these being the telencephalon, diencephalon, mesencephalon, metencephalon and myelencephalon. The 5 become the 5 major regions of the adult brain. Muscles are beginning to be controlled by the brain, even though the mother unaware of such contractions. Foetus ¾ inch long, and weight 2–3 grams. (Abortions often take place at twice this date post-conception.)
7th week (Feb. 18)	Forward swelling of brain now as large as the rest of the neural material within the head. Also kinking very marked, and this is the last occasion for seeing the former basic simplicity of the brain. Hereafter it becomes compressed/enmeshed within itself. But brain less than ½ inch from front to rear. Neurons being added at thousands every minute.
End of 2nd month (Feb. 28)	Head now half length of body. (It will be quarter at birth, and one-eighth at adulthood.) Weight of nervous system one-quarter of total foetal weight. Foetus capable of responding to touch, first on the face, then on body.
3rd month (March 31)	Brain now with very definite form (something like a diminutive boxing glove, with the wrinkles at the wrist-end being the mesencephalon, cerebellum and medulla). Cell division and differentiation proceeding apace. Total increment per month 600 per cent but size still modest as brain only slightly more than ½ inch long and less than that from top to bottom. Neurons being added at rate of a couple of thousand every second. (Commonest time for miscarriages is at 10th week.)
4th month (April 30)	Growth period for foetus as a whole, nervous system included. From a weight of less than 1 ounce at this time the foetus must enlarge to be 7½ pounds in the next 5 months. Brain's Sylvian fissure detectable. Many reflexes now

possible, such as frowning, swallowing, thumb-sucking. A tickled foot will retract. Lips begin to protrude in early preparation for all-important sucking. All these activities are possible in an individual smaller than an adult's finger joint. Myelinisation – sheathing of the nerve fibres – begins with some of the more primitive (spinal) tracts, and the process continues until well after birth. (Fibres from higher centres, such as cerebral cortex, are last to be covered in this fashion, and process not really complete for several years.)

5th month (May 31)
Foetus now 12 times heavier than at end of previous month. Brain almost 2 inches from front to rear. Other fissures become apparent, such as central, parieto-occipital, calcarine. Foetal hiccups start. Heart beat can be heard externally (by those who place an ear on the mother's abdomen). Head now only one-third of total body length, but non-neural volume of head still relatively small (to full-term baby, and even more so to adult). Mother's weight gain now 1 pound a week, but foetus still less than 1 pound. Commissures of brain completed. Foetus now in possession of full quota of nerve cells which will make up adult human nervous system – 12 –15 billion. These have therefore been grown at an average rate of 1,300 a second over period since nervous system started to form. As there must have been a peak in this replication, cells were then grown even faster.

6th month (June 30)
Brain surface still smooth, but Sylvian fissure very marked. Front to rear measurement now 2½ inches, top to bottom 1½ inches (and therefore similar to the adult proportion). Total foetal weight is 1 pound 6 ounces, and premature life now possible (but not ideal). Can grip firmly with hands, can open and close eyelids.

7th month (July 31)
Boxing-glove smoothness starts to disappear with initiation of gyri and sulci. Brain 3 inches front to rear and head circumference 8½–

10½ inches. The eye's retinal layers completed, and the eye is light-perceptive. (Frequently considered that foetus has legal right to a separate existence after 28th week.)

8th month
(August 31)
All of the primary sulci now present (although many secondary folds will continue to appear for several months after birth). Brain 3¼ inches front to rear, and head circumference 11½–13 inches. Weight of foetus 5 pounds, and weight of nervous system now only one-tenth of the total. (At age 5 it will be one-twentieth, and at adulthood it will be one-fiftieth.)

Final month
(Sept. 23)
Considerable growth, as foetus adds 50 per cent to its weight in final 28 days. Considerable convolution of the brain – it looked simple, like a primitive mammal, at 8 months but is undoubtedly human at 9 months. Front to rear length increases to 4¼ inches, circumference (of head) to 13–14½ inches, and brain weight to 12 ounces (or one-quarter of adult brain weight). Head is a quarter of total body length, and its size is not only greatest problem during each birth but considerable evolutionary problem: length of human pregnancy, size and immaturity of neonate, maternal pelvis and pelvic canal all relate to the large (relative to other mammals) head size at birth. Despite considerable foetal activity, and the extensive reflexes, and the brain's size, and its mature appearance, there is no evidence that the cerebral cortex has any influence upon behaviour by the end of pregnancy (or for a few weeks afterwards).

Prematurity   The uterine confinement of 38 weeks or 266 days is often spoken of as the norm, and to be ahead of or behind that date is therefore atypical. In fact very few pregnancies – 5 per cent – finish on the appointed day. To be fourteen days late occasions no concern, but thereafter the talk of a possible induction becomes louder. However, normal pregnancies beyond 300 days do occur, and legally it is not considered impossible for pregnancies to be much longer. (A Mr Wood, in 1947, disclaimed paternity because he had been absent from his wife for 346 days before she gave birth. He lost his case.)

To be born early, which is more frequent, is almost certainly to be lighter than normal (below 7.4 pounds/3 kilos) but is not necessarily dubbed as premature. That distinction – a dubious one, as prematurity is hardly to be recommended – applies to the 6½ per cent of all babies who are born both early and weighing less than 2,500 grams/5½ pounds. Other definitions (which parallel the very low birth-weight) are:

i.   A crown-to-heel length of 18½ inches/47 centimetres or less. (Normal is 20 inches.)
ii. A head circumference of 13 inches/33 centimetres or less. (Normal is above that.)
iii. A chest circumference of 11¾ inches/30 centimetres or less.
iv. Disproportion between circumferences of head and chest. (A relatively large head is more foetal, less mature.)

Despite such precise definitions a maternity unit does not provide special care only for those babies born within these categories. Instead it gives extra care for all in need, and the small, the short and the disproportionate, having (probably) spent less time in the uterus, are (almost certainly) in greater need than those either of normal weight or above that norm. However, the US Bureau of the Census and the Children's Bureau define prematurity as 'the termination of pregnancy in the period from the beginning of the 28th to the end of the 37th week of gestation'. The reason for the earlier date is that not many babies survive birth before then, and for the later date is that many assessments of a pregnancy due-date are wrong. Premature care should not be withheld owing to an error in fixing the start of the last menstruation (and therefore of conception two weeks afterwards). One further hazard for the definers is that equally mature babies may not be equally sized. Even by the end of the seventh uterine month some foetuses are twice the weight of others. At birth 5½ pounds to 11 pounds lies within the normal range, both extremes of baby being similarly capable. Conversely two six-pound babies can be extremely different, one in need of every assistance, the other more than able.

Prematurity is extremely common, and is commonest in the poorest societies. To him that hath not, even more shall be taken away. Asians have least, in general, and also have the smallest proportion of normally weighted babies. Of the 73 million live Asian births in 1979 some 15 million (20 per cent) were of low birth-weight. These diminutive Asians help to bring the average Asian birth-weight down to only 6 pounds 6 ounces/2,900 grams. Africans have 3.2 million low birth-weight babies out of 21 million live births, or 15 per cent; Latin Americans have 1.4 million out of 12.4 million births, or 11 per cent; Europeans have 534,000 out of 7 million, or 8 per cent; and North Americans 270,000 out of 3.6 million, or 7 per cent. By no means is prematurity some modest problem affecting a few. Globally it is forty underweight babies born every minute.

An advantage of premature infants – for the scientist – is that they are visible illustrations of the state of neural development at that early age. It is generally believed that, whether such an infant is within the uterus or the intensive-care ward, its behaviour potential is similar. E. H. Watson and G. H. Lowrey, in their *Growth and Development of Children*, have listed some early attributes, detected of course in those that were born but presumed to exist also in those whose birth is still ahead of them:

28–32 weeks (less than 7½ months)
 Modest, fleeting movements. Mild avoidance reaction to light and sound. Grasps slightly if palm stroked. Sucking and swallowing lack endurance. No definite sleeping pattern. Cry weak or absent.
32–36 weeks (less than 8¼ months)
 Sustained, positive movements. Strong, but inadequate, response to light and sound. Strong grasp if palm stroked. Definite periods of wakefulness. Good cry. Start of Moro reflex (arms flung outwards, then embraced together following any rapid change in position). When prone can turn head and lift rump.
36 weeks to term
 Active, sustained movements. Brisk erratic following of objects with eyes. Strong Moro reflex. When prone tries to lift head. Resistance to head movement. Seems pleased when caressed. Strong sucking reflex.

The principal error of prematurity is that the foetus/infant is more likely to die: the lighter the offspring, the more likely the death. For those born with weights between 4½ and 5½ pounds/2,000–2,500 grams the risk these days is extremely modest, although it used to be 6 per cent at the end of World War II. For birth-weights of 3⅓–4½ pounds/1,500–2,000 grams there is still a substantial risk – of about 10 per cent. For the still lower category 2¼–3⅓ pounds/1,000–1,500 grams the risk used to be 50 per cent some 40 years ago but has much improved in recent years to around half that figure. In the lowest category, less than 2¼ pounds/1000 grams, the death rate used to be 88 per cent and that category has shown the most marked improvement, particularly in combating the respiratory problems that have traditionally been so lethal. Even so, it is still the most dangerous weight group of them all.

Oddly the world's smallest survival, from a birth-weight of 10 ounces/283 grams, was born – at South Shields, County Durham – in 1938 before modern techniques were possible and before intensive care units had been developed. Normal infant mortality was then about 40 per 1,000, all of them heavyweights by comparison, average birth-weight then being 11 times greater than that of Miss South Shields.

The surviving prems, or preemies, take a long time to catch up physically with the full-term infants in, for example, body length and head circumference. Even by the end of the first year these measurements are each less – by about one inch – for those born prematurely. Brain size and volume are therefore smaller relative to birth-age, but not necessarily smaller if age since conception is the guiding parameter. However, prematurity is not to be recommended as there is relatively poor mental development for the group as a whole. They may catch up physically, by age two or so, and usually do, but considerable evidence has accumulated since the mid-1950s to show that premature infants are more likely to be mentally deficient than are full-term babies. The extremely premature are most at risk and the survival rate of all prematures is partnered – to some degree – by an increase in the population of mental defectives. There may be physical causes, such as intracranial haemorrhage, and there may also be psychological reasons, for the clinical cribs that keep such minute people alive bear scant relation to the cosy lactating warmth of a maternal bosom. 'Take care to get born well,' said George Bernard Shaw. 'Take care to be born at term,' he should have added.

Two recent cases in the United States highlighted both the advantages and demerits of this form of medical advance, of – in effect – keeping late miscarriages alive. Both stories were extensively publicised. Born after only twenty-five weeks in the uterus, at 175 days instead of 266, Olivia weighed 1 pound 10 ounces/747 grams, or about a quarter of an average birth-weight. She managed to breathe on her own, had no brain haemorrhage, only mild respiratory trouble (hyaline membrane disease, the usual killer, was kept at bay) and was well enough to leave hospital before the date at which she should have been born. After two weeks she went blind. Retrolental fibroplasia, mild at first, then detached both her retinas. 'She's doing beautifully otherwise,' was one report.

Andrew was born weighing 1 pound 12 ounces/792 grams. His parents opposed intensive care, but Andrew received it all the same, suffering respiratory distress, fractures, seizures, intracranial haemorrhage. He was, in short, not ready for this world and would, one assumes, have been mentally deficient. Anyway, he died after six months, or three months after he should have been born, and his parents received a $100,000 hospital bill.

The medical profession is divided against itself, not just on the ethical side of such striving on behalf of these smallest of all people but on whether the effort has been rewarding. A London doctor, writing in *The Lancet* (June 1979), said that very low birth-weight babies (less than $3\frac{1}{3}$ pounds/1,500 grams) were still dying and being handicapped in 1975 as they were in 1960. The letter proved to be a cat among pigeons. Other dovecots reported progress, better figures, and a determination to carry on the work. 'Care of high-risk mothers and immature infants represents one of the best health care investments possible,' reported one. On the other hand, as another doctor stated, 'We're not the ones who have to go home with a severely brain-damaged infant.' Despite the old enemy of hyaline membrane, other breathing problems, colitis, displaced retinas (from wrong oxygen levels) and blindness, it is brain haemorrhage that is now the greatest scourge of the very small. From a quarter to a half of them suffer this way and, for those that survive, their brains are damaged for the rest of a life that started, externally at least, far too soon. With 21 million babies being born too soon every year the quantity of mental deficiency arising in this way must be considerable. Any proportion of 21 million is considerable.

Reflexes   The normal, healthy, full-term human baby may be the latest welcome addition at birth to the species *Homo sapiens*, but a truly objective observer could well be forgiven for believing otherwise. Ape offspring are smaller but look infinitely wiser. All monkeys are more capable at birth than are humans. And many a lower mammal, such as every ungulate, can virtually fend for itself – given a nipple of milk conveniently nearby. There are mammals equally or more inept at birth than humans, such as many rodents, cats, dogs, rabbits, but such creatures are all relatively young: a rabbit is born thirty-one days after conception, a rat twenty-two days, a golden hamster sixteen. No other animal spends quite so long developing in the uterus as man and is also quite so incapable at the end of it. Similarly no other animal is quite so casual in its subsequent progress.

At birth in particular, a full 266 days after conception, the human looks stupid, is stupid by any rational measurement, and is scarcely more than a bundle of reflexes. Nevertheless these are intriguing and make an odd assortment. Certainly they all indicate neural connections.

The Moro reflex Already mentioned, as prematures show it between 32 and 36 weeks. It is temporary and much harder to elicit two months after a normal birth date.

Grasp reflex For two months this can be strong enough for the whole body weight to be lifted. There is a similar, but less demonstrable, grasp reflex in the foot. After two months this foot reflex reverses itself: stimulation of the sole leads to the toes turning upwards. This (Babinski) reflex is reversed again at about two years when the toes turn down (grasp) once more. If Babinski persists there is probably a defect.

Rooting reflex Touch a cheek and the face turns in that direction. Later on both lips and tongue are moved that way as well.

Blink reflex Stimulated eyelashes lead to blinking, whether awake or asleep.

Sneezing Stimulated nostrils or bright light lead to this explosive reflex.

Walking A baby held vertically with feet on the ground will 'walk' if moved forwards, but only until six weeks old.

Tonic neck reflex If the baby is prone its face lies sideways (and keeps the airways open). When the head is forcibly (or voluntarily) moved to face the other way both legs and arms readjust. Those straight become flexed and vice versa. The reflex goes after 3–6 months.

Doll's eye reflex Eye movement lags behind if head is swiftly rotated. Very temporary reflex as it goes after a few days.

Crowned extension reflex If a leg is stretched, and its sole then stroked, the other leg bends and then stretches. Goes after a month.

Galant's reflex If trunk is stimulated between chest and hips the trunk will curve in on that side. Goes after the second month of life, but reappears later.

Of course there are also the more functional and significant neural attributes of the newborn. The reason it can survive, from about seven months after conception, is that the nervous system has sufficiently developed to control body temperature (at about 99.5°F rectally), direct breathing movements – 30–80 times a minute – the moment air becomes available, and organise swallowing when food is made available. However, the human baby is barely adept at these attributes, often spluttering, choking and confusing swallowing with breathing. It will quickly lose heat if conditions are cool. Observe by contrast an infant of the three large apes. It appears relaxed, content, even knowledgeable. Observe a human and it can be all a-splutter, certainly uncertain, and with only a tenuous grip upon its capabilities. Some say the human gestation period is really ten months, with the baby's first four weeks being a limbo or watershed between an aquatic and an aerial existence. It often looks that way as the baby surfaces from breast or bottle, much like some anxious swimmer after too long a period down below.

The Skull   At birth the skull bones are soft and more numerous: there are forty-five instead of the adult twenty-two. For example, the frontal bone at birth is divided by the metopic suture. The two halves start to fuse at age two and are firmly fused at six, creating just one frontal bone (save in 8 per cent of individuals who maintain their forehead suture). The parietal bone is also paired at birth but the occipital bone is in four parts. Many of the sutures vanish soon in infancy, having played their part in the apparent impossibility of such a large head passing through a small birth canal. The cranial bones can also overlap slightly to decrease the head's diameter, thus assisting an impossibility to become a feasibility. The various gaps between the bones also help during the moulding of the head, by permitting the overlap, the decrease in head size, the birth of a pint through a half-pint hole.

It should never be forgotten, of course, that the head contains the major part of the central nervous system. All this moulding, overlapping, and decreasing is happening, not to buttocks or feet but to the brain-case. As the mother's contractions come and go, and as she pushes the product of conception out of herself, it is her infant's skull that forces the opening. Mankind comes into this world with its head for a battering ram, and the precious brain within must suffer come what may. The distortion that follows many a birth can be alarming to the parents, but the displaced bones do return to their proper place as the offspring's head resumes its shape. It is hard to believe that damage has not occurred while the brain was experiencing considerable pressure and deformity, but there is no evidence among the normal run of births that anything untoward has really happened. Besides, the skull and therefore the brain are so readily moulded and flattened later on in life. The occipitoparietal area, in particular, can be exceedingly mis-shapen at three to four months. Parents are frequently worried and have to be reassured. Except for certain retarded infants the head (and brain) will have become a standard and less worrying shape by the first birthday.

There are six fontanels (the softer areas in a baby's skull) at birth. Quite the largest is the anterior fontanel (or fontanelle), lying between the frontals and the parietals, and measuring about a square inch. It is so large, and often visibly pulsing, that the other five tend to be disregarded. The posterior fontanel is two inches further back, between the parietals and the occipitals, and is therefore also on the top of the head. The two sphenoid fontanels and the two mastoids lie on both sides of the skull between the parietal and the sphenoid and the parietal and temporal bones. These other and lesser five are more triangular and not so square as the largest and most pronounced, the anterior fontanel. At all times this huge opening looks worryingly delicate, as the brain's frontal lobes lie beneath its cartilage. It may become tense at times of fever, convex in hydrocephalus, or concave during wasting or excessive diarrhoea; but it usually closes, being the last fontanel to do so, by ten to sixteen months after birth. If closure is delayed it may be due to rickets, mental abnormality, or just one more indication that human development follows a well-worn path but in its own good time.

The size at birth of the moulded, mis-shapen, squeezed, wedged, many-boned, fontanelled and precious skull is of course related to the size of brain within, but neither can be correlated with mental ability, either then or later in childhood. This fits with the fact that, at adulthood, there is also no correlation between brain size and intelligence (or with anything else for that matter). However, a very small head, below the normal range, can be due to a failure of brain growth and a very large head, well above normal, can be caused by hydrocephalus. In both microcephalus and hydrocephalus some brain damage can be expected.

Growth after birth   The head at birth is large, relative to the body parts, and it will grow larger after birth as the brain expands fourfold. At the same time it steadily becomes smaller, relative to the rest of the body, as the torso in general and the legs in particular grow to their adult proportions. If there is starvation during this period the brain and heart will continue to grow while many other organs shrink, notably the thymus and liver. A starved child can look foetal, owing to its abnormally large head. The neuro-cranium – brain-case – is very big relative to the face at birth, eight or nine times bigger. It continues to grow rapidly after birth, exceeding that of the rest of the skull, because the head as a whole – to speak extremely loosely – is no longer concerned that it will have to squeeze through the birth canal. By the age of four to five years the cranium will be 90 per cent of its adult size, a dimension it reaches at age ten. No other part of the body is quite so swift in its striving for maturity.

Neural advancement is a combination of anatomical development and of the abilities that then result. No child can perform any skill until the appropriate nervous system is in order, a fact that enthusiastic and ambitious parents can sometimes forget. Various experiments have made this point, most tellingly. Two twins were studied (by Arnold Gesell) from one to eighteen months. The first was given considerable training, assistance, stimulation, while the second was not. Gesell found that practice and exercise did nothing to hasten, for example, tower-building and climbing abilities. Two further twins were likewise separated over toilet training, and the conclusion was that no difference occurred in the acquisition of sphincter control. The experimenter (M. McGraw) considered that 'early toilet training is, to say the least, futile.'

R. S. Illingworth summed up this subject: 'No amount of practice can make a child sit, walk, talk or acquire other skills until his nervous system is ready for it.' Nevertheless there is another side to this coin, that of neglect, and Illingworth is once again concise and to the point: 'Delay in the acquisition of skills may be caused by depriving the child of opportunity to practise them when sufficient maturation has occurred.'

Of course neural development is a whole panoply of achievements – two balanced blocks, four balanced blocks, first real word, first one hundred words, first dry night, first dry year – but the following calendar is an attempt to list some of the major aspects of growth and maturation. It is therefore an extension of the prebirth calendar between pages 34 and 38, and assumes that the same baby is involved, having been conceived on January 1, born correctly on September 23 and therefore aged one the following September. The awkwardness of this birth-dating has one virtue: it emphasises that birth is a movable feast. It marks the end of pregnancy, umbilical feeding and an aquatic life with an abrupt transformation to mouth feeding and aerial respiration; but that, so to speak, is all. Differentiation and growth have been occurring beforehand. Then, following the trauma of leaving the uterus, they occur subsequently. It is progress right from the start and birth happens – somewhere – along the line from conception to maturity.

Neural calendar (part II)

At birth
(Sept. 23)

Cranium to face ratio 9 to 1. Weight of brain over 12 ounces/350 grams, therefore one-tenth of total body weight. The baby can breathe, suck, swallow, salivate, cry, smell, taste, hear, yawn, vomit, hiccup, sneeze, cough, stretch. *Homo sapiens* has a long way to go. Already over a quarter of adult length/height, but about a twentieth of adult weight. Heart beat is about 140 per minute. Eye is small and therefore hyperopic (long-sighted). (Eyeball reaches adult size at age 12–14.) A pinprick has to be strong to elicit a reaction but, having done so, the response is quite violent (and this hypesthesia lasts for a few days). Head circumference 13.8 inches.

4 weeks
(Oct. 21)

Head circumference 14.9 inches.

5 weeks
(Oct. 28)

Smiles. (Some say this is true birth-time, with previous month being period of recovery from birth trauma, and baby now a true infant rather than an advanced foetus.) Most active muscles are those of mouth and eyes. In fact eyes more advanced than hands.

8 weeks
(Nov. 18)

Taste present at birth, but now starts to be acute. (The sense of smell is relatively poorly developed during infancy.) Pinpricks do not have to be so strong to elicit response, but this is more delayed and less vigorous. Head circumference 15.5 inches.

10 weeks
(Dec. 2)

Vocalises.

3rd month
12 weeks
(Dec. 16)

Head circumference 15.9 inches.

15 weeks
(Jan. 6, the
following year)

Can control head. Weight gain since birth about 6 pounds (or 90 per cent of birth weight). Most cot-deaths occur between 8th and 16th weeks. Start of period of rapid cortical organisation involving important sensory-motor correlation.

20 weeks
(Feb. 10)

Can control hands.

25 weeks (Mar. 16)	Can roll over. Reaches for a cube on seeing it.
6th month 26 weeks (March 23)	Can localise sounds and differentiate between voices. Head circumference 17.0 inches.
30 weeks (April 20)	Can sit, after a fashion.
8th month 35 weeks (May 25)	Can grasp objects. Hand preference (and handedness) makes its appearance during 2nd half of first year. Earlier in boys than girls. Response to pinpricks less general, with a greater awareness of the point of irritation.
9th month 39 weeks (June 22)	Head circumference 17.8 inches.
40 weeks (June 29)	Can pull body up.
45 weeks (Aug. 3)	Can walk if held. Some say foot dominance exhibited at this age. Hand dominance comes later.
End of 1st year (Sept. 23, or 622 days post-conception)	Can stand without assistance. Can sometimes walk alone, after a fashion, although many parents can still wonder whether offspring destined to be a quadruped rather than a biped. Weight-gain since birth about 14 pounds (or twice birth-weight). Heart beat about 115 per minute. Can put one cube on top of another. Head circumference 18.3 inches. (The increase since birth – over 4 inches – equals the total subsequent increase between age 1 and adulthood.)
2nd year	Walks and runs. Acquires bladder and bowel control. Uses words and phrases, with about 200 words. Starts using pronouns – mine, me, you, I – roughly in that order. Half adult height. One-eighth of adult weight. Anterior fontanel closes (but may close in 1st year or, very occasionally, in 3rd). Other fontanels close earlier. The metopic suture between two halves of frontal bone now begins to fuse (and will complete fusion by age 6). Heart beat about 110 per minute. Can place 3 cubes in a row or on top of each other. Can push pants down, but not off. Two-thirds of chil-

dren use right hand for writing and picking up at 18 months and 92 per cent by 2 years. (But prediction of right- or left-handedness cannot be made with confidence until later.) Visual acuity 20/70. Head circumference 19.2 inches.

3rd year   Uses sentences. Vocabulary about 1,000 words. Begins to obey rules with an understanding of their meaning. Has accomplished three-quarters of post-natal brain growth. (Will be adult-sized at age 10.) Can copy a circle and can use 3 cubes to make a bridge. Can fold paper lengthwise, crosswise, but not diagonally. Can go upstairs alone. Feeds himself, and spills little. Can take off pants. Enuresis leads to bladder control which leads to dry nights. In drawing a man only 24 per cent give him a head, 6 per cent give him feet, and none give him a neck. Head circumference 19.6 inches.

4th year   Great year for questions. Could (just about) be self-sufficient if food no problem. Begins to play with words. A great speaking time. Can lace shoes but not tie them. Likes to choose food. Goes to toilet solo. In drawing a man 79 per cent give him a head, 32 per cent give him feet, and none give him a neck. Head circumference 19.8 inches.

5th year   Can tell (long) stories. Can hop and skip. In manner can be a small adult as opposed to a maturing baby. As Leo Tolstoy said: 'From the child of 5 to myself is but a step, but from the new-born baby to the child of 5 is an appalling distance.' Most maturation is therefore happening before the first schoolday. Weight-gain since birth about 30 pounds (or 4 times birth-weight), but weight of nervous system now less in proportion to total body weight. It was one-tenth of total at birth, and is now one-twentieth. (At adulthood it will be one-fiftieth.) Neuro-cranium now 90 per cent of adult size. Heart beat about 100 per minute. (Girls are consistently higher throughout infancy, by about 5 beats a minute.) About 15 per cent of boys and 10 per cent of girls still experience enuresis. Can copy a square. (Copying a diamond will not come until 7th year.) In drawing a man 95 per cent give him a head, 63 per cent give him feet, and 9 per cent give him a neck. (At the end of the 6th year, these three proportions are 100, 95 and 56 per cent.) Visual acuity 20/30. (Will be 20/20 at age 7.) Head circumference 20 inches.

With the human baby showing no signs of cerebral cortex activity for the first weeks of its life, with its initial abilities comprising such a modest list, with its mental development proceeding at such a gentle pace, and with all indication of *sapiens* being promise rather than reality, it is not surprising that very little can be said about mental capacity in the earliest post-natal days and weeks. Indeed, most other mammals would score higher. It is easier to state what cannot be said about the human neonate, and Professor Illingworth has compiled a list.

A baby cannot be assessed intellectually in its first month. (Certain abnormalities are detectable, and severe cerebral palsy of the spastic type, but it cannot be said otherwise if various neurological signs will be permanent or not.) An exact score for an infant's IQ cannot be given (but only a range into which the development fits) and even mental superiority cannot be diagnosed. It cannot be said if a child's development will be speedy, will accelerate, or will be slow (except by looking at other members of the family and knowing of their development). Environmental influences cannot be predicted, or diseases, or injuries which will retard a child's development. What effect opportunity will have cannot be said, nor what a child will do with his or her talents.

Of course none of this means that injuries, deprivation, love, play, disease, opportunity, experience, or genetics are not influential. It just underlines the point that proper and useful measurement of such variables is still impossible. The child books tend to be more positive, advocating this or that treatment and scorning others, and such firmness is often what parents want to hear. Some influences that are measurable can produce answers that are unwelcome. For example, Western society (and others) is against the swaddling of infants, believing that such restraint conflicts with physical and mental growth. There is, however, no evidence that this baby-binding has any negative effect upon development, and the Russians, Lapps, Yugoslavs, Mexicans and others who practise this custom will do so anyway, whether or not there is supporting evidence. We in Britain used to be of their number (before the eighteenth century), and our ancestors used presumably to be as convinced of swaddling's merits as we today are of the unfettered and sometimes furious, freedom permitted in a modern cot.

Quite what kind of personalities will develop from today's cribs, carrycots and push-chairs is, of course, quite unknown. Today we are less certain of such things than were our ancestors, presumably as some sort of reaction against earlier confidence. This rose to a peak in the first decades of this century when the simplicity of Mendelian laws (simple because he used only one or two characteristics at a time) was applied without restraint to the complexity of human character. People then were good, bad, slovenly, drunk, backward, perverted, inferior or weak because they came from similar stock. Races were also either good or bad, strong or deficient, for identical and inescapable genetic reasons. Simultaneously there were others who asserted that the environment was all that mattered. Genetics, they said, was irrelevant in the development of character; the surroundings were omnipotent. It was possible for J. B. Watson to write in 1925:

Give me a dozen healthy infants, well formed, and my own specified world to bring them up in, and I'll guarantee to take any one at random and train him to become any type of specialist I might select – doctor, lawyer, artist, merchant, chief, and yes, even beggarman and thief, regardless of his talents, peculiarities, tendencies, abilities, vocations and race of his ancestors. There is no such thing as an inheritance of capacity, talents, temperament, mental constitution and character.

Today's opinion, if it can be summarised, would state that genetics is important, that environment is important and that each child seems to follow a course of its own, paying scant regard to either genetics or environment. The same parents produce children markedly different from each other, from themselves, and right from birth. E. Glover has written: 'We have every reason to assume that within a week or so of birth infants manifest in a primitive form all the various types of response which form the basis of adult characterology.' M. M. Shirley has made the same sort of point: 'Each baby exhibits a characteristic pattern of personality trends that changes little with age.'

Every child, in attaining its own particular end, also proceeds at its own particular pace. There are late developers who will overtake, or merely catch up, or stay behind. Similarly, to the initial delight of eager parents, there are those who forge ahead, doing great things with building blocks, picture cards and the toilet, but who then slip behind as later attributes of even greater worth prove more demanding. Each child is guided/assisted by amateurs, its parents, along a unique path towards a multitude of destinations, and no wonder that general truths are so concealed by such diversity. There is so much contradiction. Albert Einstein did not speak until he was four. Illingworth quotes one baby unable to sit up until nineteen months, or walk until thirty months, whose IQ then proved to be above average, and another child who could roll over at eighteen weeks, creep at twenty-two weeks, pull himself up at twenty-five weeks, walk (with furniture help) at twenty-six weeks, and walk unaided at thirty-seven weeks, whose IQ was then well below normal. The one golden rule is that no child is mentally backward who is behindhand in a single field of development and normal in all others. The mentally retarded are late in all areas of development, save perhaps for sitting and walking.

Brain damage   Spades are not always called spades in the matter of mental abnormality. Words like backward, retarded and even exceptional are bandied about in an effort to disguise some deficiency, and presumably with the wish that the subnormal are only temporarily so. This may be commendable, but it can also be misleading. It is particularly so when the terms brain-damaged and brain-injured are used. The undoubted implication is that damage or injury has been done, and therefore that someone or something has committed this offence. (See more on this subject between pages 240 and 243.)

One author has added up those difficulties which, in his experience, have been included under the heading of brain-damage. They were hyperactivity, distractability, awkwardness, poor muscular integration, faulty perception, unpredictable behaviour, extreme sensitivity. Some have gone further, adding those with Down's syndrome and microcephaly to the list. Plainly it is incorrect to suggest brain damage in such cases: Down's syndrome, for example, results from the possession of an extra chromosome. As a consequence of inheritance various organs do not develop in a normal manner, but they have not been damaged. So where to draw the line in a defective brain between damage and some natural cause? The answer, albeit irritating, is to restrict the title of brain-damaged for those whose brains have been damaged.

Cerebral palsy is the term grouping together various conditions characterised by paralysis that occurs in infancy or early childhood. About half are spastic – they are affected by spasms – but all forms of cerebral palsy manifest themselves before the age of three. (It is extremely unfortunate that so many words with precise and unhappy neurological meanings – cretin, paralytic, spastic – are currently used so carelessly, applied in all manner of unworthy contexts. In the hope of influencing this miserable trend I will now tell a joke with the wish that readers will, in future, be more cautious in their speech. One evening a taxi service was called from a bar. 'There's someone here to take home. He's too far gone to travel himself; in fact he's paralytic.' With the aid of fellow-drinkers the man was manoeuvred into the cab's back seat. His address was in his wallet, and in due course the driver found his home. With further difficulty he got the man to the door, pressed the bell and addressed the lady of the house. 'I've brought your old man back, but he's a bit the worse for wear.' 'I can see that,' she said, 'but what have you done with his wheelchair?')

What is even more frequent than palsy is mental deficiency. As against the one in five hundred born palsied must be set the one in thirty born with severe mental retardation (or an IQ of less than seventy). Morons are said to have an IQ between fifty and seventy, and five-sixths of the mentally deficient are in this category. The remaining one-sixth, still a much larger number than the palsied, have an IQ lower than fifty. Victims of cerebral palsy, although with a brain defect, may and often do have a normal intelligence, a fact which can make the neuro-muscular aberrations yet more aggravating.

There are many more varieties of brain malfunction (described in the chapters on abnormality and damage) but the purpose of mentioning palsy and mental deficiency in this context of birth and development is to underline the fact that some subnormality is caused by the very process of birth and development. No one knows how much but, apart from the damage of anoxia and the trauma of birth, there is also the damage done by an inadequate placenta (or one diminishing before its time), by a poor umbilicus, by drugs taken by the mother. Anoxia is the best known, because it is possibly being monitored at the time, and palsy is the most easily detectable, because muscular control is either satisfactory or not satisfactory; but there are all manner of other causes and effects, with the causes being immeasurable and the effects no less so. A mother who smokes produces a baby smaller on average (by seven ounces) than normal, but no one yet claims that smoked babies are less (or more) intelligent, and less (or more) able than they might have been without the enforced addition to their umbilical diet and, after birth, to their inhalation. Even the foetuses of mothers who do not smoke, but whose fathers do, are detectably different, having suffered what is called 'tertiary smoking'. Without doubt brain damage is done during development, and during birth and infancy, but quite how much is still quite impossible to say.

Head size, brain size   The paragraphs devoted to this subject in many books refer to the cranial capacities of Ivan Turgenev and Anatole France. There is never reference, for example, to Guy de Maupassant, Leo Tolstoy or Maxim Gorky, and so curiosity is aroused. Why that particular pair of writers, and why such enthusiasm for their cranial capacities? The prime answer is that very few dead heads have been measured and, of those that have been detailed in this fashion, Turgenev and France proved to be among the most extraordinary: the Russian brain was twice the size of the French one.

In a sense the practice of measuring cranial capacities reached its zenith at the very outset. On 15 May 1832, the greatest doctors of France assembled to dissect the body of the greatest French scientist, Baron Georges Cuvier. They found nothing of significance in the torso but were rewarded when they examined the 'instrument of his powerful intelligence', as the leading physician phrased it. It was larger by far than normal, larger than any properly formed brain previously examined, and it turned the scales at 1,830 grams (4 pounds). Allegedly – the facts are thin – Oliver Cromwell and Jonathan Swift had brains of similar calibre but Cuvier produced the first detailed proof that a great intelligence was provided by a large brain. Much was to follow from that single measurement. The small-headed, whether individually or racially, were thenceforth known to be less intelligent.

The interest in head and brain size reached another peak when Paul Broca, to be rightly immortalised in Broca's area, argued strongly that study of brain size 'would lose most of its interest and utility' if size variation was unimportant. He was a great head measurer, if not the greatest, and of course cited Cuvier as exhibit No 1. Unfortunately, in the thirty years since its weighing, others pointed out that there was no longer proof of it. The brain had not been kept, and there was not even the corroborating evidence of skull size for that had not been measured or retained. Broca sought out Cuvier's hat, and it was found to be the largest standard size, but neither exceptional nor unique. Finally, as happens in such stories, someone discovered (sixty years after the event) that Cuvier's skull had been measured but it was only large (equal to 6 per cent of French scientists) and not colossal.

Turgenev came into the story when his brain beat Cuvier's by 182 grams, and the hunt was therefore on for someone bigger still. By the first decade of the twentieth century a total of 115 eminent men had been measured, but there was no pattern of correlation between their cerebral brilliance and their cerebral size. Walt Whitman, undoubtedly talented, entered the lists with only 1,282 grams, a slight advance on one of the earliest light-weights to be recorded, Franz Gall, the founder of phrenology (and discoverer of much else neurologically of greater worth). When Anatole France died in 1924, and was measured as a puny 1,017 grams, or 995 grams less than Turgenev, interest in the subject of craniometry was not just perplexed but waning.

Nevertheless it is odd that brain size is so aberrant. An adult male gorilla has a brain of 560 grams. The other anthropoid apes have smaller brains but their bodies are also smaller. Human adult males have brains which measure, on average, 1,400 grams, while their bodies are smaller than the bodies of male gorillas. Plainly brain size is not irrelevant, and every ordinary human has a brain at least twice the size of every ordinary ape. It might therefore be reasonable to expect that the most intelligent humans, demonstrating the greatest intellectual gap between man and ape, should have brains which visibly prove the point; but they do not. Of course brilliance may stem from a larger number of neural connections or of neurons rather than bulk, but such measurements are not yet available. At present cranial capacity is all that can conveniently be counted.

So, to conclude this argument, what has happened to the most formidable brain of recent times, and was it large? Well, the important organ was removed following its owner's death in 1955 and it now resides in a jar in Wichita, Kansas. If anyone has measured its capacity they have not yet announced the results. Therefore, for the time being, there is still an unknown number of cubic centimetres against the brain and the name of Albert Einstein.

PART TWO

Anatomy and physiology textbooks are never bedtime reading. The names, locations and tasks of the various parts of the nervous system can create prose of a time-table consistency. Considerable effort has here been made to derange this general rule, but the three chapters of Part Two may be heavy going. They can be skipped, but the price to be paid for such good sense is that various words encountered later in the book will reappear without further introduction. Naming of parts is always difficult, not to say tedious, but even time-tables have their uses, and this book would plainly be inadequate without the chapters of Part Two.

4. Anatomy

History / Naming of parts / Cerebral hemispheres / The lobes /
The ventricles / Meninges / Cranial nerves / Spinal nerves / The
plexuses / Blood supply

> It is highly dishonourable for a reasonable soul to live in so
> divinely built a mansion as the body she resides in
> altogether unacquainted with the exquisite structure of it
> – Robert Boyle

> The want of any consistent history of the brain and nerves,
> and the dull unmeaning manner which is in use of demon-
> strating the brain, may authorise any novelty in the manner
> of treating the subject
> – Charles Bell, *Idea of a New Anatomy*, 1811

History   Mankind discovered gunpowder, the nature of the universe, the steam engine, vaccination, Antarctica, democracy and
balloons long before it had any understanding of the brain which
gave the drive and intelligence to do all these things. There were
several reasons: a steadfast devotion to the teachings of antiquity,
objection (from church, state and almost everyone) to the practice
of dissection, an unwillingness to place visual inspection above the
accepted texts, and, of course, the innate complexity of the subject. Even so, despite early Greek enlightenment, the Arabs, the
Renaissance, the flowering of medicine in the seventeenth century,
the invention of the microscope, and the birth of modern science,
the amount of accurate information assembled about the brain by,
say, 1800 was pathetic. In fact neurology did not really advance as a
subject until phrenology arrived. This mistaken science acted as
catalyst, gadfly, stimulant to brain research, much as wars have
done in other areas.

It is timely to consider, in broad outline, how today's brain
knowledge came about. From our modern viewpoint, it is strange
that prime interest lay initially in the ventricles, more latterly in the
convolutions and most recently in the cortex. This is an inversion of
the true situation, because cortex is paramount, convolutions less
so, and ventricles least of all. Nevertheless, even though many of

us today are scarcely aware that we possess ventricles, they were of supreme interest for over a thousand years, the subject of considerable argument, the presumed centre of intellect.

The history of neurology is, like other science histories, a matter of innumerable firsts; who did what and when, and were thus the pioneers. Traditionally it is said that Alcmaeon, a pupil of Pythagoras, was the first to draw attention to the brain. A dissecter of animals, he distinguished between veins and arteries, described optic nerves and Eustachian tubes, believed goats breathed through their ears (not as daft as all that, anatomically, bearing the Eustachian tubes in mind) and stated that the brain not the heart was the seat of intelligence. He, and later Greeks, were vague – to say the least – about the physiology of the brain but just believed that its tissue, somehow, organised intelligence. Alcmaeon's writings, alleged to be the first of their kind, were in fact preceded by Egyptian textbooks inscribed almost two thousand years earlier, such as Instruction No 6 in the Smith Papyrus: 'When you examine a man with a wound in his head . . . something is there that quivers [and] flutters under your fingers like the weak spot in the head of a child which has not yet grown hard.' The Egyptians were on a different planet to the rest of the world at the time, but there is no assertion in the papyri that the brain was the organ of intelligence. That had to wait until 500 BC and Alcmaeon of Croton.

It was Herophilus of Alexandria who, around 300 BC, first drew attention to the ventricles, the cavities lying within the brain, but it was Galen who entrenched their importance by giving a firm description of them. Everything that Galen stated, in the second century AD, became gospel, and to criticise any of his statements was to perform a kind of blasphemy. If something did not seem to be as he had described it, either bodies had changed since his day or the body which refuted Galen must be diseased or wrongly formed. His word – that blood did not circulate, but ebbed and flowed, for instance – was virtual law for over a thousand years. Nevertheless he was not dogmatic about the role of the ventricles, and expressed uncertainty about the part they played in cerebral function. Not so all of his successors, such as Nemesius, Bishop of Emesia, and St Augustine who, in the fourth century AD, first proposed the so-called Cell Doctrine. Disregarding the brain tissue itself, they considered the first cell (our lateral ventricles) was the home of common sense and imagination, the second cell (our third ventricle) controlled thought, reason, judgment, while the third cell (our fourth) was the centre for memory. To us today the idea of a liquid (cerebrospinal fluid) possessing these functions, and the dismissal of brain tissue as if it were no more than a packing case, is bizarre, but stranger still was the acceptance of the Cell Doctrine for a millennium.

In an eleventh-century manuscript is the first (Western) drawing of brain function. It gives liver, heart, testes and cerebrum as the 'four principal human members', and includes 'fantasia, intellectus, and memoria' as the three mental faculties residing within the ventricles. Nothing had therefore changed, and Avicenna (tenth to eleventh centuries) was to put his tremendous medical weight behind the Cell Doctrine. He made it, as one author put it, canonical but shifted the ventricle number from three to five. Not only did other authors slavishly copy the traditional belief in ventricular importance, but almost every head was drawn facing to the left. It was a time of considerable adherence to inherited dogma. The fact that the Bible and the Koran had been written centuries beforehand did not deny their authority: on the contrary, their antiquity made them all the more respected. So too, one suspects, with the Cell Doctrine. It was venerated in time, steeped in tradition, and amended perhaps but certainly not jettisoned. With the Arabs everything was even more formal and stylised due to the hostility of all orthodox Moslems to any representation of the human form. Therefore, even if they did know the brain's true shape, it could not be portrayed.

The Renaissance, when it arrived, was truly a rebirth rather than an entirely novel event, certainly so far as anatomical description was concerned. Instead of inherited lore, and constant repetition of a dusty doctrine, the Italians in particular began to behave more like ancient Greeks. Mondino de Luzzi wrote in 1316 the first practical manual of anatomy, commendable in its pioneering but poor in its facts. The liver is given five lobes rather than two; the heart has three chambers rather than four, the uterus is given a remarkable seven cavities, and the brain is controlled by a 'red worm', namely the choroid plexus. Mondino wished to revolutionise, but Galen still ruled too firmly. So facts were written which could not possibly be supported by the anatomical evidence. Even Leonardo da Vinci, at the end of the fifteenth and the beginning of the sixteenth centuries, could not break the ancient and early medieval stranglehold. He was the first to take castings of a brain's ventricles (using an ox), and first in innumerable areas, but he still labelled the ventricles in similar fashion to the Cell Doctrine. Accurate Renaissance anatomy was therefore blended with traditional (erroneous) teaching.

Now to Vesalius, a step which, according to J. M. Ball, is 'like passing from darkness into sunlight'. He was among the greatest of Renaissance medical men. Andreas Vesalius, body snatcher (from gibbets), foremost anatomist of his day (if not of all time), called Vesanius (madman) by his teacher, and appointed professor of surgery at Padua when aged twenty-three, was the first to knock cracks in the Galen edifice. This was only gradual, as and when he discovered errors, such as his failure to find pores between the' heart's two ventricles (a fact crucial to Harvey's work one century later). A person so ahead of his period, and at a time when the Inquisition reigned (he had left Padua for Madrid), was certain to incur authoritarian wrath, and by the age of thirty his anatomy days were forcibly concluded. He did not die for another twenty years, but human anatomy as a subject had been born, with Vesalius as its undoubted father. However, even he, no fawning disciple of Galen, drew the brain's ventricles well enough but then called them reservoirs of the animal spirits responsible for the sensory and muscular activities of the body. Galen was still in power after 1,300 years.

Despite Vesalius, despite Leonardo plus other artist–anatomists, and despite the fact that many an unprotected skull was cleft open during the interminable warfare of the Middle Ages, no one yet took much interest in the most obvious and immediately visible feature of the brain, its convolutions. The old Greeks had been interested, having no stern dogma to guide them, and Erasistratus of Alexandria thought (in the third century BC) that the gyri looked like intestines. He was wrong, in that they do not make a continuous tube, but at least he had looked and had attempted a description. Then came Galen who flatly denied that the convolutions were relevant to cerebral activity of any kind. The first drawing of gyri was not made until 1345, but even then it was badly done, unconvincing and, with a final dismissal of interest, of an ox's brain rather than a man's. Another problem, doubly sinful after Vesalius's brilliant devotion to accuracy, was that artists began again to draw either diagrammatically or just wrongly: Archangelo Piccolomini (sixteenth century) drew a human brain that was more like an early Arabic representation. Giulo Casserio, whose life ended in the seventeenth century, was no less culpable: he insisted that his drawings excelled everything previously published 'in nicety, clearness, and finally in workmanship and pains', but drew a human brain that really did resemble the continuous coiling of the small intestine. The face in this picture is excellent, a rugged, bearded explorer of a face: the brain, exposed beneath the pulled-back skin, is no more than travesty.

The rest of the seventeenth century is similar paradox. For example, among the several pioneers to be fascinated by brain function were Thomas Willis (of the circle of Willis, the vascular system beneath the brain) and Franciscus de le Boë (or Sylvius, of the fissure of Sylvius). These two were the first to propose that the brain's cortex, not heard of in all the earlier debate, was of functional significance, and they undoubtedly put the first rung on the ladder of modern neuro-physiology, but their drawings were inadequate in comparison to their thinking. (The illustrator of Willis's *Cerebri Anatome*, published in 1664, was none other than Sir Christopher Wren, already one of the founding fathers of the Royal Society and soon to start, the Great Fire permitting, on an almost singlehanded task of rebuilding the religious houses of central London, St Paul's Cathedral included.)

René Descartes, contrary influence of the seventeenth century to Willis and Sylvius, was a philosopher but gave his personal authority to the ventricles by adding the pineal body to their central organisation. He defined this modest protuberance as the seat of the soul, controlling everything via the ventricles. The cerebral cortex had scant mention in his writings, but the drawings with his work were quite the most accurate representations of convolutions so far seen in the history of man's interest in his brain. The old power of the ventricles was still hanging on, and via one of the greatest intellects of the age, but simultaneously with the first real mention of the all-important cerebral cortex. Medically it was a century of transition, an adherence to tradition coupled with the birth of brand-new thought.

Just because the cortex had been mentioned did not mean instant enlightenment about the role it played. As the seventeenth century led into the eighteenth Marcello Malpighi (of the kidney's Malpighian tubules) thought the cortex was glandular. Frederick Ruysch said it consisted of blood vessels (partly, one assumes, because he was a blood-vessel fanatic, having learnt how to inject them with a substance that then solidified). And Anton van Leeuwenhoek, a great early microscopist, the first to see bacteria and protozoa, believed the cortex to be 'globules'. (As an aside many a student-user of the microscope will, particularly if myopic, see everything as globules.) The principal value of the three different guesses lay in their stimulation for other observers to guess rather more correctly.

The final conundrum in the history of the neuro-sciences came when a wrongful enthusiasm caught hold of all manner of minds with far-reaching consequences. Franz Joseph Gall, who lived into the nineteenth century, proposed the notion that certain brain areas were responsible for certain mental attributes. Out of this thinking arose phrenology, the specific mapping of the skull for the various faculties that lay beneath its uneven bumps. Gall himself was a diligent, modest man, but a pupil of his, Johann Caspar Spurzheim, pushed phrenology with more energy and passion than Gall had ever intended. For the first years of the nineteenth century it was a cult, widely popular, and inordinately influential. In the 1830s it was dying out, having overreached itself, but it had played its useful part. It had focused attention upon the brain's surface rather than its ventricles. Phrenology itself was misdirected zeal, but anything that drew man's obsession towards the cortex was bound to do good in the end.

Besides, everything was soon happening at a pace never known before. Microscopy, anatomy, physiology were all advancing on a wide front. Photography was also to play its part, the very first lithograph of the human brain being taken in 1854 (by Emil Huschke). Within a few years the convolutions of the gyri and sulci reached, as Edwin Clarke and Kenneth Dewhurst phrased it, 'the ultimate in pictorial representation'.

The final stage, not in knowing what the brain is all about but in setting the scene for all modern neurological endeavour, came also in the latter half of the nineteenth century. Various workers, notably in Paris, Berlin and London, showed the excitability of the cortex and its precise localised functions. The localities were not as the phrenologists had asserted in the first part of the century, but those early enthusiasts, with bumps for this and that, had been right in their way. Most important, they had stirred others to realise that function *is* represented in the cortex, in the surface layer of the brain. By the time that Wilder Penfield and others at Montreal were directly stimulating the cortex of fully-conscious patients, and noting all responses, the history of man's early thinking about cerebral function was at an end. It had been twenty-five centuries since Alcmaeon of Croton had first put down his thoughts and, with the arrival of direct cortical stimulation, the modern era had arrived. Today's gross anatomy of the brain is no more a matter of conjecture, dogma, doctrine and philosophical argument. Instead it is detailed in the textbooks, with the facts written down as if we have known them for all time.

Naming of parts There is very little, if anything, noticeably exquisite – to use Robert Boyle's term – about the structure of the human brain. Anatomically it is a confusion, a deterrent from the outset. A fish's brain is a model of straightforwardness by comparison, with its swellings visibly and geographically linked to the sense organs with which they are involved. In fact, a human and all higher brains can only make sense if their ancestral origins are remembered, if the fish simplicity is recalled. The trouble is that the more advanced brains are not an expansion of the lower brains, but a swelling (mainly) of part of them, of the fore-brain. A parallel would be if the stomach had enlarged enormously, to submerge and dwarf the rest of the intestinal tract and destroy the visible simplicity of the alimentary canal. Strip off the enlarged fore-brain, greedy for all available space, and the ancestral brain is at least detectable, huddled, distorted and cramped beneath the swollen hemispheres that have taken up five-sixths of the cranium.

The naming of the brain, and of its parts, might have been devised to make absolutely certain that every medical student was serious about his or her intentions. It is not simple because Greek, Latin and English compete with one another while various other parts, as in geography, are named after their explorers, such as Broca, Willis, Variolus, Monro, Reil, Rolando. A further confusion is that the namers so liked the Greek word cerebrum (meaning brain) that they used it twice. Consequently we now have the cerebral hemispheres, which grow from the fore-brain, and also the cerebellar hemispheres, which are totally distinct and arise from the hind-brain. As a result we have the cerebellar cortex, the cerebrum, the cerebellum and the cerebral cortex which are either to do with the cerebral or the cerebellar hemispheres and woe betide any student who confuses these quite separate structures. (The original logic was that the cerebellum, paired and walnut-fissured, appeared as a diminutive cerebrum.)

'Ontogeny recapitulates phylogeny' is a venerable biological phrase – the development of the individual retraces the evolution of his kind. It is certainly true with human brain development, as the embryonic neural tube swells at its anterior end and, initially at least, mimics the brain development of the earliest vertebrates. Nomenclature of the human brain also, in part, makes obeisance to the old structure. As in every tetrapod, primitive or advanced, there is a spinal cord and then a hind-brain, a mid-brain and a fore-brain. It is much harder to detect these three sections in the human than in the fish or amphibian brains and, as if to reflect this difference, the human three are also called the rhombencephalon, the mesencephalon and the prosencephalon. The prosencephalon is further divided into the diencephalon (or between-brain) and the telencephalon (or end-brain). These names are not what one surgeon might bandy to another, but they do put the human brain into its phylogenetic or evolutionary perspective by identifying its fundamental compartments.

The next set of names, which surgeons do use, refers to the portions of brain that have been developed, during human ontogeny, from those three (or four) basic zones. Again starting from the rear and the spinal cord they are: the cerebellum (in order as far away from the cerebrum as could be, and attached to the brain stem by three peduncles – or little feet), the medulla (sometimes with oblongata added to emphasise that this part of the brain is uniquely long rather than wide, elongated and not a bulge), the pons (or bridge sometimes called of Variolus – not that there is another pons – which links the hind-brain to the mid-brain) and the mid-brain itself (which is modest, being less than an inch in any direction). It too has parts, such as the tectum, the tegmentum, and the cerebral peduncles. These can also be subdivided and the tectum, for example, is composed of the superior corpora quadrigemina and the inferior corpora quadrigemina or, if those names do not appeal, the superior colliculus and the inferior colliculus.

In other words names do abound at every level. They tend to be lengthy, Graeco-Roman and do not immediately trip off the tongue. As a measure of relief the whole of the mid-brain, the pons and the medulla oblongata are collectively called the brain stem for the sound, apt and precise reason that they act like and resemble the stalk of a plant crowned by the great bulk of the cerebral hemispheres. A particular hazard is that biologists and human anatomists, working concurrently, have sometimes named the same – or homologous – feature by two names in mankind and the animal kingdom. Similarly, or contrarily, they have borrowed a name on occasion to identify a part that is only similar and not the same. Just as *Homo* was thought for a long time to be set apart from the rest of life so should human and animal anatomists now beware of each other's labels. These do not always coincide.

Finally to the cerebrum, the fore-brain, the five-sixths of cranial volume that is so critical. Again, starting from the rear (although the order is nothing like so clear as in the brain stem), the diencephalon or between-brain already mentioned consists of the thalamus (through which nearly all nerve impulses pass on their way to the higher brain), the epithalamus (important for smell, and for containing the pineal gland, about which more later), the subthalamus (which has some function in the regulation of certain muscles) and the hypothalamus (very small – one three-hundredth of the total brain – but by no means least, and about which much more later). The first three, thalamus, epi and sub, are sometimes lumped together as the thalamus (although they should not be, as there are distinctions), but no one ever lumps the hypothalamus with anything. It may be small, being less than a finger joint in size and weighing four grams, but it is the fore-brain's centre for the autonomic nervous system, which regulates temperature, appetite, thirst, water metabolism, blood sugar levels, growth, sleeping, waking, and seemingly every activity which is done without a moment's thought. Other bits of the brain's anatomy are sometimes listed with the all-wise hypothalamus (even though they are most distinct), such as the optic chiasma (which is what it says, and where nerves from the nasal – or inside – half of each visual field cross over into the other half of the brain), the two mammillary bodies (nothing to do with mammary glands but look – just a little – that way, and are actually concerned with the sense of smell), the infundibulum and the hypophysis, the former being the stalk of the latter, and the latter being – under another name – the all-important pituitary gland. As it is a hormone producer, with a controlling influence on other hormone producers elsewhere, its minute size (one centimetre in diameter) is out of all proportion to its effects. Neither it nor these other bits of brain should be bracketed with the hypothalamus as their functions do not overlap, but it is intriguing that the multi-purpose hypothalamus should be so close to the multi-powerful pituitary, one acting by nerves and the other by chemical messengers. Their location, aptly, is about as central in the head as could be.

Next, in this listing of the brain's parts, there is the second portion of the fore-brain, the telencephalon, practically all of which is formed by the cerebral hemispheres, the giant lump of tissue responsible for all our wisdom. The remainder of the telencephalon (or end-brain) is formed of the rhinencephalon (literally nose-brain) and the basal ganglia. The nose or smell-brain is the most ancient part of the fore-brain, referring back to the times when there was geographical logic to the brain's parts. The nose-part was then the foremost section of the brain, being nearest to the apex of the animal and to its nose-end. (Similarly the optic lobes were just by each eye and therefore further back, while the auditory area was further back again. With the human brain it is as well to remember these archetypal placings, although such straightforwardness has been lost as assuredly as our tails, our four-footedness and a simpler style of life.)

But even in the old days, when the rhinencephalon was so aptly situated, it must have been concerned with more than the sense of smell. Some of the lowliest and most primitive vertebrates have little more than a rhinencephalon to their fore-brain and, as this ultimately swelled into the thinking area, and as primitive creatures are often capable of quite advanced behaviour, such as learning, it is therefore assumed that they smelt *and* remembered with their rhinencephalons. Further evidence comes from the human fornix and hippocampus. These two parts of the rhinencephalon are better developed in humans than in some animals with a highly developed sense of smell. Why we are relatively well endowed with them is still unclear, despite the great antiquity of the rhinencephalon and the considerable human interest in the considerable human brain.

Not much is known about the basal ganglia, the remaining portion of telencephalon that is not cerebrum. The name itself is little help, being the Greek for knot (and which Hippocrates used for knot-like tumours before Galen took over the word and used it for knot-like bundles of nerves). The invertebrates abound with ganglia, notably in pairs, but there is nothing particularly knot-like about the human basal ganglia. (Some call them basal nuclei, as if that latter word was not already over-used in every branch of science.) Anyway, they are quite large, relative to all the other non-cerebral portions of the brain, they are made of grey matter (as against the white matter of the cerebrum) and most knowledge about their function has come from their occasional malfunction. Should the basal ganglia be diseased the patients can suffer tremor (as with Parkinson's) or rigidity or the involuntary movements of chorea (as in St Vitus's). The ganglia are plainly linked to muscular movement but how or why is, as with the unknowns of the rhinencephalon, a matter for the future to unravel.

Cerebral hemispheres   Now, at last, to the cerebral hemispheres. Every part mentioned so far, starting with the cerebellum and up to the cerebrum, is the one-sixth of the total bulk that we think of least when referring to the human brain. However, it is those 230 cubic centimetres (or thereabouts) that not only have most affinity with our distant forebears (fish, amphibia, reptiles and mammals) but permit us to perform (almost all of) our daily routine, as we walk, balance, grow lusty, hungry, thirsty, become satiated, sleepy, wakeful, and behave at the modest level demanded by the normal round and common task. These 230 cubic centimetres are even invisible should anyone have the top of his head removed, as with a hard-boiled egg, to expose what lies beneath. What is then visible is the spongy, convoluted, fissured, almost cloud-like, pinkish-greyish bulk of the two cerebral hemispheres.

This apotheosis of evolutionary intelligence, bathed in a pint of blood every minute, and liable to damage in a few seconds (allegedly seven) if that supply is occluded, looks identical from one race to the next, between men and women, and between genius and idiot. It is among the most liquid of all the body's tissues, being about 85 per cent water (therefore even more liquid than blood), and the hemispheres cannot support themselves correctly if extracted from their bony casing. They, the hard core of all our wisdom, will slump like soft jelly. Of course there are parts to the hemispheres (and scores of names) but this 85 per cent of the human brain is most uniform in appearance, certainly when compared with the various portions, already listed, of the other 15 per cent. The whole brain consumes a quarter of the body's oxygen, with most being taken by the hemispheres. They are sixteen times more demanding, by weight, than the average organ. However, there is nothing fundamentally novel about the substance of the human hemispheres: they consist of the same components operating in the same manner as in every other animal with pretensions to a brain. The only immediate external difference (apart from size) lies in the degree of convolution. As with a foetus, whose lobes are smooth at first, so are the gorilla's lobes slightly smoother than a human's, and a rat's smoother still, and a reptile's still less contorted. Once again, ontogeny recapitulates phylogeny, and a human embryo seems to go through its ancestral forms before emerging as *Homo sapiens*.

Despite the eventual confusion there is a sort of logic to the manner of cerebral creation. Supposing, to speak simplistically, there is a requirement for more brain tissue. How can it best be added without destroying the original arrangement of a hindbrain, a mid-brain and a fore-brain? To swell one of those hindmost areas would, very likely, interfere with a working arrangement; but to enlarge the most forward part would be like invading new territory, like building an extension rather than modifying the house. In increasing the vertebrate brain from a few grams to more than a thousand, the addition took place, in the main, at the anterior end of the system where there was room to grow. However, again speaking simply, it could not just expand like a rubber balloon. There is still the skull, and the requirement of the head. So human brain development first proceeds forwards, then back along the top of the head, and then from the back of the head down towards the centre again. Unlike the simple expansion of an ordinary balloon it more resembles one of the tubular (or sausage) kind being inflated within a sphere and growing first forwards, then backwards and then in on itself to meet its starting place. No wonder that the human brain is anatomically a considerable mix-up as the all-demanding hemispheres bury the other nervous components, much as a constrictor encircles its prey.

Or rather as two constrictors do because the hemispheres are paired. This fact of having the greater portion of the brain as two distinct units, linked only in part (and that a small part), is of enormous consequence. The section on cerebral dominance (page 110) attempts to explain this extra strangeness plus the unexpected benefits that go with a communication system where each half is almost wholly separate from the other.

Between the two is a gap known as the median (or superior) longitudinal fissure. Each half, either at first or even second glance, appears identical (such differences as do exist will be encountered later), and the halves are joined by a tough bridge of tissue, the corpus callosum (or hard body). This can be seen by peering down the centre of that central fissure. Each hemisphere is divided into four lobes but these are less emphatic than that central division into two halves. The four lobes are the frontal (at the front of the head), the parietal (at its top), the occipital (at its rear), and the temporal (on its sides). These names have all been taken from the bones of the skull situated roughly over those areas, but the matching between each bone and its corresponding lobe is by no means exact (and different names for the brain's parts might have been more welcome).

The four lobes are not equally distinct from each other. The frontal lobe is the most straightforward, as it is that part of the brain lying in front of the central sulcus and above the lateral sulcus. A sulcus, after the Latin for furrow, is a crevice or cleavage and, although these other words would have served, sulcus was chosen. Of all the brain's sulci the lateral is the most conspicuous as it runs backwards and slightly upwards from the temple area just behind the ear. It is also known as the fissure of Sylvius, after the French anatomist who described it in the seventeenth century. In theory, if not in practice, a fissure is a large sulcus, but the anatomists are not good at following their own rules. The second most striking cleft is the central sulcus (or fissure of Rolando, after the eighteenth-century Italian anatomist). This runs across the top of the head, from side to side, with its apex slightly aft of the central point. Therefore the frontal lobes, lying forward of and above these two main fissures, include some two-fifths of the cerebral hemispheres.

The three remaining lobes, possessing the remaining three-fifths, each have at least one margin clearly defined but are otherwise less precise. The parietal lobe (named after the parietal bone which itself is from the Latin for wall) starts just behind that side-to-side sulcus (of Rolando) and ends about halfway from there to the very rear of the brain. The occipital lobe (ob caput: against the head) is from the halfway point (which is where the lateral sulcus – of Sylvius – would reach if it persevered to the back of the head) down to the extreme rear of the brain. This third lobe is principally connected with vision and the smallest nick at the back of the head can have appalling effects upon sight. The final and fourth lobe, the temporal, does indeed lie inwards of the temples. Its forward margin, Sylvius's fissure, is clear enough but its hindmost one is merely where the parietal and occipital lobes are presumed to finish, there being no convenient sulcus to mark the borders.

Despite the importance of the four pairs of lobes as the basic continents of the cerebral map there is no outstanding difference in their appearance. They are from the same apparent mould, indented with the wandering sulci, some deep, some shallow, but adding up to the fact that almost two-thirds of the cerebral surface is buried in these grooves. The portion in between each sulcus is a gyrus (plural gyri), after the Latin for roll which well illustrates their slightly flattened, apparently tubular, podgy form. The gyri wander this way and that, seemingly without rhyme or reason, as if a child's attempts to roll out Plasticine were packed and crammed away into a hemisphere of space. It is indeed a half-sphere as the human brain occupies most of the volume of the head above a circle drawn from the eyebrows, halfway through each ear and round to the little protuberance at the very back of the head. The diameter of this dome is about seven inches, although the brain is slightly ovoid, being wider towards the rear than at the front.

As a slight breathing space to all this naming of parts, and remembering the contortions of those gyri and sulci, it is intriguing to reflect upon the brain's apparently haphazard precision. It is so vague in its anatomy and yet so detailed. The paradox is everywhere. Prick this area with a pin and a man may be immediately blind in one portion of his visual field. Push a crowbar through his head, as happened in that Boston accident, and the victim may walk away with nothing more than a limp. Stimulate this part and the little toe, or the knee, or the ear will be immediately aware of the provocation, twitching inanely or most conscious of itself. But try to stimulate ambition or drive, intelligence, love, hate, thoughtfulness or devotion, and they are nowhere to be found; at least, not yet. If one individual is a thousandfold superior to another in arithmetic or memory, music or scientific enquiry, there is nothing visible to register this fact, no parallel to the sinews of the runner or the muscles of those who exercise them most. The heart of a corpulent and idle individual looks that way. The brain of the most gifted, who aggressively tackles each new problem, appears not a whit different from that of an indolent who never tackles anything as each day draws into the next. 'Tell me where is fancy bred, Or in the heart or in the head?' asked Shakespeare's song almost four hundred years ago. It is still a good question, with the vibrant, beating, exciting heart still outwardly the better candidate.

The four lobes of the cerebral hemispheres, for all the formality of their naming and the demarcation of their frontiers, are not the totally separate entities implicit in all this definition. They are more separate in their function than, say, the lobes of the liver but nothing like as distinct as the various portions of hind-brain, mid-brain and fore-brain that precede them. To some degree they merely reflect the basic human wish to create order, to define, to name things, to compartmentalise and subdivide. Certainly they help to reduce those swollen hemispheres into more digestible proportions.

So too, in their way, do the cerebral ventricles. Like lakes on a map they are further and helpful points of reference and, like the brain itself, they are distorted reminders of a simpler past. The human central nervous system is the direct descendant of the primitive neural convolution that ran the length of our pre-vertebrate ancestors. It was a tube, an infolding of the outer skin, composed of nervous tissue surrounding a fluid-filled cavity. In the human embryo also there exists for a time this simple neural tube. Most of its length remains relatively simple, and becomes the spinal cord running from top to bottom of the back. This is still tubular as there exists a minute central canal throughout its length. However, within the brain, as can be imagined, that simplicity could not survive. What does remain is a series of ventricles, distortions of the central cavity that parallel in their fashion the varied distortions of the brain itself. Named after the Latin for little belly, the ventricles are cavities, but these are not belly-shaped, being all manner of protrusions and spikes, diamonds and triangles, occupying the space left to them by the folds, outgrowths, and swellings of the neural tissue on every side.

Nevertheless they are landmarks in their way, and there are four of them. The one nearest to the spinal cord, the fourth ventricle, lies in front of the cerebellum and behind the pons. At its upper end it connects with the much smaller third ventricle, barely more than a slit within the thalamus (or between the two thalami). The third ventricle connects, again via a narrow duct, not with the second (as might reasonably be expected) but with both the remaining ventricles. They are not the first and second (as might also be expected) but the lateral ventricles. The brain, it must always be remembered, has its cerebral hemispheres divided from each other by the all-important median fissure. Consequently the two foremost ventricles follow suit, with one in each half. They are the lateral ventricles and each, seen from above, resembles a most uneven Y, with the hook of each Y facing outwards. The total volume of all four ventricles is only 100 cubic centimetres, or some 7 per cent of the brain's capacity, and they are filled with cerebrospinal fluid.

This watery, alkaline, translucent, colourless substance of low specific gravity is constantly being produced (within the ventricles) and equally constantly being resorbed (after it has leaked from both lateral ventricles to flow over the surface of the brain where it can find its way into the bloodstream). Perhaps 'produced' is not the correct word as this fluid is essentially filtered blood, strained of white cells, corpuscles and platelets, and therefore very like plasma, the blood's liquid base. It does carry nutrients, as only the large protein molecules are filtered out, but its primary function is to protect the brain. The liquidity of our most precious asset means, as already stated, that the brain cannot support its own shape if removed from the skull. It becomes deformed; it sags. ('It slumps like blancmange,' I once wrote. 'We don't have blancmange. Does it slump like Jell-O?' queried an American editor. 'Don't know. Over in England, we have jelly but not Jell-O, and it slumps like blancmange,' I wrote back, more aware than ever of the two languages, but it certainly slumps in both of them.)

If it cannot even retain its proper form without aid, how can it possibly survive within the harsh casing of a skull? (After all, a blancmange, and doubtless Jell-O, would travel badly if placed within, say, a cake tin.) The answer lies in three layers, or membranes, or meninges (after Greek for membrane). These are not so much padding, as is used to encase delicate objects, but layers that correspond firstly to the solidity of the skull and then, via the intermediacy of the central layer, to the softness of the brain. (Perhaps there is method here that human packers could emulate, as they have as yet only imperfectly learned their trade.)

The outermost (and skull-side) zone is a tough, fibrous lining that actually adheres to the inner surface of the cranium. Therefore no space exists between its firmness and the greater solidity of the skull; hence no rattling, a prerequisite of sound packing. To call it a membrane (or meninge) implies thinness and delicacy, but it is neither. Its actual name – dura mater – is preferable, despite that reference to maternity. (The Arabs believed the meninges gave rise to all other membranes in the body, and for that reason the dura was considered to be maternal.) The innermost layer is the pia mater, or gentle mother, and its softness is as closely involved with the outer surface of the brain as is the dura's hardness with the skull. So, once again, no possible oscillation. The central membrane, which has to be soft and hard, is both firmly structural and yet delicate, a spider's web of filaments that gives it the name arachnoid. However, even these three are not adequate for the protection of the brain. There is a subarachnoid space, filled with the same cerebrospinal fluid that seeps out from the ventricles. Therefore the brain, so liquid itself, is buttressed not just by three meninges (whose inflammation can give rise to meningitis) but by liquid, by incompressible liquid whose volume can be adjusted to maintain this almost perfect barrier. (All of which makes one think of, for example, boxing – see p. 252 – whose very aim is to seek out the imperfection of this system.) The three meninges do not care just for the brain but, in a modified form, continue in their tripartite role all the way down the spinal cord.

With all this talk of protection, and careful encasement of three pounds of central nervous system, it should not be forgotten that it cannot exist in isolation, like gold bars incarcerated within a vault, but has to be connected with its outside world – the rest of the human body. It has to receive information from the sense organs in particular, and it has to send instruction to, above all else, the muscles. It has to receive blood and get rid of blood: so there have to be arteries and veins. It cannot exist *in vacuo*, cocooned, insulated and isolated, any more than any other organ can, however vulnerable. In short there have to be – for the brain itself – cranial nerves and – for the cord – spinal nerves. And there has to be a blood supply.

Cranial nerves On old Olympus topmost top a fat-eared German viewed a hop. This happening, so precise in detail and so uninspiring an event, is extremely relevant to the brain's nerves. It is known by every medical student – unless someone has thought up a different mnemonic for the vital nervous connections linking the central with the peripheral nervous systems. OOOTTAFEGVAH is the initial letter sequence of the cranial nerves, and the Graeco-German botanical incident has helped many a student keep track of a confusing situation.

Once again, as is becoming repetitious, the situation was simpler when brains were simpler. In fish, for example, there are only ten cranial nerves. They emerge from the brain in a reasonably clear fashion, with No. 1 at the anterior (or snout) end and No. 10 coming from the most posterior portion of the brain, that nearest to the spinal cord. The human cranial nerves are functionally the same as these archetypal fish nerves, and they emerge from the same area of the brain (whether fore-, mid-, or hind-); but, owing to distortion from the ancestral form, it does not seem that way. The symmetry has gone, and the simplicity has gone, but the original logic still exists, however compressed by the swollen hemispheres and the fact that man's brain has been bent through ninety degrees. The upright stance, as against a fish's in-line form, is responsible for this bending, which further confuses the picture. However, the old fish design still exists, and the cranial nerve numbering is identical, save that man has two more (Nos. 11 and 12) than the fishes.

So, remembering the botanical (or beery) German once more, the twelve pairs of cranial nerves in man are:

1. Olfactory. Connects the nose with the so-called olfactory lobes which lie at the base of the temporal lobe of the cerebrum. This is therefore quite a distance in man but in fish, where the smelling organ is at the front and connects with the very front of the brain, the nervous connection from sense organ to related brain tissue is very short indeed. This No. 1 cranial nerve, the only direct connection between cerebrum and anywhere else in the body, is a reminder that the famous cerebral hemispheres, the fountain of human intelligence, were once mainly concerned with olfaction. Evolution – to speak loosely – took over this cerebral area, conveniently placed where it could most readily expand, and turned it into something much more interesting (to our minds, at least) than a processor of smells.

   The olfactory nerve is only sensory (or afferent, after the Latin for 'carry toward'). All its impulses go towards the brain, and there are no motor (or efferent, 'carry outward') nerves in connection with it. All cranial nerves are either of this input variety, or output, or a combination of both: sensory, motor, or mixed.

2. Optic. In the fishes the nervous fibres from each retina travel in a fairly straight and certainly short line to the nearest portion of the brain (the rear part of the fore-brain or diencephalon). In mankind each optic nerve (of about a million fibres, as against about thirty for each olfactory nerve) travels for one and a half inches before entering the cranial cavity (at the optic foramina), continuing backwards to the optic chiasma (just by the pituitary, and named after the Greek letter 'chi' which is X-shaped) where half of each bundle crosses over to the brain's other side. It then proceeds still further back to the rear of the brain. (There is academic uncertainty whether the optic is a true cranial nerve or merely an extension of brain tissue to each retina, but there is no argument whatsoever that the distance travelled is almost as great as could be from visual

organ to visual cortex.) As with No. 1 so is No. 2 purely sensory.

3. Oculomotor. Literally 'movement of the eye'. This nerve supplies four of the six muscles which control each eye-ball, those that adjust the lens focus and those that move the upper eyelid. It is therefore a motor nerve, wholly so, and arises from the mid-brain. (This fact, of all but one of the brain's cranial nerves, of its direct links with the rest of the body, arising from behind the swollen hemispheres and in the brain stem, indicates again that most nervous functions, from seeing things, reacting to them, hearing, balancing, salivating, making facial expressions, etc. etc., are ancient activities, developed long before any thinking brain, and quite independent for the main part of either thought or intelligence. It can be argued that almost any animal can do almost everything that a human can do, such as use its five senses to make a living, with the cranial nerves emphasising the one crucial fact of life: knowing what is going on and reacting accordingly.)

4. Trochlear. Named after the Latin and Greek for pulley it has no pulley-like task but this smallest of the cranial nerves passes from the mid-brain through connective tissue that, according to the namers, resembles a pulley. It has a modest function, particularly when it is remembered that only twelve nerves are directly connected to the brain: this one controls one of the half-dozen muscles that move each eye-ball. It is motor only.

5. Trigeminal. Next to the smallest is the largest which, as its name states, is really three nerves in one. They all connect with the pons and are mainly sensory (of the face and head) but partly motor (control mastication). The three subdivisions are the ophthalmic (virtually everything at the front of the face and head – eyes, tear glands, nose, forehead), the maxillary (cheeks, upper teeth and gums, lower eyelids) and the mandibular (most of the lower jaw and the pinna of the ears). The dentist, therefore, incapacitates either the maxillary or the mandibular or both. A facial tic is the fault of the trigeminal. This nerve's first two subdivisions are wholly sensory; only the third is mixed.

6. Abducent (or Abducens). Entirely motor and given that name (Latin for 'leading away') because it pulls the lateral rectus muscle of the eye, and therefore leads the pupil away from the body's midline. (With the abducent and the trochlear each controlling one eye muscle, and the oculomotor controlling four, this completes the eye's muscular innervation, a system which permits the spherical object within its spherical cavity to

look, within its limitations, in any direction.) The abducent arises from the pons, but further back and nearer the medulla than does the trigeminal.

7. Facial. Mixed motor and sensory. Another pons nerve, and acts for the muscles of the face more or less as the trigeminal does for its senses. A pricked cheek has its trigeminal stimulated by the pain and its facial in effecting an appropriate grimace. Virtually all expression is created via the facial nerve, but its sensory fibres are unrelated, collecting sensation from the anterior (or most prominent) two-thirds of the tongue. (It could be accused of transmitting sensationalism rather than sensation as even minor injuries to the tongue seem magnified out of all proportion to their actual size.)

8. Auditory. Sensory. A straightforward cranial nerve, in that it receives all sensation from one organ, the ear, but made more complex by the fact that the ear both hears and possesses the mechanism for balance. This fourth nerve from the pons is therefore sometimes called the stato-acoustic (in which case the mnemonic German can no longer be 'fat-*eared*'. A 'fat, static German' would be a possible substitute for cranial nerves Nos. 7, 8 and 9.)

9. Glossopharyngeal. Mixed. Of less consequence than the title implies. Its sensory fibres run from the back (and less important) third of the tongue and from the pharynx and tonsils, while its motor nerves act on the throat muscles and those of a pair of salivary glands. The name is explicit, meaning tongue-throat. The nerve arises from the medulla just behind the cranial-nerve-infested pons.

10. Vagus. Mixed. Rightly called the 'wanderer' as it travels further and has more of a distribution than any other cranial nerve. It arises, as does No. 9, in the medulla but then sets off, either with sensory or motor fibres or both, to the throat, windpipe, oesophagus, heart, stomach, intestine, pancreas, spleen, gall-bladder and kidneys. In other words it is almost a spinal cord on its own, running from the brain to the abdominal cavity, controlling muscles and conveying sensation for a major portion of the body. But, of course, it is far thinner, is duplicated, and keeps on dividing and reuniting more as a filigree than a central cord.

11. Accessory. Motor. Arises from the medulla (and is therefore a genuine cranial nerve) and also from the spinal cord (which therefore obscures the simplicity). These latter nerves are said to be accessory to the main branch, hence the name. Also some of the fibres join up with the vagus, and are therefore

accessory to that. Anyway the muscles controlled by No. 11 lie in the shoulder (such as the trapezius), the arm and the throat.
12. Hypoglossal. Motor. Name means 'under the tongue' and this final cranial nerve, also coming from the medulla, does indeed control the muscles of the tongue plus some others in that area.

To sum up. Although the brain is the major controlling organ of the central nervous system, which itself is truly central to the body's innervation, the nerves directly connected to the brain do not pour in from every part of the body. It is not like the hub of a bicycle's wheel, with spokes arriving from every quarter. Instead it is a reminder of its past history as its direct connections link, in the main and save for the wandering vagus, with the head area. In other words, what made sense for the earliest chordates is the basic design that is still being followed by all their descendants, including man.

That basic pattern, already discussed in the earlier chapters, is of a neural tube running the length of the body. All along this tube are short nerves which connect only with that portion of the body nearest to them. That same pattern exists even at the anterior end where there are sense organs and where the neural tube swells into a brain: the connections are short and lead from tube to periphery in the simplest fashion, even though that part of the periphery may be an eye and that part of the tube is the optic centre of the brain. There is no point, so to speak, in having the connections any longer than they need be. However, there is no way, again speaking fairly loosely, of adjusting the purpose of each connection even though the evolved organism may be a gross distortion of its ancestors. The human brain, for example, does not look like the fish brain; the human head does not resemble the fish head; but each set of cranial nerves parallels the other. No. 1 is still olfactory, No. 2 is optic, and so on, and it is helpful for us to remember this fact just as the cranial nerves cannot dissociate themselves from their history.

Spinal nerves It is perhaps leaping ahead to mention spinal nerves in the same breath as cranial nerves, but they do follow on. They are entirely distinct from the brain but logically they succeed the cranial nerves just as the spinal cord itself is connected to the brain. Fortunately the spinal nerves themselves are rather more logical, in that their basic symmetry is less confused than with the cranial nerves. The ladder-like chordate plan of having each nerve control the body segment nearest to it is still apparent, but, of course and alas for the human anatomist, it has lost much of the old straightforwardness.

There are several reasons for this. Firstly, the chordate organs are no longer in the same place. As with the cranial nerves the old functional allegiance has to remain for the spinal nerves, however transposed their original destinations may be. Secondly, although there is some regularity with each pair of spinal nerves emerging from each gap between the vertebrae, there is complexity because the spinal column (of bones) is about ten inches longer than the spinal cord (of nerves). Thirdly, many of the nerves, quite distinct on leaving the cord, subsequently join up to form an intertwined mass known as a plexus (after the Latin for network or plait) from which they emerge in a different arrangement.

Nevertheless there is uniformity – of a kind. Sever the spinal cord, as bullets can with such simplicity, and there will in general be paralysis and insensitivity in the area below the damage. There will be both because each spinal nerve – except the very first – is both sensory and motor (as against either or both for the cranial nerves). The vertebrae and the spinal nerves almost match, with thirty-one spinal nerves to emerge between the twenty-six vertebrae. There are eight cervical nerves (as against seven cervical vertebrae), twelve thoracic nerves (and twelve thoracic vertebrae), five lumbar nerves (five lumbar vertebrae), five sacral nerves (one sacrum – although the human embryo has five separate sacral bones which, together with the five nerves, help to prove the ancestral arrangement), and one coccygeal nerve (one coccyx). The caudal disharmony results in the main from the loss of our tail, while the cervical unevenness of eight to seven is caused by the emergence of a spinal nerve both before the first cervical vertebra (the atlas) and after the seventh. (A judicial hanging – or even an unjudicial one – generally breaks the spine at the second (or axis) cervical vertebra and it causes death largely because the break is above the fourth spinal nerve which controls the diaphragm for the lungs.)

Other spinal nerve facts are: all of their roots are covered by dura mater, arachnoid and pia mater just as the brain itself is covered; each nerve is formed of an anterior root (containing the motor fibres) and a posterior root (of sensory fibres); the shortened nerve cord – relative to the vertebral column – means that the spinal nerves tend increasingly to run down the spine before reaching the point where they can emerge, via the intervertebral foramina, from the spinal column (for example, thoracic nerve six leaves the cord by the fourth thoracic vertebra but emerges from the vertebral column between the sixth and seventh thoracic vertebrae); the spinal nerves outnumber the cranial by almost three to one, and innervate many more muscles than do the cranial nerves, but the spinal cord from which they emanate is far smaller than the brain, weighing only an ounce for all its eighteen inches and therefore a fiftieth of the brain's swollen mass; and by no means do the spinal nerves control the muscles of or receive sensation from the area nearest to their point of emergence from the cord. As with the cranial nerves the passage of 400 million years and the amendments incurred during evolution have severely disturbed the basic chordate plan. The lower spinal nerves do innervate the lower areas but the rung-like directness has gone, and the various plexuses confuse the issue even more.

There are five of these large plexuses on either side of the backbone, all formed by spinal nerves. They are: the cervical plexus (formed by the first four cervical nerves); the brachial plexus (formed by the last four cervicals and the first thoracic nerve); the lumbar plexus (formed by the first four lumbar nerves); the sacral plexus (formed by part but not all of the sacral nerves plus some bundles from the lower lumbar nerves); and the coccygeal plexus (smallest, and formed from the fifth sacral and the coccygeal nerve). Not every part of every spinal nerve has to pass through one of these five – thoracic nerves 2 to 12 entirely fail to do so – but most do. The nerve bundles emerging from each plexus are different both in size and number from those that entered, making it difficult for anatomists to follow all the components of each spinal nerve. The most famous plexus of them all, the solar, is part of the sympathetic nervous system (about which more later).

What with the spinal nerves ramifying, combining and then splitting up again into smaller and smaller bundles, the task of discovering any destination for any nerve is not devoid of complexity. However, partly via surgery (which gradually linked nerves, particularly if damaged, to areas of skin) and partly via disease (such as localised herpes infection of the central nervous system which then renders insensitive a particular zone), the general pattern has been determined. It is known, more or less, which bit of us is associated with each spinal nerve.

Starting from the top, and dealing with the sensory element only, the following areas are associated with the following nerves (although descriptive precision varies from difficult to impossible):

(Cervical nerve 1 is unique among the spinal nerves in having no sensory component.)
Cervical 2: back of the scalp almost to the head's highest point.
Cervical 3: the neck.
Cervical 4: the upper part of the shoulder.
Cervical 5: outer shoulder and upper arm.

Cervical 6: outside (or lateral) forearm, extending as far as the thumb and forefinger.

Cervical 7: central forearm to central finger.

Cervical 8: inner forearm to part of ring (or third) and little finger.

Thoracic 1: inner (or medial) side of upper and lower arm, and remaining areas of third and little (fourth) finger.

Thoracic 2: that part of the chest wall below the section innervated by cervical 4. (The arm therefore is catered for by five of the spinal nerves.)

Thoracic 3–12: relatively simple and chordate-like, with each in turn connected to a lower portion of the trunk, so that 5 covers the nipple level, 8 the end of the rib-cage, 10 the navel, and 12 the upper portion of the hip.

Lumbar 1: the lower belly and lower back.

Lumbars 2 and 3: the forward part of the thigh and the lowest part of the back.

Lumbar 4: knee and calf.

Lumbar 5: shin, much of the foot and big toe.

Sacral 1: sole, smaller toes, and the rest of the foot not innervated by lumbar 5.

Sacral 2 and 3: some of the inner thigh, buttocks and genitalia.

Sacral 4, 5 and Coccygeal: what is left, namely the most central part of the buttocks and the perineum (or part beneath the anus). Had we a tail these lower sacral roots would assuredly possess a more significant role.

So there is, as stated, a logic to the areas connected by each emerging spinal nerve but the fundamental pattern is disturbed, partly by the limbs, partly by that lack of tail and also by the distortions that have occurred as the earliest chordates became fish, then amphibia, then reptile, and then mammal and man. There is also overlap from zone to zone. Each nerve, in part and to a varying degree, is connected to areas served by its two neighbouring nerves: a problem for the anatomists but a blessing for the victim should a single nerve be damaged or cut since the two bordering nerves can perform some or all of its duties.

Completion of the basic cranial and spinal nerve story, with all the points of origin and all principal functions, does not conclude the body's innervation. Far from it. There is, for example, the autonomic nervous system (see the next chapter) with its chain of ganglia and there are major plexuses other than those already mentioned, quite apart from the ramifications involved in connecting every part of the body with its brain. However, the basic cranial and spinal story, now completed, does provide a breathing space. It is the principal link between the central nervous system and the entire peripheral network. There are no other major connections joining those three pounds of brain and that one ounce of spinal cord with the rest of the network. The information received and the instructions meted out (almost) all pass along either the twelve cranial or the thirty-one spinal nerves. Of that total of forty-three (pairs of) nerves, three are wholly receptive (or sensory), six are wholly instructional (or motor) while the remaining thirty-four both give and receive. It is through the thirty-seven sensory tracts that the central nervous system learns what is going on and via the forty motor fibres that the muscular responses are made resulting from that information.

Essentially this chapter is still a naming of parts and an account of the main nervous area rather than a probing beneath the surface. That will come, and so will a full return to the brain; but, in the meantime, it is convenient to continue with the naming of the larger nervous components. Still remaining is an elaboration of the five plexuses, already mentioned, that lie on either side of the backbone. Many of the most famous nerves in the body arise from them.

First, starting at the top, is the cervical plexus (created by the first four cervical nerves). The main muscles it supplies are of the neck, such as trapezius and sterno-mastoid, but it also controls the diaphragm via the phrenic nerve. (Hence the collapse of breathing and of life should it be damaged.) The brachial plexus, second in line and formed by five spinal nerves, then forms five of the important nerves that serve the arm, the shoulder and the chest.

The second, or radial, is the largest and, without expecting the following quotation to clarify this nerve's meandering, even for the diligent, it may help to underline just what the anatomist is up against as one major nerve is charted for just part of its length. So herewith Lockhart, Hamilton and Fyfe from Aberdeen describing in their *Anatomy of the Human Body* (1959) just what this one nerve gets up to when it leaves the brachial plexus. It

descends behind the axillary artery running in front of subscapularis and the tendons of teres major and latissimus dorsi. In the axilla, the radial nerve sends the posterior cutaneous nerve of arm postero-medially through the deep fascia, gives twigs to the long head of triceps and before leaving the axilla sends, along the ulnar nerve, the so-called ulnar collateral nerve to supply the medial head of triceps. The radial nerve then inclines backwards between the long head and the medial head of triceps, supplying the latter by a branch penetrating the muscle to innervate anaconius. It supplies, then passes deep to, the lateral head of triceps and descends in the spiral groove behind the humerus, separated from bone by fibres of the medial head of triceps save for a small area behind the insertion of deltoid. In the spiral groove it gives off the lower lateral cutaneous nerve of arm and the posterior nerve of forearm. Reaching the front of the elbow . . .

and so on for several times that length of words for just one post-plexus spinal nerve, the radial, No. 2 out of the brachial plexus. (For those wishing to comprehend fully this quotation, a modest glossary may be helpful: axilla is armpit; humerus is the upper arm bone; triceps is the major muscle to counteract biceps; and every other unfamiliar word is yet another muscle.)

Next come all the thoracic nerves which, in not forming a plexus, are refreshingly direct in their innervation of nearby muscles and skin. However, the lumbar plexus banishes such simplicity and, after its enmeshing of four spinal nerves, gives rise to two nerves in particular, the obturator and the femoral. Both supply the legs, with the femoral being larger and attending to a greater area. The fourth plexus is the sacral which gives rise to far and away the largest post-plexus nerve in the body – the sciatic. This is about three-quarters of an inch wide at the start of its journey down the leg. It also, according to neuralgia sufferers, gives far and away the most pain, a fact reflected in its name abbreviated from the Latin and Greek for 'pain in the thigh-bone'.

Finally is the coccygeal (or sacral) plexus, the smallest, least important of the five, which might have had more to do had we retained our tail. However, the very existence of this fifth plexus, plus the fact that spinal nerve plexus No. 4 serves the legs (or hind limbs) is a reminder of the basic tetrapod form from which we all evolved. There was, in that distant shape, a lot of body behind the rear limbs. The pelvic fins of fish, for example, are a long way forward of the caudal (tail) fin and a large proportion of the propulsive musculature lies between that final fin and the two pelvics. As those rear fins became, via the crossopterygeans and the earliest amphibians, the hind legs of reptiles and mammals, it is to be expected that their innervation remained fundamentally the same. A human being may consider his (or her) toe to be the final part (of him or her), and might therefore be surprised that its nerves come from the fourth plexus. The presence of a fifth is proof that there used to be more of us behind.

Blood supply   The brain is quite the most greedy organ in the whole body for blood, and for the oxygen this carries. It also complains most abruptly should the flow be interrupted. If the cut-off is immediate the reaction is swift, with unconsciousness occurring in six to seven seconds. This is damage of a kind but not irreversible. Lasting damage only follows a loss of blood-flow for several minutes, with the actual period depending on the circumstances. A time of one minute forty seconds has definitely been endured without any subsequent, detectable drawbacks. Tolerance for oxygen lack is greatest among the very young (this is particularly relevant at birth when temporary anoxia so often accompanies a delivery) and among the very cold (whose demands for oxygen have been dramatically lowered). Experiments upon cooled monkeys have shown that fifteen-minute stoppages of blood-flow are possible without damage.

Although the brain only weighs 2 per cent of the body it receives about 30 per cent of the blood leaving the heart. That proportion occurs when the body is at rest. When it is active the percentage goes down because the muscles then receive a greater share of the blood – but not at the expense of the brain. That still gets its same requirement of about its own weight in blood every minute. If the rest of the body was as demanding we would either have to possess sixteen times as much blood (a difficult concept as the body would then be grossly larger to accommodate all this fluid) or the heart would have to beat sixteen times faster, and no less effectively, to satisfy the need. Within the brain there naturally has to exist a network of capillaries through which to supply the necessary demand for oxygen. In white matter there are about three hundred millimetres of blood vessel in each cubic millimetre of tissue. In grey matter the total length is three times as much.

All of the brain's supply reaches it by four blood vessels. There are two vertebral arteries and two carotids. The vertebrals enter the brain case (or cranial cavity) via the foramen magnum (or big hole) through which also passes the spinal cord. The carotid arteries enter via a smaller hole, the foramen lacerum (or torn hole), and thereafter pursue a much more complex course than do the vertebrals before dividing into the cerebral arteries and then giving off a multitude of other branches. The various sulci (or grooves) lying between the gyri make convenient channels for some of the arteries running over the brain's surface, but much greater use of these is made by the venous system. As a generalisation the surface arteries travel across the gyri while the veins flow parallel with them. Both arteries and veins within and around the brain have much thinner walls than comparatively-sized blood vessels elsewhere, thus making it extremely difficult for the anatomist who cannot see most of the brain's vessels unless they contain blood. The thin walls also mean that the veins, in particular, are capable of considerable distension.

In the days of 'cut-throat' razors, and possibly spurred on by that name, it was relatively common for would-be suicides to make unhappy use of these weapons. The thought, presumably, was that a severed throat would more speedily end it all than, say, a severed wrist. After all the neck does contain, and vulnerably, the arteries leading to the brain. In fact many would-be suicides remained that way as they merely cut their windpipes and not the more lateral, more embedded arteries. The converse of this tale is that many would-be self-throttlers have ended up not so much blocking off their air supply as stopping their blood-flow. Rope tension on the jugular veins will close them if it is four and a half pounds, on the carotid arteries if it is eleven pounds and on the trachea (or windpipe) only if it is as much as thirty-three pounds. Therefore eleven pounds (about the head's weight) for seven seconds is sufficient to cause unconsciousness, and more time will finish the job.

5. The Autonomic

Sympathetic and parasympathetic / Plexuses / Adrenals / Pituitary
/ Thyroid / Hypothalamus

> A clash of doctrines is not a disaster; it is an opportunity
> – A. N. Whitehead

For all the magnificence of our cerebral hemispheres it is humiliating that much of our daily round is conducted without reference to these higher centres. We can walk to our office in a trance-like, thoughtless state and achieve much, just as relatively primitive animals can carry on with the routine of their lives. During that walk, a range of activities will have occurred with little cerebral involvement. We enlarge or shrink the pupils of our eyes, secrete saliva (and more so as feeding time approaches), produce sweat as our thermostat demands, move our gastro-intestinal tract, change our heart beat, adjust our blood vessels, breathe differently, contract our spleen (to give more blood when need be to the arteries), cause glands (such as the liver) to produce more or less, and generally maintain our internal environment. 'La vie libre c'est la fixité du milieu intérieur,' said Claude Bernard, and the autonomic system gives us that freedom. Without it we would perish very rapidly, with or without our splendid hemispheres.

Not every automatic act is carried out autonomically, with important exceptions being postural tonus, i.e. just standing there and breathing; but most of them are and they all work independently of the cerebrum. Autonomic is virtually tantamount to automatic, but the autonomic (Greek for self-law) nervous system is in fact the product of two systems, the sympathetic and the parasympathetic. At once, partly because these names are so bizarre, they have to be explained. *Pathos* is a Greek word responsible for many of ours: pathetic, pathology, pathos itself, and sympathy. So different in their meanings they all manage to stem from *pathos*, Greek for suffering or feeling. The sympathetic system received its title because it was believed to respond to the body's sufferings and feelings. And so it does, in a way. If an animal (or man) suffers from or detects a shortage of oxygen it steps up its heart beat, constricts its arteries, raises blood pressure and responds – sympathetically – to the call for help.

So what is parasympathy? The autonomic (or automatic) system used to be known as the sympathetic for the reasons just mentioned, but then it was discovered, or realised, that it existed in two parts. Whereas many of its fibres arise in the upper and central regions of the spinal cord, a number of them, quite separate, arise both higher up and lower down. These other regions are the cranial and sacral areas, or head and tail. So, as para- means beside or beyond, the bastard name of parasympathetic was coined, 'beyond with feeling'. So there is historical logic to the title, even though it has ended up as an awkward, untidy word demanding a paragraph of explanation.

There is much more distinction to the sympathetic and parasympathetic than either their portmanteau names or the anatomy of their place of origin. Origin is important but functionally the two systems are also quite distinct because they countermand each other. For each action of the sympathetic there is an opposing reaction by the parasympathetic. This may initially sound unhelpful but, as with musculature, it is crucial to have a protagonist and an antagonist, a pull one way and a pull the other, a sympathetic and a parasympathetic. The former accelerates the heart beat, the latter slows it down. The arteries are constricted by the sympathetic (thus raising pressure), and are dilated by the parasympathetic. So too with the intestines – peristalsis is slowed down by the sympathetic, speeded up by the parasympathetic. In the same fashion the bronchi are dilated (for easier breathing); and constricted. The bladder is relaxed; and constricted. The iris of the pupil is dilated; it is constricted. The hair muscles erect the hairs; then lay them flat. The autonomic is a give and take system, a weight and counterweight, and both act positively. It is not a matter of doing something and then of not doing it. It is pulling in one direction or pulling in the other. It is sympathetic *versus* parasympathetic.

Structurally these opposing halves of the autonomic (or involuntary) system are very similar. There is a chain of twenty-three ganglia (nerve centres or mini-plexuses) on either side of the backbone. All the ganglia on each side are connected vertically and the two strands therefore resemble (slightly) a couple of knotted lengths of string. Each knot is connected with the ganglion lying above it and with the one below it. In addition most of the ganglia are connected both to the spinal cord and to the various organs under their control. Reasonably the inner links are called pre-ganglionic nerve fibres while those proceeding elsewhere are the post-ganglionic fibres. Equally reasonably the various ganglia are named after the vertebrae lying nearest to them. Consequently there are cervical, thoracic, lumbar and sacral ganglia on either side to form each chain.

Despite similarities there are also dissimilarities in the two halves of the autonomic, particularly in their innervation from the central nervous system. The sympathetic, controlled mainly by the brain's hypothalamus and its medulla, receives all its nerves from the thoracic and lumbar sections of the spinal cord. The parasympathetic, controlled by the mid-brain, pons and medulla, receives (almost) all its nerves directly from the brain or from the sacral region of the cord. The two halves of the autonomic, therefore, incur major structural differences. Firstly, they are controlled by separate areas of the brain and, secondly, the nerves from those areas emerge via different sections of the spinal cord. It was quite wrong in the old days to assume the autonomic was just one arrangement. Its two parts, the sympathetic and the parasympathetic, are two entities, and much more separate than their similar names imply.

The ladder-like regularity of the double row of ganglia is lost on the outer, or post-ganglionic, side because there are plexuses (which, said the student, are so named because they are both complex and do perplex). There are the five major plexuses – already mentioned – formed by the spinal nerves, and now there are three more formed by the nervous bundles of the autonomic system. Highest is the cardiac plexus which lies along its partner, the pulmonary plexus. These are often listed as a single plexus lying in the midline of the body just above the heart. Also in the midline, but lower down (everyone knowing its location who has been hit there) is the coeliac or solar plexus. It is the largest congregation of nerve cells, excluding the central nervous system, within the human body. Why it received the name solar is uncertain, and there are two suggestions: its nerves radiate in sunlike fashion and, as in an eclipse, the sun goes out and darkness falls whenever that mark is truly hit. It is also called the abdominal brain, which makes more sense and does emphasise its size, but the term solar plexus is probably too deeply entrenched to be removed. The final autonomic plexus, No. 3, is the hypogastric, which lies centrally but lower down.

As both brain and spinal cord are so well protected – by the skull casing, by the bony vertebral column, and by the packaging of the three mater layers – it is not surprising that a well-aimed blow to the relatively exposed plexuses is quite devastating. Their neurons possess no more solid protection than that portion of the abdomen which surrounds them. The solar plexus can be most painful, but a blow to the hypogastric can be almost as devastating, should an antagonist be sufficiently low in his hitting to strike well sub-belt.

Not only are the sympathetic and the parasympathetic systems distinct anatomically, being supplied from different regions of the brain, and distinct functionally, with each action partnered by a reaction, but there is also a chemical distinction. All pre-ganglionic fibres in the autonomic system secrete acetylcholine at their endings when an impulse is transmitted, and so do all post-ganglionic fibres of the parasympathetic system. The exception to the prevailing rule of acetylcholine production lies only with the post-ganglionic nerve endings of the sympathetic system. When this was first realised, and the unknown chemical released in place of acetylcholine had to have a name, it was called sympathin. Later, its composition having been found out and its similarity to adrenaline having been noted, it was renamed as noradrenaline.

Adrenals   The plot, as they say (and generally with justification), now thickens. In 1895, and in Edinburgh, it was learned that extracts from the two adrenal glands, each one two inches long, weighing ten grams, and on top of the kidneys, could raise blood pressure dramatically. In 1901 the substance was purified by a Japanese biochemist, and CH_3NHCH_2 was given the name of adrenaline. (Some call these glands the suprarenals but their all-important product is almost always called adrenaline or even epinephrine – as in the US – but never suprarenaline.)

Adrenaline, generally speaking, does the same job as the sympathetic system: it speeds up heartbeat, opens up blood vessels to the muscles, and does the same for the bronchi so that more air can be inspired. It is therefore fitting that the sympathetic, noradrenaline and adrenaline all have a chemical affinity, since they are all involved in putting the body on an active footing.

The plot continues to grow more viscous when it is realised that sympathetic fibres innervate the adrenal medulla. This is the central, dark-brown portion of each adrenal gland and, when stimulated, secretes adrenaline. The adrenal's other portion, deep-yellow and outermost, is called the cortex (after the Latin for bark). It can also be stimulated but then produces a range of hormones known as corticoids which are also needed, much like adrenaline, in periods of stress. So what stimulates the adrenal cortex? The answer is the pituitary, the ductless gland at the base of the brain, but what stimulates the pituitary? It is – somewhat inevitably at this stage in the plot – certain nerves of the sympathetic system, which themselves are stimulated by the hypothalamus.

To sum up. The sympathetic half of the autonomic, either directly (via its own actions) or indirectly (via the adrenal medulla) or yet more indirectly (via the pituitary and via its action upon the adrenal cortex), prepares the body both for immediate and more protracted activity. The parasympathetic quietens it all down again: slows down heart beat, restarts digestive activity and kidney function, relaxes general activity, and causes us to live at a less frenetic pace.

Two facts remain. The triple influence of the sympathetic, immediate and then less so by the liberation of hormones into the bloodstream, explains how some shock to the senses can cause both an immediate reaction (a drawing-in of breath, an apparent stopping of the heart) and then a more prolonged response, as the heart pounds in preparation for whatever action will ensue. The second fact is that none of this elaborate, interlocking mechanism is crucial. The sympathetic's nerves can all be cut and the adrenal medulla excised without harm or even inconvenience resulting. One might more likely be caught by an approaching predator but, these days, one would certainly lead a more placid and possibly more harmonious kind of life.

The adrenal cortex may be the other half, or rather outer half, of the same pair of glands, but its functions, secretions and general role are completely different from those of the adrenal's medulla (inner) half. Without the cortex a victim would not lead a more placid kind of life; he would simply die. It was in 1855 that the English doctor Thomas Addison described how destruction of the adrenals, generally caused by tuberculosis, led to skin discoloration (making it bronze rather than pink – in whites), anaemia, muscular weakness and, after two to three years, death. For his pioneering work he now has the dubious distinction of naming Addison's disease. Quite why death occurs is still a mystery as the cortex produces a wide variety of hormones, such as a large number of steroids (compounds resembling cholesterol). These, particularly in their unidentified days, were known as adrenocortical steroids and then, without much more delay, as corticoids, but that does not explain why their lack causes death. Many of them, as already mentioned, are of particular need in times of stress. The most famous, although not for its relationship with stress, is cortisone, first available as a drug in 1948. It too is probably made, along with other corticoids, from cholesterol which exists within the adrenal cortex in considerable quantities.

Oddly the only other human organ richer in cholesterol is the human brain. Why this should be so is largely unknown, but what every product of the adrenal cortex does is certainly unknown. The sympathetic system comes into the story both when it stimulates the pituitary to stimulate the cortex and when it directly stimulates the adrenal's other half, its medulla. To be clear-cut about the operation of the sympathetic nervous system is, to phrase it gently, an uphill task. To state that it is a bewilderment of conflicting roles is not only true but a suitable epitaph. Or perhaps the following definition from a medical dictionary will serve better still: 'The sympathetic system is that part of the nervous system from which most of the nerves that connect and regulate the various internal organs appear to take their origin.' In short, an uphill task.

Pituitary Strictly speaking, the endocrine glands (those which secrete internally, as into the bloodstream) have no place in a book about the brain. On the other hand, because their influences are so wide-ranging, they merit space in any book about any part of the human body. The adrenal glands, so supplementary to the sympathetic system, have been described and the pituitary must follow suit. For one thing the gland has already been mentioned, as intermediary between sympathetic and adrenal cortex. For another it is actually attached to the brain. And for a third reason, if a third is necessary, the pituitary exerts so much control over so many bodily functions, such as growth, sexual development, sugar level and pancreas metabolism, as well as affecting other endocrine glands, that it would be quite wrong for the pituitary not to get a mention.

Like the adrenals the pituitary is also in two quite distinct parts, separate in origin and separate in function. The posterior portion, or lobe, is an outgrowth from the brain and stays attached to the base of the brain (by the neural stalk, or infundibulum) just behind the optic chiasma. The anterior lobe is, embryologically, a piece of mouth but it becomes detached during development and attaches itself instead to the posterior lobe. The name pituitary is from the Latin for phlegm and from the days (until about 1600) when the gland, lying between the nasal passages and the brain, was thought to be the manufacturer of a runny nose. The list of functions attributed today to both halves of the pituitary is extremely lengthy. (Its name has also been lengthened to hypophysis cerebri, but the old title is proving durable and does come more easily off the tongue.) As contrast to its many roles – some say almost everything but mucus production – the pituitary is minute, even when the two halves are added together. It weighs less than one gram/ one-fortieth of an ounce (or a hundred-thousandth of the body) but has a controlling effect upon all other endocrine glands. Its importance is out of all proportion to its size.

To take one example of pituitary function – that of water control – is to realise some of its potency. Water enters the body in food and drink, and of course has to be removed, mainly via respiration, perspiration and excretion. The first two are somewhat independent of control, as the water quantities involved are linked to other parameters (such as temperature), but the amount of urine is directly related to the need, or lack of need, for water retention. In the 1940s it was discovered that pituitrin, just one of the pituitary's hormones, encouraged the kidney's tubules to retain water by reabsorbing more of it. And since then this simple story of just one hormone has become steadily more complex as extra roles, such as blood-vessel and uterine contraction, have been found to be involved via the pituitary's hormones vasopressin and oxytocin.

To have a malfunctioning pituitary is to suffer in a variety of ways. Cushing's disease (a particular form of obesity), diabetes insipidus (as contrasted with the more common diabetes mellitus, and called insipidus because urine is then tasteless) and dwarfism are from too little pituitary production, whereas giantism and acromegaly – large extremities – are from too much. The pituitary is a powerful influence, for good and ill. To be without it is to die.

Thyroid   Like the adrenals, and all endocrine organs, the thyroid comes under the aegis of the pituitary. And, like the adrenals, the thyroid's own range of hormones influence a variety of bodily functions, such as skeletal growth and sexual and mental development. To be born with an inadequate thyroid, or with a pituitary producing inadequate supplies of TSH (thyroid stimulating hormone), is to become a dwarf, probably deaf-mute, an individual without either sexual organs or secondary sexual characters (pubic hair, etc.) and almost certainly mentally deficient. Such a collection of abnormalities is labelled cretin, and is therefore distinct from, say, idiot, imbecile and moron which apply only to mental inadequacy. The word cretin is from the French for Christian, but no one knows precisely why. (A general belief is not that Christians were particularly stupid but they were the innocents, the – according to early Romans – barely human, the poor souls, the grossly inadequate.)

Should thyroid deficiency begin in adult life, when skeleton, sex organs and brain have all been properly developed, the victims will operate more slowly and suffer from apathy but they are not mentally defective. They have a low metabolic rate, thick puffy skin, and thin dry hair – as with cretins – but their slow thinking is part of a general slowing down rather than stupidity. Fortunately this condition, known as myxedema (mucus swelling), can be speedily cured by giving thyroid hormone to the patient. Even cretinism itself can be treated, and the sooner detected the better. If treatment is started early, and then maintained, skeletal, sexual and mental development will all be almost normal.

There is also hyperthyroidism, an excess of the gland's activity. With this condition the metabolic rate is increased, the eyeballs protrude (exophthalmia), the heart beats rapidly and, from a neural point of view, there is increased nervousness and tremor but not a mental superfluity to offset the mental deficiency of the cretin. An excessive thyroid, or goitre, can be treated surgically but must then not result in excessive lack or hypothyroidism.

Normal control of a normal thyroid is exercised by the anterior lobe of the pituitary and by the brain's hypothalamus. The fact that the two halves of the pituitary have their finger in so many pies has already been mentioned. This organ's multifarious influences are unrivalled among the endocrine glands but it meets its match in the hypothalamus. This one three-hundredth portion of the brain seems at times to be almost as important as the remaining 299/300ths of cerebral matter. It is particularly so with regard to automatic and involuntary functions.

Hypothalamus It is not strictly correct to be encountering the hypothalamus only at this final stage in a discussion on the autonomic and endocrine systems. It is, very largely, behind everything that has already been written in this chapter, and should therefore be at the head of it rather than the rear. However, a better understanding of its influence and potency is perhaps possible now that its ramifications have to some extent already been unravelled. In brief, the hypothalamus controls the sympathetic system, the parasympathetic system and therefore everything else that these two systems control. So it is not just that the pituitary controls the adrenal cortex which supplements the actions of the sympathetic but that the hypothalamus controls the pituitary controlling the adrenals and so forth. It is *the* major power in the autonomic world.

Its very modest quantity of fore-brain lies behind the optic chiasma, beneath the floor of the third ventricle and therefore under the thalamus (hypo means beneath in this context). Basically it looks after all those bodily operations which are called primitive, such as the metabolism of fat, of carbohydrates, the regulation of water and thirst, sleeping and waking, growth, the cycles of the reproductive system, appetite, temperature control, blood-vessel size, digestive secretions, much behaviour and emotion, and by this stage it is easier to wonder if there is anything in which the hypothalamus is not involved, all four and a half grams of it (one-sixth of an ounce). It is even being said, after experimental work on rats, that a piece of it is a pleasure centre. If probed with an electrode it provides a pleasurable sensation, banishing all thoughts of sex, food, sleep. If it could readily be stimulated (and without the unpleasantness of a needle reaching the central base of the brain) the possibilities that arise, so Isaac Asimov has written, 'in connection with a kind of addiction to end all addictions are distressing to contemplate'.

That the hypothalamus can do so much, and be so small, is yet another indication that the human brain is either unreasonably large for its performance or that it possesses capabilities as yet untapped and undeveloped. The tasks, and successes, of the hypothalamus are not simple just because they are primitive (which means that they appeared early in evolution). For example, many mammals can detect changing day-length extremely accurately, whatever the weather is doing, and therefore bring their reproductive cycle into operation during the optimum week, thanks to their hypothalamus. Water needs can be so regulated that a human thirst arises and is slaked by, say, a third of a pint of water, or about a four-hundredth of the water present in the body. Similarly, even though a body runs, sits, sleeps, digests and even becomes unconscious, it can maintain – via the hypothalamus – temperature with considerable precision. A rise of ½°F over normal for that hour of day can cause us to suspect fever or other malfunction. Even those who grow fat, and wish the extra ten or twenty pounds would go away (without any assistance on their part beyond assuaging all appetite), should remember that we process about 120,000 pounds of food in a lifetime of maintaining one 170-pound body. To retain an additional twenty pounds of that tonnage is not bad regulation, particularly when deposition of fat for the lean times used to have such selective advantage.

In 1966, and in a leading article on the hypothalamus, the *Lancet* wrote: 'Obviously it is immensely important, and it is also immensely complex.' It is possible to go even further and say that, come the day when all the functions of the hypothalamus are properly understood, the day will not be far ahead when all of the human brain is also understood. For instance, it is not so surprising to read in more recent *Lancet* issues certain articles implicating the hypothalamus in 'primary depression', in 'dementia' and in 'anorexia nervosa'. Inevitably, with this minute piece of brain controlling both the autonomic and (virtually) all the endocrine systems, its implications will increase in the years to come. The autonomic may be the lesser, less exciting, less bulky and less advanced portion of the body's nervous system, but its role and significance seem to be gaining all the time, not at the expense of the central nervous system but with an increasing realisation of what an autonomic system has to do.

The hypothalamus may even help to solve one of the biggest man-made problems of them all: overpopulation. A baby sucking at the breast stimulates the hypothalamus which, in its turn, triggers the release of prolactin from the pituitary. This hormone, in its turn, suppresses ovulation, and anything which suppresses that cannot be bad for a small and crowded planet. The hypothalamus, it seems, controls almost everything. We, perhaps, should seek to control the hypothalamus.

6. Physiology

The neuron / Impulses / Conduction time / Synapse /
Neuro-transmitters / Brain waves / Feedback / Blood-brain
barrier

> Whatever it is, I'm against it
> – Groucho Marx

Put at its very simplest the brain is composed of nerve cells which conduct impulses and pass these on to other nerve cells. Put more confusingly each nerve cell is able to conduct an impulse from one end of itself to the other, liberate a chemical to convey that impulse to another nerve cell, and then recharge itself so that it is ready to convey yet another impulse. Finally, and possibly to put it with a bewilderment that many will find intolerable, the brain's 15,000 million nerve cells are able to conduct these impulses at speeds of a couple of hundred miles an hour, the chemicals they liberate at their nerve endings are extremely varied (for over thirty have so far been discovered), and there are about a thousand nerve endings for every nerve cell, or ten thousand on occasion. To keep this whole system going (and whether or not the brain is actually 'working' is irrelevant) requires fifty millilitres of oxygen a minute, or a quarter of the amount used at rest by the remainder of the body. The energy equivalent of brain metabolism, of all this conduction, liberation and further conduction, is twenty watts.

The neuron has to be the starting point. It is often referred to as the building block of the brain, being the basic nerve cell. (However basic, there is not agreement about its spelling. Neuron was the classical word for nerve or tendon, and the word neurone was subsequently coined for the actual nerve cell of each nerve. Somewhere along the line that final e started to slip, and did so faster in the United States. There are still neurones and neurons in circulation, but this book favours the shorter version.)

To some degree nerve cells are similar to all other bodily cells, in that they possess a membrane enclosing cytoplasm and a nucleus. Their general biochemistry and metabolism are also similar. It is their dissimilarities that are more intriguing. Each neuron has a unique shape, varying from round-ish to pyramid-ish but always indescribable. They (almost always) possess axons, very long and very thin extensions, as well as branching dendrites, wisely named after the Greek for tree. Neurons are among the most delicate cells in the body, and occasionally among the largest. The brain's grey matter is often spoken of as if it is the important part as distinct from the less valuable white matter. In fact the cell bodies of neurons, which always contain the nucleus, form grey matter while axons and dendrites form white matter. All parts of the cell are equally vital, whether white or grey. Essentially the dendrites collect information while the axon distributes it elsewhere.

It is easy to speak of the brain as if it contains only neurons, but there are other kinds of cell. There are the neuroglia, or glial cells, which fill up the space between the neurons. What they do is by no means understood, but they must assist structurally, metabolically and, so recent research would suggest, are even involved in some mental activities. It used to be said they were as numerous as neurons, but it is now believed there are ten times as many, meaning one hundred thousand million in the human brain. There are also Schwann cells (named after the early nineteenth-century German zoologist Theodor Schwann, pioneer of cell-study in general and neurons in particular). These surround the axons of neurons, but in such a way that there are gaps, roughly every millimetre, known as the nodes of Ranvier (after the French histologist Louis Ranvier who described them in 1878). These nodes are necessary for the transmission of nerve impulses, while the Schwann cells are responsible for wrapping each axon in an insulating layer known as myelin. Myelination occurs in human foetuses and babies well after the fibres have been laid down and, possibly because the sheathing acts as an energy conserver, a myelinated fibre conducts impulses faster than one without this casing. There are also blood vessels within the brain, necessary for delivering oxygen and removing waste products, but more intensely so owing to the brain's extreme demands.

Consequently, it is more accurate to say there are some 15,000 million neurons in the brain, which are heavily outnumbered by blood-vessel cells, protecting Schwann cells, and supportive neuroglia. The building blocks are, therefore, eclipsed by the rest of the building. Nevertheless, the neurons provide the crucial wiring, which is both extremely able and extremely rapid.

Take speed first. Ever since the arrival of computers there have been assertions for and against their similarities with brains. In truth they bear scant relation to each other, and nowhere more so than in speed of impulse conduction. Electricity, which powers the computer, travels along wires almost at the speed of light – 186,000 miles a second. Human neurons cannot compete, being exceptionally leaky (some say one million times leakier to electricity than a well-insulated cable) and even more resistant (about one hundred million times more than a copper wire). The top speed of impulse transmission is about one hundred metres a second (as against those tens of thousands of *miles* a second for electricity). Nevertheless, if viewed on its own, and without the repeated comparison with computers, a transmission time of 328 feet a second or 225 miles an hour is not inconsiderable. From top to toe of man is, therefore, one-fiftieth of a second. Even from snout to fluke of the blue whale, assuming similar transmission, impulse time is only three-tenths of a second. Then, of course, there has to be reaction, the sending of an impulse back to appropriate muscles. Assuming a near-instantaneous turn-round at the brain the human big toe could twitch away from danger in, say, one-twentieth of a second. The nervous network is not a silicon chip, but its haste is commendable none the less.

In 1846 the German physiologist Johannes Müller, discoverer of Mullerian ducts (important in embryology) and much else besides, carelessly stated that no one would ever be able to measure nerve impulse speed. Only six years later a fellow German physiologist, Hermann von Helmholtz, proved him wrong by the elementary procedure of noticing how long it took a muscle to react after its nerve had been stimulated at different points. Since then a major part of the work done on impulse transmission has been with the kind assistance of the squid, or rather of its giant axons. These are up to one millimetre in diameter whereas human axons are only about one-hundredth as wide. Diameter is (more or less) proportional to speed of impulse, and the squid's abilities – at detecting and then reacting from some danger – are worthy of study. An extra advantage lies in the actual fibre size: something a hundred times thicker and in an experimental animal is easier to manage. Finally, everything discovered in the squid neuron appears to be applicable to every other nerve fibre, including those of humans.

On, therefore, to the method of transmission. The composition of every cell is different from that of the material in which it exists. This is equally true of neurons, and particularly so in its possession of sodium and potassium ions. (An ion is a charged atom or molecule, most fundamental to electricity, and certainly fundamental to nervous impulses.) The striking feature of a neuron at rest is that its contents are one-tenth as rich in sodium ions as the external fluid and, simultaneously, ten times richer in potassium ions. Inevitably, as there are channels in the cell membrane, there will be leakage; sodium ions will leak into the cell and potassium ions will leak from it. Therefore, the membrane possesses pumps to offset this flow, the devices in question being known as sodium-potassium adenosine triphosphatase pumps. Cunningly, and most crucially, these can steadily exchange three sodium ions for two potassium ones. Every neuron contains about a million pumps – each one is a slight bump on the cell membrane – and every pump can swap about 200 sodium ions for 130 potassium ions every second. (It is hard thinking in terms of the many thousands of millions of neurons in the brain. That difficulty takes a mega-leap when contemplating each atomically, and realising that total of 330 ions exchanging places every second in every one of those million pumps in each of those multitudinous neurons.)

Anyway they do. The pumps manage to maintain that sodium/potassium imbalance, and, therefore, keep the inside of each neuron at seventy millivolts negative to the outside. It is this steady maintenance that helps to explain the near-permanent demand for oxygen, whether the individual concerned is mentally active or not, whether awake or asleep, dreaming or even unconscious.

Then comes an impulse. It was in the early 1950s that the sequence of events executed in every transmission was first worked out (and Nobel prizes were rushed to the relevant scientists – A. L. Hodgkin and A. F. Huxley – in less than a decade). There is, at first, a change in the electrical state of the nerve cell, and this hurries along the axon in advance of the impulse. It is partnered by an alteration in the permeability of the membrane, a change permitting sodium ions to pour into the cell. There are channels in the membrane allowing this flow of sodium ions, and it is self-promoting: the more the ions rush in the more other channels are opened to increase this torrent. Suddenly, with a change in the membrane potential from negative to positive, these sodium channels close. Another group then opens, permitting potassium ions to flow out, and they do so until the original potential of minus seventy millivolts is achieved once again.

The impulse, therefore, travels along the nerve as flame runs along a fuse, but with the overriding distinction of returning the fuse to normal as soon as the flame has passed. The transmission of an impulse is not electrical, as used to be thought, but – to quote one definition – 'a physico-chemical change associated with electrical alterations'. The so-called spike, marking the shift in membrane potential between -70 millivolts and $+40$ millivolts, is the electrical manifestation of each nerve impulse. It may seem like hair-splitting not to refer to nervous transmission as an electrical impulse, but there is plainly more to it – with channels opening, pumps operating, and sodium scurrying back and forth – than in the conduction of an electrical impulse along a copper wire. The wire is a conductor, and no more. The axon of a nerve is very much more than that.

A further difference is that wire can conduct electricity continuously. The neuron can only transmit in impulses – continually. During the time of the spike no other stimulus to that nerve can have effect. The neuron is then said to be absolutely refractory, or inexcitable. Only when all those physico-chemical-electrical changes have taken place, and when the neuron is back to its resting potential, can another similar impulse be made to travel along it. However, even small fibres can recover in a hundredth of a second while large ones are about ten times quicker. To have a system of sodium ions rushing through the channels, then removed via the pumps, and then rushing in again at speeds of a hundred times a second, and to have the voltage flicking back and forth faster than the usual fifty cycles of alternating current, can be no less mind-boggling than the colossàl number of ions involved in just one cell, or the vast assortment of cells involved in just one brain.

To give slight breathing space not all human nerve fibres conduct impulses at 100 metres a second (or 120 m/second in some textbooks). Those that do, known as group A fibres, are the large myelinated nerves of the sensory and motor systems, those which receive sensation and instruct the muscles. As might be expected this aspect of behaviour, of learning and reacting, receives most urgency. Relatively sluggardly are the smallest fibres in this A group, with diameters one-twentieth as large. Their impulses travel at three metres a second, or one-fortieth as fast as the largest. Even so the slowest messages could still get from toe to top and back again in not much more than a second. Group B and C fibres include some nerves in the autonomic system as well as unsheathed nerves. These also conduct impulses at the modest pace of three metres a second or, with some of them, at no more than one metre a second. In general the autonomic system can be more leisurely over its tasks of bodily control. (With regard to speed in general a flash-back to the animal anatomy chapter may be helpful. The central fibres of the earthworm can conduct at fifteen to forty-five metres a second, which is among the fastest such time of all invertebrates. Even jellyfish nerves are conducting at half a metre a second. The fastest human times are, therefore, speedier than both jellyfish *and* earthworm, but only double the earthworm's fastest time.)

Most of each impulse's travelling, whether slow or fast, is along the axon. The main body of the neuron also possesses dendrites, in fact a very large number of dendrites. The usual textbook drawing of a neuron inevitably simplifies the situation. Its axon is probably just a couple of inches long instead of, as frequently happens, several feet. The dendrites are perhaps four or five in number, looking like the few roots of some uprooted sapling, instead of a thousand or so, or even ten thousand. It is easy to sympathise with the artist in his economy. It is also possible to suspect that generations of students remember the five-rooted sapling rather than something perhaps a thousandfold more complex. A neuron does not have just a few endings from which to conduct each impulse on its way; it has a multitude. Consequently, the possible ramifications and interconnections do not run into a few dozen after two or three neurons are involved; they run into many millions. In this sense the textbooks do harm. They imply a simplicity that does not exist.

The synapse is the point of union between one neuron and the next. It may be from axon to dendrite, or dendrite to dendrite. Until the 1950s it was generally believed that an impulse bridged this gap in some electrical fashion (partly because the brain is tingling with the so-called brain waves, detectable externally, and the material for electroencephalograms, discussed later in this chapter). It is now known to be chemicals that pass information from one neuron to the next, each of which is a neuro-transmitter. The time taken to bridge the synapse was not consistent with electrical transmission, and the actual chemicals involved were gradually identified. Initially it was presumed that only two would exist; one for excitation and another for inhibition, for enhancing or diminishing the message. After all much of the body works on this simple principle: nerves transmit, nerves do not transmit; muscles contract, muscles relax; the sympathetic speeds, opens, enlarges; the parasympathetic slows, closes, shrinks. There was ample precedent for a two-way, binary, on-off system.

The truth was somewhat different, and so far thirty neuro-transmitters have been identified. This deluge has also led to the prevailing certainty that many more will be encountered, isolated, identified. The first generation, generally called amines because of their nitrogen, included acetylcholine, noradrenaline (mentioned on p. 88 in connection with the adrenal gland) and dopamine (mentioned on p. 269 in the section on schizophrenia). In the early days acetylcholine was presumed to be particularly important, the main neuro-transmitter with the enzyme acetylcholinesterase nullifying it with the kind of immediate haste necessary when hundreds of impulses are being transmitted every second. Since then it has been realised that it and the two other amines mentioned account for only about 5 per cent of neuron connections in the brain. The remaining transmitters are, almost entirely, amino-acids. This discovery was surprising because these molecules, present in every cell that is creating protein (which means, in effect, every cell), are the stuff from which proteins are made. Essentially a protein is a long strand of amino acids, perhaps a hundred or so. The surprise, therefore, is that molecules so heavily engaged in manufacturing protein should also have a quite distinct, alternative and equally vital role, namely passing an impulse from one neuron to the next. There is scope, as it were, for the two tasks to become confused, relying as they both do upon the same raw material.

Nevertheless that is the system. The most recent neuro-transmitter research merely emphasises this point as peptides have now been recognised, along with amines and amino-acids, as further conveyors of impulses. A peptide is a group of amino-acids linked together, and a protein is either a string of amino-acids or of peptides. From an outsider's point of view this amounts to the same thing. From the biochemist/neurologist viewpoint the facts are more intriguing: they add to the plethora of neuro-transmitters; they raise questions about the many kinds of impulse being transmitted (and of different forms of information passed on by so many different transmitters); and they confuse the issue still further about that dual role of protein raw material also doubling as conducting agent. (Among the peptides being liberated at nerve endings are the recently – 1975 – discovered enkephalins and en-dorphins, apparently the brain's own pain modifiers, and discussed in the section on pain.)

If any single fact has been gleaned from the preceding two paragraphs it should be that neurons do not just fire and not fire. Via all these transmitters they must be capable of passing on much more subtle information than yes or no. They are not just hammers hitting the next nail, either more frequently or less so. They are, to complete this analogy, a carpenter's kit, with screwdrivers, pliers, pincers, mallets – and hammers. The wide range of transmitters is also exciting pharmacologically. It is generally assumed that most drugs affecting brain function do so by interfering with the trans-mitters. If this assumption is correct the quantity of transmitters means a corresponding wealth of interference possibilities. Possibly some of the modern drugs, acting effectively but without revealing how they act, are merely influencing transmitters as yet undiscovered.

Transmission is one thing; reception is another. The synapse is the gap between one neuron and the next. Therefore, it witnesses the release of a transmitter but also the recognition by the second neuron that this is a message, an impulse, and something to be forwarded. There are receptor sites on the next neuron, which are large protein molecules, but how they recognise that an impulse has come their way, and how they then translate that recognition into another impulse, is still a riddle. 'It is,' said Solomon Snyder, professor at Johns Hopkins University, 'one of the fundamental mysteries of neurobiology . . . akin to the genetic code of molecular biology.'

How a particular chemical liberated at a nerve ending is translated into impulse may seem of fringe interest to the major questions hanging over the brain, how it sees, memorises, thinks, and recollects. Nevertheless it is vital. The statement made in varying forms throughout this book that 'information is processed' on its way to the brain or that 'three synapses lie between sense organ and cerebrum' suggests activity, selection, adjustment, influence. An impulse does not just travel from point to point, much as Morse Code blindly departs and arrives with its dots and dashes. Each neural impulse is transformed along the way, and nowhere else than at the synapses. Therefore, what they do, how they inhibit and excite, liberate this or that transmitter, use this or that pathway, go faster, go slower – all of this is basic to the working of the brain. It is not fringe. 'It is one of the fundamental mysteries . . . akin to the genetic code.'

Brain waves   Non-invasive investigation has always been attractive, both to patient and doctor. Taking temperature is one example; feeling the pulse is another. Not only does nothing have to disrupt the system (painfully, expensively) but the body is giving a truer statement of itself. All invasion is a disturbance of the internal state. Hence excitement in the electroencephalographs – electric head writers – that are able to record, from the outside, changes in electric potential happening within. Known as EEGs, great things have been expected of them, in determining malfunction, in theoretical research, in predicting and confirming mental breakdown. It had been hoped, at the very least, that they would mirror the usefulness, in diagnosis and display, of ECGs, the electrocardiographs. (-graphy is the process, -graphs are the devices, and -grams are the recordings. A secondary blessing of the initials for ECGs and EEGs is that they slide over the necessity for these different endings.)

However, rather like each new drug, brain-wave recording has oscillated from early lack of interest (when its possibility was first reported) to tremendous enthusiasm to downright scepticism and finally to a grudging acceptance that it does have a role to play, though uncertainty still exists as to the nature of that role. In one sense the story is already a century old. In another its first half-century has only just passed. In a third sense, that of the most sceptical, it has not yet begun because the uncertainty is still so intense.

It was an English physiologist, Richard Caton, who in 1875 applied electrodes directly to the brains of animals. With the modest equipment available to him he was just able to detect electric currents flowing through their brains. It was hardly non-invasive, as the cerebral hemispheres had been exposed for the purpose, but it was the first outside measurement of the brain's own electricity. Mankind's electricity, manufactured externally, had already been applied to the human brain. According to Ritchie Calder, diligent delver after extraordinary kinds of fact, the first electrical experiments on the human cerebrum were performed on the Sedan battlefield in 1870. Various skulls had been conveniently cleft open, and two Prussian medical men, allegedly named Fritsch and Hitzig, applied current to exposed brains before noting the muscular twitching that resulted. They were able to confirm that left-sided applications led to right-sided movement.

Caton's work was advanced slightly in 1913 when Prawdwicz Neminski produced the earliest graphic records, rather than mere observations on a galvanometer; but he, like Caton, had first to expose the brain (of a dog) to achieve results. It was Hans Berger, the psychiatrist of Jena, who opened up the subject in 1929 by leaving the skull intact. *Über das Elektrenkephalogram des Menschen* was disregarded (and how often has such a statement been written when mentioning crucial work of pioneers?) until Britain's Lord Adrian, grand old man of neurology, gave it the nod of approval five years later, having checked the system with better apparatus. 'Berger rhythms' were finally applauded.

Berger persevered, whether he was being noticed or not, and detailed four principal electrical rhythms: Alpha, the dominant wave, particularly when the mind is at rest (8–13 cycles a second, and usually near 10); Beta, most noticeable when the brain is consciously attentive (more than 13 cycles/second); Theta, related to drowsiness (4–8 cycles/second); and Delta, only usually present in deep sleep (less than 4 cycles/second). Since Berger's time EEGs have so improved, in amplification and technique, that the greater wonder is how he managed to make any observations whatsoever. Perhaps, to be facetious, the work was easier in the near total silence that greeted his earliest labours.

It is easy to understand the feeling that EEGs ought to be informative. Certain electrical events within the brain are not just existing but must be revealing something. The strip-chart exuding from an EEG is so packed with fact, in shifts of potential, spikes and troughs, and at a rate of an inch a second or 350 feet of paper every hour. It all looks so fascinating, and indeed there are some facts to be gained from all that information. It can show if the individual within the skull is a child or adult, asleep, waking, or dreaming, has eyes closed or open, possesses dead areas (perhaps caused by tumours, provided they are in the cortex), is suffering an epileptic attack (such as one that cannot be observed clinically), or is dead. This last attribute may not seem of tremendous consequence but the use of EEGs is important for current definitions of death (there is much about this subject between pages 295 and 302).

An accurately positioned and sensitive thermometer could fulfil the same sort of role, disclosing general activity in an area, excess of blood, lack of it, or death, and perhaps the EEG should be seen as a similar aid rather than a giver of neat, water-tight answers. It cannot say if a patient's epilepsy is improving – only the frequency and severity of the fits will do that. It cannot say if someone is insane – dementia is often partnered by brain-wave changes but these do not identify the madness and, in any case, diagnosis by other means is relatively simple.

Nevertheless, EEGs are useful (so too the thermometer) and a *Lancet* contributor once listed some virtues. They can

> contribute to the assessment of recovery from head injury, the control of cerebral symptoms from hepatic failure, the control of hypothermia, the detection of intra-cerebral haematomata in subarachnoid haemorrhage, and of recurrence of excised cerebral tumours.

The principal problem is that no accepted normal range of brain-wave activity exists, nothing equivalent to 'normal' in temperature regulation (even though that normality ranges wider than customarily believed, with 'normally I am below normal' being an acceptable remark). Save for the fits of epilepsy – as distinctive on the EEG as the fits themselves – there are no wave abnormalities immediately specific for any one disease. A temperature of 102°F also indicates nothing precise, save that the individual is at that temperature.

Dr W. B. Matthews, of Derby, the author of the *Lancet* article, had, along with others, been optimistic about the potentialities of

EEGs, hoping them to be of both theoretical and practical value. But 'before these assumptions could be verified' various EEG departments, 'usually precariously staffed', had spread 'thick and fast throughout the country'. They were increasing the 'thousands of recordings made every year' and 'apart from wasting time, space and money, deluding the medical profession and the general populace, and debasing scientific methods of thought, no great harm resulted from this premature expansion because the investigation was at least painless and safe'. However, as he added, darkly, 'This was too good to last.' The wavering traces on print-outs often produced inadequate fact; hence a growing interest in what is known as activation. The non-invasive policy is abolished, electrodes are implanted within the skull, general anaesthesia is necessary, various drugs are injected, sometimes 'dangerously', and the procedure is becoming 'routine'. Hence Dr Matthews's concern. 'Activation . . . may sometimes provide information necessary for the welfare of the patient or the advancement of knowledge . . . [but its] increasing use . . . as a routine measure when no such information can be hoped for' had caused him to pick up his pen.

His article was written in 1964. Since then the role of EEGs has wavered back and forth, but forth more than back because they are each year more numerous. (Even so only 10 per cent of British hospitals have machines suitable for producing the flat tracings compatible with certain criteria for brain death.) It has occasion-ally been felt that EEGs would be superseded rather than sup-plemented by more modern techniques, but supplementation has been the rule and EEGs are not yet being wheeled into the street. Perhaps they are more acceptable because their limitations are better known. They do sample only about a quarter of the convo-luted outer surface of the brain. Neither is the brain stem assessed, the one-sixth of brain tissue involved in every basic function, nor is the under (or inner) surface. They have not yet disclosed much about the nature and location of whatever is generating the various rhythms. There can even be completely flat tracings from some children, from the very cold, or from the badly poisoned. They also require expert practitioners to decipher whatever it is they are producing upon the 350 feet of paper every hour. (Some writers have even dismissed EEG departments as 'another waste-paper store'.) It has also been necessary for clinicians to learn how to interpret the EEG interpretations prepared for them. 'This record is compatible with epilepsy' can mean practically anything as, according to the ebullient Dr Matthews, the remark 'applies to every record ever taken'.

What Hans Berger could not possibly have foreseen was the development of other techniques likely to overshadow his invention. The past twenty years have witnessed great advances with radioisotopes. Hardly non-invasive, in that radioactive substances are introduced into the body, there is still minimum disturbance; the individual is not anaesthetised, the functions are as normal, and the recording of information is performed externally. In this fashion blood-flow can be measured, region by region. Areas can be detected that receive sensory messages, generate muscular response, participate in thought. What are called the functional landscapes can be determined, investigated, assessed. These are different at rest, during mental effort, during pain, among the demented, the schizophrenic, the autistic. Not only can blood-flow be recorded but metabolic changes, such as glucose uptake. The procedure is costly, requires yet another kind of expert, and is only possible (with Britain) in a 'handful' of centres, but at least comprehensible features are being examined. The basic trouble with shifting potentials in the EEG is ignorance. Just what is being measured, apart from those changes in potential?

It was ten years after Berger started work upon his waves, and five years after his first published account, before the world took note. Such laggardliness would not be possible in neurology today. Any new scheme is leaped upon, discussed and analysed at considerable conferences with well over 2,000 delegates, and either promoted or shelved. The fact that EEGs are still in existence, still growing, and still producing facts must be partly due to that nagging curiosity over their very nature. They are recording natural events within the organ that is the fountain of all wisdom, and yet combined scientific wisdom does not know what is being recorded. It is most strange to sit, wired up and with electrodes attached to one's own scalp, to watch the needles flickering and hear their measured potentials translated into sound. Close one eye and the noise changes gear. Close both and the alpha waves leap into prominence, trembling as they do at ten or so cycles a second. This is oneself speaking. The noise is not mundane like the rumbling of an intestine, or simple like the ebb and flow of blood within the heart. It is the electrical background of 15,000 million neurons at work, maintaining thought, emotion, perception and the status quo.

Feedback is a modern word with ancient affiliations. In the context of EEGs it has a most particular meaning. Essentially it is closely related to governor, and governors have their origins in engineering technology. Steam-regulated valves were early examples of feedback; the more steam produced the more it closed the valve to diminish its supply. In short (and possibly too short) the input is governed by the output. Such a system obviously has parallels outside engineering, and the word cybernetics was coined (in 1947 by Norbert Wiener, of prodigy and genius fame in Chapter 12) to cover the entire field of control and communication theory. (It was later learned that André Ampère had used the word in his *Philosophy of Sciences*, published in 1838, but much new coinage proves to be melted down old currency.) Feedback, cybernetics, governor, gubernator are all variations upon the same theme, and feedback is the most commonly used within biology.

This preamble is to introduce the most remarkable (thus far) example of the feedback mechanism: people have learned to adjust their brain rhythms. The first to do so was a physicist at a Massachusetts research laboratory. With electrodes attached to his head, an amplification system near by, and two good ears, he learned how to switch his alpha rhythms on and off. It became possible for him to communicate by code, such as binary or Morse, without lifting a muscle, let alone a finger. Countless others have learned this trick since then – there are even biofeedback classes, much like meditation, where groups learn to control their cerebral rhythms; and, indeed, the brain sets out to control itself as soon as it is wired and amplified. The rhythms are dependent upon the kind of activity within the brain; therefore the brain learns to adjust its activity in order to alter the rhythms.

Feedback is everywhere. An arm is instructed to move, and then signals return from that arm telling of its movement so that further movement may be appropriately adjusted. What is so strange about brain rhythms is that they are fundamental to brain activity. Yet, by hearing them or even seeing their actions on an oscilloscope, they can be adjusted. The brain is able to control and organise even this most basic happening. This ought in theory to make brain waves more comprehensible. The converse, or so it would seem, is much nearer to the truth.

Brain physiology is far more than impulse conduction, neurotransmitters, shifting potentials and their control by feedback. There is, as with every bodily tissue, metabolism; how brain cells receive, alter and despatch the various metabolites necessary for their welfare.

For example, considerable attention has been paid to the 'blood–brain barrier'. The existence of some structure of this kind was first postulated in 1909 when it was realised that certain substances, such as dyes, did not reach the brain. If injected into the blood they arrived swiftly within every other tissue but not the brain or spinal cord. Later experiments confirmed that there did seem to be some sort of barrier (and with more interesting substances than dyes which may be too dilute to be observed). There was apparent restriction both to foreign substances (sucrose, insulin, penicillin) and natural ones (urea, sodium, potassium, creatinine). By comparison with muscular tissue, where there is equilibrium between blood and tissue for the injected substance within seconds or minutes, such a balance in the brain may take hours.

On the other hand the barrier seems not to exist at all with, for example, ethyl alcohol. So too with various anaesthetics, such as ether and chloroform, or the sulphonamides. Barbitone can take a long time to induce unconsciousness; thiobarbitone is almost instantaneous. The common denominator of the speedy substances is their high solubility in fat. The concept, therefore, of some barrier protecting the brain becomes less positive when everything fat-soluble can seep through so rapidly. Besides, the restraint that exists is never complete; everything gets through to some extent in the end. The most restricted are the very large substances that are also water-soluble, such as insulin and proteins. In recent years, though everyone acknowledges that the brain behaves differently with regard to its absorption of different substances, the idea of a specific barrier has waned. Perhaps the brain is more resistant to inflow merely because it cannot afford to be casual, encased as it is within the skull. Any swelling would be disastrous, as every owner of a headache will willingly testify.

In general the human brain is both attractive and unattractive to physiologists. It can absorb drugs, and then recount their effects, but this does not explain what is happening metabolically. It can be anaesthetised and made comatose, but most bewilderingly as there is no equivalent to consciousness in any other organ. It is both an easy subject for study, and an impossible one. It is like nothing else. Neuro-physiologists must at times wish they had chosen some simpler objective, such as the spleen or pancreas; but there is no greater challenge than the human brain, and no wonder that human brains have tried to tackle it.

PART THREE

The properties of the human brain are, of course, en-meshed with its anatomy and physiology, but are also sufficiently distinct to form a separate portion of the book. The characteristics of dominance and consciousness, of memory and general ability, and the various attributes of the sensory system are not all uniquely human (although some are) but they are all consequences of cerebral function and can be conveniently grouped within Part Three.

7. Dominance

Symmetry and asymmetry / Right side, left side / Dominant hemisphere / Split-brain / Hemispherectomy / Left hand, right hand / Left-sided speech / Digital dexterity

Let not thy right hand know what thy left hand doeth
– Matthew 6:3

And he shall set the sheep on his right hand, but the goats on his left
– Matthew 25:33

Why [the right hand] was chosen is a question not to be settled, not worth asking except as a kind of riddle
– Thomas Carlyle

Beware of the devils on your left-hand side
– Tibetan proverb

Symmetry and asymmetry Man is bilaterally symmetrical. Not every animal is – think of snails, starfishes and the protozoa – but it is the rule among vertebrates. However, like all rules, it is broken, time and again. Even the paired organs of mankind are dissimilar, such as the kidneys (where the right one is lower down the back), the testes (where the left is lower) and the lungs (where the right is heavier than the left). There are singleton organs, centrally placed (nose, penis, vagina), which do not conflict with the symmetry but there are others, equally unpaired, that do, such as the heart, stomach, spleen, pancreas, liver, intestines. Not one of these is central in the body. Very rarely is there any rearrangement of this asymmetry which, for humans, has the heart and stomach on the left, the liver on the right, the spleen on the left. Very, very rarely is the heart alone transposed to the right – dextrocardia – while all other organs remain in their normal placing. Less rarely (about 1 in 10,000) is there a complete switch (known as situs inversus totalis), a mirror-image of normality. (I remember watching a doctor in Brazil applying his stethoscope with nonchalant confidence, but frowning increasingly as he moved it here and there, and only grinning when he placed its disc below the patient's right nipple rather than the left. It was the first inversus he had met.) Situs inversus is much commoner in adults than dextrocardia partly because those with only their hearts transposed have a much higher death rate than those where the switch is total.

The brain, as befits its status, breaks rules and generalisations. Anatomically it is a bilaterally symmetric organ, and much more symmetrical than most, but functionally there is extreme dissimilarity between both sides. A human can lose half his brain and yet carry on living in a reasonable fashion; but if a small part of the other half is lost he can become an idiot, speechless or dead. There is a dominant half – so called, although it does not dominate – and there is the other half which is never called recessive or submissive but occasionally (notably in the earlier years of brain research) subservient, minor or non-dominant. The brain is primarily a supreme communications centre, passing impulses from neuron to neuron with extreme facility. But its symmetrical form, and the separate bulging of its fore-brain into two fore-brains, meant that these two halves of the walnut could only communicate between each other with relative difficulty. This fact is both an advantage and a disadvantage. The disadvantage, to speak lightly, is that the left side is less immediately aware of the right's activity. The advantage, to use a different image, is that there are not two heads of department vying for supremacy. A particular function, such as all-important speech, can be kept to one half without need to involve the other half. The errors of dyslexia, it has been said, are caused by two right-hand halves fighting with each other.

Although the brain's regular form with its irregular function is exciting (and most germane to this book) it needs first to be examined in relation to the body's other unevennesses. Just as the brain's two halves look largely alike – but lose their uniformity on close inspection – so are some other parts of the body less identical than at first sight. For example, the humerus is larger on the right side (by 1 per cent) and this asymmetry occurs even before birth, which suggests that it is not a cultural influence. The radius, the bone mass of the hand, the scapula, the pelvis, the frontal and parietal bones of the skull, the jugular foramen, the skin sensitivity of a baby, the testes and ovaries (whether adult or foetal), the position of the foetus, skin thickness, ridge count on fingerprints and the ridge count on the sole, all favour the right side, being greater or more numerous or just (as with the foetus) more inclined that way. The scalp's hair whorl is most frequently on the right, and more often clockwise (which direction is allied with rightness, but more dexterity on this subject under the heading of handedness).

Partiality to the right does make an odd list. So do the items that favour the left. The ridge count is greater on left palms (and therefore distinct from soles and fingers), the femur is larger (and therefore different from the equivalent arm bone), the skull's malar bone is larger (as against the frontal and parietal being bigger on the right), the rate of skeletal growth is faster and the sodium in sweat is more concentrated on the left. It is hard to ponder the reasons for all such general differences. (And, of course, more and more dissimilarities will be found as and when people choose to discover them.)

Coupled with these anatomical and physiological asymmetries are those of disease and malformation. Yet again they make a strange assortment, and examples commoner for the right side are: club foot, congenital inguinal hernia, tumour of the ovary, mallet finger, trigeminal neuralgia, pulmonary tuberculosis and lung cancer. (Blood is circulated differently round the apex of each lobe and this fact leads to a different susceptibility to these diseases.) Commoner on the left side are several congenital abnormalities such as polydactyly (more than five fingers), polythelia (more than one breast), varicocoele (distended veins of the testicle which hardly ever occur on the right-hand side), dislocation of the hip (which, as an extra abnormality, is six times commoner in female babies), absence of a limb, and cleft lip. Affecting adults more on the left side are breast carcinoma, ankle sprain, optic neuritis, blockage of the kidney artery, and osteoarthrosis of the hand.

In short, for a bilaterally symmetrical body, there is considerable asymmetry: gross – as with the intestines; distinct although paired – as with the lungs and testes; and barely detectable – as with the brain. To ask why there should be differences is to pose a question with few answers, but some are merely consequences of others. Right-handedness is associated with quite a few, and left-heartedness – a word worth the coining – must be responsible for others (such as the right-sided location of the liver). But why should the heart be left rather than right? As I. C. McManus put it the query is 'neither simple nor trivial'. There must be, one has to assume, selective advantages in left-heartedness and right-handedness. There must also be merit in having a dominant cerebral hemisphere, for that dominance to be – in general – located on the left.

As a digression it is relevant that the snail, *Fruticicola lantzi*, can spiral both to the right and to the left, but the rarer left form is less able to cope with starvation. This is the only animal symmetry to demonstrate a selective advantage, and that sort of proof of natural selection is not available for mankind, for left-hearted, left-brained and right-handed mankind. It is also very odd that the mirror-image of situs inversus can occur quite frequently with no considerable disadvantage. Similarly left-handers thrive and so do those with a dominant right cerebral hemisphere. The human rule, to say it again, is there to be broken.

Right side, left side   As further introduction to the symmetry of form in the brain and the asymmetry of its function some generalisations are possible (with qualification). For example, the brain is a symmetrical organ (but closer examination, as of the planum temporale, reveals asymmetry: its posterior portion is generally greater on the left). The brain's left half both controls the muscles of and receives sensation from the right-hand half of the body. This switch-over, of the left controlling the right and vice versa, is true for most functions (but others, such as speech or spatial thought, are almost entirely related to one half of the brain). Speech, for example, is organised in the left-hand half of the brain (except in those people where it is right-sided). Right-handedness is the customary human trait (save for those who are left-handed or who are ambidextrous). It is fatal for a stroke to kill off half the brain (save when that half is the non-dominant side). It is critical for humans to have communication between each side of the brain (but the point of union can be severed without fatal results). The brain is a highly specific organ where the most minor damage can have awesome results (but the most awesome damage can also have minor results). The left side is plainly preordained for certain functions (but these can be performed perfectly satisfactorily on the right side if the left side is damaged at a sufficiently early age). Right-handedness is a basic human faculty, and has been for thousands of years (but it is not present in the most likely animals to share this trait, the big apes).

In short, it is not easy making any kind of remark about the brain without immediately adding a contradiction. (It has been likened to conversation with an adolescent: every opinion uttered is instantly rebuffed.) Nevertheless, bearing that contradictory element in mind, it is possible to be positive about the brain's asymmetrical symmetry. Two happenings, one natural and one unnatural, are particularly helpful here, namely handedness and split-brain. The former, called by Thomas Carlyle 'the oldest institution that exists', is the human preference for being right. (His interest in the subject magnified when he was forced to switch from right- to left-handedness.) The latter, or split-brain, results entirely artificially from the surgeon's knife. In an attempt to cure epilepsy the commissure union between left and right hemispheres is severed – with possible benefits for the epilepsy but undoubted benefits for mankind's knowledge of his brain. However these two phenomena must wait until further facts have been detailed about asymmetry. They shed light on and also confuse the picture simultaneously.

Hopefully they will shed light on, as an editorial in the *Lancet* called it, 'a paired organ in which the halves display a remarkable degree of functional integration'. Most paired organs, such as the kidneys, lungs, testes, ovaries, perform the same function but independently. However, the brain not only performs integration but, conversely (or perversely), also has its two halves performing different functions. Ever since it was realised (first by the French anatomist Paul Broca in 1861) that a particular injury led to a particular defect, it has been known that there were specialised regions in the brain. He learned that damage to a part of the cortex (lying just ahead of the motor cortex, just up from the Sylvian fissure and now known as Broca's area) invariably led to speech disorder, or aphasia (literally speechlessness). As this area was so near to the zone controlling muscles of the face, tongue, jaw and throat it is immediately arguable that the speaking defect is caused by a failure of muscles vital to speech; but the argument is no less speedily refuted by the further fact also discovered by Broca that damage to the same area on the brain's right side causes no aphasia. Ergo: speech is a one-sided matter, and almost always left-sided. Curiously, those afflicted with Broca's aphasia can generally sing, allegedly with ease and elegance, in total contrast to their halting, inelegant, ungrammatical and ugly style of talking.

Much more about speech under Speech (p. 152) but Broca's work was then compounded by that of the German investigator, Carl Wernicke. In 1874 he discovered that another area (now known as Wernicke's) on the brain's left side was crucial to speech. Not even in the frontal lobe or forward of the Sylvian fissure, it lay in the temporal lobe and behind that fissure, but damage to it caused a different kind of damage to speech. Essentially Broca malfunction leads to jerky, slow, telegraphic speaking ('Broken' if the mnemonic helps) whereas Wernicke error is gramatically sane but semantically wandering. Once again the brain is therefore precise but imprecise: speech is (primarily) a function of its left side but at different locations on that side.

As speech is a uniquely human attribute, as humans are predominantly right-handed, and as both speech and the right side are controlled by the brain's left half, it was inevitable that efforts should be made to correlate these facts, to equate right-handedness with the left-sidedness of speech. Once again, as with so much cerebral research, the affliction of injury, whether accidental (trauma) or man-made (surgery, ECT) has been both a spur and a boon to discovery.

Facts revealed in this fashion include: damage just to the brain's right side in a right-hander rarely leads to speech defect; some 98 per cent of right-handers with such defects have left-sided lesions; about one-third of those with right brain damage and speech defect are left-handers; the application of ECT to the left brain is more injurious to speech in right-handers than a similar application to the right brain; and all such results are much more variable with left-handers. (Genetically right-handedness can be defined as an absence of left-handedness, but more on that subject later in this chapter.) What the facts do not say is that we are (largely) right-handed *because* our speech centres are (very largely) left-sided. Neither do they say the other half of that statement: we have speech centres on the left because that is where our dexterity is controlled. Nevertheless the wish to associate the two will persist because speech is mankind's most distinctive attribute and its location in the brain is so neatly linked with mankind's most distinctive prejudice, a partiality for the right.

Hearing is more two-sided than speech, but less so than vision. A normal right-hander listens more (or better) with the right ear than the left, whereas left-handers are less preferential. In fact the more tests that are conducted – on almost any characteristic – the more it seems that asymmetry is the rule. In the early post-Broca and post-Wernicke days it was assumed that any extra asymmetry discovered was somehow related to the well-documented and universally accepted asymmetry of speech. Now the pendulum has swung to the other side. It is wondered if there is any higher function of the brain that is not asymmetrically represented.

Examples are legion and varied. Newborn babies turn spontaneously to the right four times more frequently than to the left. Three-month-old babies grasp longer with the right hand than with the left. Damage to one side of the brain causes the victim to look to that side more frequently than to the other, undamaged side. If something is balanced on a finger the time before it topples is generally longer if it is a right finger. However, the converse is true if the balancer is also speaking at the same time. Damage to the speech centres of the brain will have permanent effects if the victim is either adult or of school age. If the child is less than four it will reacquire normal speech within a few months, the speech centres having been (presumably) relocated on the other side.

Amputations above the right knee produce more phantom limb sensation than corresponding amputations on the left thigh. Conversely, amputations below the right knee lead to less sensation than if they were carried out on the lower left leg. With mastectomy there is often pain or perception after the operation, as with limb removal, but this disappears more markedly with time if the left breast has been removed rather than the right. This coincides with the more general fact that skin on the body's left side is more sensitive than right-side skin. Certainly the left breast is more sensitive, even before mastectomy, than the right. (Which is just as well for in sex it can be favoured. 'Poor right breast, it's not fair, the left one gets all the loving,' wrote Douglas Hayes, making this point, in his novel *The War of '39*.)

On more cognitive matters the brain's asymmetry is considerable. The right cortex, for example, is dominant for various aspects of music, for the recognition of difficult visual patterns, for the expression and reception of emotion. In fact it is *the* hemisphere for virtually every form of spatial ability. The more elementary this ability the more it is precisely located within the brain's right half. Put another way round, the right's speciality is anything nonverbal, such as facial recognition, which is only fair (or to be expected) if the left is paramount for speech and words. Experimental confirmation of this verbal/non-verbal arrangement is possible with cooperative friends. Stand one of them directly facing you and ask a question. While searching for the answer the friend's eyes will probably be averted, either to the left or right. It is customary that they go to the right while seeking the answer to a verbal or arithmetical question (what is 59 from 82?). They should look to the left when solving a spatial problem (what lies immediately beneath a first-floor object on the ground floor?). The eyes, receiving so much information, temporarily favour the side which gives less information to the brain-half that has to solve the problem. Look right, provide relatively less optical data for the left half (due to cross-over) of the brain to absorb, and that left half is then more able to solve the verbal or arithmetical problem processed in the brain's left side. Of course, friends do not always comply with expectation, but a sufficiency of friends should demonstrate obedience to this general rule (providing they are not totally contrary and close their eyes to concentrate yet more effectively).

Even consciousness is said (by some) to be asymmetrical, with the left hemisphere playing the greater role. Also, from the kindergarten upwards, we tend to draw faces with a bias, favouring one side, one profile to the other. This may be just another manifestation of our handedness or a reaction to spatial thought being largely in one half of the brain. The recording of alpha wave activity has helped to resolve this kind of double answer, the change in activity being greater in that half of the brain more involved with some signal. Give a verbal stimulus and the alpha change is most marked over the left (verbal) hemisphere. Give a musical stimulus and change is more detectable on the right (spatial) side. This is true for adults, children and infants, which indicates that the brain very early on is designating different hemispheres for different tasks.

A neat experiment rounded off this regional distinction with admirable aplomb: whistling a tune decreased alpha activity in the right (musical) hemisphere, saying the words of that tune made a similar change in the left (verbal) hemisphere, and singing the song (words and music combined) produced a result midway between the two. Game, set and match to Schwartz, the experimenter.

Reduction of alpha activity in the more active half of the brain may seem contrary, and was indeed contrary to expectation in the early days, but that is what happens. Suddenly to close both eyes, for example, and considerably reduce nervous input to the brain, leads to an immediate rise in alpha activity. Needless to say, with so much cerebral asymmetry being discovered, alpha activity is itself asymmetrical, being customarily more pronounced in the right (non-dominant) hemisphere. But even that unevenness is uneven. The temporal areas show more asymmetry than do the parietals for brain waves in general and, for alpha waves in particular, there is greater symmetry regarding muscular tasks than sensory ones.

It is almost easier at this stage, and in despair, to think of the brain as two distinct organs united only by a similar appearance. The more that is discovered about their roles the less uniform the two hemispheres appear to be. Nevertheless there is union between them. The principal direct link is the corpus callosum (or 'hard body', already mentioned in the anatomy chapter). This is by far the largest fibre tract within the central nervous system, being three and a half inches long and a quarter of an inch thick, and it is that bundle which is (generally) cut during the operation that severs right from left (performed mainly on those with severe or intractable epilepsy). This form of cerebral bisection, or commissurectomy, does assist epileptics but also helps to explain the disunity of our united brains or, if vice versa is preferable, the unity of our disunited brain.

Split-brain The surgical procedures for separating the two hemispheres were first developed (on the cat) in 1955. Since then they have been both modified and applied to humans (starting in the early 1960s although the first actual severance occurred in the 1930s during the removal of a tumour). A surprising and general result is that the operation does so little harm to the patient (and may, for the grossly epileptic, do great good). After all, to make the point again, the largest nerve bundle in the central nervous system has been cut; but muscular coordination, for example, is hardly affected. However, at a higher level, there is considerable confusion. What has happened is the creation of what could be called a Siamese mentality. Conjoined twins are two different people who share, in part, a common body. A commissurecto-mised human has two spheres of consciousness, and is two diffe-rent people – of a kind – who share a brain stem and the remain-der of one body. In short two minds exist in one head.

Certain experiments have helped to make this point. For exam-ple, if some picture – of, say, a triangle – is shown only to the left visual field, and therefore only to the right hemisphere, the speak-ing half of the brain – the left – will claim that it has seen nothing. The cutting of the commissures has cut off that knowledge from its grasp. If the patients were then asked to retrieve from a bag (of assorted shapes) what they had seen, they would, and with their left hands, correctly pick out a triangle. If then asked what they had done they would reply, 'Nothing'. The triangle had been seen only by the right hemisphere and then picked up by the right hemi-sphere. As far as the left half was concerned it had seen nothing, done nothing and therefore it said, 'Nothing'. The two-mind concept enters this experiment because the right hemisphere, seeing something and then selecting that something from a bag, is presumably conscious of what it is doing even though, unequipped with the power of speech, it cannot relate this experience. The left hemisphere, ready to speak about any action, knows nothing of the triangle and therefore cannot describe the experience. One half is mindful of it; one half is not. The two minds are leading their separate, severed lives.

Other experiments upon divided brains suggest that the corpus callosum transmits what is called high-order information. It does not just send across all the signals received by the other side, like some demented office bureaucrat photocopying every departmen-tal document for every other department. Instead it seems to filter or process or encode that information. The wording is vague because these are early days in an understanding of the corpus callosum and of its so-called callosal code, but it is the only fibre tract in the brain known to act in this fashion. Therefore it is currently the object of considerable study, principally in the cat (whose brain presumably operates in a similar fashion in this regard to that of humans).

Strangely, for those people who have experienced/suffered commissurectomy there is not a feeling of loss. Normally only the callosum is cut, or even just a part of it, but there are other, relatively minor interhemispheric systems, such as the anterior and posterior commissures, the habenular commissure, those of the superior and inferior colliculi, and the interthalamic commissure. Therefore connection – of a kind – still exists, but it is modest and also further down the brain. Nevertheless, however severed from its right partner, the left hemisphere neither complains nor seems to be aware of its loss. Indeed, as Michael S. Gazzaniga has remarked in *The Bisected Brain*: 'One would miss the departure of a good friend more, apparently, than the left hemisphere misses the right.'

The fact that brains are bisected, however interesting the results to the rest of us, may evoke the earliest (late 1930s) scalpel attacks upon the frontal lobes. Lobotomies were frequently performed to quieten certain varieties of anti-social behaviour. They succeeded, often only too well, and quietened the individual in a most inhuman fashion. The commissurectomies are also performed to quieten, but only epileptics whose condition cannot yet be controlled in any other fashion. The idea is to contain the seizure. Normally an epileptic attack is an accelerating process, something akin to a loudspeaker's shriek when its sound is picked up and then increasingly magnified by its microphones. Eventually the entire brain is convulsed, or enough of it to put the victim, helpless and unconscious, on the floor. Brain severance is an attempt to restrict the seizure to one hemisphere. The other, hopefully, stays unaffected and is therefore able to maintain at least its half of the body in a fairly normal manner. The attack is contained – in theory – by the severance (usually) of both the corpus callosum and the anterior commissure. (During the 1940s there was a joke reply to the medical student's query about the function of the callosum: 'It transmits epileptic seizures from one hemisphere to the other.')

Certainly many of the patients have been extremely cooperative afterwards and their split-brains have produced some fascinating facts. For example, that inability to know consciously about the observed triangle, even though its shape is correctly extracted from a bag, can be duplicated simultaneously. The image of an orange was flashed to one patient's left hemisphere just as an apple image was flashed to his right brain. Immediately afterwards his left hand picked up an apple and his right an orange, even though he was incapable of saying (and of knowing) what had been flashed to his left field or had been picked up by his left hand. Yet more intriguingly (for the rest of us, if not for the patient) is the shining of a red light to one hemisphere and a green light to the other. Both lights are observed, of course, but the observer is unaware of the difference in colour.

This lack of correlation between one side and the other can lead to contradictory, Jekyll-and-Hyde behaviour. One patient would sometimes be found pulling down his trousers with one hand and pulling them up with the other. Or shaking his wife violently while, with the other arm, protecting her and trying to control the aggressive limb. However, the correlation, or awareness of the other side, is not totally lacking. A nude picture was flashed to the right hemisphere of a brain-divided girl. She said, with her left brain, that she saw nothing, but she chuckled as she did so. Asked for an explanation of her mirth she could not give one, but believed something 'funny' had happened. When the same picture was flashed at her left hemisphere she laughed again and reported instantly upon the picture's nudity.

Evidence is accumulating that the human baby has a split-brain. It seems that the structures linking the hemispheres are not behaving normally at birth, or for quite a time afterwards. Anatomically the neonate's callosum does not resemble the adult's, being smaller and less developed than might be expected. Functionally the very young brain acts as if it is in two halves, with language, for example, being developed equally in both hemispheres. By the age of two there are signs that the left half is beginning to take over language, insofar as the two-year-old is able to exploit language, and lesions to that left half are increasingly disruptive thereafter. Dominance, as one author put it, is thenceforth waxing while information duplication wanes.

By the time that infant is adult, and the left has waxed as the right waned to their mature levels, the overriding question remains: why is half the brain relegated to such a lowly state? It can be destroyed, as in a stroke, with so little effect. Also its particular and higher abilities make such a meagre list: a very little involvement with language (being able to react to some nouns but no verbs) but more with music, spatial perception and such attributes as facial recognition. Doubtless the list will grow, but the huge quantity of neural tissue on that right side is relatively unemployed when compared with the left side. To comprehend language fully, to assemble it correctly and to express it properly is a task that has no equal in human capability. To do all this (or virtually all of it) in just one half of the cerebrum is one of the most extraordinary facets of our extraordinary brain. Flying is an amazing event: to fly on just one wing, leaving the other idle, would be yet more astonishing.

Hemispherectomy   Perhaps the enigma will come nearer to earth, and be more comprehensible, when there are more left hemispherectomies walking about. Occasionally the presence of tumours demands that an entire half-brain – if that is a valid phrase – is removed. Removal of the right half is certainly not undertaken lightly, but at least that hemisphere is the minor one with its modest list of attributes. The patient is not 100 per cent afterwards but very much better than dead.

The first hemispherectomy was performed in 1928 – on the right half. The first two left hemispherectomies survived for 17 and 113 days, and for years it was felt that this would be the inevitable kind of consequence if the dominant half was excised. Now both children and adults have survived the loss of a left hemisphere. The adult's survival is more surprising because an adult's brain is more set in its ways, less ready (or so it was thought) for change, less able to lose its all-important, all-powerful (almost) dominant half. However, in 1966 a forty-seven-year-old man from Omaha experienced this loss and almost immediately, to everyone else's astonishment, began uttering words. Admittedly most of them were curses, for he was frustratedly incapable of finding the right words, but words of all kinds were believed to be the property principally of the brain's left half. And for him that had gone, along with its glioblastoma; but progress continued. Within eight months he was able to walk (with a stick), close his right hand, lift his right arm, and surprise everyone intellectually. On non-verbal tasks he was as good as he had been. With tests involving language he was very poor at first, but after six months could always discriminate colour correctly and usually select the requested picture from the assortment set before him. The most crucial fact of all, not to be forgotten in this set of achievements, was that he stayed alive.

Since then others have lived. Their continuing right-only existence has helped to modify thinking about that minor, allegedly redundant hemisphere. Plainly it is nothing like so negative as was formerly believed. If it can find words, or feel frustrated at not finding them, and if it can learn some of the left brain's functions at the advanced age of forty-seven, its ability is undoubtedly on a higher plane than was traditionally believed. It has, in short – and to borrow a useful phrase – more of a mind of its own than we gave it credit for, and the notion of two minds in one head has gained ground. An analogy is that the right hemisphere has been like the moon's dark side, the side we never see from earth. Of course it is there and crucial but the half we know most about, the facing half of the moon and the brain's left side, has been so much more blatant, so much easier to study, and more obtrusive, that we have tended to relegate the dark side, the right half, to some lesser role. As with the moon in recent years the brain has increasingly been regarded in the round. Contrarily this advance has occurred largely via those whose brains have been sliced in two or half has been removed.

One modern idea is that the right side acts as an echo chamber for the left, a modifier, or a qualifier for the left's personality. A medical metaphor is that the right provides a second opinion. It gives time for consideration (much as some of us count to ten before acting upon some impulse) and for evaluation. Seen in this light the famous case histories of the split-brained make more (or at least different) sense. There was the man doing up his dressing-gown cord with one hand while undoing it with the other, the mower of a lawn who could never guide his machine consistently, as left vied with right, and the reader who had to sit on his left hand to stop it turning pages before he had finished them.

It has always been a conundrum that such a mass of neural tissue, the right hemisphere, appeared to have so little function. No wonder we called it minor, non-dominant, subservient. 'I've half a mind to do this or that,' we would say, as if echoing this belief in half a brain. But we knew we had a whole mind – somewhere – and right and left are beginning to get together at last. The question is now being asked whether every mechanism is, to some degree, common to both sides, and whether we need to have two minds to have one that really works.

Left hand, right hand   Certainly they make a mixed bag: Charles Chaplin, Harpo Marx, Paul McCartney, Tiberius, Michelangelo (as the Sistine ceiling confirms), Horatio Nelson (but force majeure for he lost his right), Jack the Ripper (whoever he was), Sir Thomas Browne (who thought it was 'a vulgar error' to believe the heart was on the left), Danny Kaye, Leonardo da Vinci (perhaps – the possibility is still being argued), Rex Harrison, footballer/cricketer Denis Compton, and about 10 per cent of the population. There are more boys than girls (12.8 per cent as against 9.6 per cent girls in a recent survey), and the percentage in mental institutions is higher still (sometimes 30 per cent). The habit starts at birth – if not earlier. Historically it goes back a very long way, in fact to the beginning. And no one can say why there should be this largest minority of them all, the 400 million or so who are more able with their left hand than with their right.

There is undoubted prejudice against them. Linguistically they are gauche, sinister. Their opposites are right, dextrous. Even when both hands are equally able this is called ambidexterity, or doubly-right. The Bible has 1,600 references to rightness or right-eousness, almost all hostile to the left, the goat side. (Who counts such things? A left-hander certainly.) Spiral staircases were (and still are in the main) built to favour right-handed defenders, retreating upwards and anti-clockwise. Modern tools with a hand-edness to them normally favour right grips, although the large left market has created a trade in left grips. Politics are left for radical, right for traditional (although the terminology may have had its origins in the French post-Revolutionary Assembly, with con-servatives sitting right of the President, revolutionaries left, and moderates central). Eating is a right-handed matter in the Middle East, neatly leaving the sinister left for toiletry. With language, hygiene, custom, religion and technology all involved the pre-judice against left-handedness is indeed very strong. It used to be stronger still with everything cack-handed being devilish, anti-clockwise or just widdershins – the wrong way.

No one knows where the prejudice began. The big apes are often right-handed, showing a distinct preference for that hand, but they are equally often left-handed. In some surveys the largest number are neither left nor right being not so much ambidextrous as ambiguous or psephological 'don't knows'. It is commoner that there should be a favoured hand, but no uniformity between the species over a favoured side.

Humans do seem to have opted for right-handedness ever since they were humans. There is some evidence that Australopithecines used the right hand more than the left (in attacking skulls) and, leaping on a couple of million years, that the cave painters did so. Hand imprints are generally of the left, indicating (probably) preference for working with the right. Leaping forward another 30,000 years the skeletons of burial sites are, if damaged, more wounded on the left side, suggesting right-handed attackers (or a more vulnerable left side). In Renaissance paintings four-fifths of all Madonna babies are, if cradled maternally, held on the left side. This leaves (four-fifths of) right arms free for the more demanding tasks of feeding, amusing and caring for the offspring. (However, there is considerable tradition in such art, and, even if it was no more than customary for the child of each Madonna to be held that way, the 80/20 disproportion is just another aspect of human one-sidedness.)

At all events humanity has ended up with, in every grouping so far studied, a partiality for right-handedness. The ratio of right to left varies, generally between 5 and 10 per cent, but not the preponderance to the right. It is easy to argue why one hand should be so favoured – it is used more and becomes yet more skilled, it becomes stronger, there is less hesitation over which arm (or leg) to use – but less easy to say why right should be preferred. The heart is on the other side, but so it is with the ambidextrous apes. Speech and the body's right side are controlled by the left hemisphere, and there may be some merit in having these two particularly human traits closely allied in the brain, but that only pushes the question one stage further back: why is the dominant hemisphere not on the other side to make us (nearly) all left-handed?

The inconsistency, the 5 to 10 per cent abnormal, is also odd. Most abnormalities are much rarer. For example, the possession of a speech centre in the right hemisphere is much less frequent than left-handedness. Very much rarer still is the abnormality of a right-sided heart (see p. 110). A proportion of us also have three breasts, six fingers on a hand, a divided palate, or an outward-turning spine, but these aberrant features are uncommon and generally unwelcome. A strangeness of left-handedness is not only that it is so frequent but is apparently without disadvantage (the many left-handers in mental homes have left-handedness as a result of their mental deficiencies rather than as a cause of them). As it occurs all over the world, among so many lifestyles, and races, and (almost) equally between the sexes, there does not seem to be a selective disadvantage. Eye colour and hair colour, for example, might seem at first sight to be irrelevant to natural selection, but this cannot be the case. Blue eyes and fair hair do not occur in many areas. Not so with left-handedness. This abnormality seems entirely normal – for the 5 to 10 per cent who are so blessed/afflicted in this fashion.

Such defects as have been discovered relate, not so much to any wrongness in being left-handed but to the rightness of being right. There is hysterical paralysis which predominantly affects the right side. Patients also prefer treatments to their right half and being right-handed and right-footed might explain why Parkinson's disease seems to be more damaging to that side. In short, having the asymmetry does lead to a multitude of asymmetries, some clear-cut in their cause and effect, some obscure. Just as it is odd that partiality to one side should oscillate from right (generally) to left (occasionally) so it is strange that complete ambidexterity can occur without detectable drawback. Sir Edwin Landseer, the artist, was able to transform his abnormality into a party trick. With one hand he would draw a stag. With the other, and simultaneously, he would draw a horse. Left partiality, right partiality, and impartiality, are all – or so it would seem – perfectly acceptable.

The most fundamental fact is the prevailing preference for the right. It runs in families. It runs in mankind as a whole. The point has been made, notably by Napier, that we could not manifest handiness (as *Homo habilis* did) until we acquired handedness, but that still does not explain why right was right. Or why there was evolutionary benefit to such an extent that there is now a genetic basis for our dexterity. It is suggested that two genes control our handedness, the one for right being (usually) dominant, the one for left being (usually) recessive, and therefore what is known as partial penetrance of the left-handed gene in heterozygotes. This fits in with the fact that most heterozygotes (mixed inheritance) develop right-handedness but in some the recessive gene will produce tendencies to left-handedness. This sinistrality – not even such a happy word as dexterity – varies from strong to weak, with there being differing degrees of skill for the right hand. Left-handers are usually far less absolute in their preference than are right-handers – which fact fits in with the genetic 'model'.

It is very easy to go along with the idea that a dominant right hand and left hemisphere go together, and that the two powerful attributes of speech and rightness are somehow linked. This suggestion of union is reinforced by the alleged relationship that stuttering and unwilling right-handedness go together. Unfortunately (for the argument) this link is less widely acknowledged these days. Whereas the *British Medical Journal* wrote in 1966 that '. . . the enforced use of the right hand in some cases of strongly left-handed children has led to a stammer' the same journal was writing in 1979 that the theory suggesting most stammering 'occurred in left-handed children made to use the right hand . . . has not been confirmed, and nowadays few therapists or theorists believe this'.

Perhaps, as the *BMJ* suggests, there is a genetic association. Left-handedness is commoner in twins and five times as many twins stammer as in the general population. Hence the idea of a genetic link between twinning, stammering and sinistrality. However, if it exists, the association is weak because most twins neither stammer nor are left-handed. In fact the entire inheritance of handedness is somewhat vague. For example, about 10 per cent of the children of two right-handers are left-handed, but the proportion goes up to 20 to 25 per cent if the parents are mixed (right and left) and to 30 per cent if both parents are themselves left-handed. With identical (one-egg) twins about 20 per cent are not identical in their handedness, which is odd bearing in mind their similar upbringing, similar uterine environment and uniform genetic make-up. Just as intriguing is the fact that more one-egg twins are left-handed (about 15 per cent) than are two-egg twins (11 per cent). There may be even some form of sex-linkage. Children of left-handed mothers are more likely to be left-handed than the children of left-handed fathers.

The expected and longed-for association between a dominant left hemisphere and a strong right arm is no more clear-cut than the inheritance of handedness. About 90 per cent of right-handers and about 65 per cent of left-handers have the left hemisphere dominant for speech. The remainder, 10 per cent of rights and 35 per cent of lefts, talk, so to speak, with their right hemisphere, but 10 per cent of all right-handers (90 per cent of the population) and 35 per cent of all left-handers (10 per cent of the population) add up to only 12.5 per cent of the population (9 per cent plus 3.5 per cent). It is a proportion similar to the proportion of left-handers, but the two do not coalesce. It would be so convenient, and neat, and straightforward if they did so; but they do not. The general cack-handedness of left-handedness stays paramount.

Thomas Carlyle, forced to use his left hand when he could no longer use his right, was righteously indignant when he said that our preference for right provoked a question not to be settled, and not worth asking except as a kind of riddle. A hundred years later the question is still not settled, but its asking has provoked a multitude of riddles. One suspects, particularly with his interest in minorities, that Carlyle would have been fascinated by all of them. One day they might explain what he termed the oldest human prejudice, our favouring of the right-hand side.

8. Consciousness

Definition / Unconsciousness / Concussion / Stupor / Coma /
Sleep / Active and normal / Dreams / Hypnosis / Convulsion /
Epilepsy

I love and I hate, you ask me how can I do it? I know that I
can, and it hurts, for I'm going through it

– Catullus

One not only knows but knows that one knows. Other
species do not

– Anon.

What are you thinking about? – Maynard Keynes. Nothing, dear – his wife. I wish I could do that – M.K.

What is Matter? – Never mind. What is Mind? – No matter

– *Punch*, 1855

Even the dictionaries have different notions of consciousness. The
Oxford English Dictionary calls it the 'state of being conscious;
totality of a person's thoughts and feelings'. *Chambers* defines it as
'the waking state of the mind; the knowledge which the mind has of
anything: awareness: thought'. Perhaps dictionaries are not the
best arbiters of complex issues, such as consciousness. So herewith
other attempts, culled from a wide range of opinion. Consciousness, according to them, is:

the outside world going through the inside framework of the
brain – J. M. R. Delgado

the most obvious and the most mysterious feature of our minds –
Daniel C. Dennett

the knowledge which a man has within himself of his own
thoughts and actions – Jonathan Swift

[proof that] the self is a relation which relates itself to its own
self – Sören Kierkegaard

a process in which information about multiple individual modalities of sensation and perception is combined into a unified multi-dimensional representation of the state of the system and its environment, and integrated with information about memories and the needs of the organism, generating emotional reactions and programmes of behaviour to adjust the organism to its environment – E. R. John

the perception of what passes in a man's mind – John Locke

that immediate knowledge which we have of all the present operations of our mind – Thomas Redd

a non-entity and has no right to a place among first principles – William James

the organism's state of general excitability – W. R. Hess

something within the head which determines behaviour – Donald Hebb

the experienced integration [of] functioning parts – A. Fessard

a natural, innate property of the human life form, one that is integrated in a precisely structured brain – Colwyn Trevarthen

a vital part of living which defies definition – W. Ritchie Russell

a dizzying phenomenon [and] it is not even clear that those who use the word always refer to the same thing – D. M. Armstrong

The last two quotations make particularly pertinent reading in the light of all the others, but many problems lie behind all attempts to define consciousness. Over the centuries people have argued whether animals possess it (if they do when did it begin?), whether plants possess it (a photosynthesising plant is not unaware of the sun's presence), whether human babies possess it, whether those sleeping or dreaming do so, whether the unconscious and comatose are truly without consciousness, whether it is an intrinsic part of the human brain or any brain, and whether it can be maintained or even initiated in the absence of external or internal sensory inputs. A definition bringing many of these strands together (by Chris Evans in his *Dictionary of the Mind, Brain and Behaviour*) states that consciousness is being aware of oneself as a distinct entity, separate from other people or things in one's environment. The awareness is probably present to a varying degree in the higher animals as well as man, and presumably a function of the complexity of the living brain and its integrative power.

The word itself, from the Latin *conscientia* (equivalent to the Greek *syneidesis*), means 'with knowledge'. The first derivation was conscience, with consciousness being more recent. Most recent of all is the stripping from this word of all moral overtones and self-knowledge. We may feel a sense of identity in consciousness, even a soul and a spirit, but scientifically it is now the concept of wakefulness, alertness, and responsiveness to stimulation. Although it is just one word, it no longer means the same for man, higher animals, and those lower down the scale. Colwyn Trevarthen, of Edinburgh University, defined what he sees as the three main strands of our mental condition, of human consciousness.

1. Conscious intentionality. Knowing why and what one is doing.
2. Conscious awareness. Perceptive of reality. Knowing what is being seen, heard, touched, sensed.
3. Conscious sharing. Knowledge of personal feelings, of others, of their feelings.

'The growth of the mind is the widening of the range of consciousness,' wrote C. G. Jung, neatly tying up the suppositions that consciousness varies and personal identity varies along with it. Consciousness does not belong to man alone but, by no means, does the consciousness of other animals equate with the human kind. Monkeys and apes, for example, are believed to have some manifestations of it plus intelligence, communication (via signs and sounds), recognition of their own image, and other mental attributes such as (on occasion) an ability to mimic. Humans have these faculties plus a grammatical language, culture, creativity, and all manner of extra mental qualities. There is no suggestion – these days – that mankind is unique in his consciousness; but, to remember Jung, he does have a wider range of it and therefore a greater mind. The principal biological complexity of mind is that it did evolve and yet seems to have no reason. It is part and parcel of consciousness, and consciousness seems part and parcel of perception, and perception comes from a sensory system that can take note of the outside world, a system possessed by the lowliest of animals. The uniqueness of mankind lies in other areas, such as – to name one, and possibly the only one – his cultural evolution.

'I see no reason,' Trevarthen has concluded, 'to look for the mechanism of consciousness anywhere but in the organised processes of brain activity.' Or, as R. W. Sperry has phrased it, consciousness has emerged as the 'principal and most unified brain function, which puts it "in the driving seat", able to subordinate the elementary interneuronal processes to its own integrative states'. Consciousness is what we know to be true. It is the most important thing about each and every one of us. It is our very life – and curiously indefinable; as is proven, most contrarily, by the torrent of definitions now firmly ended.

Unconsciousness For all our awareness of ourselves the event of being unaware is an easier state to comprehend than consciousness itself. The comatose body exists, functioning in its fashion, but the mind does not, or rather it is not aware of itself doing so. To refer back to Trevarthen's three distinctions there is neither intentionality, nor perception of reality, nor knowledge of feelings. Instead there is unconsciousness. Or rather there are different forms, and levels, of it.

A gentle hit on the head, not sufficient to produce visible damage, can so stretch and disturb nerves that unconsciousness (unawareness) and amnesia will result for seconds, minutes or hours. This is concussion (Latin for 'shake violently') but no one knows what is happening, or has happened, to make the brain both unaware of itself, and incapable of recording events but capable of erasing past memories. Acceleration and deceleration of the brain are more effective producers of concussion than truly damaging blows. Bullets, crowbars and tamping irons have all passed through human brains to create either minimal or no concussion whatsoever, but many current sports, such as boxing and football, and motor accidents give countless humans a taste of concussion and amnesia. The degree of concussion is not a measure of the degree of damage done.

Medically there is imprecision over the naming of levels of unconsciousness, mainly because a neurological examination of the patient is inevitably limited. Reference is made to semi-coma, semi-consciousness, stupor, coma, and unconsciousness. Coma is deepest, and refers to patients who show no reflex response to any stimulus. The deepest comas of all are tantamount to death (with even the blinking corneal reflex being absent). Stupor is shallower, and its patients can be roused by painful stimuli. They make noises, of a kind, and withdrawal movements away from pain. The semi-states are the halfway stages, for consciousness is not always either on or off, as victims of concussion ably demonstrate. First they mumble, then ask where they are, then ask again, and again, and finally comprehend their situation. Only rarely do they remember the accident that led to their concussion, or the time both before and after it.

Most cases of concussion do not lead to further complication. Given time the affected brains recover totally from their insults, leaving the patients merely astonished that consciousness is such a delicate and tenuous possession. Eyes do not go blind for a couple of hours if they are hit, nor do muscles fail, but the brain can halt its consciousness. A kicked footballer can continue with the game, score a goal perhaps, shower, dress, and travel home while totally unconscious. The rest of him has worked perfectly; only his consciousness has gone – until it chooses to return and make him whole again.

The temporary paralysis of concussion tends to recede in similar fashion for each of its victims. It is therefore possible to tell how deep it is, how much longer it is likely to last. First is a return of simple reflex activity. Second comes restless and purposeless movement. Third is a state of more purposeful activity which, despite apparent normality, still does not mean that unconsciousness has ended. Fourth comes the onset of talk, often spasmodic and jerky. Fifth is a return of proper speech, but not yet a proper brain because amnesia is still present. Sixth is a rearrival, at last, of proper orientation, behaviour, and general comprehension, with the capacity for rational thought being the last to arrive.

Everyone must have a concussion story, and I was recently able to see those six stages only too well. My son, having fallen from his skateboard, was quite motionless with a mouth hung open when we took him to the hospital. There he lay, unmoving. When he moved I spoke to him, but no word came back. Eventually he too spoke, but meaninglessly. When he did produce a sentence, asking clearly where he was, I was fooled into thinking he had quite recovered. Only when he asked again, five minutes later, and again, and again, did I realise that my identical answer each time was falling, so to speak, on barren ground. About ninety minutes after the first question, and after my telling him for the twentieth time that he had fallen in the park, landed backwards and was now in hospital, did he truly hear and comprehend. 'How daft,' he said, for the twentieth time, meaning it no less fervently but remembering now what I had said and what he in answer had replied. He had been unconscious for six hours and never did recall that day's events before the accident or until those hospital hours had passed.

For my own part, and to conclude this personalisation of concussion facts, I recently experienced one traffic statistic. We reversed into a main road and I, sitting at the back, received the major force from the other car. I know nothing about the return of purposeless or purposeful activity, but I was aware of the rearrival of deliberate thought. With a feeling of pride I stitched together two observations. There was glass on my lap, and glass missing from the windscreen. 'We have been in an accident,' I reported, a statement of dazzling tedium to the assembled police, ambulancemen, witnesses and passers-by. Worse still I could remember the driver, a friend from student days, but could not recall my lady's name. 'I know you are more important than he is,' I told her worried eyes, 'but I just cannot remember who you are.' Some fifteen minutes later, with a further sense of triumph, I did so, but the thirty minutes before the crash never came back. Both observers and observed see concussion as a bewildering hiccup to normality. It invariably does no harm, but it leaves all parties yet more mystified about the state of consciousness, what it is and where it goes when a piece of tarmac or another car arrives too speedily.

Coma can never be regarded so casually. A recent report (with facts collected from hospitals at Newcastle-upon-Tyne, New York and San Francisco) gave the outcomes of 500 patients admitted with non-traumatic coma (unpartnered by wound or injury). All patients were checked for 'verbal responses, eye opening, oculo-cephalic (doll's eye) and oculovestibular (caloric) responses, corneal responses, extremity motor responses, deep tendon reflexes, skeletal muscle tone, and respiratory tone'. In other words, how deep was the coma, how absent the reflexes, and how disturbed both fore-brain and brain stem? Outcomes were classified as no recovery, vegetative state, severe disability, moderate disability, and good recovery.

The poorer the responses the worse were the prognoses. For example, of the 253 admitted without spontaneous eye movements only 21 subsequently gained independence. Of the 162 without motor (muscular) responses only 10 did so, and of the 144 without corneal response only 6 recovered. Comatose patients may look similarly dead to the world, but they possess varying abilities and these can foretell the probable outcome, not so much for individuals but for the group in which they lie. A lack of corneal response means a 4 per cent chance of recovery. Relatives are less good at appreciating percentages, being determined that their loved ones will recover, much like punters invariably betting on horses who run at twenty-five to one.

In contrast to those poor recovery rates were the patients who made sounds of any kind on admission (23 recovered out of 57), or who showed full eye movements in response to head movement (59 recoveries out of 277). Time was also important. Of those who regained full eye and muscular responses within three days more than half were finally discharged with either good recovery or moderate disability. Conversely if patients had not regained any cognitive (thinking) ability by the end of a week none recovered fully and only 5 per cent achieved any degree of independence. One trouble – for doctors and relatives – is that precise percentages do not dictate precise policies. Only 57 per cent of those still vegetative or in coma at the end of a week never improved; therefore 43 per cent did so to some extent. All patients must be assumed as belonging to the 43 per cent rather than the 57 per cent. Decisions become easier as time progresses. Of the twenty-five who were still vegetative after a month 'not a single one ever followed commands or regained even a measure of independence.' No one bets on horses at twenty-five to nil. They are just not in the running.

Nevertheless such patients are still not dead. The first month of deep coma is generally the most likely time for infections to attack, and conveniently to absolve doctors and relatives from awkward decisions about prolonging life. After that month, with the patient still lying there, uninfected and still alive, doctors are understandably unwilling to turn Hippocrates upon his head and withhold care. Relatives, never before confronted by the option of encouraging or delaying death, are equally nonplussed. Their loved ones are unblinking, unthinking, and helplessly in coma. What should they do or recommend? (These dilemmas and issues are discussed in the section on brain death on page 295 when they are at their most extreme.)

Generalities and percentages can make it easy to forget that individuals are involved. To restore the balance, and show that new techniques, and hopes, are on the way, the singular story of Darren Marcz may help. Aged eighteen months he fell into his parents' swimming pool at Long Beach, California. On reaching hospital he was 'clinically dead', having no respiration, no heart beat, no pulse, and a temperature of 81°F. He was already on a respirator, but was immediately prepared for 'cerebral resuscitation'. This involves the insertion of a small device through the cranium to monitor intracranial pressure. (A lack of oxygen causes brain pressure to rise damagingly.) The boy was then drugged into a colder and more comatose state for three and a half days, giving the brain time to recover but with oxygen demand much reduced. He was then warmed up over eighteen hours, and one week later attended a press conference held in his honour. He still could not walk, but was relearning fast and improving every day. Normally only 5 per cent of near-drowning victims come round from their unconsciousness, but cerebral resuscitation has doubled that proportion. Darren Marcz proved to be one unit of that 10 per cent.

A final point is that we, as a society, are confused over the seriousness of concussion. We hit our heads a fearful crack upon some miserable beam, 'see stars', know that we have assaulted our most precious possession, and do not bother to see a doctor. We may even knock ourselves out, for seconds or for minutes, but consider that all danger must be over once we have our wits about us again.

Neurologists say that unconsciousness can never be dismissed as trivial; blood clots can form, oedema may result, and any change in behaviour after recovery should be suspect. Nevertheless we do seem to be extremely resilient over insults to our head. For every 5 patients admitted with a head injury (to the Birmingham Accident Hospital) 4 were then sent home. Of the 1,000 head injuries admitted in any year, only about 70 spent longer than 24 hours within the hospital, and less than 20 spent longer than a week. Our brains may be the most sensitive organ, but we frequently damage our heads (resulting in about a quarter of acute surgical admissions to an average hospital) and yet damage their contents most infrequently. We can survive skull fracture, generally without detectable damage to the brain within, and must therefore admire yet again the pia mater and dura mater packaging of the central nervous system. We must also admire unconsciousness. No one knows what is happening, save that it gives our cerebrum the rest it needs after tarmac or blunt instrument has come its way at sufficient speed.

Sleep   If unconsciousness and coma are one puzzle, and supplying more questions than answers, sleep is another. This form of relaxation, both of body and of mind, might be expected to provide helpful information about body and mind, and recuperation, and regeneration, and what goes on in an organic system that regularly, necessarily, curiously, and lengthily shuts down a considerable part of itself. It is then no longer alert, ready to attack or retreat. It is not just resting; it is asleep. Such thoughts as may be going through its mind are uninspired by events in the immediate environment; they are, if mankind's dreams are not exceptional, an amazing hotch-potch of past happenings, deep anxieties, longings, and irrational events.

On therefore to some facts. Sleep seems to occur in all warm-blooded creatures, with most of them showing signs that they experience the two kinds of sleep, known as orthodox and para-doxical, as normal and active, non-dreaming and dreaming. The second kind, also called rapid-eye-movement, or REM, is now known to be a crucial ingredient of all sleep, but was not even discovered until 1953. Sleep times vary. The giant sloth drops off for twenty hours a day; rabbits, pigs, echidnas, guinea pigs and man for about eight hours; and cows, elephants, donkeys, sheep and horses make do with two to three hours. It is harder to know if the cold-blooded animals, frequently so lethargic, are sleeping, but some reptiles have different brain-wave patterns when apparently asleep, all amphibia appear to show sleep-like immobility, certain fish seem at times to be asleep (with parrot-fish even wrapping themselves in a slimy envelope at night), and all insects show at least one period of inactivity per day. By no means is sleep a human-only attribute, a consequence of swollen hemispheres, of cerebral activity.

Insofar as animal intelligence can be judged (for who can say if the sloth is wiser than a donkey, or wise at all?) there is no parallel between mental ability and sleep requirement. An understandable relationship exists between prey species, with most to fear from inattention, and short sleep. It takes a giraffe ten seconds to stand up after being roused, and this species only sleeps for two hours a night, but it does sleep for those two hours. The advantages, whatever they are, must clearly outweigh the dangerous disadvan-tages. The blind Indus dolphin, always at risk from the fast streams in which it lives, sleeps in ninety-second bursts, minimising the hazard of sharp rocks but emphasising a need for sleep. The bottle-nosed dolphin, whose language and secrets are still (almost entirely) a closed book, sleeps with one hemisphere at a time. Moscow's Severtsov Institute discovered also that one eye stays open, the other shut, during this split-brained performance. Nor-mally both dolphin hemispheres are in perfect partnership with each other. The one-sided arrangement, akin to one sentry sleep-ing while the other keeps watch, has such benefits it is easy to wonder why the system did not evolve with other species. Perhaps it did, with few researchers troubling to observe both sides of the beast they study.

REM sleep, originally named paradoxical, is now more com-monly called active because it is both active and arguably less of a paradox than normal sleep. During active sleep the brain waves are more similar to those of wakefulness than of ordinary sleep. Heart beat and respiration are more irregular, brain blood flow is in-creased, and there is extra arterial flow also to the genital areas in both sexes, leading to male erections but not to a correlation with erotic dreams. Humans have longer active sleep periods later in the night, but the ninety-minute interval between these bouts stays (fairly) constant. The heavier the animal, man included, the greater the interval between active sleep periods. This fact, seemingly so strange in partnering a cerebral activity with body size, may help to explain active sleep. Perhaps it evolved to meet the needs of warm-blooded animals; the bigger the body the slower the rate of cooling, and therefore less immediate the need for active periods to raise the temperature.

So far no generally accepted theory has arisen. Maybe active sleep is linked to heat control. Or to some kind of recovery which is impossible during normal sleep. Or there may be advantages in lighter sleep at regular intervals, in greater awareness of the external environment (temperature, predators, change of any kind) and of the internal one (full bladder, hunger, thirst). Or normal sleep may have evolved after active sleep, which contrarily is deeper, filling in the gaps with bouts of lighter, environment-monitoring sleep. All such theories beg the question that sleep itself, whether active or inactive, is understood. This is not the case, the few available facts being of little help.

For example, growth hormone (from the pituitary) is released considerably just after human sleep starts. So perhaps sleep is for growth? Countering this possibility is the fact that most mammals do not liberate growth hormone in this fashion. Therefore, the hormone may be connected with the starvation of sleep, the fast we break on waking up, and the need to preserve protein. Normal cell division occurs most in mid-sleep, but it happens within the small hours whether we are sleeping or not and has nothing to do with the liberation of growth hormone. The idea that sleep is a time for bodily restitution is knocked by amino-acid oxidation and protein synthesis being both reduced at night. The two should rise if restorative work is proceeding. Humans and animals undoubtedly need sleep. They cannot be deprived of it for ever, or even for more than a few days. Therefore sleep deprivation ought, in theory, to demonstrate where and when and how the body suffers.

Unfortunately practice is different. Less than a hundred people have withstood eight days without sleep under scientific observation, and only one man for eleven days. The subjects became tired (understandably), irritable and suspicious (yet more so), disoriented with time, and unable to speak without slurring words. There was some hand and eye tremor, increased skin sensitivity, and occasional problems with vision. Intellectually the subjects found concentration difficult, particularly if the task was boring, but could perform normally with chess and IQ tests. The EEG tracings remained standard, save with some patients possessing a history of epilepsy. Most remarkably no signs of mental ill-health were observed in any sleep-deprived subject, either during or after the considerable deprivation. Those of us who miss, not eight days, but a night or two of sleep may feel, or look, or behave like zombies but, under the harsh light of scientific examination, we appear markedly unchanged.

Internally the detectable alterations are also modest. Cortico-steroids, which customarily rise with stress, are maintained at normal levels. Blood pressure does not change greatly. Nor does heartbeat (or rather it diminished in five subjects, gained in three, and stayed normal for the remaining nine in one study of seventeen volunteer-insomniacs). Nitrogen excretion in the urine, a guide to protein metabolism, did not alter. So far as bodily restitution can be measured – direct measurements are impossible – no ill-effects have been found. Also the capacity to perform work is unimpaired by lengthy sleep deprivation. In short, the changes that might be expected both mentally and physically have not yet been dis-covered. A third of our lives is spent in sleep (five-sixths for the sloths), and all those who kept awake for science's sake fell asleep in the end; but, in minds and bodies, we show no obvious need for it beyond the one glaring, undeniable, wholly measurable fact that all of us go to sleep, throughout our lives, if not every day, then very frequently. Those who are sleep-deprived do sleep lengthily once the experiment is over, as if trying to catch up – on some-thing; but those deprived of eight consecutive nights (sixty-four hours) did not sleep for more than sixteen consecutive hours thereafter, and within a day or two were back to normal.

It is alleged, from several countries, that an occasional human requires no sleep whatsoever. A certain Señora Palomino of Spain is said to have dislocated her jaw (by yawning) and, coincidentally, never to have slept again. Some very short sleepers have been investigated scientifically, one averaging sixty-seven minutes a night for a week, and several only two to three hours of the twenty-four, but the various Señoras Palomino are generally pre-sumed to sleep a little. Many an ordinary person will wrongly claim a sleepless night, if only because it seemed that way. Besides, society exerts pressure on all of us to sleep. It does so when we are infants, as lullabies, cradle-rocking and soporific car-rides coerce us to sleep against our infant will. Pressure continues when we are adult. Buckminster Fuller, the architect, trained himself to sleep only four hours in every twenty-four, but resented being unable to make phone calls or meet people for so much of his new working life, and so ended the experiment.

Sleep-related diseases do not help our understanding of this basic, cyclic, physiological need. Narcolepsy, first described by Gelineau in 1880, is an irresistible urge to sleep, initially in easy places (office, buses, theatres) but later more awkwardly (at dinner, between mouthfuls, standing up). Plainly there must be cause, presumably related to the alerting mechanism which wakes us up, but there is no structural disease. When narcolepsy is advanced there can also be cataplexy, in which sudden weakness follows some emotional trigger. The weakness can be partial (head or jaw drop) or total (falling to the ground), but there is never unconsciousness. The narcoleptic and cataplectic patients sleep differently at night: they fall straight into active sleep instead of, with normal people, deep sleep that changes later into active sleep. (Catalepsy is something different, being a sudden form of unconsciousness quite unrelated to cataplexy.)

Perhaps sleep is solely for energy conservation, a semi-hibernation that is daily rather than annual, an immobile retreat from life. It is not unconsciousness, as the sleeper can readily be roused. It is not a time for bodily restitution, as ordinary rest is better for such repair. It is not, as used to be argued, an occasion primarily for dreaming, with such mental exercise being the prerequisite of a healthy, active brain. (This theory, wrote one author, is now a dead duck, but it is one that will not lie down.) However, sleep is still a vital need. No normal person has yet stayed without it for longer than eleven days, which is less time than it takes to die from water lack, in temperate conditions, and far less than the time for starving to death.

Most importantly of all it may have no greater relationship with the nervous system than with any other. If sleep is a device for energy conservation, a switching off as far as possible, the heart and lungs must still continue, but not every organ need do so. The brain is oxygen-demanding, energy-consuming, and remains so even when asleep. However, by closing down, it shuts down other organs and diminishes their needs. Sleep, according to this argument, is not a bodily sacrifice for the good of the brain but the brain's sacrifice for the body's general good.

Dreams It was fifty-four years after Sigmund Freud earned fame, very little cash, considerable ridicule and immortality (so far) by writing *The Interpretation of Dreams* that Nathaniel Kleitman published his breakthrough paper on dream sleep. This active sleep, already mentioned, is the kind that dreams are made on. Eye-balls roll (in most people), wave-patterns change (in all people), sleep is deeper (but waking is more likely after active sleep) and people who are forcibly woken at this time can generally recall dreams. However, it cannot be called dream sleep because that implies dreaming to be the purpose of it, or a necessary ingredient. The 'dead duck' argument that dreaming is a mind sorting itself out, pulling itself together after the sensations of the day, sifting through experience and jettisoning unwanted memories – all of this is contradicted by the facts that children experience active sleep (for 30 per cent of the total) more than adults do (20 per cent), babies experience it (40 per cent) more than children, and premature babies (50 per cent) more than normal babies. It is assumed that the foetus, still too young for birth of any kind, is probably actively sleeping for 60 per cent of its total sleep time, an even greater proportion. Perhaps all of early foetal sleep, as soon as the brain is so capable, is of the active kind. And, if so, this is another indication that active sleep is the archetypal form, the first to evolve, the orthodox kind and not the paradoxical.

Volunteer sleepers, who are repeatedly denied active sleep, prove that it is a necessary part of the dream cycle. If they are woken when showing signs of falling into active sleep they soon fall asleep again but into the quiet, inactive kind. However, as the experimental nights wear on, the woken volunteers fall into active sleep more and more frequently, and therefore have to be woken more and more often. On the first night of one trial they were woken five times, but by the fifth night the numbers of wakenings ranged from twenty to thirty. When the subjects were permitted normal nights again they slept, on average, for double the length of time in the active state, namely 40 per cent of their total sleep against the normal 20 per cent. As active sleep and dreaming go together it is tempting to say that dreaming is a necessary feature of active sleep, and the volunteers seemed to prove this by dreaming more after being deprived of dream time. It is more accurate to say that active sleep is a necessary component of total sleep. Both kinds somehow fulfil a physiological need.

Although there is association between active sleep and dreaming, humans do dream at any time of the night. ('In the Spring a young man's fancy lightly turns to thoughts of love. It also happens in the autumn,' wrote Bernard Shaw in another context.) There are also day-dreams, where the dreamer is not so much asleep as unaware. And there are lucid dreams where the dreamer can, to some extent, control the action. This is also a twilight area where the dreamer is definitely asleep but, according to one of its researchers, 'can maintain critical awareness and even convey information to the real world'. Dr Keith Hearne has added that

> differences between the subject's reports and responses in the lucid dream condition and in wakefulness could give significant insights into the physiological bases of those processes and of the functions of REM sleep . . . lucid dreams could even give an inkling of the physiological activity connected with consciousness.

Outsiders would be more than content if they could give an inkling into even the reason for sleep or the nature of dreaming. It was all very well for Freud to interpret dreams in 1899. The questions almost a century later are much more fundamental: why sleep and, as a corollary to that, why dream?

Hypnosis The word was not coined until the middle of the last century (by James Braid, a Manchester doctor), and he quickly regretted naming the mental state of hypnosis after the Greek for sleep. It is not sleep, but his and others' efforts have not erased the word: it is plainly here to stay. Hippocrates knew of the condition, and spoke of 'what the soul sees quite well with shut eyes'. In the eighteenth century Franz Mesmer brought renown to the phenomenon, called it mesmerism, thought it involved magnetism, and incurred the wrath of Louis XVI of France who cured rather fewer people with his royal touch. After being condemned as a quack Dr Mesmer retired to Switzerland but his baton was picked up by others, principally John Elliotson, a founder of London's University College, introducer of the stethoscope to England, top medical man of his time, and then victim of considerable attack for favouring mesmerism. Does he 'treat the harlotry which he dares to call science' with respect, queried the *Lancet* when it heard he was to give a prestigious lecture on the subject in 1846. In that same decade Braid coined the new word but was refused all opportunity to demonstrate hypnosis under any name before the British Medical Association.

Not until the earliest years post-World War Two did the medical establishment's shell start to crack. The British Society of Medical Hypnotists was founded in 1948. An equivalent American society was started one year later. Stage hypnotism, always a thorn in the dedicated hypnotists' side, was prohibited in Britain in 1952. And both the British and the American medical associations officially recognised hypnotism in the 1950s. What the soul sees with shut eyes had finally arrived.

Just as the hypnotic state is not sleep it is also not unconsciousness. Instead it is a bit of both. The knee-jerk reflex, still present in most concussions, is absent in sleep but present in hypnosis. EEG waves during hypnosis are similar to the waking state and not to the sleep patterns. Heart beat and respiration are as in wakefulness. The sleep idea originated when it was realised, contrary to Mesmer's first beliefs, that a patient had no need of convulsions to enter the trance-like state. A certain peasant boy just closed his eyes before one of Mesmer's disciples and 'went to sleep'. However, it was no ordinary sleep, as he both talked and thought more intelligently than when awake. The lad had entered, to borrow a modern definition, 'the peculiar psychical state in which the mind is particularly susceptible to suggestion'.

Usually it is necessary for an operator, or hypnotist, to induce this state, but self-hypnosis is also possible. Not every hypnotist can hypnotise everyone; far from it. The frequently quoted adage is that 'everybody can be hypnotised by somebody and everybody can hypnotise someone'. Normal, healthy people make the best subjects. The nervous and anxious are more difficult, but can be improved (made more susceptible) with training. Sigmund Freud took up hypnotism, but was neither a good operator nor willing to concede defeat. 'When I discovered that in spite of all my efforts I could not hypnotise by any means all of my patients I resolved to give up hypnotism.' Hypnosis lost, and psychoanalysis gained.

So what is the trance-like state of hypnosis that is neither sleep nor unconsciousness? One theory states that it is a concentration of the mind, a form of attention 'far greater than that which is possible in the ordinary waking state'. A normal mind, so this theory claims (and as most of us would concede), is a hurly-burly of thoughts, from then and now, past event, future possibility, current happening. Any suggestion made by a friend, for example, has to compete with counter-suggestion from one's own mind, with present mood, with other thought and odd-remembered happenings. So much is occurring that concentration is always difficult. Hence the theory that less is happening in hypnosis: a cutting down has been achieved and the patient can therefore listen as never before. Be that as it may the hypnotic state is yet another form of consciousness. It is also another bewilderment which will, when solved, form one more piece of the mental jigsaw.

Convulsion   One in fifteen children experience it during their first seven years of life, and one in two hundred adults do so. It is generally partnered by a fall, and was called an invasion of the devil. Those with it have twice as many accidents on the roads as do those free of this disease, despite restrictions on their acquisition of driving licences. Like practically every malady, or so it sometimes seems, the sickness was known to Hippocrates when it was named the sacred one. Some sixty thousand schoolchildren in Britain are said to have it, and yet there is stigma, as if it were indecent and shameful. It can be brought on by almost anything, with the bright lights of Space Invaders being recently indicted. Doctors not wishing to use its ancient but emotive name can call it cerebral dysrhythmia but, for all practical purposes, it is known as epilepsy.

The ailment is a paroxysmal or episodic disorder of cerebral function. Less formally, it is a brain gone berserk, disorder where there used to be order, a firing of neurons that somehow gets out of hand. It is listed in this chapter because unconsciousness, almost always, however fleetingly, is one of its effects. There are many others. Intracranial pressure rises three or fourfold, and can last for twenty minutes after the convulsion. The increase is due to the exceptionally heavy oxygen demands of the excited and discharging neurons. So blood-flow is stepped up, and the resulting pressure can cause obstruction of the venous outflow. This, in its turn, can lead to diminished arterial supply, an increased oxygen lack, an excess of carbon dioxide, an accumulation of lactic acid, and eventual cerebral oedema. Such a swelling will, if sufficient, cause irreversible damage to the brain cells. Epilepsy, in short, is unwelcome.

Nevertheless, although it can lead to death or serious disability, such grave forms are rare. With modern treatment epilepsy can be controlled in some 75 per cent of patients. Initially doctors almost always have to learn of epileptic fits from witnesses or the victims themselves, but there is no difficulty in knowing such an attack has occurred. From the epileptic's point of view the description can be both vague and quite clear: 'I was going there on my own but there was nothing I could do to bring myself back into the real world . . .' From the witnesses' viewpoint the epileptic generally falls down, is convulsed, and provides a sight extremely disturbing to those who have never before seen a cerebral seizure.

There are several kinds. Commonest is the major fit or *grand mal*. Consciousness is lost almost instantaneously as the patient (often) cries out and (always) falls down. All limbs are rigid, with the legs stretched and the arms bent. These then relax only to go rigid again, with gradually increasing intervals between the spasms. At first breathing is stopped and the lungs are emptied. As the contractions die down breathing begins again stertorously until it too relaxes. During a convulsion the patient may have bitten his tongue, emptied his bladder, or even injured himself in the fall.

Unconsciousness lasts for some fifteen minutes or more and, on coming round, the patient probably has a headache, may vomit, and may even fall asleep. Much later he may have muscular pain, understandable from the contractions' severity.

A second type is *petit mal*. The name implies it is less severe, which it is, but it is not just a minor form of *grand* epilepsy. Instead it is quite specific, occurs almost entirely in childhood, is accompanied by an abrupt loss of consciousness, as in *grand mal*, but without any falling down. The most diagnostic feature can be detected only on the electroencephalogram, namely a three-per-second wave-and-spike activity quite distinct from all other wave formations emitted by the brain, whether waking, sleeping, active, resting or agitated. The unconsciousness of *petit mal* is very brief – just a few seconds. The departure from consciousness may even be concluded without the person/child being aware that it has happened. They stop whatever they are doing and then start again. The attack is often more conspicuous to others, for there is a sudden blankness of expression, sometimes called the 'absence'.

A third epilepsy is the Jacksonian fit. Instead of a total seizure, as in *grand mal*, or a fleeting unconsciousness, as in *petit mal*, there is a spreading of the effect. Tremor starts on one side of the body, at the mouth's corner, the big toe, the thumb, and then progresses away from that initial area. Sometimes the spread coincides with neighbouring zones in the brain's cortex, as if – which is surely happening – the seizure is travelling through the brain. The various muscles twitch and shake as and when the spasm reaches their relevant control centres. The effect dies out on its own accord; or it may end in one tremendous convulsion immediately partnered by unconsciousness.

For all the antiquity of this sacred disease neither the nature of the abnormality nor the nature of the trigger is known. Fits can follow many of the ordinary vicissitudes of life, such as fright, worry, excessive work, over-breathing, awakening, or being in the pre-menstrual phase. (The most bizarre case of recent years occurred in Wisconsin when a thirty-five-year-old man proved to be a musicogenic epileptic. The *1812 Overture* and strident rock 'n' roll left him unmoved, but the gentle rhythms of 'Stardust' or 'Abide with Me' had him staring, twitching and sometimes falling down. Treatment was devastating. They played 'Stardust' at him 6,000 times, in dozens of variations, until it too left him unmoved.)

If signs of epilepsy are found in a brain at autopsy they have more frequently been caused by the convulsions than were the cause of the epilepsy. *Grand* and *petit mal*, in particular, are known as idiopathic epilepsy because there is no discernible cause. Nevertheless there is plainly fault. Whatever normally prevents an impulse from building up, and then overtaking the whole brain with its energy, is failing. It should contain the explosion, but it does not.

Most of those who suffer epilepsy remain otherwise mentally normal during their lives. The many epileptics in mental hospitals are probably there because brain damage is responsible both for the epilepsy and other disorders. Treatment for epilepsy of unknown cause is by drugs, such as phenobarbitone. The difference between *grand* and *petit* is emphasised by drugs good for one being usually bad for the other. The problem of epileptic drivers will presumably never be resolved. In the UK an epileptic may normally regain his driving licence if he has had no fit during waking hours for three years, whether or not he is on anti-convulsant drugs. Other countries tend to have shorter fit-free times, unless the licence is for a heavy-goods or public-service vehicle. In these cases the custom, as in Britain, is to refuse a licence for life. In the United States there are, as is frequent, about as many laws as there are states. In some the physician has to inform the authorities of all epileptics known to him. Doctors have been held responsible, legally and financially, for accidents attributed to unreported patients. A Department of Health, Education and Welfare publication (of 1978) stated that the primary responsibility of reporting lay with the patient. The doctor had only to advise him correctly, of the risks of epilepsy and the need to report. Despite the British three-year ban the accident rate of those known to have been epileptic is twice that of the general population.

Because there is stigma about epilepsy, the word often being allied – quite wrongly – with madness, it is not only applicants for driving licences who hide their history of the disease, with 'my doctor said I have a seizure disorder which is not epilepsy' being one form of denial. Another is straight untruth. At a 1980 meeting of the Epilepsy Society of Massachusetts 80 per cent of the attendance spoke of suggestions by their neurologists to deny or cover up their epilepsy, particularly in dealings with an employer or insurance company. Genetically a link exists but no single, or simple, mechanism has been identified. The disease occurs in some families, either in generations or among siblings, but the parents of most epileptics have never themselves been affected. If only one parent is epileptic the risk to any offspring is negligible, or about 200 to 1 against. If both parents are epileptic they are generally advised against child-rearing even though, to quote one correspondent to the *New England Journal of Medicine*, 'risk figures for genetic counselling [on epilepsy] have been scattered, inadequate and often conflicting'. Very rarely does an epileptic fit lead to violent crime. This is a common worry among the general population, but a 1981 study of 5,400 epileptic patients from four countries only discovered fifteen with 'aggressive phenomena' during their seizures.

According to the World Health Organisation the disease strikes three to ten per thousand of the total population. Assuming the higher figure this means forty million epileptics in the world. As the WHO statement blandly added: 'It is an important and very common mental health problem.' It is a form of unconsciousness whose unravelling should say much about the normal working of any brain, and about consciousness itself. Just as it is not known why the brain is not in a continual seizure, so is it facetiously reported (as mentioned under Dominance) that the inter-hemispheric commissures are the brain's means of ensuring that epilepsy can occur. They permit the seizure to swamp the whole brain instead of half or part of it. The simple epileptic may yet contribute to neural knowledge; the severe ones have already done so. Cutting those commissures is a last-ditch measure when drugs are unable to keep repeated seizures at bay. The resulting so-called split-brains, described on pages 117 to 122, have provided fascinating facts about the human mind. Many ill winds have power to do good, for others if not for the patients themselves. Also, those who possess consciousness as an inexorable part of their daily routine should contemplate what it must be like losing it for seconds or even minutes at a time. How then would they view such simple acts as shopping, swimming, bicycling, driving, minding their children or just holding down a job? A distressing number of the world's people already know the answer.

9. Ability

Learning / Intelligence / IQ / Speech / Language / Reading / Music

Unless you know what it is, I ain't never going to be able to explain it to you

– Louis Armstrong (on jazz)

I wish I could be as certain about anything as Lord Macaulay is about everything

– Lord Melbourne

Man is not a reasonable animal but only capable of reason

– Jonathan Swift

Learning 'O! this learning, what a thing it is' despaired (or exulted) Shakespeare in *The Taming of the Shrew*. Four centuries later mankind is similarly baffled, still desperate but still excited. Even definition is difficult. As Patrick Bateson, zoologist at Cambridge, wrote: 'Defining learning is almost a bad joke among people who study behaviour.' A problem, as Professor Marie Jahoda pointed out, is that 'learning cannot be observed, it is always an inference from behaviour or experience.' Or, to retreat to Shakespeare, 'learning is but an adjunct to ourself.' It is also an adjunct to memory, and memory is but a piece of consciousness. Any nervous system, with any degree of complexity about it, gives rise to learning. Therefore, it is, in part, the possession of a nervous system.

Learning, wrote Sir Peter Medawar, 'is learning not to think about operations that once needed to be thought about'. In fact the process is twofold, for he continued: 'We learn to make the processes of deliberate thought instinctive, and we learn to make automatic and instinctive processes the subject of discriminating thought.' Alfred Whitehead made the same sort of point in writing: 'It is a profoundly erroneous truism, repeated by all copy books, and by eminent people when they are making speeches, that we should cultivate the habit of thinking what we are doing. The precise opposite is the case.'

There is also discrepancy about the brain's ability to learn. Many graphs seem to prove that mental abilities are virtually concluded after the age of twenty or so. Some suggest a peak at twenty-five, with decline proceeding apace thereafter. Individuals demonstrate this fact (if their lives are examined) and so do populations. Conversely every single one of these statements has been vigorously contradicted. It is not the number of neurons that is important (this does diminish with age) but the number of inter-connections (about which there is no proof). Also intelligence may actually increase with age. As Patrick Bateson phrased it: 'The search for a single global concept of learning is utterly hopeless.' Interestingly most books on the development of young humans, or on abnormal development, make no reference to learning in their indexes.

To quote from Chris Evans' *Dictionary of Psychology* learning is 'The acquisition and subsequent storage of information by an animal in a way that allows it to modify its behaviour in the future.' It, therefore, involves memory (storage) and remembering (extraction from storage) because learning without memory is as unthinkable as memory without learning. It is not even known at what stage a human neonate begins to learn. There is an orthodox assumption that no learning happens until the age of eight to twelve months. Until that time everything is reflexes and activities such as imprinting, the phenomena first studied in goslings (by Konrad Lorenz) which impels the young birds to follow the first large creature that they see. Undoubtedly young humans become familiar with certain objects (mother, bottle, cot), and with certain happenings, but such increased awareness is not everyone's notion of learning. More recently, it has been suggested that babies begin learning between twelve and twenty-one days. Experimenters made gestures in front of babies (lip protrusion, lip pursing, etc.) and watched for imitation. The work has been criticised, partly because babies have such a limited repertoire (lip protruding and pursing being a major part of this capability), and will react – in any way they can – to any stimulus. The case is, therefore, still *not* proven as to when true learning starts.

Every parent should also remember the existence of so-called backward learning, that undressing comes before dressing, emptying boxes is achieved long before they are ever filled, and a mess is made – repeatedly – before anything is tidied up. Much of learning proceeds from trial to error and only belatedly to success. We must first fall off our bicycles, and much of learning is achieved by being given the opportunity to fail.

Scientific advance often occurs through study of malfunction rather than normality. Haemophilia had much to teach about the clotting of blood, and diabetes of the role of insulin. However, neuropsychology textbooks have little to offer about learning disorder. One child (or one adult) can learn; another cannot. There must be a reason for this variance but, as with consciousness, as with memory, as with thought itself, the unravelling has scarcely begun. 'O! this learning, what a thing it is,' said Gremio. And so, with not much advance, say all of us four centuries afterwards.

Intelligence   Louis Armstrong's remark about jazz is worthy of a second telling with intelligence in mind – 'Unless you know what it is, I ain't never going to be able to explain it to you.' In one sense the word is much like physique for general physical ability. In another it cannot compare because intelligence implies superior intelligence whereas everyone has a physique, whether good, bad or cadaverous. Chris Evans' dictionary, so precise in other areas, is forthrightly vague about intelligence: 'One of the most important concepts of psychology and at the same time one of the least understood.' We all have intelligence but only a fraction are intelligent. It is one thing; it is a multiplicity of things. We have more than any other species but, having got it, we seem hard-pressed to know what it is.

Dr George Stoddard made an attempt in *The Meaning of Intelligence* where he wrote that intelligence is

> the ability to undertake activities that are characterised by Difficulty, Complexity, Abstractness, Economy, Adaptiveness to a goal, Social value, and the Emergence of originals, and to maintain such activities under conditions that demand a concentration of energy and a resistance to emotional forces.

Another definition might be the wit to understand fully Stoddard's statement. Yet another definition, and less didactic, is 'a quickness of response, a scanning of possible solutions, and the capacity to perceive new relationships between aspects of a problem'. It has also been defined as 'versatility of adjustment'. Although *Homo* is the only species dubbed *sapiens* it is not a uniquely human ability, but occurs wherever learning occurs, and where behaviour is not solely a matter of instinctive response. Intelligence is plainly lodged within the cranium, but how and where and what it is are much less obvious.

Ordinary dictionaries point up one aspect of the problem: intelligence is 'intellect, understanding', whereas intelligent is 'showing a high degree of understanding'. The words for grades of intelligence at the upper end are not distinct while, strangely, the lower end is much better defined. One classification ranges human intelligence from: Idiot, Imbecile, Moron, Borderline, Dull, Normal, Superior, Very Superior, to Gifted. There are words such as wise, brilliant, genius, but they have no precision to them.

Genetically some statements are possible. According to C. O. Carter, the 'natural children of professional men are, on the average, significantly more intelligent than their adopted brothers, while the natural children of unskilled workers are significantly less intelligent than are their adopted brothers.' He considered 'about half' the variation in general intelligence among schoolchildren is due to 'genetic endowment' and added that this proportion would increase when opportunity and living standards 'become more uniform'. The common belief is that clever children are weak in health and strength. The truth is that they are healthier and stronger than the average.

IQ Mention of genetic and environmental endowment must be followed by mention of tests for intelligence. Few try to measure general physique but mental ability has been measured since the earliest years of this century. The work may have been well meaning initially, but it is easy to believe that the argument on racial difference, rife at the time, spilled over into desire to prove this difference in quite the most sensitive area, that of intellect. The Alpha and Beta tests used by the US Army to classify one and a half million recruits during World War One acted as a springboard, both for considerable claims concerning racial difference and for resentment over the methods used plus the wholesale indictment that resulted.

Ever since then, and possibly even before, there has been controversy. Against IQ testing it is argued that: what is being measured is not what is generally understood as intelligence; the value or worth of a person is not being tested; the judgment is being made about certain abilities only (such as comprehending verbal symbols); and, as geneticist Theodosius Dobzhansky put it, 'The IQ is certainly not independent of the environment, of the family background, schooling, and the circumstances under which the test is administered.' In favour of tests it is stated that: there is correlation between them and educational success; there is negative correlation with mental defect as judged by conduct; the more demanding jobs are occupied by people with higher IQs and vice versa; and, as Professor Hans Eysenck phrased it, 'People generally regarded as intelligent score higher than people regarded as dull.'

Hence the controversy, which has broadened occasionally into vitriolic furore. *Intelligence: The Battle for the Mind* was jointly written by Eysenck (of London) and Leon Kamin (of Princeton). Each outlined the opposing viewpoints, and a subsequent reviewer accused Kamin of 'sarcasm', a 'relentless anti-Eysenck diatribe' and 'disgraceful and gratuitous insults'. Not always in the IQ war does each side listen to the other. In a *New Scientist* debate between Eysenck and Steven Rose (of Britain's Open University), who were alleged to be on opposite sides, Eysenck wrote: 'Intelligence is not some *thing* that exists somewhere out there . . . [it] is a *concept*, like mass, or temperature.' Rose wrote (on the very same page): 'The fallacy that "IQ" tests measure intelligence is a classic example of circular reasoning, based on a series of untenable assumptions: (a) that intelligence is a sort of *thing*, a fixed quantity . . .' Unlike much scientific debate the IQ wrangle has turned each set of protagonists into zealots for their cause. As two observers (both from *Psychology News*) despairingly pointed out in 1982: 'We have found no sign of any leading psychologist in the UK changing his or her position on the issue in the past few years . . .' They then added, yet more despairingly, 'It is not clear what sort of evidence would make psychologists change their minds.'

All debate can become entrenched, but there are aggravating extras in the IQ argument. If intelligence can be assessed, or estimated, or predicted, what then? Will fewer educational resources be allocated to those individuals with least need of them, such as individuals scoring worst or best in the tests? If races or other groupings of mankind do score differently, what then? Will – assuming one group consistently scores 1 per cent less – it receive 1 per cent less money (or 1 per cent more)? Also, as the relative importance of genes and environment (nature and nurture) have figured in (almost) every IQ discussion, what will happen if it is generally accepted in one community that genes wield, say, 80 per cent of the influence? Even if that remark has any meaning in science, does it have meaning for that community? In short, it is neither known if the IQ debate can be resolved, nor what should be done with the information if it is generally acceptable.

Further entrenchment (if that is possible) has come from several recent developments. Firstly, some of the evidence, so frequently cited, concerning the inheritance of intelligence has been shown as fraudulent. Sir Cyril Burt's research has been subject to particular enquiry. Secondly, a federal judge in California has outlawed the use of IQ tests for labelling black students as mentally backward. The relatively high number of such students in classes for the mentally retarded resulted from their inability to perform well in tests. This, said the judge, constituted cultural and racial discrimination. The banning, which came at the end of an eight-year law suit, technically only applies to California at present, and to one particular use of one type of test, but it is certain to have repercussions.

Thirdly (and in favour of IQ testing) the speed of nervous action in the brain – responding to flashing lights, etc. – has been shown to correlate well with high IQs. Therefore, there may be something innately better or faster about clever brains. Fourthly (again favouring tests) it has been shown that evoked brain waves, those which change according to outside stimuli, can also be correlated with IQ. In other words, there is detectably different behaviour in the brains of dull and bright people. Or, as Hans Eysenck put it: 'A concrete, measurable biological basis has been found for IQ.' Alan Hendrickson, who did the work on evoked potentials, goes even further. The results did not just demonstrate a biological foundation for intelligence: they suggest what IQ actually is. Others have inevitably been quick to assert that claims of finding the root of intelligence are, as swift deductions go, not notably intelligent.

The debate is, therefore, still active. For some critics IQ tests merely test a person's ability at performing in IQ tests. Each recognisable group will only do well when that group sets the tests. The converse argument is that any scheme which tests intelligence, mankind's most exciting attribute, is worthy of examination, and then of improvement. If found acceptable it would undoubtedly be useful. A third point of view is that the concept of intelligence is just too diverse to end up as a single number. Karl Popper and John C. Eccles wrote:

> It seems likely that there are innate differences of intelligence. But it seems almost impossible that a matter so many-sided and complex as human inborn knowledge and intelligence (quickness of grasp, depth of understanding, creativity, clarity of exposition, etc.) can be measured by a one-dimensional function like the 'Intelligence Quotient'.

Two final points can conclude this section. Children, apparently, cannot be tested for their IQ until they are six, by which time their nature and much nurture have already been applied. Secondly, in a world increasingly bewildered by the Japanese skill at comprehending everyone's commercial wishes ahead of time, and at providing an industry to satisfy that need, the nation with the highest mean IQ is Japan. It is published as 106.6 while the British figure is, for example, just 100. However, even this differential has been exceeded. In May 1982 *Nature* carried a report by Richard Lynn, of the New University of Ulster, which specifically compared a sample of Japanese children with a similar sample of Americans. He found a difference of eleven IQ points between the two groups – in favour of the Japanese.

Speech Most animals can communicate, but only mankind can speak. Via language mankind is able to achieve what the cleverest animals cannot even contemplate, such as accumulate knowledge, relate experience, discuss an issue, plan the future. The 'loom of language', Plato's phrase, has woven the fabric of human culture, and it was and is through a cultural evolution that mankind has diverged from a wholly biological evolution. 'Speak that I may see thee,' said Ben Jonson. Speak, all of us, so that we may know what is happening.

No one knows when speech began. In fact no one knows to within a couple of million years, or even longer. A great deal of prehistorical information exists about bipedalism, stance, gait, brain capacity, dentition, dexterity and artefact, but speech neither fossilises nor leaves clues (as does dexterity via artefacts) concerning its existence. It is arguable that speech must have existed for mankind to have leaped forward, as artist, as technician, as skilled hunter, from the less able individual that had existed beforehand. It is less arguable, by far, that speech was in existence beforehand, and during the thousands of Acheulian generations lasting one and a half million years when cultural progress hardly advanced, at least as judged from artefacts.

Another unknown is whether speech was well formed, with syntax and a good vocabulary, almost the moment it began. Or whether there were innumerable millennia with *Homo* grunting most inarticulately, much as Hollywood made Indians speak in the earliest days of sound. (So imbued was I with this form of Amer-Indian talk that it came as quite a shock, when I first encountered such people, to hear them prattling and jabbering much as any humans do.) It is difficult to think of speech arriving piecemeal, remaining perhaps at the level of a current two-year-old for countless centuries – I see elephant, Mummy see elephant?, both see elephant. On the other hand it is impossible to know.

Brain casts have been helpful, but hardly conclusive. When latex rubber is poured into an ancient and fossilised cranium it picks up a very slight impression of the brain that once resided there. On a few of the casts from two-million-year-old skulls there is a barely detectable bump over Broca's area. This region achieved fame (and its name) when Paul Broca identified it with speech in the last century, having discovered that its removal would leave the patient speechless. A similar, barely detectable bump over Wernicke's area, also connected with speech (but with the grammar rather than speech itself), has been found in some equally ancient skulls. The facts are interesting, but cannot create conclusions about the onset of speech. Besides, modern apes have a lump over the equivalent Broca region. They may be on their way to speech, but they do not speak as yet.

It is tempting, as an outsider, to state that mankind's speech began, abruptly and most effectively, in the late Pleistocene (Greek for 'most recent') just when mankind started upon his present course, say 40,000 years ago. For thousands of generations before then he had made near-identical tools, and seemed to be hunting and gathering in similar fashion throughout that time; but within one thousand generations afterwards he had domesticated animals, he had crops, many kinds of dog, religion, villages, jewellery, and all manner of art. He could not – or so it is easy to believe – have contrived so much without the gift of speech. Similarly, or so it is even easier to believe, he would not have made such slender progress beforehand had he been able to speak.

The development of a baby gives a few clues about the possible development of speech. The foetal larynx is similarly placed as in all other mammals. Even if it had the desire and mentality to speak, when in the womb or at birth, the human foetus/baby could not do so because it would be impossible anatomically. The neonate is capable only of crying. It is also a nose-breather; and, should its diminutive button of a nose be blocked, will die for lack of air unless a tube is pushed into its larynx. It cannot breathe through its mouth, at least not unless or until the larynx and jaw are pulled down. In normal development the larynx starts to drop into place at six to eight months, making the vocalisation of speech then possible.

However, the baby has been communicating before then. Crying is no one thing almost immediately, there being various shades and forms – a general unhappiness, hunger, actual pain. The second noise phase is cooing. Mother and infants can spend time not just imitating each other but communicating after a fashion. The smiles and coos go hand in hand. Thirdly, after about eight weeks, appears babbling. This series of vowels and consonants is gibberish and often performed, unlike cooing, by the infant on its own. Otto Köhler was the first to realise that every normal baby, whatever language was used nearby, babbled in similar fashion, making the same kinds of noise.

At about nine months, when the larynx has dropped, and when speech is ready to begin, babbling can stop. It is as if the child suddenly realises what speech is all about, and feels inhibited. It starts to imitate adult babbling and uses actual words rather than the rich, tumultuous variety of sounds it had been creating earlier. At age one it has the wit and means and wish to learn a language. Articulation is still difficult, but by the end of its fourth year the child can master most of the requisite sounds (or phonemes). It then not only speaks the language of its locality but has learned its dialect. In some respects the child is superior to the adult, in that it shows more variability in the pronunciation of vowel sounds. This ability wanes to adult level at age eleven or so.

Initially, at least, a baby's development of vocalisation has some similarities with the sound-making (or phonation) of other young primates. There is a fixed pattern of development, independent of the kinds of noise and of language being used in its vicinity. Squirrel monkeys raised with mute mothers can vocalise immediately after birth and go on to make all kinds of adult sounds. The human difference only occurs when its early vocalisation is steadily replaced by pre-programmed changes. It is this ability, of knowing at age one or so, that babbling, shrieking, crying, screaming, laughing and cooing are somehow inadequate, which has helped mankind to be such a different species from the rest. 'One of the first products of the human mind,' said Karl Popper, 'is human language'; but it is difficult to imagine the human brain, the human mind, and the human language arriving independently – they seem so enmeshed, each with each. Nevertheless, human language cannot exist without a brain to make and organise it. So the brain must have had pride of place, with language as its offspring.

Language also cannot exist without a larynx with which to speak it. Initially this organ functioned solely as a valve at the head of the pulmonary air tract. It was developed by the tetrapods in response to breathing, but only in frogs and toads, some lizards and most mammals is it now a vocal organ. (Birds have a larynx but it is lacking vocal cords. Their voice comes from the syrinx, an organ similar to the larynx, which is lower down the air passage near its division into the bronchi.)

The human larynx is some two inches high. Its vocal cords are neither cords nor cord-like. They are flat bands and, therefore, more like reeds. They are white, and whiter still in females. In length they range from 17 to 25 millimetres in males (up to an inch) and 12.5 to 17 millimetres in females (½ to ¾ inches). Both cord length and cord mass contribute to the pitch of the human voice, higher with the lighter, shorter cords of children and women. The source of sound is not the actual vibration of the reed-like cords but the repeated interruption of air-flow caused by their valving action (yet another reason for not calling them cords, for they neither resemble nor act like the cords of a stringed instrument). There must be air pressure to force the cords apart, which during ordinary conversation is only about twenty centimetres of water gauge (one-fiftieth of an atmosphere). Loud shouting demands a pressure of 95 centimetres water gauge (one-tenth of an atmosphere). Singing can occupy a similar range, and requires also a flow rate of 100 to 200 millilitres a second. As the maximum air volume, after a maximum inspiration, is about five litres, this means a note can be maintained for some forty seconds. (Mankind's singing voice has been nicely defined by T. A. Sears of the Institute of Neurology, London, as 'the oldest musical instrument, rich in harmonic content, of wide tonal compass, eminently portable, and completely idiosyncratic in performance being played by its owner alone'.)

There are sexual differences apart from length of cord and difference in pitch. Girls tend to speak their first words sooner than boys, and develop larger vocabularies in the earliest years. In proper speech both girls and boys are similar until, at about three to five years, the girls take the lead. They also do better than boys when reading begins. The male lag is eventually overcome, but it is argued that the female lead in language skills may encourage her along a different intellectual path to that of the (initially) less linguistic males. Any difference tends to manufacture other differences, and some of the adult male/female distinctions in cerebral performance may be due to the earlier divergence in the acquisition of language.

A controversy almost as bitter as the IQ debate concerns ape ability to master language. They cannot speak, not having the equipment to do so, but the discussion has concentrated on their faculty for comprehending and learning language. The most famous ape, possibly of all time, has been Washoe, a chimpanzee taught (by Robert and Beatrice Gardner in Nevada) in the 1960s to communicate via ASL or Ameslan, the sign language used in the US by the deaf and dumb. From age one to four and a half Washoe learned 132 signs (for Come, Banana, Washoe and so forth), a total that increased to 180 by age eight. Those who argued that this was language-learning were particularly excited by Washoe's ability to put two signs together intelligently. There being no sign for duck in her vocabulary she called one a 'water bird'. Another chimpanzee, successor to Washoe, labelled a watermelon as 'candy drink'. These particular students even acquired syntax of a sort, have passed on signs to offspring (without human intervention) and have undoubtedly shown considerable cleverness. On the other hand, and according to the detractors, learning to associate signs with objects, colours, concepts, events, is not demonstrating language.

The debate has been surprisingly violent. It was particularly acrimonious at a meeting of the New York Academy of Sciences held in May 1980, when both attackers and defenders gave as good (or as bad) as they got. For those not involved in such cut-and-thrust the issues seem fairly clear. Patient, dedicated work, notably with chimpanzees but also with orang-utans, has shown apes to be more talented than had generally been presumed. Nevertheless, what they have learned has been far short of what a human will learn at an early age without dogged persistence from diligent researchers. The clever apes are, by human language-learning standards, no more than idiots. Mankind and the apes must have had a common ancestor some time in the past, but neither mankind nor the apes much resemble that ancestor, not least in the ability to communicate or use a language.

The major question, which Washoe and Co. did not begin to answer, is why and how ordinary communication turned to speech. Animals do communicate, and presumably hominid ancestors were just as good as modern apes, if not more so. They then learned to speak, to use language and directly cause the 2,000 languages in use today (give or take different definitions of dialects). It was an amazing leap which can never be examined; but it is very possible that it occurred, or came to fulfilment, in synchrony with all the other leaps around 40,000 years ago that led, in a few more bounds, to neolithic man. 'Language most showeth a man,' said Ben Jonson. Would that it could show us how men began their language.

Reading Intellectually (and to make this point yet again) mankind is equipped with a brain developed and evolved for a hunter-gatherer. Nothing has happened, so far as is known, since the era of modern man began to change that ancient brain, to render it more fit for modern times. Primitive *Homo*, living off the countryside, has had to become technological man, living in cities, surrounded by equipment, suffering all manner of new pressures, and still with the same old brain. The point merits a second telling (and a third) because it is so believable, when surrounded by books, music, mathematics, science, that such things have always been. They have not. They have been grafted to and developed by that hunter-gatherer's mind.

Reading is a prime case in point. To uneducated man it must be a bewilderment when someone selects a book, and smiles or laughs or frowns or cries at what the letters say. (Watching a Japanese with the far more complex Kanji can imbue a European with similar astonishment.) All reading is being performed by a mind fashioned for nothing of the kind. Nevertheless, the medical literature, when commenting on the ability to read, lays 99 per cent of its emphasis on reading disability, as if reading (or writing) was like every other function, like digestion, vision, and all normal attributes, and should work perfectly. However, malfunction can give helpful clues to function, and a damaged brain is always of interest if the wound is partnered by some inability to perform. Alexia, also called word blindness, is the inability to read. It is caused by damage to the temporal lobe, and more specifically to 'the left angular gyrus down to the underlying white matter', as the *British Medical Journal* outlined it. Coupled with the alexia is (probably) agraphia, the inability to write, and some aphasia, or difficulty with speech. If the nearby posterior superior temporal gyrus is damaged there will certainly be aphasia. If it is bad enough to create reading problems, it is called aphasic alexia. If there is alexia without agraphia the damage is not to the angular gyrus but to nervous pathways from that gyrus to the visual cortex. The writing of these people, though it exists, has been likened to normal efforts with eyes closed.

A problem in the location of reading within the brain is that three major tasks are involved: visual recognition (of letters); conversion of these symbols (into words sounds, phonemes); and semantic comprehension. So there can be letter blindness as well as word blindness, both probably caused by distinct faults in the visual cortex. Semantic problems, sometimes known as paralexia or just deep dyslexia, can result in puppy being read as small dog, or vice versa. Sometimes the answer is less immediately comprehensible, such as: NICE – a small town in France; KIEV – Odessa; ITALY – republic; or (as quoted by Max Coltheart, psychology professor at Birkbeck) 'HOLLAND – it's a country . . . not Europe . . . no . . . not Germany . . . It's small . . . it was captured . . . Belgium. That's it. Belgium.'

Word blindness has been in use as a term since A. Kussmaul coined it in the *Cyclopaedia of the Practice of Medicine* published in 1877. He emphasised that speech and intelligence could still be normal, and generally are. Dyslexia, the more modern term for the same condition, is often defined as a disorder of word perception when not due to a deficiency in intelligence. A school medical officer in Britain, Dr James Kerr, was in 1896 the first to mention that it created a problem in education. It is still a problem, largely because education is so much a matter of reading. Severe dyslexia can, contrarily, be less of a problem, being easily recognised. The child is then switched to oral teaching. Modest dyslexia can be mistaken, as the *Lancet* phrased it, 'for laziness, carelessness, or stupidity, to the sad detriment of the child'.

Many possible causes for dyslexia have been cited, such as: an inherited constitutional factor; an incomplete hemisphere dominance (as dyslexics are often ambidextrous or left-handed); and cerebral injury at birth. It is essentially curable, treatment requiring individual attention and the repetitive association of visual patterns with sounds. If no help is given, the children can experience misery and despair, as well as a complete emotional blockage to all forms of learning. According to an article in *World Medicine* 26 per cent of schoolchildren have some form of learning disorder, of which poor reading is often a contributory element. The article, by Audrey Wisby (consultant in remedial education), suggests that all children accused of dyslexia should be given 'as a starting point . . . a full-scale audiometric, ophthalmic, orthoptic, and neuro-physiological investigation'. Eyes, ears and brains all need to be tested to define more closely what is wrong. It may just be eye movement that is faulty, in being weaker or more erratic with an abnormal proportion of regressive or backward glances. It may be nothing to do with the interpretive side of the brain.

There are also what are called the pseudoalexias caused by, for example, the inability to read aloud, mental deficiency, psychiatric disorder, or a psychogenic problem such as schizophrenia. A trouble with labels is their very convenience. Dyslexia is one such classification, with more being grouped under its umbrella than is justified. Perhaps, to reverse the *Lancet*'s statement of two paragraphs ago, some laziness, carelessness, or stupidity is today being classed under its heading. At least there is now more flexibility of thought. Not only is it being appreciated that some intelligent individuals cannot read correctly, but it is also understood there is more to reading than was at first assumed. The hunter-gatherer's brain is, yet again, proving itself cleverer than was originally believed. There should perhaps not be astonishment that 1 per cent have some degree of dyslexia, but considerable amazement that 99 per cent can read with such facility.

Music 'Of all noises I think music the least disagreeable,' said Samuel Johnson, adding on another occasion that it was 'the only sensual pleasure without vice'. Even this least assiduous music-lover was naming it as something on the plus side of human experience. Others have gone rather further, calling it the most ancient of all the arts. Aldous Huxley proclaimed that music 'comes nearest to expressing the inexpressible – after silence that is'. L. Newman said (in 1919) it 'is an idea, addressing us in its own language, with a force and a logic as great as any that words can command'. A couple of centuries earlier Joseph Addison, in his 'Song for St Cecilia's Day', had written: 'Music, the greatest good that mortals know, And all of heaven we have below.' In short, as practically everyone knows, music can be exciting, stimulating, conversant after a fashion, and yet bewildering. There is no reason for it, at least not by strict evolutionary requirements, like food, survival, procreation.

It is one more uniquely human attribute. Birds sing, and musically to our ears, but a chaffinch locked in a chamber where only backwards chaffinch song is played will only learn that backwards noise. Whales sing, according to people, but there is no information that the sounds are musical according to whales. Music is always an art, states one circular argument, and only mankind is capable of art. R. A. Henson (of London) has written that music 'is concerned with the expression and communication of musical ideas . . . Speech deals in words and the suggestion that it is more precise than music probably stems from the universally greater familiarity with words.' Many centuries earlier, writing in *What Music Can Do* between AD 622 and 633, Isidore of Seville would have agreed: 'In battles the sound of the trumpet rouses the combatants, and the more furious the trumpeting the more valorous their spirit . . . music soothes the mind to endure toil, and the modulation of the voice consoles the weariness of each labour.' So why?

Apparently music can: increase bodily metabolism; alter muscular energy; accelerate respiratory rate, and make it less regular; enhance perception; exaggerate knee-jerks; lower the threshold for various sensory stimuli; affect blood pressure, and thereby alter blood circulation. However, as Macdonald Critchley, neurologist, pointed out, each item on that list 'might equally well be the product of noise as opposed to music'. Different kinds of music do work differently (as, presumably, different kinds of noise do). Dance music and orchestral marches produce predominantly muscular response, while other kinds are more respiratory or cardiovascular. According to G. Harrer and H. Harrer (of Salzburg) the highest pulse frequencies during the act of conducting 'are not reached at moments of greatest physical effort but at passages producing the greatest emotional response'. Heart beat can then be twice normal.

There has been considerable debate whether musical understanding is located on the left or right side of the brain. Initially it was ascribed to the right half, occupying an equivalent position to that of language in the (probably) dominant left half. Critchley found it difficult to accept the notion because

> it is straining credibility to imagine that music, as comprising at one and the same time song and articulate language, should stem from the activities of opposite halves of the brain . . . If we talk with our major hemisphere and sing with our minor, by what cerebral legerdemain do we contrive to cope with those intermediate vocalisations, chanting and recitative?

By 1974, according to Antonio R. Damasio (of Portugal and Iowa), the idea gained ground that the left hemisphere becomes dominant in those for whom music becomes increasingly important. Choirboys have supported this concept. A group of young singers were found to have a right ear superiority for musical processing, this differential between right and left growing more and more marked with increasing musical experience. What the right ear hears is organised by the left hemisphere.

Another group, who did not at first support the choirboys, were able to recognise melodies better with their left ears (and were therefore more effective with their right hemispheres). The plot then thickened – and made more sense of the choirboys – when further work showed that 'non-musical subjects' were more discerning with their left ears while the 'musically experienced' were better with their right. What seems to be happening, and in the words of Maria A. Wyke (of London), is 'a differential pattern of cerebral specialisation . . . for musically sophisticated and musically naive subjects'. A tentative conclusion is now possible: musical execution is performed by the right (and usually minor) hemisphere, while musical perception develops into a left hemisphere dominance in those who are active musically. (Critchley's bewilderment over left and right, expressed in the previous paragraph, can therefore be resolved. The musically experienced do indeed sing and talk with the same hemisphere, while the musically 'naive' may be using both sides for their songs.)

A search has also been conducted, not just for knowing which brain half is involved with which aspect of music, but for which part of each half is so concerned. Dogs have been used as experimental animals. Conditioning, developed by Ivan Pavlov in the early years of this century, can have animals salivating if a sound is consistently made whenever food is imminent. If a musical note is employed the dogs will show that they can detect a semitone difference. If it is middle C they will salivate; if it is faulty by half a tone they will not. If that correct note is within a chord they will again detect it; if the chord is repeated without it they will know the difference. It has subsequently been argued that dogs have absolute pitch, a faculty enjoyed (or perhaps unenjoyed when instruments are poorly tuned) by only a small percentage of humans.

The animal experiments suggest that certain projections in the temporal lobes, corresponding (in humans) more or less to the transverse convolutions of Heschl, are the musical centres. Complete amusia, the inability to recognise or reproduce tunes, is often partnered by damage to the same temporal area in the dominant (usually left) hemisphere. A similar wound on the other side is linked with partial amusia, notably in the expression of music. (Just as music must be – and is – incomprehensible to those with amusia, to the totally tone-deaf, so is the power of music bewildering even to those able to sing tunes. Try whistling a familiar song solely on one note.)

Musical ability tends to manifest itself at a younger age than in other areas of art. Graphic artists can show early skill, but rarely is this youthful work good enough for exhibition. (Exceptions have been Dürer and Picasso.) Mozart, Beethoven, Handel, and J. S. Bach all, for example, not only showed early ability, but composed work of adult stature before they reached their adulthood. Even more striking is the ability, in some, to compose when deaf. Beethoven's deafness (possibly from an early attack of typhus) and Smetana's (perhaps from neurosyphilis) did not halt their genius. On the other hand there are those who prefer quiet. Ernest Newman wrote that he would rather experience a silent, ideal performance at home with the scores than attend a concert with all its imperfections.

Archbishop Isidore's statement, now thirteen and half centuries old, can be repeated and with the question that succeeded it. 'Music soothes the mind to endure toil, and the modulation of the voice consoles the weariness of each labour.' But why? What on earth has this to do with the evolution of a hunter-gatherer?

It is not possible, and certainly not within a single chapter, to be in any sense conclusive about human mental ability. To travel from intelligence to learning to speech to reading to music may give some notion of the breadth but hardly of the range of human wisdom, thought, perception and inventiveness. Somehow, as was discussed in this book's very first chapter, an ape became a hominid who then became a species with the wit (and presumption) to alter the planet on which it found itself. And with the skill even to leave it, briefly, but to leave it none the less. There is no comparison between the mental capability of man and of every other species. The human brain might have been formed on another planet since its three-pound mass is of a different order from the brains of other animals. They may be more suited to their environments, less destructive, less greedy and ambitious, but in thought and reason, dexterity and adaptability, they are all as nothing when each is compared with man.

A small story, culled from science fiction, can serve as epitaph. It emphasises both the ability of mankind and what happened when biological evolution became cultural, when men could learn from men. Once upon a time, a future time of course, an interplanetary rocket was fired from Earth to a planet in another system. On board were half a dozen humans. Their instructions were to transmit a message back home within a year. If they did so, they would be retrieved with some other vehicle. If they failed, it would be assumed they had either perished or the planet was generally unwelcoming. Naturally they carried radio equipment with which to report their news.

Unfortunately, on arrival, the rocket and everything on board sank at once within a bog. The six crew struggled to the shore. They saw about them a planet precisely as Earth had been, with trees, grass, seas, lakes, and hills. It was entirely welcoming; but there was no radio. Instead the place had all the elements and ores, the deposits that Earth once had. It was, therefore, up to the team to build a transmitter to request the retrieval that would carry them home again. As they had nothing from the rocket beyond themselves, it was vital to find the necessary deposits, make heat and energy, valves and aerials, and then make known their presence upon the distant land. In short, they had to do in one year more or less what mankind has done since the Neolithic, but with the advantage of knowing that iron, glass, electricity and radio were all quite feasible.

In the story they transmitted on the very last day. The eighteen pounds of brain with which they had landed had just proved adequate. Via memory, reason, intuition, endeavour, foresight and desperation they had exploited every facet of mankind's intelligence, just as mankind has done on earth. They had spoken to each other, written messages, planned, imagined, and made music along the way. No other species can begin to operate in such a fashion (at least none we know of) and the story dramatically relived much of the technological progress of recent centuries.

There was yet another side to it. The six on board were particularly able. Most of us alive today can do very little technically. How many of us can find coal, make steel, fashion glass, produce cement, or – even with all the parts to hand – create a radio? That has been the strength of cultural evolution. Mankind has done all these things via its cerebral hemispheres. Mankind has then stored away this information, and most men and women have proceeded with other kinds of lives. So learning is also forgetting, or rather putting on one side. That ability is perhaps the most astonishing, and therefore Sir Peter Medawar's neat account of it demands a second quoting: 'We learn to make the processes of deliberate thought instinctive and automatic, and we learn to make automatic and instinctive processes the subject of discriminating thought.' We learn, and then we unlearn in order to learn some more.

10. Memory

Definition/Understanding of memory/Theories/Short term,
long term/Amnesia/Retrograde, post-traumatic/The
mnemonists

Man differs in memory from brutes, and this is because
there is record only of man
                                    – medical manuscript of AD 1380

What we can put on our shelves we should not put into our
brains
    – Auguste Forel

If we remembered everything we should be as ill as if we
remembered nothing
                                                    – William James

Just as mankind's nervous system makes use of the same kind of
neural units as are used in much of the rest of the animal kingdom,
so is memory not a uniquely human attribute. Almost every kind of
creature, from man to the simple coelenterates, has been proved
capable of memory. No one is suggesting that *hydra* is able to
remember and recognise another *hydra*. Instead, much of memory
is no more or little more than a better reaction to a repeated
stimulus. In this sense a coelenterate can remember to avoid a
certain area (which is unpleasant) or will have a swifter reaction to
such an area (if encountered repeatedly). Its particular impulses
are carried along specific nerve tracts; so too, or so it is assumed,
every memory. Even protozoa, single-celled animals, have been
shown to possess the simplest, most basic, most ordinary kind of
memory because learning, it would seem, also plays a part in their
lives. This form of benefit from experience cannot occur without a
form of memory. Learning, at its simplest, is no more than
habituation. Every recurring event has an effect upon the nervous
system that records it and reacts to it.

Therefore, as with the nervous system in general, the human
memory arrangement is no more than an extension of simpler
arrangements, but the advance is formidable. It is the comparison

of a single dwelling with an entire city. The human capabilities are megalithic by comparison, and of quite a different order to those of animals. It is customary, if not the rule, for human beings to decry their individual memories, as if nothing short of perfection is expected; but, in truth, our storage and retrieval abilities are as astonishing as our intelligence, if not more so.

It is difficult to list these accomplishments, but each of us must know hundreds of faces (even if we cannot put names to them), thousands of locations, hundreds of smells, hundreds of tunes. We can tell very speedily if we have seen that film before (with its thousands of images), heard that joke before, read that story. We seem weakest over what might seem easiest, such as phone numbers, names, dates. We are best at what might seem hardest, such as faces. Each one is (generally) just another rearrangement of the same old features – some hair, two eyes, two eyebrows, one nose, one mouth, a chin, a colour – but each is far better remembered than any phone number. So too a room, a street, a picture. We even know if something has changed, although hard put to identify precisely what has altered. And on top of all this passive memory there are all the end results of experience: how to speak, to behave, to drive, to cook, to perform as *Homo sapiens*.

Retrieval is possibly even more bewildering. If memory is much like a library, how much more superior is the brain that can, almost instantaneously, bring every required fact to the surface? Have you been here before? No. Is this your coat? No. Do you like water melon? Yes. What is the next number after 14,576? The answers come so speedily that, or so it is easy to suspect, most of the time before the answer is given is used in opening the mouth to say it. Fancy being able to affirm that this particular location is a new experience! Fancy being able to know, and to know that one knows!

Speech itself, necessitating the steady retrieval of suitable language, is possibly even more astonishing. That particular sentence, one assortment of fourteen words, can be spoken far more speedily than written. A fast talker uses three words a second, which all pour forth in a logical, grammatical and meaningful manner. Virtually simultaneously someone else's speech may be arriving at the speaker's ear, requiring interpretation of its sounds so that a suitable answer may be thought up, put into fresh words, and then delivered. The retrieval system, unlike some demented librarian hurtling from source to source, is working calmly, efficiently and with amazing haste. If it stumbles, producing one word instead of another, or failing to recover a particular name, we are immediately offended with ourselves. We should, conversely, be constantly astounded at our brilliance. We speak, remember, describe, recollect and retrieve (almost faultlessly), and all via the three pounds of matter encased within each cranium. Or rather, there being other tasks for the brain to accomplish (like thought, bodily control, sensory comprehension), via that part of it not already fully committed. No one knows how much cerebral tissue is involved in memory, and no one knows much about which areas are principally involved, but how extraordinary that we should ever reprimand ourselves for not being able instantaneously to put a name to a face last seen in a public house just a dozen years ago.

Yet more remarkable are those individuals with memories out of all proportion to the normal run. Frequently quoted are: Mehmed Ali Halici, of Ankara, who in 1967 quoted 6,666 verses of the Koran in 6 hours; Hideaki Tomoyori, of Japan, who has memorised the first 20,000 places of π; Hans von Bülow (mentioned in the first chapter) who read once through a symphony unknown to him and then conducted it that evening without a score; Arturo Toscanini who, on being told that the second bassoonist had damaged the key for the lowest note, thought for a moment and then said it did not matter because 'that note does not occur in tonight's concert'; the Shasa Pollak – Polish talmudic memorists – who could always give the right word if told the page, line and word number of the traditionally printed Babylonian Talmud; Ben Jonson who, allegedly, could recite all that he had ever written; Themistocles who knew the names and faces of 20,000 Athenians; and Solomon Veniaminoff, the Russian generally referred to as S., whose memory was apparently total (Luria, the psychiatrist, 'had to admit that the capacity of [S.'s] memory had no distinct limits').

The phenomenon of such complete recall is plainly undesirable (and will be discussed later), being a form of malady. Memory needs to be both effective and yet ineffective, a sort of sieve – though this term is used disparagingly by individuals aware of memory's imperfections. The brain must retain knowledge and must let it go. The better brains, presumably, are those with better sieves, more able to retain important facts, more ready to let the others go. Arguably the most skilful memorisers, Halici, Tomoyori and all other memory men, are less able than the rest of us. We can forget. We can also remember for a hundred years, if we live that long. And we do all this, the learning, the forgetting, the life-long remembering, the steady storage of new fact, with a mass of neural tissue about the size of our fists. Computers still have much to learn about micro-processing.

Understanding of memory is poorly understood, to say the least. In 1949 R. W. Gerard (writing in the *American Journal of Psychiatry*) commented that our comprehension of it 'would remain as valid and useful if, for all we knew, the cranium was stuffed with cotton wadding'. Despairing souls might agree with him today. The lack of understanding does not mean a shortage of theories. On the contrary, as always, they proliferate rather as weeds do when nothing else is growing. In brief, there are neural theories (which suggest that brain cells change anatomically as a result of experience), electrical theories (which suggest subsequent changes in the electrical field) and biochemical theories (which suggest changes in the cells' molecular structure). There are also other theories involving, in part, each of the big three.

Perhaps a definition makes a suitable starting point. According to Chris Evans' excellent little dictionary (of the mind, brain and behaviour), memory is 'essentially that property, shared by a large number of living organisms, of storing information about past experiences so that these can be acted on later to improve the animal's chances of survival'. The information is, therefore, stored by the process of learning, it is remembered by the process of retrieval, and actual memory is the information in store. The statements may seem simplistic – or are simplistic – but it is as well to absorb the threefold nature of memory. (Some talk of memory's three Rs: registration, retention and recall.) Any theory, whether anatomical, electrical, biochemical, has to explain how memory is acquired, how it is kept, and how it is brought to the surface when need be. And at such speed. And so correctly, with such aplomb. 'Hello, Jo,' we say, 'I haven't seen you for some six years. And is it still Mabel, and engineering, and two kids, and North Wales?' What ability to come forth with all such fact, merely because one particular assortment of eyes, eyebrows, nose and mouth has suddenly loomed in the crowd!

Plato likened memory to a wax tablet. 'We hold the wax to perceptions and thoughts and in that receive the impression of them . . . we remember and know what is imprinted as long as the image lasts.' No one today speaks of such impressions – the analogy is possibly too strong, or too primitive – but modern terms do not really advance Plato's description, now 2,350 years old. Memory trace or synaptic record or biochemical engram are scarcely more than wax in other words, but words that reflect their user's prejudice or enthusiasm for a biochemical or electrical solution to the problem. Thirty years ago, after a flush of enthusiasms for explaining memory, one reviewer of the subject (B. R. Gomulick) wrote that the thirty different twentieth-century theories 'all have serious drawbacks and show a lack of agreement not only on the problem as a whole but on every single aspect of it'. B. D. Burns, writing a few years later in *The Mammalian Cerebral Cortex*, said none had proved 'a wild success'. Modern authors might well be tempted to reiterate these earlier appraisals when reviewing to-day's notions of the subject.

The theories took a leap forward in the first year of this current century when G. E. Müller and A. Pilzecker published in Germany their idea that memory occurred in two stages. No one now denies this concept, save for those who insist upon three (or more) stages; and even the ordinary citizen is happy to go along with it. There is plainly a difference between knowing what someone has just said – a phrase, a number – and knowing a fact for life, a birthday or 1066. One is ephemeral, fleeting; the other permanent, fixed, solid (well, fairly so).

In 1949 psychologist Donald Hebb advanced the two-stage idea – with some saying that modern memory science, therefore, started in that year. In phase one electrical activity, vulnerable and impermanent, holds the memory in place. With phase two there is some structural change, perhaps involving protein synthesis, to retain the memory more securely. Hebb's suggestion, although well received, unfortunately caused other researchers to look for quick solutions to the problem. By subjecting brains to electric shocks they hoped to block memories linked to electrical activity. Similarly, by tinkering with protein synthesis (and using inhibitors, for example) they hoped to prevent long-term memory, that linked with structural change. Unfortunately such procedures were too all-embracing. Disrupting the brain by giving it shocks, or less protein, or intense cold (hypothermia was also used), or any other violent treatment is inordinately savage. Computers also use electricity, but no one would learn much about their operation by firing volts through them. It became plain that such experimentation was altogether too severe.

Only slightly less crude was the subsequent approach. All manner of drugs were used in efforts to alter the two phases of the memory process. The *Lancet*, in assessing this work, listed 'lithium, codeine, endorphins, phosphodiesterase inhibitors, ergot derivatives, vasodilators, benzodiazepines, some central stimulant drugs, anisomycin, colchicine, vinblastine, and marijuana'. Such a wide range smacks, probably not unfairly, of an alchemist proceeding happily along his shelves, hoping that chance and the right mixture would yield the philosopher's stone. Or of Thomas Edison trying everything (including his wife's hair) to act as long-lived filament in the incandescent lamp.

The latest approach – if it is possible to generalise from a multiplicity of approaches – is to be more specific, both in the kind of drug and with the area under investigation. For example, to quote work published from Sussex University, the team attempted 'to interfere with the normal functioning of only a discrete region of the brain'. Thus, 'by selecting drugs with known pharmacological actions . . . we have been able to use behavioural experiments to separate out three different phases of memory formation.' These are a 'potassium conductance increase', 'sodium pump activity' and some sort of 'protein synthesis'. In other words, the various neurons which were involved in the learning experience of the experiment were altered, part physically, part biochemically. Provided the same experience is repeated, or that particular assortment of neurons is somehow reactivated along the same path (perhaps by thinking over the experience), the first two phases can become the third and most permanent phase. However, on this final point these are still very early days, as the Sussex researchers emphasised: 'No suggestions have yet come out of our studies as to how protein synthesis retains the trace.'

It may be helpful to stress at this stage the fundamental role of memory. The ability to memorise is often mentioned as if some sort of extra, like the stomach or taste or speech. It is possible to imagine humans without these attributes for they could live more or less like ordinary people, eating differently (less at a time but more frequently) and communicating differently (by signs, gestures and written words); but a person without memory is a wholly different kind of person. Indeed memory has even been equated with consciousness for it is an intrinsic part of intelligence, of learning, of living. It is not an extra but an integral feature of the nervous system, a most basic property. To discuss memory is to discuss nerves, why they are as they are. To expect a ready solution is, therefore, to imagine that all of neurology will be laid bare. It may be some day, but not just yet. The nervous system – and its memory – will have to wait awhile.

Nevertheless there is advance. One form of it, as in any area of knowledge, occurs when previous certainty is replaced by uncertainty. Until the 1960s, for instance, it was widely believed that electrical impressions formed the basis of memory, with polarity changing as the circuit was used. These lasting patterns were known as engrams, and Karl Lashley, neuropsychologist, was the most diligent engram searcher. His experimental animals were rats and, after training them to perform certain tasks, he then set about destroying their cortex in the hope of destroying the relevant memory. Various chunks of brain were removed, but always the memory persisted. He struggled with the problem for decades; in fact for the major part of his life. Eventually, and in words to extract sympathy from the harshest reader, he declared: 'The necessary conclusion is that learning is just not possible at all.' His life's work had been one long advance from certainty to its very opposite. Nevertheless it had been progress, of the depressing kind.

Apart from steady current progress at the biochemical and molecular level there are discoveries at what could be termed the macro-level. For instance, it has been learned that electrical stimulation of the exposed surface of the human brain can cause the remembering of long-forgotten memories (notably in epileptics). The temporal lobes are the most effective for conjuring the past in this fashion; so too the minor (as against the dominant) hemisphere. Another point is that commissurotomy, which effectively creates a two-halved brain, enables each half to remember its kind of interest, namely verbal and numerical for the left side, and spatial and musical for the right. (On commissurotomy in general see pages 117–122.) The surgeon's knife has also been instructive when it has cut through the hippocampus. This small nervous substance lying deep within the cerebrum (and indeed shaped like a seahorse) was initially thought to be linked solely with smelling. However, its removal (or rather of the two hippocampi from both sides) leads to almost complete failure in the establishment of new memories. The old ones stay good but new experience can no longer be translated into new memory. A friend's death, for example, will provoke sadness, but this is short-lived. A retelling of the news will lead to further sadness of the same kind, and then a further speedy recovery.

Presumably better comprehension of memory will come from both kinds of work, macro and micro. Presumably also no one can foresee which will be more revealing. Or maybe solutions will arise from yet another source, the complete lack of memory. In these accident-prone days it happens often enough and is revealing in its fashion.

Amnesia   often partners unconsciousness after a blow to the head and, of the two, the degree of amnesia can be a better indicator of internal injury. Named after the Greek for forgetfulness this form of memory loss can be either of events before or after the accident. It is known either as retrograde amnesia (shortened to RA) or post-traumatic amnesia (PTA). Of the two PTA is more significant, in terms of assessing the internal injury. In general an ordinary accident involves a bit of both, a blank period leading up to the trauma and a similar lack of memory afterwards. PTA is assumed to exist until continual awareness has returned. So-called islets of consciousness may occur, which are interrupted by periods of relapse. Only the full return of memory and of consciousness – the two are difficult, if not impossible to separate – marks the conclusion of PTA.

As mentioned in the section on unconsciousness (page 130) a bullet wound to the head can appear less damaging than a knock-out blow in that the victim may not even fall down. The famous Phineas Gage lost neither consciousness nor memory when the tamping iron went through his cranium. In one survey of penetrating war wounds 25 per cent of survivors experienced no amnesia. A further 20 per cent from the same survey did experience it but for less than one hour. By comparison many a minor tap to the head can cause PTA for several hours, without greatly concerning anyone. The brain is particularly susceptible to sudden acceleration; so too whatever is occurring during the earliest phases of a memory.

Electro-shock can also cause both kinds of memory loss. According to the severity of the insult the amnesia lasts for minutes, hours or days. The longer the period of PTA the greater the severity of, to use the medical term, closed head injury. In fact PTA provides 'the most reliable form of measurement' of what is happening internally, according to one book on nervous ailments. Naturally there can be external inspection of open injury, as from bullets; so there is less need for secondary guides, such as amnesia. Naturally also there is no question of knowing the degree of RA until the unconscious individual can relate how much of his earlier memory has been lost.

Quite what has been disturbed in an accident to prevent the normal working of memory is still unknown. The fact that earlier memory is erased and the further fact that memory after the event is prevented for a time are not necessarily related. Sudden acceleration causes them both, but there may be different disturbances involved in the obliteration of memories from one hour before the accident, one minute before it, and one minute or one hour after it. The creation of a memory does not appear to involve just one process. Therefore, the prevention of that creation is likely to be similarly wide-ranging with disturbance being no one thing.

Memory loss in general can be caused by a variety of ills, such as nutrition defects, alcoholic dementia, multi-infarct dementia (many small strokes), depression, and infection. Memory capability also diminishes with age, but advancing years are an easy excuse for a memory that was always far from perfect. When psychologists speak of memory loss they are rarely referring to ordinary decay. For example, a severe amnesic may score reasonably on intelligence tests but be unable to relate either backwards or forwards in time. Even current happenings cannot be recalled. The so-named amnesic syndrome entails a loss of all memory except the short-term. With this disease there is both anterograde amnesia (loss of memory for events occurring after its onset) and retrograde amnesia (loss of memory for earlier events). Such individuals can even become lost in their own homes. Normal personal memories may sometimes seem inadequate, but are hardly in that class.

There is also what can be called partial amnesia. At a Ciba Foundation conference held in 1969 reference was made to an individual whose comprehension of the abstract was much better than his understanding of more concrete terms. Whether this was a one-sided deficiency in some aspect of memory or of a different mental function is unclear, but the result was striking. When asked to define Blacksmith, Hound, and Macaroni, his three answers were 'I've forgotten', 'An animal' and 'No idea'. When asked for definitions of Soul, Opinion and Perjury, the answers were at quite a different level: 'Your basic interior element', 'Having own view' and 'People behave in a damaging manner – telling untruths'.

Possession of total memory is at the other end of the scale from amnesia and forgetfulness. Theatrical 'memory men' are often said to have this ability, but may have no more than good memories. One individual reported to have a 'tape-recorder mind' was John Dean, a central figure in Washington's Watergate story. When the famous tape-recordings made by President Nixon were eventually made public it was discovered that Dean's memories, although good in their broad outline, were inaccurate in detail and biased in favour of Dean. However, there are other individuals, such as the Russian Solomon Veniaminoff already mentioned, who are not just at one end of the normal human range. They are giants in their way and, much like giants of stature, are aberrant and not of the common throng.

S., as he is generally known, became a journalist during the 1920s. At briefing sessions he never took any notes and was initially reprimanded. It was then discovered that notes were indeed quite unnecessary because S. remembered everything. Professor Alexander Luria, mentioned elsewhere in this book for his interest in the war-wounded Zasetsky, immediately investigated the young S. and realised his memory was virtually perfect. It was also adaptable in that he could, for instance, abolish pain. He formed an image of pain in his mind, and then coerced that pain to vanish out of sight, thereby forcing the real pain to disappear as well. He could make himself warmer by imagining translocation to a hot place. Similarly he could cool himself by thinking of the Arctic. Unfortunately, the blessing of such a perfect memory was not always advantageous. Not everything would disappear, however much he willed it so. He became increasingly concerned by the problem of his memory, and this fundamental problem grew more aggravating every day, as is lengthily described in Luria's book *The Mind of a Mnemonist*. It is impossible for others to contemplate a near perfect memory. It was impossible for S. to get rid of it. As William James wrote: 'If we remembered everything we should be as ill as if we remembered nothing.' Somehow S.'s mind, according to one book discussing the case, had 'triggered on to the way in which memory functioned, and he simply functioned in that way for the rest of his life'.

A co-worker of Luria, Pyotr Anokhin, was also struck by S.'s achievements which helped him formulate ideas on cerebral potential. If S. could work such wonders, stumbling upon new techniques by chance, what about future possibilities? 'No man yet exists who can use all the potential of his brain,' wrote Anokhin. 'This is why we don't accept *any* pessimistic estimates of the limits of the human brain. It is unlimited.' It would almost seem, remembering S.'s unhappiness, as if the normal human mind imposes limitations upon its capabilities. It is too clever for its own good. Or, as Arthur Koestler phrased it, 'In creating the human brain, evolution has wildly overshot the mark.'

Some further points provide a conclusion, pointing up other areas of ignorance in the matter of memory. It used to be said, notably by psychoanalysts, that everything is remembered, with individuals either suppressing unwelcome facts or deliberately failing to remember them. This notion is less acceptable today, mainly because forgetting or not even learning the fact is such a vital requirement. Memory must be defective to be effective. Secondly, it is difficult to know whether a missing piece of memory is due to the original learning being faulty, or to the storage, or to the retrieval. What is the capital of Peru? asks someone. Presumably we have all been told in our time, but those of us who cannot remember do not know if recall, or storage or learning is at fault.

The old suffer from poor memory, at least according to the old. It is argued by others that they experience not so much bad memory as bad recall. Work in Canada, involving people aged twenty to seventy-five, flashed twenty-four words on to a screen before asking the subjects both to remember what words had been used and to remember them if and when they were shown in the middle of other words. The first part – straight remembering – was performed worse with age, and steadily so. The second part – recognising when one of the twenty-four was shown again– was performed equally well by young and old. Recall, therefore, was the elderly failing, and many an old person – say over twenty-one – will fail to remember a name, a fact, a date, until someone else remembers it. The correct answer is then pounced upon by all concerned. They exclaim loudly that they knew it all the time. Their recall had been at fault, not their memory.

There is also the unknown of memory's permanence. There is no way, as yet, to prove either its permanence or its impermanence, partly because revision plays such a part. We either bring a fact to the surface, and help ourselves to remember it anew, or we are reminded of it. What is most certain is that we are frequently in error about our certainties. The testimony of witnesses, given in good faith and with absolute conviction, has been proved as false, again and again. Experimental bank attacks have caused all manner of misidentification. And all of us, if we are honest, have realised that innumerable, positive, sure-fire memories have been shown as wrong when confronted by the facts.

About the most crucial point raised in this chapter is the importance of forgetting. It is important for individuals but also for communities. As Sir Ieuan Maddock, British scientist, once said: 'All development . . . requires an interplay between "learning" and "forgetting".' Or, as Harold Laski, political commentator, phrased it a generation earlier: 'In politics while there is death there is hope.'

11. Senses

Seeing / Hearing / Smelling / Tasting / Touching / Hot, cold,
pressure / Proprioception / Pain / Phantom limbs / Enkephalins
and endorphins

> What we perceive comes as much from inside our heads as
> from the world outside
> – William James

It is perhaps easier to say what the sensory system is not than what
it is. It is not a collection of just five senses, or even of six. It does
not give us a true picture of the outside world. It can easily be
fooled. All sensation is linked to perception, to interpretation (just
as all facts are said to speak through an interpreter, the one who
uses them). As Vernon B. Mountcastle has written: 'Each of us
believes himself to live directly within the world that surrounds
him, to sense its objects and events precisely, to live in real and
current time. I assert that these are perceptual illusions . . .' In
short, sensation is an abstraction, not a replication, of the real
world.

Aristotle was most responsible for ossifying the concept of five
senses: seeing, hearing, smelling, tasting, and touching. Did he
never feel the difference in size between two coins in his pocket,
and thus suspect proprioception? Or was he not aware that
touching temperature seemed different from pressure or from
feel? There are five different kinds of nerve endings in the skin
alone. And pain is one of those sensations, if not strictly a sense.
We can sense if we are falling over, can know if a bladder is full, and
when thirst or hunger is important. These last may not measure
the outside world, but they are sensation. Also, as Isaac Newton
recognised, the light rays he split in the prism did not become
coloured. They became a form of energy that interacted with the
eye's pigments, causing the brain to interpret the varying energies
as different colours. This all-important sensation of colour perception is, therefore, a phenomenon we (partly) fashion for ourselves.

It is possible also to be wrong about the word sensation. It
implies a consciousness of feeling, but most sensation is received
(and acted upon) quite subconsciously. Standing vertically is an
example. Proprioception is self-awareness by the body of the

location and action of its limbs and muscles. It keeps us upright, lets us retrieve an object, and certainly could have told an ancient Greek whether a half drachma, or more, or less, lay within his tunic. As every sense can be fooled, every sensation can, therefore, be wrong. Visually we can be tricked by all those optical illusions. Audibly we can be made to mis-hear in similar fashion. So too with the skin, called by anatomist Wood Jones the 'external nervous system'. Put a hand in hot water, and move it to tepid which feels relatively cold. Then put a hand in cold water, move it to the same tepid bowl, and the contents will feel warmer than formerly. There is also phantom sensation (about which more later) from breasts and limbs no longer there.

A final introductory point is that the human sensory system conceitedly suggests it is providing a complete record of outside events. A study of animals should speedily contradict this belief. Many of them can see deeper into both ends of the light spectrum, the ultra violet and infra red. With some odorous sources a dog's nose is one million times more sensitive than a man's. Salmon do, somehow, rediscover the river of their birth. Birds can fly the oceans, using magnetism as guide. Certain invertebrates seem able to detect nuclear irradiation. Eyesight of hawks and eagles puts ours to shame, and owls are better still. Prawns know depth to within a centimetre. Bats and dolphins, among others, use echo-location with extreme skill. Worms are extraordinarily sensitive to earth tremor. Some moths can smell each other a mile away.

By comparison mankind is virtually insensitive, seeing quite a bit (particularly if it moves), hearing a little, smelling hardly anything (unless he jams his nasal system right into the rose), tasting even less, touching fairly well (but much better if he files off all dead skin), detecting temperature very poorly, knowing of magnetism or irradiation not at all, and generally blundering through the environment. Practically every animal is more aware than he is of the world about them both. Birds and mammals have seen, heard, or smelt man coming for an age beforehand. Even the mosquito knows how to find him, however much he cannot find it, or rather her. (I once sat on a bare and fallen tree trunk in central Brazil. Scarcely a minute passed before ticks were advancing towards me from both ends, 100 per cent aware – somehow – that largesse had arrived in their locality.)

Mankind's sensory system may, on occasion, seem pathetic or inadequate, but it is his only means for directly examining the outside world, its heat, light, force and chemical composition. Everything else is logical inference. Colin Blakemore defined reality as 'that which it is biologically necessary for a particular animal to detect'. Mankind is rather better at logical inference than most. Therefore it might be expected that the sensory necessities have waned in consequence. Nevertheless they do exist, with vision as the best of them.

Seeing   Vision, from a camera's viewpoint, is simple. A lens focuses the three-dimensional world on a two-dimensional surface. The image may be smaller, upside down or even distorted, but it still resembles the object. Human vision has no such simplicity. Each eye's lens focuses its image on the retina but that part of the system can no more see than a camera can see. All the seeing, the interpretation of electrical impulses that travel along the optic nerve, is performed by the brain, or rather (in large measure) by its visual cortex on the occipital lobes lying at the rear of the cerebrum. The retinal information, initially straightforward, is confusingly scrambled on its way to the cortex. The neurons there have to unscramble it, make sense of it, and portray for each of us an apparently three-dimensional image. The picture has, in effect, to be reconstituted. A second confusion – and there are plenty more – is that each occipital lobe, so cut off from its other half (the brain being almost an organ in two parts), receives information from each of the two eyes, but only the right half of the visual field goes to the left lobe and vice versa.

The human cortex, described by the neurologist John C. Eccles as possessing a 'level of complexity, of dynamic complexity, immeasurably greater than anything else that has ever been discovered in the universe' is the reason for mankind's brilliance. It contains about one hundred thousand neurons in each square millimetre of its surface. Therefore, as its total area if spread and smoothed is 1.5 square feet (1,350 square centimetres), the whole cortex contains about ten thousand million nerve cells. Only a part of that cortex is concerned with vision, about one-ninetieth of the whole, or 2.2 square inches (15 square centimetres), which means – assuming equal distribution of neurons – about one hundred million for seeing things. (A 1963 article in *Scientific American* inadvertently attributed twenty square feet to the cortex. Quick to reply was a neuroanatomist from Toronto: 'It should be 1.5 square feet, at least that is what Canadians have.')

About a million nerve fibres convey the information from each eye to the visual cortex. Every axon in this bundle leads directly from the retina but not directly from its light-sensitive area. Other cells have recorded the optical information and have then passed it on to the cells of the optic nerve. Some of this bundle makes, as it were, a detour to the lateral geniculate nuclei, a group of cells deep within the brain. From these nuclei, one on each side (or hemisphere), other cells convey the information to the so-called primary visual cortex. It is primary because the information it receives is then passed on yet again, via synapses and other cells, to still other areas of the cortex, to yet other regions of the brain and even, in part, back to the lateral geniculate nuclei.

Remembering, therefore, the one million fibres leading from all the retinal cells to the hundred million neurons of the primary visual cortex, and not forgetting that detour on the way or that the visual cortex is only the first stage in the brain's handling of optical information, it is hardly surprising that the network has not yet been fully deciphered. As David H. Hubel and Torsten N. Wiesel, collaborators on vision research for twenty years, wrote about the eye in a review article of 1979: 'Understanding of this large and indispensable organ is still woefully deficient.'

The few years since then have possibly seen more progress than in all previous years, in mapping, in understanding how the brain tackles the problem of vision, how groups of neurons have particular tasks, how a single line seen by the eye becomes a set of regularly spaced patches within the cortex. It may seem like disorder, when the numbers of cells, synapses and interconnections are initially investigated, but it plainly is order, and the researchers have a finger-hold upon the process being used. There is even a possibility that vision, when effectively unravelled, will provide clues for understanding the even greater problems, such as memory, retrieval, learning, and thought. At least vision can start with something simple, like one straight line applied to just one eye. If that can be followed – and it has been – something outstandingly more complex like a face, or memory of that face, might eventually be traced.

Much recent work has concentrated on stereopsis. Named after the Greek for solid sight it is the ability to see depth. It needs two viewpoints, such as two eyes, to be focused upon the same object, but at once there is paradox. In the first place both animals and men can judge distance very well with just one eye. There have, for example, been extremely capable cricketers with monocular vision. Even those individuals, normally binocular, who cover up one eye can get by without immediately encountering all the furniture. And straight distance-judging – how far away is that person, that box of unknown size, that rock? – can also be fairly accurate with just one eye. Besides, approximately one in fifty of the population is essentially one-eyed; the two they do possess are not cooperating correctly. (Such people can even be unaware of their defect until an optician points it out to them.) It has been said that the prime evolutionary advantage of bearing two eyes, to which Cyclops would testify, is that one remains if one is lost. The second part of the conundrum, therefore, follows from the first: if one eye can judge distance, what other system is being employed that makes two eyes judge better?

The work to answer this problem started 150 years ago when Charles Wheatstone (whose bridge for measuring resistance is well known in the physics classroom) invented the world's first stereoscope. This enabled each eye to see a slightly different picture and thereby provided a suggestion of depth. The work now involves what are known as random dot stereograms. By misaligning part of the random design the brain can be tricked into believing that that part is either further from or nearer to the eye. Interest in this work stems principally from its lack of other clues to distance definition. Normally the human visual system uses everything within its grasp to judge distance, such as head-movement parallax, a moving head being better than a stationary one, particularly if just one eye is used. The random dots give no such clues, but are as effective as Wheatstone's stereoscope.

This most astounding fact about human vision is not that distance can be judged but that it can be estimated accurately and unhesitatingly even when there are no other guidelines. If a carpet has an identical pattern, frequently repeated, and if that carpet fills the viewer's field of vision, it is still possible to estimate its distance. Each piece of pattern is seen correctly by both eyes, and the information collected by one eye is precisely matched with the other eye's information. So too with the random dots. The brain has nothing sensible on which to latch its focus and its interest, but it still operates just as effectively as when confronted by any normal scene. Understanding this ability has been called by John P. Frisby, in his *Seeing With Two Eyes*, the 'central theoretical challenge which current research on stereopsis is confronting'. And stereopsis, he could have added, has received in recent years the bulk of research effort dedicated to the number one human sensory system, namely vision.

So skilled is human stereopsis that the suggestion has even been made that it was not primarily developed to aid in judging distance. The random dots were spur for this proposal because they are not form but formlessness. Where in nature is there similar disguise, save in camouflage? The brain is excellent at finding form when all manner of trickery has been employed to deceive it. The tiger can be seen amongst the vegetation; the moth can be observed pressed flat against the bark. Judging distance is child's play by comparison; just one eye can do that. Seeing the obscure is very much harder, needing two good eyes and an excellent brain. Both distance assessment and detection are useful for survival and maybe detection is the more important.

The colour blind can make better entomologists in that they are less distracted by colour, looking instead for the form and seeing through the camouflage. This may help to explain the strikingly high proportion of humans, particularly men, known as colour-blind but more correctly labelled colour-confused. The male percentages (with female percentages in brackets) are that grey is confused with: Blue, green, or red in 1 per cent of men (0.02 per cent of women); Reddish purple in 1 per cent (0.01 per cent); Pale red in 1.5 per cent (0.03 per cent); Pale purple in 5 per cent (0.4 per cent); and violet or yellow very rarely in both sexes. Although there may have been colour-blind advantages in past ages, and in past styles of life, modern man created a grave disadvantage when he decided that red and green should be the universal signals for danger and safety. These happen to be the two most indistinguishable colours among those individuals (8 per cent of males) with colour vision defects. Most employees are given no colour-discrimination tests, though they then drive cars, use colour-coded wiring, buy tomatoes turning red from green, check diamonds, oversee weaving, and try to turn company accounts from red to black. Colour is important to modern life, and yet has blinded us to the fact that a considerable proportion do not see its full range. Most mammals are poor at discriminating colour. Only the higher primates have a colour appreciation which approaches that of man, even all the men who are colour-confused.

The eye may be the visual organ, but it is the brain that sees. The camera, with shutter and lens, takes the picture, but all the processing is done via the film. So too with the pupil, lens and retina. Processing is done by that part of the nervous system which interprets the information arriving along the optic nerve.

The brain can also see without any need for external stimulus, as in dreams. There are hallucinations or false perceptions, which are convincingly real save that the eye has, once again, not observed them. An illusion is similar, but is a distortion of perception rather than the invention of one. Both hallucination and illusion can seem equally true because reality is what the brain creates within itself, fed and stimulated perhaps by the sensory nerve endings, or perhaps not. Sensation – to repeat a sentence already used – is an abstraction and not a replication of the real world. The brain sees, and also chooses what it wants to see.

The visual system is, therefore, not a copying device, with the two-dimensional image focused on the retina becoming a two-dimensional vision of the world. For one thing that image is scrambled and then re-formed. As Colin Blakemore phrased it: 'What does the brain do with the visual information after it has taken the image apart? If it only reassembles the features in some way to recreate the image, then why did it take it apart in the first place?' Vision, in short, used to be what the eye did. It has now shifted and is what the brain does with the facts that come its way via the optic nerves.

Hearing may seem a straightforward sense, at least compared with seeing. However, as with sight, there is nothing direct about the nervous connection between ear and brain. Reading about the pathways involved can cause the reader both despair and wonder, initially from their complexity and then from amazement that so much unravelling has already been achieved. The textbooks are somewhat bland as they reproduce this information and, in the expectation of creating both wonder and amazement (or despair) in others, herewith a quotation (in part) from one of them, *The Essentials of Neuroanatomy* by G. A. G. Mitchell and D. Mayor.

The auditory pathway from the cochlea to the cortex is as follows. The primary neurons are in the spiral cochlear ganglion and their central processes end in the ventral and dorsal cochlear nuclei in the pons. The secondary relay of fibres resulting from these synapses pass through the corpus trapezoideum and the striae medullares ventriculi quarti (slender transverse bundles of fibre arising in the dorsal cochlear nuclei which cross the floor of the fourth ventricle and sink into the median sulcus) before turning upwards to form the lateral lemniscus. The fibres in the lateral lemniscus end mainly in the medial geniculate bodies, the lower auditory centres, and in the inferior colliculi. The new relays of fibres originating in the lower auditory centres pass through the homolateral internal capsule . . . Fibres arising in the inferior colliculi enter the tectospinal tracts . . . Some fibres from the lateral lemniscus end in the substantia nigra; others form synapses in nuclei . . . which fibres enter the medial longitudinal bundle . . . Certain fibres from the vestibular division of the eighth nerve . . . may follow routes similar to the cochlear fibres and many vestibular fibres also enter the medial longitudinal bundle.

Human hearing is both astonishingly good – from the faintest to the loudest detectable sounds involve a billionfold alteration in energy – and astonishingly poor relative to many other animals. Mankind is said to have the most limited range of all the mammals. Certain rodents and bats can hear two complete octaves higher than man can hear. Any human being in a natural setting is humbly aware that virtually every creature is a better detector of sound. Or rather they are better detectors of sounds interesting to them, such as a rival of the same species or approaching danger. Mankind's hearing is best suited to hearing speech.

The general rule among animals is that the smaller the head the higher the frequency which can be heard. Small-headed bats can hear up to 115 kilohertz (115,000 cycles per second), rats up to 72 kilohertz, dogs to 44 kilohertz, man to 19 kilohertz, and elephants only up to 10.5 kilohertz. Body size used to be considered relevant to this difference in hearing higher notes, but the distance lying between both ears is now generally believed to be more important. Explanation rests with direction discrimination, and with the brain's ability to note the difference in sound reaching the two ears. The nearer the ears are to each other the shorter the wave length (and, therefore, the higher the frequency) necessary for discrimination. This acoustic fact has been responsible for species evolving a hearing system able to detect the frequencies most suitable for the distance between their ears, namely the highest for the smallest heads, and the lowest for the biggest. Mankind may be different in possessing speech, but the human range – from 20 hertz to 20 kilohertz – fits in well with human size, and the distance between each human ear.

The external ear, or pinna, is not only indefinable in shape but different on each side, this difference being an aid to the localisation of sound. If the various (indefinable) contours are gradually eliminated, by smoothing down their ridges and valleys, the ability to locate a noise is equally gradually reduced. The pinna's convolutions reflect some of the sound, thereby delaying its arrival at the tympanum, and the brain is able to make use of this difference between direct and delayed sound to help it place the noise. In fact there are many differences; such as the direct sounds to each ear, different on each side, and also the indirect reflections from each pinna. The brain is able to interpret these differences, and turn the head accordingly to face the sound. (Microphones have even been placed in artificial pinnas to make a better orchestral recording, or rather recordings that make more sense to human listeners. Even the location of actual instruments in the orchestra can then be correctly identified.)

The nature of sound has itself helped to elucidate how hearing works. A tone is tantamount to a series of impulses, the number of impulses per second being its frequency. Transmission of information along a nerve is also a sequence of impulses, the sequence (for hearing) being generated by the inner ear. Therefore it might be expected, if a pure tone is played, that its frequency should be mirrored by the number of pulses travelling along each auditory nerve. For some tones this is indeed the case; there are as many pulses per second travelling along the nerve as in that tonal frequency. However, the rate of impulse transmission along a single nerve fibre does not exceed three hundred or so per second. So other nerves have to respond to the higher frequencies. They still cannot fire at more than three hundred impulses a second, but the brain interprets their firing as registering a higher frequency. How it comprehends all this information, with one nerve firing at, say, two hundred impulses a second meaning quite a different tone from another nerve firing at the same rate is – to use the hallowed scientific phrase – not entirely clear.

The nature of sound also helps to explain why higher frequencies can be less correctly located and how cunning the brain is in its powers of discrimination. From the moment that a sound wave hits the ear to that later moment when the relevant impulse reaches the auditory cortex is about twenty milliseconds (one-fiftieth of a second). These two moments are, for the same sound, slightly different for each ear. Assuming the source is neither directly ahead nor directly behind the observer, the sound – travelling at 1,100 feet per second – will take slightly longer to reach the more distant ear. Human head size being what it is, the sound takes about one two-thousandth of a second longer to travel the greater distance if it originated at 90° to the direction the head is facing.

However, the brain can discriminate time differences of the order of sixty micro-seconds, which is eight times better. The sound source need not, therefore, be either directly right or left for the human listener to know on which side it exists. A much smaller arc of location is possible, which becomes smaller still if the head is cocked to increase the time difference of the sounds falling on each ear. High frequencies cannot be located because, particularly above 1,200 cycles per second, their wave lengths become less than the distance between the two ears. If, for example, the high point of a sound wave reaches one ear precisely when the high point of the next wave reaches the nearer ear even the most discriminating brain can make nothing of the information it receives. So far as it is concerned both ears have received the same information at the same time, and the sound is, therefore, straight ahead or straight behind. So too, in effect, with all higher frequencies; their time of arrival at each ear has become irrelevant.

Essentially the animal kingdom uses the same system (or rather mankind is using the system already evolved for the animals). However, there are differences. The barn owl, able to locate small rodents scurrying in the dark, possesses ears more asymmetrical than the human pinna. One owl ear is both higher and larger than the other, thus increasing sound discrepancy. The green tree frog has an internal passage linking its ears, and each ear, therefore, receives sound from two directions, one as normal and one through the head. The result, yet again, is enhanced discrepancy. Birds have small heads, but are more efficient than similarly-sized mammals at locating sound. They still seem to rely on time difference, even though sound takes about one thirteen-thousandth of a second to travel the inch between one ear and its fellow.

The most baffling property of the human ear, which may also exist among animals, is its ability to single out a sound, pay attention to it, and dismiss other noise. A hearing aid delivers all sound to its wearer, sometimes – as at a party – rendering its helpfulness marginal at most. Individuals with normal hearing can listen to just one voice, no less single-mindedly than the eye focuses upon the face pronouncing it. How this happens, to quote one author who varied science's hallowed phrase, has not yet 'received a satisfactory explanation'. However, it is not the ear that is discriminating, or so it is assumed; rather it is the brain that chooses to hear what it wants.

In general every individual can hear his or her voice more clearly than can another who stands nearby. Some work with monkeys has contradicted this point: the cells in their auditory cortex were inhibited when they themselves vocalised. If the human ear is suddenly subjected to a loud sound there will be a near-immediate reflex of the tympanic muscles which effectively dampen that sound. However, they do not work quickly enough (which would be difficult) to block the noise instantaneously; nor do they continue to work if the noise is prolonged. As a result the ear is often damaged, either by abrupt noises (rifle fire, back-fire) or steady

There is generally legislation concerning permitted background sound – in Britain the day-long level is allowed to be ninety decibels – but industrial noise is responsible for much ear damage. A recent British report stated that 18 to 20 per cent of all adults may suffer from 'significant hearing loss', which means they cannot hear any noise softer than twenty-five decibels. What is intriguing, particularly in a book dedicated to the brain, is that the sense organ itself, whether eye or ear, is much more frequently the cause of sensory defect than the cortex or other nervous tissue. The brain seems to have a resilience which mere lenses, tympanic membranes, cochleas and corneas do not. They fail, frequently. The brain, or so it seems, will continue to interpret, analyse, comprehend and decipher whatever comes its way. Or perhaps its role in the feeble-sighted and hard-of-hearing has still to receive a satisfactory explanation.

Blind people have frequently confirmed that their sense of hearing is far more capable and acute than that of normal people. Two doctors from Derby reported in 1981 about a woman, blind since the age of twenty-seven, who began to suffer deafness a few years later. 'I can no longer hear the silence of lamp-posts,' she said one day. They discovered she had been able to walk through woods, and neither collide with trees, nor trip over logs, roots or brambles. She could tell if a vehicle was a car, a van, or a lorry, and on one occasion was mystified by an object on a wall. It made no sense until she felt it, and discovered a rolled-up fire-hose.

In truth it is the brain which is more capable and acute than is traditionally believed by normal people. Perhaps the Derby woman was partly smelling things rather than hearing them (although increasing deafness made her realise how much hearing was involved) but she just knew things were there as any normal person knows things to be true. The brain receives its information, and then decides how best to interpret and analyse. It makes a kind of reality which is not the truth but the kind most suitable for its possessor. The hearing aid comes nearer to the truth, but a sensory system possesses – to put it over-cleverly – more sense about it. It discriminates, and selects; but the brain, of course, rather than the ear, plays this skilful role. The ear just sends its information and the brain then deals with it. As with the seeing of the eye it is the brain that hears rather than the ear.

Smelling   At least it is known how the eye works. It is also known how the ear works, in broad outline if not with the detail some would like. However, not so with the nose as the smell sensory system is still, in the main, a matter of conjecture. Do molecules smell as they do because of their molecular structure, or their vibration, or their effect on the smell receptors (perhaps by puncturing them)? The receptors lie (unhelpfully) out of the mainstream of inspired air. Existing in a blind alley they are formed of cells with long cilia attached to them. The cilia cannot wave about because they are embedded within a layer of mucus. Therefore, every odour has to be soluble in this substance for detection – by the cilia – to be possible. Each smell organ is about 2.5 square centimetres (0.4 square inches) in size, yellowish in colour, and is believed to possess several different kinds of receptor. How many is unknown, and it is absolutely unknown how they operate, and why burning rubber and burned toast, cloves and cinnamon, chalk and cheese are so immediately identifiable, and memorable, and highly individual.

It is said that mankind can detect thousands of odours, and more than ten thousand with practice, but it is not said how this feat is achieved. Or how the brain unscrambles whatever it receives by way of impulse along the olfactory nerves. It is not even known whether smells have affinities with each other, and can be classified. There have been attempts – ethereal (as in fruits), aromatic (as in almonds), fragrant (as in flowers), ambrosial (as in musk), and so forth – but there is no general acceptance of such headings. Neither is there belief that classification will help in the understanding of smell, any more than noise classification has assisted in comprehending hearing.

Humans are traditionally contemptuous of the human olfactory organ, mainly because many animal noses are of quite a different calibre. Dogs, as mentioned elsewhere, can be one million times better than man with certain odorous substances. Mankind, in short, has to wait until that smell is one million times more concentrated before it is detectable. The great virtue of the olfactory system, in dogs or humans, is that it continues to serve when other senses no longer operate: the predator, or prey, still has a smell even when invisible in the dark and when inaudible or stationary. However, humans in such circumstances fare very badly. In acquiring and growing their cerebral hemispheres, they made use of the fore-brain, that division of the ancestral vertebrate cerebrum principally dedicated to olfaction. No creature is expert at everything, and mankind has favoured vision and intelligence at the expense of other attributes, not least of which is smell.

Nevertheless, human olfaction is much better than customarily supposed. (Science talks of olfaction, commerce of fragrance, behaviourists of scent, and humans of smells – unless they are Dr Johnson who said, 'Madam, you smell, I stink.') The nose of mankind can detect the mercaptans which skunks produce in times of stress at concentrations of one molecule in every 30,000 million of air. It can do even better with the chemical 2-methoxy-3-hexylpyrazine: the detectable dilution is one part in a million million (which, for those who like this sort of comparison, is the same proportion as one cubic kilometre is to the total volume of the Earth). Humans can also track, if prepared to kneel and sniff the floor where a stockinged foot has walked not too long beforehand. According to research at Vanderbilt University people can even smell out their relatives. Not only were nineteen of twenty-four children able to identify their siblings by used T-shirt smell alone, but sixteen out of eighteen parents could single out their offspring just by smell. Primitive peoples, living more straightforward kinds of life, are often said to possess exceptional powers. Perhaps they just exercise the abilities latent in us all.

The olfactory system is unique in being in direct contact with the external environment. There is no specialised receptor cell in the nose equivalent to the rods and cones of the retina or to the bony and membranous transmission system in the ear. Instead the cell body of what is known as the primary neuron lies actually within the receptor organ. Each such neuron leads via its axon to the olfactory bulb. Within this bulb are synapses, and therefore connections with other bodies, such as (initially) the mitral cells, and then the granule cells, and also the olfactory cortex. In other words, as with both the visual and the auditory systems, much processing of information received is carried on before the actual cortex gets to know of it. The smell centre within the cortex lies, to quote from a text on the subject, 'in the uncus and the anterior part of the hippocampal gyrus (pyriform area) closely related to the temporal lobe'.

Other intriguing smell facts are: one-sided loss of smell usually causes no symptoms; two-sided loss, known as bilateral anosmia, is generally accompanied by inability to taste (causing life to lose much of its savour); parosmia, or distorted smell sense, can be yet more unpleasant as all food may, to quote from a book on neural disease, 'have the same repellent flavour'; the commonest cause of continuing anosmia is a blow to the head (thought to disrupt the olfactory fibres), is generally permanent and, if recovery does occur, may only be from anosmia to parosmia (sometimes called dysosmia); and pheromones – chemical substances given off by animals which induce oestrous, courtship, aggressive behaviour, etc. – are being increasingly studied from the human angle, as they can lead to, for example, earlier menstruation or, in confined female communities, synchronised menstruation. The medical profession is objecting increasingly to irritant perfumes – sometimes even called pheromones – added to seemingly everything from nappies to sheets to tissues with the stated intention of making them 'close-up fresh' (whatever that is) or 'baby soft' (which must be difficult for a smell).

A final point. Knowing how easy it is even for humans to detect when some rain-sodden or, far worse, well-rolled dog has walked into the room it is interesting to speculate on the dog's millionfold ability to detect humans, whether sodden or otherwise. Why is the smell not unbearable? And why do they not resemble those creatures in T. H. White's story who 'lived on smells but could be killed by a stink'? Besides, as Dr Robert Rouse, of Clwyd, queried in *World Medicine*, if dogs' noses are that acute 'why do they have to get so close to me – with special reference to the sharp nasal nudge to the groin so many of them seem to find essential to my full acquaintance?'

Mankind mourns in general for the blind and the deaf. It scarcely sheds one tear for the anosmic; it hardly knows the word.

Tasting Often spoken of as allied to smell it bears little relation to it, save that talk about the taste of something should often be more properly applied to the smell of it. Unlike the thousands of detectable smells there are only four taste stimuli – sweet, salt, acid, sour. (There is even argument that only two truly exist.) The taste receptors lie in some five thousand buds, largely at the front, back and sides of the upper part of the tongue (and, therefore, missing out the centre). Other buds lie on the palate, throat and tonsils. A similarity with smell is that the method of information collection is still unknown; whether taste buds or olfactory cilia the procedure is not yet understood. Loss of taste ability tends to advance with advancing years, but is very rarely total (hypogeusia). There is also dysgeusia, or malfunction of the taste system.

Unlike the complexities of seeing, hearing, and smelling, all of which are difficult even to contemplate, the business of tasting is elementary by comparison. Nevertheless, the neurologists still have a long way to go before this fourth sensory system is unravelled. The tongue is innervated more complicatedly than might be expected, bearing in mind that it is but one protuberance. In the words of W. B. Matthews and Henry Miller the impulses from the taste buds 'converge on the nucleus solitarius in the medulla by strangely devious routes'. Nerves from the front and two sides lead via the lingual to the trigeminal nerve, one of the brain's twelve cranial nerves. The lingual element leaves the trigeminal after a while and passes through the middle ear (of all places) to join the facial nerve, yet another of the brain's cranial nerves. (Whether or not the taste buds at the end of this wandering nerve are doing their job of tasting can be discovered with the terminals of an ordinary torch battery. The tingling is a taste, and not some muscular effect. If it is present the buds and nerves are operating; if not they are not.)

The back of the tongue plus its contingent of taste buds behave as if they are part of a different organ. They join up with neither the trigeminal nor the facial cranial nerves, but with the glossopharyngeal. The tongue, therefore, involves cranial nerves, 5, 7, and 9. The other sense organs are less casual. Every nasal sensation travels along cranial nerve 1, the olfactory; every visual sensation travels along 2, the optic; and every hearing sensation travels along 8, the auditory. The tongue, so unimportant by comparison, uses three times as many cranial nerves, and has much less to say about the outside world than eye or ear or nose. Oddly the back of the tongue cannot be satisfactorily tested for its tasting ability by the electrical method.

Of the four tastes, bitterness is easiest to detect (at one part in 2,000,000), sourness is second easiest (at one in 130,000), saltiness third (at one in 400), and sweetness last (at one in 200). The selective advantages of possessing a taste system – rejecting harmful foods, for instance – are quite outclassed by the sense of smell, which can identify individual substances.

Being hypogeusic, and without taste, can be symptomatic of either trivial or severe causes (as with virtually every other form of bodily failure). It can be a feature of depressive illness (or part of the cause of that depression), of lack of thyroid secretion (hypothyroidism), of drug action (as with lithium carbonate, griseofulvin, penicillamine, for example), of certain epilepsies (in which case the taste inability is not permanent), of smoking, of radiotherapy, of various local and other diseases (such as influenza, the common cold, and Bell's palsy, but almost certainly not cerebral tumours), and all this lack of taste may be one-sided or total. The commonest cause is a deficiency of zinc (remedied by taking zinc sulphate). Drops of bitterness, sweetness, etc. can be used to test taste, but are more time-consuming and generally less clear-cut than the electrical system.

Just as anosmia is rarely known (as a word), so is hypogeusia. Nevertheless, according to a clinic at Washington, DC, which is one of the very few to specialise in smell and taste disorders, there are from two to ten million Americans so afflicted. Treatment with zinc is successful only for those with zinc deficiency, such people forming the minority of the 1 to 4 per cent of the population without taste or smell, or both. 'I don't think we understand how difficult these problems can be,' said the director of the Washington clinic. 'Eating is more than refuelling . . . and living in a tasteless, smell-less world is not only boring, it's unbelievably frustrating and depressing.' Perhaps the better evolutionary advantage of smelling and tasting is the zest and excitement they add to life, and to refuelling.

Touching This traditional fifth sense should be independently sufficient to banish the notion that there are five senses because touch is not a single entity, with a single kind of receptor, but customarily (and erroneously) embraces five distinct sensations: pressure, pain, heat, cold, *and* touch. The various receptors, named after their discoverers, are (chronologically from the time of each discovery): Pacinian corpuscles for pressure (Filippo Pacini, Italian, 1830), Meissner's corpuscles for touch (George Meissner, German, 1853), Krause's end-bulbs for cold (Wilhelm Krause, German, 1860), and Ruffini's end organ for heat (Angelo Ruffini, Italian, 1898). There is no specialised receptor/corpuscle/bulb/organ for pain. Its nerves just end, as befits this form of sensation. (In any case, pain merits a separate section, and will be described when the other forms of touch have been concluded.)

Touch, in all its kinds, is also different from sight, hearing, smell and taste in having no special organ equivalent to the eye, ear, nose and tongue. Touch – so far as the skin is concerned – is everywhere, and is known as a general, rather than a special, sense. The receptors are unevenly distributed so there is no uniformity of sensation on each individual's twenty square feet of skin. On the back there are fewest, on forearm and legs there are more, on the palms more still, on the nose's tip even more, and on the fingertips as well as certain genital areas most of all. Hairs are insensitive, but have receptors near their roots that detect hair movement (a capability at its most refined in animal whiskers). There are about two hundred thousand receptors for cold and heat, some five hundred thousand for touch and pressure, and about four times their joint total for pain's nerve endings. All this innervation, even if on the tongue or up the nose, is essentially external, and known as exteroceptive.

The internal form of sensation, called proprioception (after the Latin 'received from self'), is as much a sense as everything gathered from the outside. Specific nerve endings, attached to certain muscle fibres, ligaments, tendons and joints, are the means whereby the body knows what it is doing, where its limbs are located, and whether it is about to fall over. Proprioception works extremely well, without much personal awareness of its activity (if any) and with great precision. Making two fore-fingers meet behind the back is a telling example. As J. H. Green elaborated in his textbook on physiology:

Consider the number of joints involved: interphalangeal, meta-carpophalangeal, intermetacarpal, carpometacarpal, carpal, wrist, elbows and shoulder . . . Not only can the resultant position be calculated, but another limb, connected to a different part of the trunk, [is] taken to an identical position in space.

It is very easy to discriminate between the size of two coins, to touch nose-tip, ear-lobe or knee even when blind-folded, and certainly to stand vertically, more or less, when carrying out all the daily routine. If seeing, hearing, smelling, tasting, touching, and detecting pressure, heat, and cold, are the first eight senses, proprioception makes a most able ninth to swell the total.

Should proprioception fail, whether to a greater or lesser degree, there can be considerable compensation by vision. Instead of the fore-fingers finding each other, and out of sight, they can be brought together in front of the eyes and then correctly coordinated. However, a blind-fold or night-time will render any proprioceptive defect much more conspicuous. The disease known as tabes dorsalis is a case in point. This late manifestation of syphilis, which may appear twenty years after the original infection, ably demonstrates, certainly for the legs, the disabling loss of this important sense. Gait becomes ataxic, which means the legs are thrown about, somewhat uncontrollably, and feet are lifted unnecessarily high off the ground. There is an inability to retain balance if the feet are together when the eyes are closed, a feature known as Romberg's sign. Even temporary blindness, as in face-washing, can cause imbalance and the sufferer may fall most damagingly.

The sensory pathways from the various forms of touch take complex and varying routes between each receptor organ and the brain. All enter the spinal cord via the posterior nerve roots, but thereafter the sensory fibres follow three main paths. The first, involving both touch receptors and proprioception, leads initially to the medulla, then to the thalamus, and then to the sensory cortex of the cerebral hemispheres. The second, involving pain, temperature, and touch receptors, leads initially to the spinal cord, then to the thalamus, and finally to the sensory cortex. The third, involving just proprioception, leads to the spinal cord and then to the cerebellum. Each stage necessitates another synapse and, therefore, another neuron, or nerve cell. Consequently there are three, three, and two neurons in these three principal pathways between receptor and brain. With all of them there is cross-over, the curious attribute of the left half of the brain organising the right side of the body, and vice versa. The brain's sensory cortex lies in the postcentral gyrus and immediately behind the central sulcus. In other words it is a band stretching roughly from the top of the head down to each ear. Each half of this band, dealing with the opposite half of the body, is also contrary in its arrangement from the apex of the head down to each ear. At the top lie the nerve endings whose pathways originated in the feet and hind limbs. Then are those which came from the trunk, then from the arm, and finally from the head. Sensation, therefore, not only ends up on the opposing side but upside down as well.

Despite the variety of receptor organs, and their location up and down the body (and inside with the proprioceptors), there is a simplicity to their operation not matched in the big four senses already described, in sight, hearing, smell, and taste. The greater the pressure, or warmth, or touch, or cold, the more nerve endings are triggered into activity, and the more frequent their impulses. However, the longer that the sensation is maintained the more insensitive become the relevant nerve endings. In this fashion the steady pressure of clothing is disregarded, although lack of pressure can also be noticed if, for example, a wrist-watch is suddenly missing. To some extent the thalamus, a more primitive part of the brain than the cortex, can detect where a sensation is located, but finer distinction has to wait until the impulse reaches its destination in one or other cerebral hemisphere. Quite apart from everything else that it does proprioception should at least be a permanent reminder that Aristotle has much to answer for in imprinting the notion of five senses. Even if temperature sensation seemed like one rather than two sensations, and no more than a form of touch, the sense of proprioception is undoubtedly extremely different. And so, for that matter, is pain.

Pain Proprioception works well, and there are few complaints about it. Pain works most unsatisfactorily, and criticism is loud. The quantity of pain is poorly related to the degree of injury. A pinprick, one tooth, or a lumbar vertebra can yell, as it were, so loudly that all other action, thought, deed, is virtually impossible; but a tumour can grow with no accompanying pain at all. Pain is even a poor protector against injury in that its onset (almost always) occurs too late to be useful as a preventive measure. There is no direct relationship between an injury and the sensation of pain caused by that injury; in moments or days it can feel very different. The footballer will only notice his wound when the game is over. The child will disregard the slap and its pain unless it was intentional. The cancer victim is said to feel pain more because of its portent, all pain being influenced by the three Ms – mood, morale, and meaning.

Pain is also different from the other senses, possessing qualities they do not. It is essentially private; only the individual concerned is aware of it. Secondly, there is no such entity as pain unless and until it is perceived; there are noises, light energies, and temperatures whether or not they are perceived. Thirdly, pain is no more and no less than the perception of it, and cannot be doubted; the standard senses are all fallible, with hallucinations, illusions, after-images, ear-buzzing, tinnitus being errors of perception. (An apparent exception is phantom pain, about which more in a moment, in that pain is attributed to a non-existent region. However, the pain perceived is no less real and painful for all that.) Nerve impulses can be measured to assess the intensity of a signal, say from an injury (and these are most uniform between individuals), but nothing can assess the intensity of pain save for the individual concerned. Finally, just as there can be pain without injury so can there be injury without pain. And pain can even be pleasurable.

What pain does is initiate a different form of behaviour. It cannot prevent injury in the first place, but it can help to protect that injury from further damage. The hand is tucked away; the body becomes more cautious; a different lifestyle is imposed. Pain, therefore, is more allied with, for example, hunger and thirst. These signal not only a bodily condition but the start of a new form of behaviour. When severe they completely dictate that behaviour; when moderate they merely influence it. Other sensory systems have no such direct relationship with such drives. To see water is perhaps to drink it; to sense thirst, hunger or pain is always more straightforward. There is what has been called (by T. J. Crow) a 'dichotomy of sensory modalities', with vision, hearing and touch on the one hand, and smell, taste, hunger and pain on the other.

C. A. Keele, considerable expert on pain, identified three skin layers from which different sensations can be evoked. The epidermis and immediately underlying dermis (the outermost layers) give itch, a quite distinct sensory impression from pain. The main part of the dermis creates a bright, superficial pain. And the deep dermis and subcutaneous tissue produce an appropriately deep, aching pain. Itch is unpleasant, and is reacted against, but differs from pain in that it: feels different; provokes scratching rather than withdrawal; is abolished by warm water (41°C) which intensifies pain; can be made worse by morphine, which abolishes pain; and can only be evoked from the exterior skin. Pain may be a mixed blessing, slow to warn, slower still to go away, incapable of measuring severity, but itch seems entirely valueless. Perhaps the scratching it provokes can disturb ectoparasites, but it more frequently aggravates the injuries they cause.

Attempts have been made to measure pain, with dol as the unit of sensation. One dol has been rated equivalent to two just noticeable differences of pain, with 10½ dols marking the ceiling of pain intensity. Other pain researchers have preferred a simpler scale, one descending from very severe, to severe, to moderate, to slight, to no pain. Maximal pain can be sustained only briefly; all pain of long duration must be of low intensity. The rate of tissue damage required to create severe pain (of 5–8 dols) is probably sufficient to destroy the pain fibres in that area. According to Keele: 'So-called intractable pain must . . . be either of low intensity, periodic, or must not be truly pain at all, but rather a combination of non-painful sensations which are interpreted by the individual as unpleasant and unacceptable.'

Whether something is interpreted as pain, or is actual pain, it is painful and (generally) unwelcome. Nevertheless it is frequent. (According to the Interagency Committee on New Therapies for Pain and Discomfort some seventy-five million Americans – about one-third of the population – suffer chronic pain of various kinds.) One study, entitled 'Undertreatment of medical inpatients with narcotic analgesics', showed that 73 per cent of those being treated for pain experienced moderate to severe discomfort. 'This is not for want of tools,' wrote Dr Marcia Angell when reviewing the subject in 1982, before adding: 'It is generally agreed that most pain, however severe, can be effectively relieved.' 'There is no lack of therapies from which to choose,' wrote Geoff Watts in *World Medicine*, before listing some of them: 'Simple and opioid analgesia, analgesic adjuvants, local anaesthetic and neurolytic nerve blocks, neurosurgical interruption of pain pathways, electrical stimulation, cryotherapy, acupuncture, hypnosis, operant conditioning, biofeedback, psychotherapy . . . and others.'

Unfortunately, for those in pain, there is almost as long a list of reasons for the lack of treatment, such as fear of side-effects (notably respiratory distress), fear of addiction, a belief that higher doses (of pain killers) will provide no added relief, an affection for routine (and for the drugs to be administered at fixed times), an unwillingness among patients to create a nuisance, a difficulty in summoning nurses, a belief among doctors and nurses that frequent requests for drugs suggest a growing dependence, and a general feeling on both sides that stoicism is admirable. To be in pain and not to ask for aid earns nods of approval; to request a drug often achieves no more than cluckings of dismay.

The solid evidence, according to Dr Angell in her review, is that less than 0.1 per cent of those who receive narcotics for pain relief will become addicted. The side-effect of respiratory distress is likely to be no more than 1 per cent. As for those with terminal illness the modest risk of addiction or breathing troubles is quite irrelevant.

I can't think of any other area in medicine [she concluded] in which such an extravagant concern for side effects so drastically limits treatment. We are used to a closer balance between risks and benefits . . . Pain is soul destroying. No patient should have to endure intense pain unnecessarily. The quality of mercy is essential to the practice of medicine; here, of all places, it should not be strained.

But it is. The recent trial in Fall River, Massachusetts (Commonwealth v. Ann Capute) gave wide publicity to the charge that a nurse had murdered a patient suffering from cancer secondaries by the administration of morphine. After five weeks she was acquitted, but hospitals have allegedly reacted as if she had been found guilty. Pain relief, it seems and in general, is now being rationed even more. In a *New England Journal of Medicine* 'special article', Dr Eric J. Cassell broadened the subject to include suffering, a word so frequently coupled with that of pain. 'The relief of suffering, it would appear, is considered one of the primary ends of medicine by patients and lay persons, but not by the medical profession.' The conquest of suffering, which may or may not include physical pain, is plainly harder than the conquest of pain. Nevertheless, pain abolition is a good starting place, particularly as it is (almost always) something medicine can do. The Stoics and the Spartans are living yet, or so it would seem, and most notably on behalf of other people.

Nevertheless, the last dozen years have witnessed considerable change in attitude. There was the First World Congress on Pain (in 1976) and the establishment of the International Association for the Study of Pain. Pain clinics have sprung up, with Britain, for instance, possessing 130 by early 1982. They are generally managed by anaesthetists, and vary in size from a once-a-week outpatient session to twenty-four-hour care with inpatient facilities. Britain also has its Intractable Pain Society, swollen from 12 to 200 members since 1968. And an announcement was made (in 1978) that money will be found to build the world's first institute of pain relief. 'The most satisfying aspect of the pain scene,' wrote the *Lancet* in a 1982 editorial, 'is that our ignorance has come into the open.'

As a result of the new (and recent) interest in an old (and distressing) condition many novel techniques are being tried. To relieve post-operative pain the nerves around the surgeon's incision are (occasionally) being frozen. This cryoanalgesia is particularly interesting for the major intrusions, such as chest surgery, where subsequent pain is notorious. Pain management can also involve (on the placebo principle) steadily giving the same volume of medicine but reducing the amount of medication in it. It looks like the same dose, but is not. New drugs are always coming on to the market, partly – to view it crudely – because the potential sales are so attractive. (About 10 per cent of the world's population suffers from arthritic pain, and appears to have done so since Neanderthal man. Aspirin is still the treatment of choice, but often in doses of fifteen to twenty tablets a day. At such levels pain and inflammation can be suppressed, but other features can be aggravated – ulcers, stomach, haemorrhage. The potential market is colossal, and is growing at one million a year in America alone.)

Patient control of drug flow is another new idea. The individual in pain can adjust the drip, for instance, as and how she or he needs the pain-killer. A general finding is that less drug is consumed in this fashion. Women in labour at Cardiff, South Wales, have been permitted to adjust the flow of pethidine by pressing a button. Afterwards they considered their labour no milder than normal, but they did take less of the drug. Perhaps the rate of drug flow is more important than its quantity. The Clinical Research Centre, London, has shown that a trickle is more effective for post-operative patients than hefty shots. A hospital in Sydney, Australia, reported in 1979 that it had found continuous, intra-venous, narcotic infusions to be particularly satisfactory against post-operative pain, the method used being cheap, reliable, not prone to over-dosage, and less conducive to side-effects. Drug combinations are also more favoured these days, such as anti-depressants together with analgesics. So too is the truth that a drug is not worth giving until it reaches its effective level of concentration. As Dr Jon D. Levine, of San Francisco, said: 'No matter how much morphine you give a patient, it's the last 5 mg (milligrams) that turns on the body's pain-control system.'

Other modern forms of treatment are: injecting alcohol into the pituitary fossa (work which originated in Rome); cutting out a dorsal root ganglion from victims of chronic, intractable, low back pain (not a cure for the trouble but a palliative, none the less); blocking the nerve, as distinct from cutting it, by numbing the general area; and giving drugs by mouth rather than – which causes extra pain and apprehension – injection. Morphine, most frequently used for severe cancer pain, can even be given orally. St Joseph's Hospice, London, renowned for its sympathetic care on behalf of the dying, reported (in 1977) that of the last 400 to die in its care only 160 had 'ever needed any injection of any kind. The majority were able to take oral medication to within four hours of their death.'

The overriding problem in pain treatment is that the patient alone knows the level of suffering. As Dr Levine said: 'Physicians don't have good tools for analysing pain, and therefore they don't do it very well.' Patients have different injuries, different attitudes to their pain, differing abilities to voice complaint or description, and yet can often be given the same, average treatment. There is even a special language. At a meeting of the Society for Neuroscience (held in Georgia, USA, in 1980) it was reported that 'Yes, I do now feel a little better' means 'I am exactly the same.' Patients, as well as doctors, can be at fault in creating pain relief.

Phantom limbs   Described initially in 1551 by Ambroise Paré, the famous and pioneer military surgeon who had ample opportunities for observation on the French battlefields, this pain that comes from a severed limb is still a problem. Almost everyone who loses a leg or arm reports upon its presence afterwards, but only 5 per cent or fewer report and suffer pain after some time. Captain Ahab was one of the few, presumably so, as the carpenter related how 'a dismasted man never entirely loses the feeling of his old spar, but it will still be pricking him at times.'

The cause of it is unknown. The pain is not so much a pricking as dull and aching with occasional stabbing and shooting. It can last for seconds or days, be precipitated by physical stimulation or psychological stress, be intermittent or continuous, and temporary or permanent. It is also not limited to limbs, or rather to the lack of them. The amputation of a breast or external genitalia can have similar effect: the missing part may still seem to exist, and may even be painfully absent. (For further information on whether the left or right side is likely to create more pain see the chapter on Dominance.)

Treatment of phantom pain is about as unsatisfactory as knowledge of its cause, which stands to reason. Some argue it is a disruption of the central nervous system; others that it is wholly psychological; but there is, as yet, no general remedy. This fact has not stopped claims for success, with the allegedly beneficial procedures including: the implantation of electrodes; hypnosis; various surgical incisions in the brain; psychotherapy; hitting the stump; cutting various nerves; injecting anaesthetic as near as possible to the missing, painful part; and several drugs. Analgesics, normally given to quell pain, do not work, presumably because there is no normal pain to quell. Such drugs can, despite their impotence, create addiction to them and, according to a review article in the *British Medical Journal* (of December 1978), 'should be avoided'.

Phantom limb pain is not the same as stump pain, although both may coexist. Stump pain is genuine (if that word has meaning) and is stimulated locally. Phantom pain is, whether psychological in origin or induced within the central nervous system, a more general problem. An injection of saline can bring it on, or a pinching of the skin at particular spots on the body (and on the same or the opposing side). Hence the belief that some form of counter-irritation can work and disrupt the pain, as with electrodes implanted at appropriate points.

Convincing others of intractable pain is always a problem, particularly if an alleged pain-killer has already been administered. Convincing others of pain from phantom limbs, breasts or genitalia must be doubly problematical, particularly if the usual forms of pain-killing have achieved nothing whatsoever.

Enkephalins and endorphins Encephalon is a term for the complete brain. However, an enkephalin, literally meaning 'within the brain', is a brand-new term, coined in the mid-1970s. It identifies a molecule found in the brain that has considerable similarities to morphine. In fact, two new molecules were found; met-enkephalin and leu-enkephalin. Although quickly dubbed as natural opiates they are both chemically different from morphine. They are peptides, or sequences of amino-acids that form part of a protein. (Morphine is an alkaloid, and contains its nitrogen as part of a ring.) The reason why their discovery was so exciting had three different angles: they could answer the ancient query why morphine has such an effect on the brain; they showed that the brain produces its own opiates; and they hinted at the possibility of producing the most effective pain-killer of them all by stimulating the brain's natural pain-killing system.

These first two endogenous opiates were discovered in 1975 by two Aberdeen researchers, John Hughes and Hans Kosterlitz. The excitement they generated spurred on similar work, and very speedily other such chemicals were discovered that had even greater opiate potency. The extended form of met-enkephalin, known as beta-endorphin, is much more powerful. So too the extended leu-enkephalin, known as dynorphin. What seems to be happening is that these substances permit (or cause) the brain to control its own pain threshold. Everything is intertwined; the opiates affect the brain amines, the brain amines affect mood, and pain appreciation is thereby inevitably altered. In a loose sort of way such a system had long been suspected: the soldier does not feel his wound in the heat of battle. He may even be glad thereafter that it permits him honourable retirement from the war. Similarly the very unevenness of pain had led people to suspect that some dampening system existed: a pinprick is so hurtful but a wound tenthousandfold more damaging does not create a proportionate quantity of pain. Therefore, it is very neat that the power of morphine (derived from plants) is both satisfactorily explained and, in that unravelling, explains how pain itself is modulated.

The work really began in 1973 when a team from Johns Hopkins School of Medicine, Baltimore, proved the existence of special recognition sites within the brain for morphine-like compounds. The search was then on for such self-made compounds – plainly the brain had not prepared its receptor sites for the day when mankind would learn how to extract opiates from plants – and the Aberdeen researchers were the first to come up with an answer. The work and the search have now moved on to question how this new-found mechanism can be put to use. Can it be of help clinically in the control of pain? Does it explain the curious merits of acupuncture? Is there relevance in the body's self-administering of opiates to stress, to drug-dependence, to tolerance?

Unfortunately – for simplicity – current work is merely banishing much of the straightforwardness that seemed to exist beforehand. Firstly, there are now known to be several different kinds of receptor site. Secondly, morphine (of the type from plants) and enkephalins (self-made) do not appear to work in similar fashion as was originally believed. Thirdly, the inevitable pursuit of a morphine-like compound that is non-addictive seems to be receding from its goal. Fourthly, when beta-endorphins are measured in patients with acute pain their levels are very low; there is no easy relationship between degree of pain and degree of natural pain-killer. And fifthly (although the list is longer still, and apparently endless), naloxone does not appear to be effective. This drug is a specific antagonist to opiates and, therefore, should counteract the pain-killing attributes of endorphins. A very mixed bag of experiments has been carried out on an assortment of techniques, all of which induce analgesia (of a kind), such as hypnosis, placebos, nitrous oxide anaesthesia (laughing gas), acupuncture, and even the fakir's bed of nails. Naloxone has been found both to enhance the effect, to diminish it, and also to be without any influence whatsoever. As A. Goldstein wrote in 'A Critical Review' of this subject the effect of naloxone on pain 'has been negative, ambiguous, or conflicting, and even the positive results have been less than dramatic'.

Acupuncture has been studied with particular devotion in the hope that this ancient art could be explained by some very modern knowledge. It so happened that the man-made opioids (which are also made by animals for themselves, having even been discovered in the earthworm as well as higher forms) were achieving world publicity just when Chinese surgeons were most publicly showing that open-heart investigations could be performed with no more anaesthesia than is granted by the twiddling of a few needles. Plainly, or so it was immediately assumed, acupuncture liberated natural opioids. The patients, or so it was imagined, had merely anaesthetised themselves with their own endorphins.

So much for plain thinking. The facts were rather different. As was written in an article on the 'Biology of Opioid Peptides' the compounds appeared 'to create euphoria not only in experimental animals but also indirectly in the investigators themselves'. It was learned that the use of acupuncture for surgical anaesthesia had not been known before Mao ruled China, and it was, therefore, suspected that the specifically Chinese, non-Western form of medicine was being stretched unduly for political gain. Even so, only 10 per cent of patients were given surgical acupuncture, and their number was carefully selected. Moreover they were given supplementary anaesthesia (by other means) and, despite this, only a third of them achieved satisfactory anaesthesia, at least according to an article by T. M. Murphy and J. J. Bonica. (This last name is of no casual worker in this field, but of the man to whom most credit should go for the establishment of pain clinics, for the fresh approach to pain relief, and even for the International Association for the Study of Pain.)

In a *Lancet* leader summing up the surgical merits of acupuncture, entitled 'Endorphins Through the Eye of a Needle', there is not only an abnormal degree of levity but a general condemnation of the Maoist approach. It states that such 'anaesthesia' tapered off rapidly after the Gang of Four had fallen. Two Chinese professors even denounced surgical acupuncture as 'a myth and a political hoax' in a Shanghai newspaper. The *Lancet* added that 'at least a dozen studies have shown that the traditional Yin-Yang meridian points are not essential', that pain relief after acupuncture 'did not differ from that in placebo groups' and even the 'needles are, in fact, needless'. In traditional acupuncture the 'monotonous task' of rotating needles manually can be simulated by passing electric pulses through them, but the needlessness arises because 'stimulation with surface electrodes is more effective'. In stating that 'acupuncture has not fulfilled expectations' the *Lancet* conceded that 'it has helped to advance our knowledge of pain control'. Its recent discovery 'has served both to satisfy a taste for things

Oriental and mystical, and also to promote work on the physiology and control of pain in general and on stimulation-analgesia in particular'.

As for the endorphins and enkephalins, work on them is still proceeding apace. Other opioid peptides are being found in the brain. The processing of pain is plainly only part of the story, and perhaps the minor part. People also vary greatly in their opioid levels, which may explain why responses are so different and experiments so confusing. Even the placebo effect has come under scrutiny. This diminishing of pain for no apparent cause may actually result from self-made opiates. Proof – of a sort – has come from the manner in which naloxone, the opiate blocker, can actually create pain in someone recently relieved of it by a placebo. The human placenta has been found to contain extremely high concentrations of endorphins, temptingly situated to suggest a role in suppressing child-birth pain. Although the botanical opiates are generally addictive there is, as yet, no simple explanation why man-made opiates are not equally so. What is becoming plainer, with every score of papers published on the subject, is that the body's opiates are not independent items, performing one precise, well-defined role. They are part of the system, located almost everywhere, linked to the endocrines, associated with behaviour, influential in mental breakdown, critical in pain control, most relevant to sex (when endorphins rise dramatically), and one more branch of human chemistry. The more staggering fact is that this crucial aspect of neurology has only surfaced within the last decade. What next of equal importance, it is easy to wonder, is waiting in the wings?

PART FOUR

It is easy to speak of the human brain as if it is one thing, like a replicated product of industry. Instead it is highly variable, ranging from genius to idiot, with 'abnormal ability' indicating both ends of the spectrum. It can also be badly made, as in the congenital malformations, and each brain can be damaged during its own lifetime. Part Four is of these aspects, the different kinds of abnormality.

12. Abnormal Ability

Genius / Precociousness / Prodigy / Norbert Wiener / Education / Mental deficiency / Mental institutions / Causes of retardation

> Great wits are sure to madness near allied
> — John Dryden

> No great genius is without some mixture of insanity
> — Aristotle, as reported by Seneca

> Good sense is the absence of every strong passion, and only men of strong passion can be great
> — Comte de Mirabeau

> No man is a hero to his valet-de-chambre – *the proverb to which Georg Hegel added:* but not because the former is no hero, but because the latter is a valet

> If you can keep your head while all about you are losing theirs, perhaps you've misjudged the situation
> — Kipling and Anon

On the day before his fifth birthday Francis Galton picked up a pen and wrote to his sister:

> My dear Adèle, I am 4 years old and I can read any English book. I can say all the Latin Substantives and Adjectives and active verbs besides 52 lines of Latin poetry. I can cast up any sum in addition and can multiply by 2, 3, 4, 5, 6, 7, 8, (9), 10, (11). I can also say the pence table. I read French a little and I know the clock. Francis Galton, February 15th, 1827.

Numbers 9 and 11 are here bracketed because, due to delayed truthfulness or modesty, one was scratched out and the other pasted over. Presumably the letter was one of stock-taking rather than revelation for Adèle had been instructing him since his earliest years and earliest months. She taught him all twenty-six letters so that he could point to them before he could speak. He knew all the capital letters by his first birthday, and both alphabets (upper and lower case) by eighteen months. Before he was three he could read and sign his name. By the age of seven he was absorbing Cowper, Pope and Shakespeare for pleasure, and needed only to read a page twice to be able to repeat it. Sir Francis Galton was an undoubted prodigy and he became an undoubted genius. His IQ has been posthumously assessed at 'not far from 200'. (He achieved the 'Sir' when aged eighty-seven, and two years before his death.)

Galton, apart from being one himself, took a great interest in geniuses. The end of the nineteeth century and the start of the twentieth was a period of keen concern over human origins. Much of it became side-tracked into racism, where the belief spread that human inheritance of, say, intelligence was as simple as the transmission of haemophilia, blue eyes, or any single gene characteristic. However, much of the work was a straightforward attempt to discover where human excellence or deficiency sprang from. Undeniably some traits were created or adapted by the environment. Equally undeniably others were inherited. Yet others were both born and made, genetically conceived and then nurtured wholesomely, like water poured on seed. Because the most distinctive human attribute is intelligence, and because some men and women soar above others, there was naturally tremendous interest in the parents they had, what signs they showed, and whether the brilliance was echoed in succeeding generations.

Cesare Lombroso of Turin University was one such seeker after genius truth who, in 1905, published the essence of his findings. For example, he gave lists of those who were geniuses *and* had some other distinction, such as:

Short stature – Alexander, Aristotle, Archimedes, Attila, John Hunter (5'2"), William Blake (scarcely 5'0"), St Francis Xavier (4'6". Discovered after his coffin was opened in 1890.)
Deformity – Aesop, Giotto, St Bernard, Erasmus, Newton, Adam Smith, Boyle, Pope, Nelson, Wren.
Odd-shaped head – Dante, Machiavelli, Robert Bruce, Kant.
Receding forehead – Byron, Humboldt, Ximenes, Donizetti.
Hydrocephalus – Milton, Linnaeus, Cuvier, Gibbon.
Stammer – Aristotle, Aesop, Demosthenes, Virgil, Charles Darwin, Charles V.
Vagabondage – Byron, Tasso, Goldsmith, Sterne, Petrarch, Cellini, Cervantes.

The labour involved in his *The Man of Genius* was outstanding but the general statements made possible by Lombroso's research were very few. He was fascinated by the deficiencies of the great: 'Genius is often associated with anomalies in that organ which is the source of its glory.' The fact that nearly all men of genius have differed as much from their fathers as from their mothers 'is one of the marks of degeneration'. Exceptions to this rule were Julius Caesar, Napoleon, Sterne and Voltaire whose 'degeneracy' lay in their deviation from the norm. (In Lombroso's view degeneracy was a deficiency of normality. It was degenerate to be different from the rest, whether superior or inferior. Similarly in evolution, so he argued, it was degenerate to lose a tail, or hair, or a quadrupedal stance and become a bipedal, hairless, naked ape.)

Disappointingly for Lombroso, but still fascinating, was the elucidated fact that so few geniuses left their mark genetically. Bacon had earlier made the same point: 'The care of posterity is most in them that have no posterity.' So too Michelangelo: 'I have more than enough of a wife in my art'; and Adam Smith who 'reserved his gallantry for his books'. Certainly many geniuses were celibate, such as Kant, Newton, Beethoven, Galileo, Descartes, Spinoza, Florence Nightingale, Leonardo, Copernicus, Handel, Chateaubriand, Flaubert, Cavour. Many others left either no children or children who had not occasion to pass on their all-important genetic inheritance. It has even been said that 'not one' of the great English poets had, in this sense, any posterity, among them Shakespeare, Jonson, Milton, Dryden, Pope, Goldsmith, Addison, Keats, Shelley. To be a genius, it seems, is quite sufficient.

Havelock Ellis, better known for his writings on sex, published *A Study of British Genius* in 1904. He sought generalities, and found that thirty-six was the average age of those who fathered geniuses (with very few fathers under thirty). Mothers too were relatively old, averaging thirty-one, with scarcely a single mother under twenty-five producing a British genius. One parent dying after the genius birth occurred in 'a large number' of the cases. Musicians were rarely offspring of great musicians (Bach's predecessors were 'craftsmen'), and many geniuses were either first or last of the brood. Of the 1,030 investigated by Ellis, 7 were born at seven months, 14 were not expected to live at birth, 110 were 'delicate in childhood' and 213 had a generally weak physique, although many of these weak infants became strong adults, such as Jeremy Bentham, Burke, Constable, Dickens, Galt and Hobbes. For the British Isles in general Scotland produced an above-average number (per unit of population), Wales less than average,

Kent was pre-eminent, and East Anglia was particularly good for women.

So who, one wonders, was a genius? According to Ellis anyone with more than three pages in the sixty-six-volume *Dictionary of National Biography*, save for those who did not merit such an entry (many royals, and 'miscreants' such as Titus Oates) and those who should have had three pages but did not owing to a lack of fact about them. The *DNB* of his time had 30,000 entries and his chosen 1,030 therefore amounted to 3.4 per cent.

A particularly diligent delver into past intelligence was Catherine Morris Cox whose *The Early Mental Traits of Three Hundred Geniuses* was published in 1926. She investigated such items as family standing, interests, education, school standing, friends and associates, reading, production and achievement, evidence of precocity – all up to the age of seventeen. Despite scant data for many subjects she classified everyone into IQ groupings, 100–110, 110–120, and so on upwards. The lists produce strange bedfellows; such as, for the 100–110 group, Bunyan, Cervantes, James Cook, William Cobbett, Copernicus, Drake, Faraday, and Mehemet Ali of Egypt. Others investigated were, for example, Schiller, William H. Seward, Rubens, Kepler, Dumas (père), Carlyle (all 140–150), Walter Scott and Longfellow (150–160), Coleridge, Voltaire (170 –180), Goethe, Pascal (180–190), and John Stuart Mill (190–200). The infant Carlyle made his very first sentence at eleven months, but most showed 'no evidence of precocity'. Quite a few demonstrated very little evidence of anything, such as Thomas Cromwell: 'Interests – no record; Friends – no record; Reading – no record; Production – no record; Precocity – no record'. He is listed as 110–120, partly because his Puritan schoolmaster reported him having 'quick and lively apprehension, a piercing and sagacious wit, and a solid judgment'.

Precociousness need not be a forerunner to genius, but often is. Mozart was playing the piano at three, picking out thirds at four, and composing at five. Pierre Gassendi, the French philosopher/ scientist, preached little sermons at four, explained the movements of the moon at seven, and harangued a bishop in Latin at ten. Torquato Tasso, Italian poet, spoke at six months, studied grammar at three years, and was allegedly 'pretty well acquainted' with Latin and Greek at seven. The future Cardinal Wolsey took his BA at Oxford aged fifteen. William Thompson (later Lord Kelvin), scientist, entered Glasgow University at ten. Albrecht von Haller, Swiss polymath, preached to the servants at three, and made lexicons at eight which contained all Greek and Hebrew words in both testaments. Jeremy Bentham, English philosopher/reformer, learned his letters before he could speak, and Latin and Greek at four. John Stuart Mill, philosopher/economist, maintained at five an animated conversation with Lady Spencer on the merits of Marlborough and Wellington. There must be legend in many of these facts, but there is also truth that brilliance can shine extraordinarily early.

Schools seem to be poor judges of genius enrolled among their number, it being almost a cliché among biographies and autobiographies that the great ones did poorly when at school. Isaac Newton's undergraduate studies were not distinguished, and in 1663 he failed a Cambridge exam owing to woeful inadequacy in geometry. (Six years later he was appointed to the chair of mathematics, and published a detailed account of his discoveries in optics.) The Duke of Wellington (to be) left Eton at fifteen because he was unhappy and unsuccessful there (although his Waterloo was allegedly won on its playing fields). James Maxwell, the physicist, failed to distinguish himself at Edinburgh Academy before the age of thirteen, but thereafter suddenly developed his intellectual powers. (Sir) Edward Grey, Britain's famous foreign minister, was sent down from Oxford for incorrigible idleness. Presidents Washington, Lincoln and Truman never went near a college. Albert Einstein was troublesome at school – 'your presence in the classroom is disruptive and affects the other pupils', was eventually expelled, and published his theory of relativity eleven years later. Charles Dickens, Mark Twain and Maxim Gorky did not reach the equivalent of secondary school. Other early drop-outs were George Stephenson, Thomas Alva Edison, and the Wright brothers. Walter Scott was 'a dunce'; Hume 'uncommon weak-minded'; and (Cardinal) Wiseman 'dull and stupid, always reading and thinking'. Fanny Burney did not even 'know her letters' at eight, but then leapt ahead to write poems and stories at ten. Charles Darwin gained 'little benefit' from Shrewsbury School, and Edinburgh University made it clear that medicine was not for him. For many of the famous-to-be school was not for them.

> I was found unable to answer a single question in the Latin paper. I wrote my name at the top of the page. I wrote down the number of the question '1'. After much reflection I put a bracket round it thus '(1)'. But thereafter I could not think of anything connected with it that was either relevant or true.

Thus a good many schoolchildren in their time, both the brilliant and the dull, but that particular abstraction was by Winston Churchill.

Admittedly Churchill had a busy, largely absentee mother and a harassed, largely absent-minded father, but the critical role of parents is a recurring theme. Many geniuses were driven on by their fathers in particular, educated at home, taken away from school. If they had no ambition it was often coerced in them, sternly or just doggedly. In compelling everyone to attend school, and taking education away from home, the opportunity for eccentricity, of which genius is a part, was diminished. It is easy to wonder what would have happened to one genius of modern times, the creator of cybernetics, professor of mathematics at the Massachusetts Institute of Technology, and undoubted prodigy. Unlike great brains from the past about whom so little is known – every certain fact about the life of William Shakespeare would not cover one sheet of paper – Norbert Wiener (who died in 1964) wrote an excellent account of himself in *Ex-prodigy: My Childhood and Youth*.

He was curious about his endowment, wondered what might have caused it and wondered how and when it showed itself. At the outset he makes the valid point that

> it is impossible for the child, whether he be prodigy or not, to compare the earlier stages of his intellectual development with those of other children until he has reached a level of social consciousness which does not begin until late childhood . . . In one's earlier stages of learning, one is one's own norm, and if one is confused, the only possible answer is that of the Indian, 'Me not lost, wigwam lost'.

Wiener started reading at three and a half, was 'not yet fluent' at six but was an 'omnivorous reader' by eight, preferring true adventures of naturalists to those in story books. He was then banned from such exercise by 'rapidly advancing myopia'. An interest in chemistry at seven provoked his father to organise a 'little laboratory' in the nursery. (Many a child loves test-tubes; few fathers set up laboratories.) His arithmetic at the time was 'adequate but unorthodox' for he preferred short-cuts such as adding 9 by subtracting 1 and adding 10. He was still inclined to do sums on his fingers, with arithmetic being his chief deficiency as the 'manipulative drill' bored him. So his father took him out of school until the lad was ten, put him on algebra rather than arithmetic, and took over all his teaching, whether directly or indirectly. Algebra was not hard for the boy, although my father's way of teaching it was scarcely conducive to peace of mind. Every mistake had to be corrected as it was made . . . By this time I was weeping and terrified . . . My lessons often ended in a family scene. Father was raging. I was weeping and my mother did her best to defend me. She suggested at times that the noise was disturbing the neighbours . . .

(Fathers, it would seem, who trouble to set up laboratories are not plain sailing.)

The young Wiener entered high school aged nine as a 'special student', and went to Tufts College aged eleven. (His father turned down the idea of Harvard partly because publicity would surround such a youthful entrant.) At Tufts he was 'already beyond the normal freshman work in mathematics' and, there being no suitable course, one was created for him on the Theory of Equations. He graduated *cum laude* aged fourteen, but failed to be elected Phi Beta Kappa. 'Thus my graduation from Tufts forced me to face one of the greatest realisations that the infant prodigy must make: he is not wanted by the community.' Wiener admits a theory exists that prodigies burn themselves out, collapse early and are doomed to 'second-rateness, if not to the breadline and the madhouse'. In countering, or explaining, these presumed eventualities he adds, 'My experience leads me to believe that the prodigy is desperately unsure of himself and underrates himself . . . Hence, he goes through a stage when his mass of conflicts is greater than that of most other children, and he is rarely a pretty picture'.

This particular ugly picture entered Harvard in 1909 aged fourteen, together with four other infant prodigies. At least three, says Wiener, came from homes with very ambitious fathers. He tried uniting the group, but failed. To be a prodigy was 'no more a basis for social unity than the wearing of glasses or the possession of false teeth'. In 1910, and when fifteen, he discovered he was Jewish. Clues – if not too modest a word – advocating this fact had been several: his father's mother always took a Hebrew newspaper, his cousin said he was a Jew (although his mother contradicted her), and his father had translated some Yiddish poetry into English. It can seem strange that any offspring, even faced with parental denial, would not have realised such a truth; it seems stranger yet that one of hyper-intelligence should have failed to do so. He found it doubly shocking on learning his mother's maiden name of Kahn was but a less blatant variant of Cohen. The discovery of Jewishness increased his 'feelings of resentment, despair and rejection'. At all events, after a spell at Cornell, he returned to

Harvard, when almost seventeen, as a candidate for a philosophy PhD.

He had three siblings: two younger sisters and a brother eleven years younger. His father, aware of success with Norbert, tried the same teaching technique initially upon the girls. It failed. They were undoubtedly cleverer than most, but did not respond to paternal tuition. 'This was laid to their being girls, unable to stand up to the severe discipline.' Although the younger boy was frail, and without detectably exceptional powers, he too was given the stern, parental training, and the adolescent Norbert was expected to assist. Unfortunately father Wiener had written 'in ineffaceable printer's ink' that his number one success was 'not so much a result of any superior ability . . . as of his training'. According to Norbert this statement 'declared to the public that my failures were my own but my successes were my father's'. The degree of fraternal cooperation soon became nothing more than might be expected between a seventeen-year-old and his six-year-old kid brother.

Readers of *Ex-prodigy* will find little remarkable to parallel the academic achievements. Wiener seems to have been a fairly ordinary boy in other spheres, totally forgetting the language (French) he learned early and moved away from, falling in love aged eleven, worshipping and then judging his parents, and being fairly destructive of school chemistry equipment. The only recurring abnormality is his age at which various academic achievements came to pass, coupled with the remorseless hot-house fervour from Wiener senior; but Weiner junior was an undoubted prodigy, not just ahead of most but a whole leap ahead. A prodigy, it seems, is akin to a human giant or dwarf, not just taller or shorter than others but a different kind of size. Perhaps something occurs equivalent to the causes of giantism or dwarfism, or perhaps a stern, demanding, aggressive, ambitious father is of a totally different order to the weary, harassed, un-single-minded teacher who may give least attention rather than most to the brightest in the class.

The young Wiener eventually left home and became an adult. 'I had to learn to study away from the example of my dominating father, and to regulate my affairs among people to whom my record as an infant prodigy meant exactly nothing.' His accomplishments, which were legion, 'did not begin to take their full form' until his mid-twenties because a scientist is not at his best 'until he has learned to draw success from confusion and failure, and to improvise new and effective ideas on the basis of procedures which he has begun fortuitously and without purpose'. As to a prodigy being a candle that burns too brightly and too soon, 'the early start I have had does not appear to me to have impeded me from showing a period of productivity continuing reasonably late, and has greatly increased the level at which I started this productivity.' 'Thus,' he concludes, 'it has added years to my useful life.'

Nowhere in his book does Norbert Wiener describe which of his childhood mental achievements were most astounding. That may be just as well in a world which, almost entirely, still fails to understand the excellence of, say, Einstein's initial theory, a piece of history now three-quarters of a century old. Maybe the brilliance of the brilliant can be understood only by the nearly brilliant. 'Are you a genius?' someone once asked of Lev Landau, the Russian theoretical physicist. He answered: 'Niels Bohr is, and Einstein is; I'm not. But I'm very talented. Yes, I'm very talented.' Only geniuses or the very talented can comprehend such fine distinction.

And how many of us can begin to appreciate what is going on in the brains of those extraordinary arithmeticians who have achieved honours in the *Guinness Book of Records*. Mrs Shakuntala Devi, of India, multiplied 7,686,369,774,870 by 2,465,099,745,779 to reach the correct answer of 18,947,668,177,995,426,773,730 in just 26 seconds. (The two initial numbers were picked at random by a computer.) William Klein, of Holland, found the 13th root of a 100-digit number in 2 minutes and 9 seconds. Like prodigies such people are not just better. They tower above the base-line of normality, not in everything by any means but in their particular skill. One-third of the adult British, by comparison, cannot divide 65 by 5 correctly or even add 1 to 6,399. The human arithmetical mind, it would seem, is either pathetic or incomprehensible.

Education 'It is surely ironic that the most able and talented children in western societies, such as Britain, the United States and Canada, by and large receive the worst education,' wrote Philip Vernon in his book on gifted children. Public education systems often make provision for unfortunate children, the physically or mentally handicapped, but are less willing to make similar arrangements at the other end of the scale. The very clever are undoubtedly able and this militates against them. They have advantage; so why give them more?

Some facts. Just as there are 2.3 per cent of the population with an IQ less than 70, who are classified as feeble-minded or moron (40–69), low-grade or imbecile (20–39), and idiot (0–19), so is there another 2.3 per cent with an IQ of 130 and above. At the chronological age of ten a few children in every large group will have the mental capacity of fourteen to fifteen year-olds, while others will be like seven-year-olds. Such differentiation is less among the five-year-olds, but is perhaps less important then. Girls more often excel linguistically (though not in vocabulary), in memory, and finger dexterity. Boys are best in mathematics, the physical sciences and general information (according to Vernon). Almost all tests, wrote J. P. Guilford in 1950, are 'convergent'; the pupil is expected to arrive at, or converge to, the one right, fixed answer, without opportunity to display novelty. Leta Hollingworth, psychologist, said the student of IQ 140 wastes half his time in the ordinary classroom, while an IQ 180 wastes almost all of it.

Schemes to isolate gifted children have often been condemned as élitist. Euphemistic initials have arisen to obscure the issue, such as MGM (mentally gifted minors), HAP (high academic potential), and AcTal (academically talented). A Canadian questionnaire stressed what to look for in seeking out the gifted, the HAPs, MGMs, and so forth. The youngsters are not necessarily those with the highest marks, or are the most attentive, or docile, but: the hardest to keep busy and interested; the quickest to learn; the most fluent and grammatical; those with the most remarkable range of knowledge (whether general or specialised); the askers of awkward or unusual questions; the most curious; the creators of imaginative work often technically inaccurate; and those who show most concentration and initiative in their chosen subjects. Least frequently discovered are the gifted in three main groups: minorities (or those of 'low occupation status'); girls; and rural children. (Only 5 per cent of Cox's geniuses came from the homes of semi-skilled or unskilled workers. Notables in this category were Kepler, Gauss, Faraday, Burns, Pasteur, Luther, and Kant.)

So what happens to the gifted, even if detected? The answer, in general, is very little. In Britain they are allowed to advance one year (some 5–10 per cent), perhaps two (less than 1 per cent), but hardly ever the kind of quantum leap they merit. The recent case of Ruth Lawrence, who passed her O-level Maths at nine (normally taken at fifteen to sixteen), her A-level Maths at ten (normally eighteen) plus a special more advanced paper at the same time, attracted considerable publicity. She had, it is almost needless to say after Wiener's story, been taken out of school and taught by her parents. Surprisingly she was accepted by a university at twelve, which was her wish, rather than eighteen. The so-called special regulation has permitted quite a few children to attend university at sixteen, but a two-year advancement is insignificant for the 1 in 1,000 who are exceptionally gifted. Among the forty-five universities in Britain there are only fourteen, including Oxford, that do not specify a minimum age. At a recent conference in Cambridge on the Gifted Child a statement from Oxford University suggested that brilliant young mathematicians should be 'discouraged for a few years' because there has been no precedent for extremely early entrance since the Renaissance.

When Ruth's parents proposed that she should take further A-levels at her local technical college, such exams being a prerequisite to university acceptance, the local government authority demurred, suggesting she should first see a psychologist. There is a suspicion among many that promotion according to mental ability rather than number of birthdays will lead to distress, but Philip Vernon has pointed out that students advanced in the first quarter of this century, when the system was less inflexible,

> not only fully maintained their academic position and achieved better results than their older classmates, but showed no more social or emotional maladjustment than occurs among non-accelerated bright students . . . There can be little doubt that greater harm is done to the development of many children's personalities by refusal to accelerate than by acceleration.

Quite the most impressive long-term study of exceptional ability is that initiated by L. M. Terman. Called *Genetic Studies of Genius*, and published in five volumes (so far) between 1925 and 1959 by the University of Stanford Press, it followed and is still following the progress of a thousand gifted children. They were selected by teachers, by IQ (all were 135 or above) and other tests, and represented the brightest 1 per cent of children in the state of California at the time. (Their mean birth year was 1912 and so the group has now reached its early seventies.) Facts discovered were: physical health and growth were above normal from birth onwards; marriage rates were normal with divorce rates being below normal; 68 per cent graduated from college (or eight times normal for California); and acceleration, via grade-skipping or early college entry, produced no ill-effects, such students fully justifying their promotion. Ternan died in 1957, but the work is continuing. More reports are to be published, including data on the children of that class of 1912.

Education, by and large, is addicted to birthdays, even though age of maturity is most uneven. One child may be a foot taller than his similarly-aged classmates. Puberty is a change that occurs from nine to eighteen among normal children. Intelligence is a similar variable. The standard school curriculum lasts from five to sixteen. Some pupils could happily achieve the same degree of learning in half that time. Others should take longer. Some will always be half a dozen years ahead of their age-mates; others will be six years behind. The schools may try to suppress these facts, but the variables exist. The argument that catering for the super-intelligent would create an élite has been countered by many, such as Philip Vernon: 'This minority already exists whether we decide to ignore or repress it, or to educate it as it deserves.' Britain has ESN schools for the educationally sub-normal. It has none for the educationally above-normal. The Soviet Union has more special schools than any Western country. Russian educators, according to one author, 'regard the absence of selection of the talented as a waste of the nation's most valuable resource'. Intelligent mathematicians, for example, are extracted from the general system at fourteen, and are given five more hours of maths a week at a much higher level. So too with linguists.

It is said by many a sociologist that childhood is a recent invention, largely Victorian in origin. Until then children were just small people, less strong, less wise, less capable of earning a living. With the invention has come a belief that children should be permitted to behave in their own childish way. When the brilliant cellist Yo-Yo Ma (taught from the age of four, with a one-sixteenth size instrument, by his father) was taken before the grand old man of the cello, Pablo Casals, the patriarch retorted: 'What are you doing with this child? You must let him go and play in the street.' Presumably the young Ma would have been happy to do so, instead of playing the passage correctly three consecutive times after any mistake, one of his father's strictures. Even Wiener, so self-aware, has no easy answer: 'I was not so much a mixture of child and man as wholly a child for purposes of companionship and nearly completely a man for purposes of study.' Society itself is confused. A mother living in the Manchester problem area of Moss Side was told her son aged nine had an IQ of 167. 'But he's such a nice boy,' she replied.

Mental deficiency   Just as there are individuals well above normal, so are there others well below. There are the efficient and the deficient, both ends of the Bell curve. In contriving to refer to the bottom of the scale by less direct titles than idiot, imbecile, moron, retarded, feeble-minded, and so forth, the Americans in particular have called them exceptional. This arch unwillingness to call spades as spades is not wholly welcomed, but is perfect for the context of this chapter. Both the quick-witted and the dim-witted are equally exceptional, being equidistant from the central norm.

Nevertheless society as a whole views the matter differently. Even though the very, very tall are considered to be just as aberrant as the very, very short, and to have six fingers is as odd as to have four, the mentally backward are not regarded in the same fashion as the mentally forward. We do not see them as equally deviant from the mean. If the mentally deficient were allowed today to roam the streets, like the village idiot in the past, we might have a better perspective; but, in general, we do not let them roam. We scarcely let them work or form a part of public life.

The brilliant, talented, and exceptional at the upper end of the scale are not classified into genius, intellectual, brainy, or any such category. However there is considerable classification at the bottom, partly because society has to care for such individuals to a greater or lesser degree.

In Britain there are 50,000 people living in hospitals for the mentally handicapped, and 20,000 of them have been there for twenty years or more. The total number of mentally handicapped people is almost three times that hospital figure, with home rather than any institution caring for them. In India, with its greater population, the numbers are of course far larger. An official conservative estimate puts the totals as five million for the chronic psychotics, five million for those with severe mental subnormality, and two million epileptics. The World Health Organisation, in surveying the planet as a whole, considers that severe mental illness affects 1–2 per cent, mental retardation 1–3 per cent and epilepsy 1 per cent. Assuming the lower percentages this means a total of 135 million with gross mental abnormality; but assuming the higher ones the total is 270 million, or more than the population of the United States.

It is always good to be reminded in any general discussion that individuals are involved. A recent letter to the *British Medical Journal* pointed out that many inmates of British mental hospitals had been inside since World War One. Some were celebrating their diamond jubilee, if that phrase is apt. In the Meanwood Park Hospital, Leeds, there was one sixty-year inhabitant and thirty-five others with over fifty years out of a total of 350 residents. The letter continued even more disturbingly:

As might be expected, these longest-stay patients represent mainly the more intelligent group of residents who would never be accepted in hospital today. In a sense they are a lost generation of their time, people who have spent a lifetime in hospital, which should never happen again. They were the victims of a system which society now acknowledges to have been wrong.

The current tendency to take people out of institutions whenever possible may err on occasion, may transform one form of care into another, or may merely lead to repeated admissions; but anything sounds better than a lifelong stay which society then acknowledges to have been wrong.

Causes of retardation   Mental retardation may be caused either genetically or environmentally. Even if the influences are environmental they were probably at work before or shortly after birth. Therefore retardation is almost always a problem for life. According to geneticist Lionel Penrose a few years ago some 20 per cent of mental retardation is known to be due to environmental factors, 15 per cent to chromosome abnormalities, and 7 per cent to single gene disorders, of which 5 per cent are recessive, 1 per cent dominant, and 1 per cent X-linked. A further 15 per cent are due to a more muddled form of inheritance, the 'accumulation of unfavourable alleles at many genetic loci', as a leading article in the *Lancet* phrased it. The remainder of mental retardation, some 43 per cent, has no known cause at present. There are more males than females both in this category and in the preceding one where many genes are involved. Therefore, the obvious searching place for extra deformities is along the sex chromosomes, providing as they do the principal inherited difference between men and women.

Penrose's pointing up of the male predominance in mental retardation – about 30 per cent more than females – was made in a Medical Research Council (London) report of 1938. The next significant paper on this subject was published by Herbert Lubs during 1969 in the *American Journal of Human Genetics*. Entitled 'A Marker X Chromosome', it provided the sort of news that everyone had been waiting for, a deficiency on the male's singleton X-chromosome. (Females have two X-chromosomes, males only one, and therefore an X-chromosome deficiency is most likely to become evident in males. With females the presence of one deficient X-chromosome is likely to be masked, or rendered unimportant, by the presence of a normal X-chromosome.) Lubs had discovered a family in which many members carried an X-chromosome with an abnormal constriction near the end of the so-called long arm. Sometimes this arm had actually broken at the site of that constriction, as if its thinness had made it delicate. The condition thenceforth was known as the 'fragile X syndrome'. Those of the family with the single fragile X were mentally retarded, while the remaining males with a normal X were not. It was a most significant observation and was, therefore, as so frequently occurs (making a running refrain in this book), largely neglected. As the *New England Journal of Medicine* phrased it (in a review of 1980), the 'report appears to have been given inadequate immediate attention'.

The story then moved to Australia. There Dr S. Weiner encountered eight families similar to the one found by Lubs. He published this news in 1977, and so stirred the subject that it is now estimated about one-third of families with X-linked mental retardation are affected with the fragile X syndrome. In fact, as the *New England Journal* concluded: 'Next to trisomy 21 (Down's syndrome), it is the most common of the causes of mental retardation that can be specifically diagnosed.' More important still, and because it affects families, the genetic defect actually affects or concerns more people than does trisomy 21. Down's syndrome has only a very slight relationship with families, and comes both unheralded and unexpected, a bolt from the blue.

Not so with the fragile X. It behaves more like other X-linked errors, such as haemophilia, and everyone within a fragile X family is in need of genetic counselling. Most women in such families are unaffected (as with haemophilia), even those who have given birth to fragile X boys, but affected females are now being discovered. In one survey of 128 schoolgirls all with low IQ (55 to 75, and, therefore, mentally deficient), five of them were found to possess the fragile X. The families of these five girls were then examined (by G. Turner and her colleagues) and eighteen more heterozygotes were discovered. They were heterozygote because they had one deficient and one normal X-chromosome, and six of these eighteen were mentally retarded. It is odd that the mothers of fragile X boys, who might be assumed to be heterozygotes (and, therefore, similar to Turner's affected schoolgirls), are only very rarely mentally backward. Usually, with sex-linked abnormalities, the mother is the secret carrier of the abnormality as only she provides the X-chromosome for her son, the father's equivalent contribution being a Y. With mothers of fragile X boys something else is apparently happening as they are breaking the proper, genetic rules. It is also strange that some (six out of eighteen in Turner's survey) of the heterozygotes are affected mentally, and some not. This irregularity is also breaking rules. So too, as final confusion, the discovery of fragile X males with normal intelligence.

Further work will no doubt bring further enlightenment. After all it is only half a dozen years since Weiner found his eight affected families, and already it is being suspected (and occasionally confirmed) that over 2 per cent of all male mental institution inmates are inside because their solitary X-chromosome is of the fragile kind. And 2 per cent of the mentally retarded runs into hundreds of thousands of individuals, remembering that WHO estimate of 1–3 per cent of the total population being backward in this way.

Despite advance with fragile X, with trisomy 21, with other chromosomal abnormalities (less important than the first two), and other genetic defects (also less important numerically) plus all manner of environmental influences (atmospheric lead and vitamin deficiency being two under the current spotlight) the causes of mental retardation are still for the future to unravel. It is easy to say that some particular percentage of babies are born with Down's syndrome, thereby adding to the grand total of retarded adults, but the actual cause is still missing. Why that proportion? Why more to older mothers? Why that assortment of defects, in stature, palm prints, speech – and mentality? About five in a thousand live births have severe mental handicap. In about one-third is there a specific syndrome (of which the commonest is Down's). Most of the rest have structural defects of the brain that are not known to be hereditary. There is presumably a cause, somewhere and at some time, to make the brain not so much less than perfect as less adequate than normal. A further five in a thousand (or so, the figures varying widely according to different countries and differing definitions) have a slight mental handicap. Such people do not have severe mental abnormality but do need assistance for their survival, from either their loving ones or the social agencies. Therefore, a total of about ten in a thousand are mentally handicapped to some degree, whether or not a precise name is attached to their condition, and whether or not there is known inheritance.

'Insanity is hereditary; you get it from your children' runs the modern version. It might as well be true for all the gain that arises by believing it to be the other way about. Much of mental subnormality is inherited, but the actual causes – what leads to that extra chromosome No. 21? why the thinning or even snapping of the X? why faulty construction of the brain? – are still unknown. Until then the causes will continue to operate, and one in a hundred babies will be born with mental handicap. Or, taking the higher WHO figure, three in every hundred in the world.

Society has two needs in connection with the mentally ill: it must protect itself against those who are dangerous and it must care for them, whether dangerous or not. The dilemma is not a new one, having always existed. To some extent it will always exist. Each year in Britain about twenty thousand people are compulsorily detained in psychiatric and special hospitals. To be committed in this fashion only needs the say-so of one doctor, the responsible medical officer. Most of those detained have not been before a court of any kind, and will not have committed any offence punishable by law. The rights of the ordinary individual, acquired over centuries and enshrined in law and privilege, do not in general apply to the mentally sick. They apply far more to murderers, rapists and even enemies of the state than to those locked up because a doctor believed they should be. Criminals are awarded finite sentences. The mentally ill are given no such term; their sentences can be for life. They are just locked up and, unless released, will stay inside until they die.

Much of the procedure, according to MIND (Britain's National Association for Mental Health), is contrary to the European Convention of Human Rights. In fact Britain has been criticised by the European Court on more than one occasion for its handling of the mentally subnormal.

A committee of enquiry was set up in Britain in 1979 under the chairmanship of Sir John Boynton after a television documentary had been transmitted concerning Rampton Special Hospital. In 1980 this Boynton Committee published its findings and the *Lancet* in a leading article thought its description of the patient's day was 'particularly chilling'. During the night

> patients spend 11 hours locked in their rooms with no personal belongings, not even a radio. At about 8 a.m. they are woken, their beds are stripped and searched, and they proceed in single file to the sluice with their chamber-pots. They then collect a set of day clothes from a store and change in the main corridor under observation, handing their night clothes into the store. Patients make their beds and stand outside their rooms to have them inspected. Meals are eaten in silence. At lunch-time patients are allowed to watch the television, but anyone wishing to smoke has to leave the lounge to light his cigarette on a wall lighter in the corridor. Having lit his cigarette the patient waits on the threshold of the room and says 'Please can I come in sir?'

It is difficult to remember, after such a description, that the inmates are patients, not criminals, and they are sick. The difference is that their sickness is of the mental and not the physical kind. The Boynton Committee made 205 recommendations but, as the *Lancet* concluded, 'Time will tell whether the outrage evoked by this report is anything more than pious bluster.'

Britain, in general, is becoming increasingly aware of the mental health problems, and is blustering, and is on occasion amending the law, but it cannot point to any other country as being either ideal or better in its treatment of the mentally sub-normal. This is usually the easiest of arguments – A has a better system than we do; therefore, let us emulate A – but it is conspicuously absent in all the self-flagellation about the British condition. There is, in short, a universal wrong concerning the rights of the mentally abnormal.

After such gravity a little levity might be in order. The following story, worth reprinting in its entirety, comes from the *Hampstead and Highgate Express* (of London).

> I remember a Sunday afternoon in Hyde Park at Speaker's Corner being challenged by a heckler to prove that I was not mad. I found the situation somewhat tricky, so, hoping to play for time, I challenged the heckler to prove that he was not mad which, to my discomfiture, he did by producing his discharge certificate from a mental institution.

Game and set to the heckler, but lingering anxiety as to why the man had been inside, and for how long.

This chapter is headed Abnormal Ability, dealing as it does with both ends of the mental spectrum, the abnormally well constructed and the abnormally poorly made. Different in every particular they seem to have one overriding similarity: no one knows how best to deal with them. The very bright are suspect, inadequately educated and frequently poorly used thereafter. The feeble-minded are also suspect, poorly treated and frequently incarcerated as if alien to the human race. Normal, ordinary, run-of-the-mill is what we seem to prefer. No one should be exceptional.

13. Malformation

Neural tube defects/Spina bifida/Anencephaly/Hydrocephalus/
Hydrancephalics/Down's syndrome/Huntington's chorea

> All I can say, doctor, is that the boy never got anything
> congenital from my side of the family
> – quoted in *Medical News-Tribune*

> I am happy to tell you that your daughter is a mongol
> – paediatrician to British actor Brian Rix and his wife
> (in 1955)

Neural tube defects The conviction of *Homo sapiens* that its
nervous system is the most striking, subtle and highly developed of
all organs is mirrored by the facts about nervous malformation. If it
is the most complex system it might be expected that its manufacture is most frequently at fault and this, in general, is the case. In
Britain (and in other countries but particularly in Britain) neural
tube malformations, namely those that affect the development of
the brain and spinal cord, are the biggest single cause of still-birth.
Moreover, for the babies that survive birth, their nervous system is
still the commonest site for major error, such as anencephaly
(brainlessness), spina bifida (literally a spine split in two, but more
accurately a partial lack of fusion of the spinal canal), and hydrocephalus (excessive liquid within the cranial cavity). One or a
combination of these three occurs once in every 150 births.
Anencephaly is (almost always) incompatible with life, whereas
spina bifida cystica is compatible with it for varying lengths of time,
only about a quarter of its victims actually dying at birth. In the
earlier days of pregnancy there is a higher proportion of wrongly
made central nervous systems, about one in sixty. Of this number
of neural tube defects some two-fifths are aborted naturally (spontaneously), another two-fifths die at birth (such as the anencephalics), and the remaining fifth survive with varying degrees of
disability.

The central nervous system's defects vary greatly from country
to country, from mother to mother, and even with time. For
example, the incidence of spina bifida is extremely low in Finland

(about 0.2 per 1,000 births), and then rises via Norway (0.3), France (0.5), Sweden (0.7), United States (0.8), Spain (0.9) and Germany (0.9) to Canada (1 per 1,000). Such variance has not yet been explained, and is further compounded by the British situation. England has 2 cases per 1,000 births, Scotland 3 per 1,000, Wales 3.5 per 1,000, Northern Ireland 4.3 per 1,000 and South Wales on its own 6.5 per 1,000. The relatively modest differences between Finland, Sweden, Canada and the US are therefore swamped by the differences existing within the borders of Great Britain.

There is also a genetic relationship. If one parent has a neural tube defect there is a 4.5 per cent risk that an infant will do so. If a child has been born with an NTD (as it is abbreviated) there is a 5 per cent risk of the next sibling also possessing an NTD. If two children are so afflicted the risk goes up to 10 per cent, and if three it becomes 21 per cent. On incidence in general the British birth-rate fell fairly steadily from 1960 to 1980, but the number of NTDs dropped even more dramatically. For instance, in the districts of Liverpool the NTD ratio per 1,000 births ranged from 5.56 to 7.91 at the start of those two decades. At the end of them the combined proportion was 2.4 per 1,000. The declines of both spina bifida and anencephaly have tended to partner each other in each district, but this diminishing trend has not been partnered by a general reduction in congenital abnormality as a whole. In those same twenty years the percentage of NTDs to total malformations has fallen from 26 per cent to 12 per cent.

Other general points are: there are more NTDs among the poorer people in western Europe, more among girl infants, and more (in Britain) among those of Celtic descent, Celts being the islands' pre-Roman inhabitants. NTDs are Britain's biggest cause of still-birth, and about 20 per cent of all surviving malformed infants have NTDs. Many countries, such as some in Africa, experience an almost total lack of such neural defects. It would therefore seem as if poverty, under-nourishment and disease were somehow beneficial; but the less privileged of western Europe suffer more, the children of unskilled workers being twice as affected by NTDs as are the offspring of professional and managerial families. There are relatively fewer such defects among those born in the summer (and conceived in the autumn), and more among the firstborn and from both the youngest and oldest mothers.

All these varied clues do not identify a cause. The striking British figures ought at least to clarify the problem, but do not. For a long time potato blight was indicted since it tallied with the social class difference (poor people eat more potatoes), the seasonal variation (new potatoes, blight-free, arrive in July), the south-east to north-west difference (both potato consumption and blight incidence increase in the same direction) and the recent fall in NTDs (roughly equivalent to a higher standard of living and fewer potatoes being eaten); but the neatness of these correlations is not always precise. For example, the degree of blight varies considerably from year to year, while the NTD numbers stay more constant. Few potatoes are eaten in Taiwan and India but they experience many anencephalics. Much potato is eaten in Sweden and France, but there are few anencephalics. And farmers confuse the blight situation, with its seasonal correlation, by tending to put their diseased potatoes on the market as early as possible. Consequently, and currently, the blight/NTD relationship is out of favour.

Soft water has to some extent taken the place of blight but, once again, the relationship is imperfect. One prevailing difficulty lies in the actual birth number of NTDs as against the conception and development of them. A more capable uterus, one better nourished in a rich, as opposed to an African, country, might be more capable of retaining a malformed foetus instead of aborting it. Unfortunately facts about abortions are less well collected than facts about births at term. It is known that many spontaneous dismissals from the womb are badly made, and much more so than those who survive nine months, but details and numbers are relatively unreliable.

These days it is unfashionable to look for genetic causes of defects, owing perhaps to an overenthusiasm in this regard earlier this century, but genes are undoubtedly involved to some degree. Just as the Irish produce more NTDs than the rest of the United Kingdom, so do those of Irish extraction living in Massachusetts produce more than, say, its Jewish people. And if social class, or wealth, is thought to explain this differential the incidence among east coast American Negroes is lower than among the Jews, a fact that partners the low numbers in Africa itself. Beyond the general affirmation that genetics and environment are both likely to be involved there is as yet little solid proof both about the degree to which this is true and which environmental factors are guilty.

Congenital malformations may be crippling mentally as well as physically but are not equivalent to mental retardation. That is a different category, a malfunctioning of the brain rather than a malformation, and distinct from the big three of spina bifida, anencephaly and hydrocephalus. Spina bifida is the commonest, and in that sense the most crippling, as almost two thousand babies are born with it each year in the United Kingdom. There are two kinds. The first, spina bifida cystica, is what is generally meant when just the first two words are used. It is always blatant at birth, and is itself of two sorts. In the less damaging form only the meninges (or coverings) protrude through the gap in the spinal cord, producing a meningocele (or hollow/enlargement). The spinal cord itself is (usually) normal. Therefore, none of the paralysis traditionally associated with spinal damage occurs with this variety of cystica. Unfortunately the more crippling form of cystica is much more common. It occurs when actual tissue of the spinal cord protrudes to form a myelomeningocele, also called – with justification – a myelocele, or a swelling of the cord. Paralysis of the legs, incontinence, skeletal malformation of the feet, and other defects partner this form of cystica. The severest cases (about 25 per cent) die at birth, and most of the remainder would die later (frequently from meningitis, owing to infection following damage to the parchment skin that grows over the wound), were it not for surgery.

Such intervention, thought to be a universal blessing as soon as surgery was able to tackle the problem, quickly proved of doubtful benefit. The preservation of every bifida life – paraplegic, wheelchair-bound, overweight, incontinent, with failing kidneys and bed-sores – is not everyone's interpretation of the Hippocratic oath. As for the victims their votes seem to go both ways. Some find it difficult suggesting they should have died while others curse the choice to let them live. The current medical stance is that surgery profits most those who are least affected, and should be reserved for them. The severer cases are both permitted and helped to die. One doctor, racked with anxiety over his answer if he were ever asked 'Why did you let me live?', prepared the reply: 'Your parents believed they could bring you up to be emotionally whole, though physically crippled.' There is no doubt that such a person, however balanced emotionally, will be a cripple, severely or moderately, but a cripple none the less.

The other form of spina bifida to cystica is occulta (or hidden) and affects 10 per cent of the population. Either it is completely masked by skin or there is a dimple, a patch of hair, a birthmark to suggest the spinal imperfection lying internally. Generally the defect is not partnered by any disability, and so this variant of spina bifida is, in the main, not significant. In any case, occulta is never in the same league as cystica.

So how to diminish the birth of bifid babies? For most parents it is preferable to discover the existence of an NTD infant when abortions are still possible. For medicine it is also preferable that a higher proportion of normal babies are brought to term. In fact the *British Medical Journal* called (in 1978) the ante-natal diagnosis of foetal defects 'the greatest advance in perinatal medicine for a generation'. Diligent enthusiasts of this pre-birth knowledge even suggest that every pregnant woman should be subjected to amniocentesis, the withdrawal by syringe of amniotic fluid. Examination of this sample is revealing about many congenital malformations, notably chromosome errors and NTDs. Unfortunately there are also disadvantages: universal testing would be both expensive and hazardous. A major British survey, completed and published in 1978, listed the risks: an excess chance of abortion (1–1.5 per cent); of haemorrhage (1 per cent); of breathing problems for the newborn (1 per cent); of bodily deformities such as club-foot and hip dislocation; and of rhesus difficulties. Overall there were twenty deaths in the amniocentesis group as against eleven in the control group, a most significant differential.

The report concluded that these extra risks had to be weighed against the likelihood of a malformed foetus being present. If the mother was old (over forty), or had already produced a child with a chromosomal abnormality, or had a high level of alpha-fetoprotein in her blood (about which more in a moment), the risks of amniocentesis were outweighed by the increased chance of detecting a foetal abnormality. In other cases the issue was less clear-cut. Certainly a doubling of the perinatal mortality should not be undertaken lightly and mild curiosity is plainly insufficient.

The financial cost of the procedure may seem irrelevant, or ought to be irrelevant, but utopia has not yet come to pass and money is an ingredient in every medical argument, particularly with major screening programmes involving, as with amniocentesis, every pregnant woman. However, the existence of any malformed offspring is (probably) expensive, both to family and state. It would be cheaper, for everyone, if there were no malformations. Unlike risks (of perinatal mortality) which have to be set against chances (of foetal abnormality), thus involving the comparison of like with unlike, money is directly comparable with money. In one recent report it was calculated that the screening of mothers-to-be over forty paid off in cash spent now (on the screening) to save money later (in rearing Down's babies). From age forty to age thirty-five the financial benefit becomes increasingly less obvious until, for mothers below thirty-five, 'the costs of screening would exceed the economies achieved in health care and education.' National health services are more able to calculate the risks of amniocentesis, chances of malformation, and problems of malformed upbringing as a profit and loss account than are parents, but money is highly relevant to both, whatever the qualms in mentioning it.

What made the equation more problematical in the past, whether of risk against risk or just cash against cash, was the number of false positives (identifying a normal foetus as abnormal) and false negatives (identifying abnormal as normal) among the tests. The existence and awareness of alpha-fetoprotein has improved matters. All foetuses produce it, but it leaks from open neural tubes, either from the top (anencephaly) or the bottom (spina bifida). This leads to high AFP levels in the mother's blood, but such levels can also be high if she has twins, a dead foetus, or is wrong about the start-date of her pregnancy. So Stage 1 is to check her AFP. Stage 2 is to use ultra-sound. Its picture will clarify the situation, eliminating the false positive causes in Stage 1. Stage 3, amniocentesis, is performed to discover AFP levels within the amniotic sac. If they are high this is still not absolute proof of an NTD foetus, but the odds against a wrong diagnosis have been shortened by this three-stage attack. And been made cheaper, amniocentesis being the costly procedure. The British started using AFP kits in 1974, but the Americans – via the Food and Drug Administration – delayed their use until 1981, partly because it was feared that more abortions might follow. The anxiety is that more normal foetuses might die (and there is a considerable anti-abortion lobby in the US just as there are considerable pro-abortion groups), but the British experience has been that only 0.06 per cent of all the abortions carried out due to high AFP levels proved to be normal foetuses.

All this advance, and discovery, and clarification, and cost of neural tube defects does not, as yet, prevent them. Abortion merely deletes them. Deliberate neglect of the severely bifid baby also removes them – at a later stage. Surgery of the less severe cases permits a better kind of life, but does not repair the neural damage. That has been at fault ever since, during the second month of pregnancy, something went wrong, and it stays at fault. The work on potato blight was an attempt at prevention. It was even suggested that an entire community, such as that living in controllable fashion on the Isle of Wight, should be starved of potatoes for a season or two. If blight was proven guilty steps could be taken, either by refining blight to discover the faulty agent or via the cruder process of banning potatoes, to reduce the number of NTDs. Prevention is generally better, cheaper, and wiser than cure, but there is still no recommended course.

Professor C. A. Clarke, of Liverpool, has listed efforts in this direction. 'The mean potato consumption, method of peeling, use of gloves, help in preparation, maternal age, paternal age, birth rank, cigarette consumption, inoculation history, and keeping of pets' had not differed between ordinary mothers and those with spina bifida children. However, there was a difference in the eating of meat, eggs, fish, cheese, fruit and salad – the ordinary mothers ate more, had fewer illnesses during their pregnancies, took less medication, and ate more of their potatoes from green-grocers than from chip shops. Unfortunately no one difference stood out as of major importance, the culprit, the means of prevention.

Currently more interest is being shown in vitamins (a survey in South Wales seemed to confirm this theory), the inter-pregnancy gap (Britain's falling NTD rate has been partnered in recent years both by a fall in the birth-rate and by siblings more spaced apart), and better diet in general. Britain was eating more wisely in 1980 than in 1960, a period of decline in NTDs, and one Welsh experiment counselled a number of women to do better still, to cut down on refined sugar, potatoes, cream buns, sweets and soft drinks. A similar number did not receive such advice and they produced five NTD infants while the three NTDs produced by the other group were all from women who had neglected the recommendations. Nothing is proven as yet but it is easy to wonder if the British affection for appalling food will be diverted by the modest extra likelihood of an NTD offspring. After all, the extreme indictment against cigarettes has scarcely affected sales of this proven killer, and dietary habits are also well engrained. Prevention can be difficult or impossible even when medicine has decided what it is that should be prevented.

Hydrocephalus The third member of the congenital malformation trio affecting the central nervous system after spina bifida and anencephaly is hydrocephalus. It too has no known cause, save that it is part genetic, part environmental and part associated with spina bifida. It also has no prevention, as yet. Essentially it is water on the brain, or rather an excess of cerebro-spinal fluid, possibly over a hundred times too much. Unlike the other two of this unwelcome trio hydrocephalus is only rarely blatant at birth, but becomes rapidly conspicuous within weeks or months of life. Occasionally the foetal head has swollen considerably, causing survival after birth to be brief; but, in general, most swelling occurs later. A normal head has a circumference of 35 centimetres (13.5 inches) at birth which increases to 43 centimetres (17 inches) by six months. A hydrocephalic skull can enlarge by 5 centimetres (2 inches) a month, or almost four times as fast. The faster the rate of normal swelling, the greater the problem, but at least the more rapid swelling is obvious, causing tight fontanelles, dilated scalp veins, a sinking of the eyeballs relative to the expanding skull, and increasing skull circumference. The less dramatic forms can be overlooked, partly because an infant's head is so large relative to its body at birth, and even more so if it is premature. However, no hydrocephalus should be permitted to advance as it will lead to mental retardation, optic damage, and various forms of paralysis and weakness.

There are different reasons for the abnormal retention of cerebro-spinal fluid. There may be blockages which can be removed or punctured by surgery, but relief from the excessive pressure is generally achieved by placing a valve between the jugular vein and the lateral ventricles, part of the ventricular system within the brain. Pressure reduction is therefore obtained whatever the cause, and the chance of damage to the growing brain is reduced or nullified. Often hydrocephalus is associated with spina bifida – the latter may help to cause the former – and surgical work on the protrusion from the spine may aggravate rather than placate the hydrocephalus, underlining the association but bringing no comfort to the spina bifida victim, already confronted by repeated surgery elsewhere.

Hydrocephalus is not always treated. It may be considered, by parents and surgeons, that the young life is damaged beyond useful or merciful repair. In general these extreme cases die, from brain damage, infection, or a battery of other causes. One such boy was born in Florida in 1973. To everyone's surprise he survived. To even greater surprise his mental ability stayed nearly normal, and it was thought an operation might not only treat his hydrocephalus and meningomyelocele but give him a chance of becoming normal mentally. At the age of six, his head circumference was 74 centimetres (29 inches), larger than an adult's head, and still growing. He could neither sit up nor turn his swollen cranium without assistance. He had been bedridden from birth, in a sense pinned down by his head. The surgeons then set to work, rebuilding his cranium, rearranging its bones, draining his ventricles, and generally permitting his huge head to become normal. Its volume was diminished by over 2,000 cubic centimetres, by 63 per cent of the size it had reached. He suffered no neurological damage during the operations and, although still confined to a wheelchair (the spina bifida sees to that), his surgery was undoubtedly successful. Few hydrocephalics are so lucky. Normally, with this abnormality, the swollen ventricles damage the brain irremediably and tend to kill their owner, sooner or later.

Or so it was thought. Opinion on this subject began to change in the mid-1960s following publication of a paper in *Developmental Medicine and Child Neurology*. Written by John Lorber, of Sheffield University, it described two children – hydrancephalics – who had water rather than brain where the cerebrum should have been. (Hydrancephalics must not be confused with anencephalics, the brainless individuals whose neural tube did not close properly at its top/head/anterior end.) Professor Lorber's paper affirmed that neither child showed any evidence of cerebral cortex and yet their mental development appeared normal. One then died at three months, but the other was still healthy at twelve months, normal mentally so far as could be judged but still, despite repeated medical experiment, providing no evidence of cerebral tissue, even residual cerebral tissue compressed by the excessive cerebro-spinal fluid. The liquid had been drained to a correct pressure, but the cerebral signs were still nil, save that the child behaved like any other one-year-old.

As a contributor to *World Medicine* wrote in 1980, Lorber's paper 'suffered a fate like that of much of the literature of phenomenological science: it was neglected'. However, the work progressed, and other living hydrancephalics were discovered and examined. In particular one man with an IQ of 126 achieved a first-class honours degree in mathematics at Sheffield University; but, according to Lorber and the CAT scanning technique, he had 'virtually no brain'. A pair of identical girl twins were also studied. One had a big head, gross hydrocephalus and an IQ of 105, while the other had a normal head, no hydrocephalus, and an IQ of 106. A man who had had gross hydrocephalus as an infant recovered after the shunt operation (which drains the fluid) to lead a normal life and hold down an ordinary job. Unfortunately the shunt broke down in early adulthood, causing him to die. The coroner performed an autopsy, and found a high degree of hydrocephalus plus a minute rim of brain tissue, but knew nothing of the man's early medical history. So he called the parents, his next-of-kin, expressed grief that their son had died but also 'relief' that such a 'vegetable' had ended his days. The dumbfounded parents explained to the then dumbfounded coroner that the lad had been at work two days beforehand. Had they shone a torch through his head in a dark room when their child had had the delicate bones of a baby they would have discovered what is called transillumination – the light would have shone from one side to the other. It is easy to imagine many parents not relishing this particular experiment, however illuminating. Perhaps severe hydrocephalus should no longer be called water on the brain but, apparently whimsically and more accurately, water on no brain.

The Sheffield group has classified hydrocephalics into four groups: those with small ventricular enlargement; those with ventricles up to fifty times their normal size; those whose ventricles are so gross that they fill 70–90 per cent of the intracranial cavity; and those with extreme enlargement, such as the most transillumi-nant, whose cerebro-spinal fluid fills 95 per cent or so of the cavity which should be, almost entirely, brain. The final category might be expected to be the most deformed mentally but, of the 9 (out of 253) hydrocephalics allocated in Sheffield to this group, 4 had IQs above 100 (ordinary average) and 2 had IQs of 126. One of these was the mathematics graduate.

So what are they using as a brain? The answer, briefly, is what they have got by way of a brain. Normal infants have a cerebral thickness of 4½–5 centimetres (1.8 inches) but those with gross hydrocephalus have this thickness reduced to 0.5 centimetre (0.2 inch), or even less. At adulthood the gross hydrocephalic brain, which barely registers on the scanning pictures, can be 1 millimetre (0.04 inch), or thinner still. This tissue is not some ancient, unused, unwanted portion of the brain – not that the more ancient areas of our brains are any less welcome – but the neopallium, the pre-sumed location of mankind's mental superiority over all other creatures, the part most in need when it comes to mathematics degrees or appearing normal to fellow humans. The fact of the skull being enlarged, caused in the main before treatment of the hydrocephalus, partly explains the brain's thinness: it has been stretched thin. An extra centimetre added to a normal head circumference of sixty centimetres increases the volume of a 1-mm layer lying beneath the skull by 3½ per cent. The increment is considerable, and hydrocephalics can have head circumferences ten centimetres above normal, but the quantity of brain matter is still minute relative to that in normal heads. As Lorber once pointed out, perhaps too graphically: 'You can put a needle in these babies' heads, and you can roam around with your needle to encounter no resistance whatsoever.' Nevertheless such infants can thrive, provided the excessive ventricular pressure has been shunted to normal.

What happens to brain tissue abruptly relieved of pressure is unknown, but it certainly becomes more capable. Normally, all brain cells are present at birth, but the repaired hydrocephalics improve their skills and behave as if they are manufacturing brain cells. Or perhaps there is regeneration of brain tissue. Or growth of fibres, or of interstitial tissue. The patients who become most normal, and who would be the most interesting to examine, are also the least likely to die. Surgical intervention, and histology, would answer many of the questions, but the surviving, intelligent, and so-called brainless hydrocephalics are still young, and have no intention of providing themselves for autopsy, however illuminating the facts might be.

A different question also needing an answer is why asymmetric hydrocephalus does not provide the expected results. Ventricles on one side may be extremely dilated and normal on the other, owing perhaps to the location of the shunt, or to the ventricles themselves. It was naturally expected that the more abnormal side of the brain would have most effect, such as paralysis and spasticity, on the opposite side of the body. A fundamental fact about the body's innervation is that left controls right, and vice versa; but hydrocephalics are upsetting neuroanatomy just as much as they are overturning traditional ideas about regeneration or the need for brain bulk. If ventricles on one side of the brain are grossly enlarged, and those on the other side are normal, there is in general no difference in muscular control, for example, on either side of the body. One asymmetrical patient at Sheffield did have one-sided paralysis, but on the *same* side of the body as his one-sidedly swollen brain. The temptation to examine his brain in detail, and discover precisely what is happening, must be almost unbearable, as nothing of the sort can happen until the patient dies.

The matter of redundancy is the most intriguing hydrocephalic fact of all. Human brains are two or three times larger than those of the great apes, and humans are unquestionably superior mentally. Plainly – or so it is said – the increased bulk of brain tissue, plus the extra connections possible with all the extra neurons, are together responsible for this superiority. Gorillas are idiots by comparison with us, but along come the hydrocephalics who reverse this convenient notion. A millimetre thickness lining a larger head may contain more tissue than we expect, but the total mass is still minute compared with that in normal human brains. And in ape brains. And, one suspects, in many a mammal's brain. It is plainly extraordinary that gross, transilluminable, and highly improbable hydrocephalics can walk or eat properly, let alone appear normal to their workmates, to their parents, or to their degree examiners.

The human body is full of considerable redundancy. A quarter of one kidney is sufficient for the task of excretion. A modest piece of liver is adequate for the myriad roles a liver must play. The stomach is unnecessary, and the twenty feet of intestine can be trimmed to a foot or two. One eye or one ear will do almost as well, but the brain, or so it was felt, is different. People have lived with half a hemisphere, and can do so with little mental impairment after a stroke (provided it affects the correct half); but the cerebral cortex was thought to be in a special category, the cream of the cream, the god-head. Now, not only does cerebral bulk seem less vital, but even its cortex can be a fraction of its normal self – and such a brain can still acquire a degree in mathematics.

The last word on this subject – for the time being, and until hydrocephalics provide more facts to help answer the questions they have posed – can be given by Professor Noel Dilly, a neurobiologist, fascinated by near-brainless intelligence. 'We almost have to follow these people like hawks,' he said in a broadcast, because 'it would be a tragedy to lose the opportunity to see why they have been so successful in surviving when, apparently, all the cards have been stacked against them.' It is easy to sympathise with the hydrocephalics who have one more card, the medical profession, to contend with, but it is even easier to understand Dilly's hawk-like manner and intent. The clever hydrocephalics seem to be breaking all the rules, and upsetting practically all of neurobiology learned thus far.

Down's syndrome The major single and congenital cause of severe mental subnormality, named after the English physician Langdon Down who first described it (in 1866), is due to a medium-sized but extra chromosome (No. 21). About 30 per cent of all severely retarded children in Western Europe and North America are victims of this extra chromosome and of the syndrome partnering its existence. A syndrome is a group of signs and symptoms, with the Down's assortment being as wide as any: short, broad hands with a particularly stubby little finger; distinctive palm and sole prints; a round face and broad head, also most distinctive; a narrow, high palate, plus an accompanying speech manner; a small, flat nose; forty-seven rather than forty-six chromosomes; considerable infertility; a thick, furrowed tongue, also involved in the distinctive speech; a particular but variable distortion of the epicanthic fold above the eye; and a diminished intelligence. They are known also as mongols, and the syndrome as mongolism.

A superficial similarity to Mongoloid people exists, according to European eyes, and due to that epicanthic fold, but the naming is unhelpful (and also hurtful to oriental people, particularly when the syndrome is bluntly called 'mongolian idiocy'). The comparison with Mongoloid people becomes even less justified when Negro people and, yet more importantly, Mongols suffer from it. ('Mongol mongolians' has even appeared in a medical journal.) Dr John Langdon Haydon Down is not blameless in having his syndrome given, so frequently, another and less satisfactory name: he actually initiated this alternative.

As medical superintendent of the Earlswood Asylum for Idiots, Surrey, his experience with the mentally retarded caused him to publish 'Observations on an ethnic classification of idiots'. The paper appeared in the very year that he first described Down's syndrome. His belief was that idiocy could be on occasion a reversion to a less intelligent form. As the various races of mankind stood at different levels of excellence, and as there were different kinds of idiot, he therefore correlated the two. Among Caucasian idiots he was able to see features/signs reminding him of African, Malay, American Indian, and oriental people. As a consequence he knew how far these unfortunate Europeans had regressed. It may be some comfort to oriental people to learn that 'mongolian idiocy' was the highest category, the smallest regression into the primitive past, the least idiotic. His argument, therefore, provides an even sounder reason for referring to Down's syndrome sufferers as Down's syndrome sufferers and not by any other name. (Curiosity prompted me to ask oriental friends how their people commonly called this chromosomal aberration, which was, of course, in existence long before Dr Down put his name to it. The Japanese, as oriental and slant-eyed as any but non-Mongol however Mongoloid we call their race, refer to Down's children as 'mongolashu' or mongol disease. So on to China, where the people are both Mongoloid and – some of them – descendants of Mongols. 'Oh we call them *bai chai*,' said a friend. 'What is that?' I asked. '*Bai* means white and *chi* means idiots,' she replied.)

No one knows why chromosome No. 21 so frequently errs in its division. It is believed there is non-disjunction during the mother's meiosis (or reduction division). Or, to rephrase that, the creation of an egg means halving the normal number of chromosomes, and the halving does not always occur correctly. In fact, chromosome numbers 8, 13 and 18 as well as 21 are occasionally found as a threesome in live births instead of the twosome (one from each parent) they should be. Trisomy-21, yet another and preferable name to mongolism, is the commonest, occurring about once in every 600 births. (It is, therefore, not so common in Britain as spina bifida, but commoner than anencephaly.) Certain trisomies, such as 22, fail to survive even to birth, and spontaneous abortions have a 'high frequency' (no one is clear about the proportion) of chromosome abnormalities. It is thought that about 65 per cent of trisomy-21 fail to achieve birth, and some of the remaining 35 per cent die at birth or shortly afterwards. There is a figure, frequently quoted, of Down's syndrome individuals dying 'on average at 16'. If those dying in the earliest years are not included the average age leaps up. Professor Clemens Benda, a Down's authority, has said that if such a child reaches the age of five there is no particular reason why he or she (both sexes are equally involved) should not live another fifty-five years – at least. Certainly Down's survival has improved markedly in recent years, mainly because most now live at home whereas most used to be in institutions.

A numerical contradiction is that Down's offspring are much more likely when the mother is over forty, but most such babies are born to women under forty. The explanation is that women in their early twenties are producing most children, a time when the Down's risk is low (3,000 to 1 against for a woman of twenty). Women over forty produce only a small share of the babies (1.5 per cent in New York) but have the odds against their production of Down's offspring lowered to 100 to 1. The arithmetic works out (in New York) at 16 per cent of Down's babies born to women over forty and 84 per cent to younger mothers. However, the higher risk to the older women does mean that any screening technique, such as amniocentesis (to detect the extra chromosome in discarded foetal cells floating in the amniotic fluid), can be applied more effectively, and where there is greatest likelihood of detecting a Down's. Unfortunately, owing to the small number of babies from older women, only a few of the Down's total will be encountered. Even if the screening age were lowered to thirty-five, which would involve 7 per cent of all pregnancies (still New York figures), only 35 per cent of the Down's babies would be detected. Assuming that every over-thirty-five-year-old then decided not to proceed with her discovered Down's pregnancy there would be all the Down's babies born to the under-thirty-fives. The gross rate would then be 1 in 1,700 births, still a sizeable number for a country producing over two million babies a year. The idea of screening every pregnant woman is unwelcome because the risks involved in amniocentesis (at least, by current methods) outweigh the potential benefits – (see p. 226). In other words, for the time being and the foreseeable future, part of mankind will continue to have three chromosomes of No. 21, and will be the happy-natured, slightly slant-eyed, round-faced, generally unintelligent (but the range is considerable) group of individuals who live by the name of Dr Down.

Or maybe methods will be found of reducing their number, and better ways than just killing off those discovered during gestation. For example, it is interesting that Catholics conceive Down's babies more than Protestants do, and Protestants do so more than the remainder – in Europe at least. Figures from Holland, which possesses the world-highest Down's incidence at Nijmegen (80 per cent Catholic), make this point. In Friesland the Down's ratio per 10,000 inhabitants is almost 5 for Catholics, 2.5 for Protestants, and less than 1 for others. Around Groningen the proportions are 2.5, 1.5 and 0.5, fewer but similar. Why the differences? Sexually the Catholics practise rhythm or safe-period birth control more than the others, they have shorter intervals between pregnancies, and longer reproductive periods. As a consequence their eggs may be over-ripe, and the older kind of egg may be more prone to the aneuploidy of an extra chromosome. A different point of interest, first noted in Jerusalem, is that the birth of the sibling before that of an affected baby tends to occur after a Down's baby had been born in the same hospital. In other words, and surprisingly, it seems as if an infective agent is at work, one picked up from the Down's baby (or its mother) during the previous confinement.

It will be difficult altering Catholic habits. The current Pope (John Paul II), who is breaking down barriers, coming close to political intervention (as in the Falklands War), and the first head of Rome's Church to visit Britain, has proved himself quite inflexible over contraception. His flock in Friesland, Groningen and elsewhere is also likely to be adamant. It would be far more satisfactory if there does prove to be an infective agent, if this can be attacked (rather than dogma and belief) and mothers made immune to it. The Jerusalem story has first to be confirmed, and the agent then has to be tracked down – if agent there be. The task is daunting, but may prove easier than instructing people to change their sexual ways.

A final point is that the law, medicine and parental wishes are rarely in unison. As generalities the law tries to find clear-cut answers, medicine makes more of an attempt to see things in proportion, and parents will obey laws but have their opinions formed largely by their doctors. A recent British case – Re B (Minor) in 1980 – set medicine against the law with the parents (and the child) set somewhere in between. The case occurred because a Down's baby was born with an intestinal blockage which would prove fatal if an operation was not performed. With an ordinary baby the operation is performed without more ado. With a Down's baby the parents and doctors can feel that the infant should be allowed to die, nature having presented them with this option. The British Medical Association and the British Paediatric

Association consider that this decision should be taken without legal interference and certainly without a hard set of rules on the matter. The basic legal position, as expressed after the case, is that criminal law does not distinguish between benevolent and evil motives in determining the guilt of an individual charged with causing the death of another. The decision to let a baby die should not be taken in the absence of a clearly defined legal process. The *Lancet* immediately expressed considerable concern: this finding 'apparently means that the parents of a child with Down's syndrome do not therefore have the choice of accepting medical advice which would lead to early death'.

Nevertheless, doctors frequently withhold treatment. They do so at the end of life and at the beginning, as with severe cases of spina bifida. It is easy to suspect that doctors and parents will connive over Down's babies, assessing the degree of subnormality, the likely intelligence and potential happiness in the family that is to raise them. Parents, particularly after a malformed birth, are highly subject to medical advice, and the doctors are usually ready to give it. They have done so in the past, and wish to carry on – at least judging by that *Lancet* editorial, which continued: 'Those reformists with the strongest sense of rectitude will accept nothing less than the discounting of parents' wishes and the suppression, if necessary by the law of murder, of what they see as presumptuous medical advice.' The law and medicine will have to fight it out – and then inform the parents. The child's stigma is its possession of an extra chromosome which, among all its other attributes, generally causes mental subnormality. The other drawbacks are irrelevant by comparison: it is unintelligence that people find so hard to bear and which lies at the root of every argument about Dr Down's syndrome.

Huntington's chorea   It has been called the most vicious disease known to man. Indeed there is a certain evil to it, its onset occurring after the responsible gene has already been passed to the next generation. The American physician George Huntington, after whom this chorea (or dance) and degenerative disease of the nervous system is named, first described it in the *Medical and Surgical Reporter* (of 13 April 1872). His description still stays virtually as good as any:

> The hereditary chorea, as I shall call it, is confined to certain and fortunately a few families, and has been transmitted to them, an heirloom from generations away back in the dim past. When either or both the parents have shown manifestations of

the disease, and more especially when these have been of a severe nature, one or more of the offspring almost invariably suffer from the disease, if they live to adult age. But if by any chance these children go through life without it, the thread is broken and the grandchildren and great-grandchildren of the original shakers may rest assured that they are free from the disease . . . Unstable and whimsical as the disease may be in other aspects, in this it is firm, it never skips a generation to again manifest itself in another; once having yielded its claims, it never regains them.

What he was describing, in the years after Gregor Mendel had done his work but before its language had become known, was the hereditary pattern of an autosomal dominant transmission. It is autosomal as it affects the sexes equally, and dominant because it manifests itself whenever the errant gene is present. Either parent, as Huntington said, can pass it on but if the children 'go through life without it', as he also wrote, they and their descendants have escaped this dread inheritance. The most damning factor, which he pointed out with elaboration, is that the disease hits its victims 'if they live to adult age'. Its symptoms most frequently begin in the fifth decade of life.

First signs can be laziness, clumsiness, or disinterest, probably assumed to be unimportant and a normal part of life. Within a year the clumsiness can lead to injury and the laziness to involuntary movements, initiating the chorea (Greek for dance, as in terpsichore). At first these spasms are slight – facial twitches, restlessness, fidgeting – but they become more all-embracing. There is no pattern to them, but a distinctive sign is that the tongue cannot be protruded and stay protruded. The muscular contractions march on, becoming more severe, until the victim is physically and mentally disabled. Cachexia is the final state, a malnutrition accompanied by damage to the brain. The disease is undeniably vicious, its genetic disability having already been passed on to half the victim's children, or maybe none of them, or maybe all of them.

The only blessing is that the sufferer may not realise what he (or she) is suffering or has (probably) passed on genetically, causing others to follow. The single merit of a diseased brain is its inability to recognise its own deficiency. The demerit of Huntington's is that the children, each with an even chance of possessing the gene, have seen their parent die from it. If there is Huntington's in the family, and if the parent on that side has not yet shown signs of it, the children must note each twitch, stumble, or uncoordination with alarm; but as that parent grows older and does not succumb they can start to hope more realistically. If the parent reaches the age of fifty his or her chances of carrying the gene have dropped to 5 per cent.

Fortunately the disease is rare. In Britain about four thousand have it, or one in twelve thousand people. Proportions in other countries are similar, and the number living under the threat of it depends upon family size. There is no method of pre-natal diagnosis and no treatment to arrest the mental decline (although drugs can halt the involuntary movements). The faulty gene causes the premature death of specific nerve cells (the cortex diminishes by about 20 per cent), and it is believed that the muscular symptoms are due to an imbalance of the neuro-transmitters, such as dopamine and acetylcholine. George Huntington, who died in 1916, was presumably a kind and sympathetic man. His name, however, is now one of the most dreaded and dreadful, immutably linked as it is with the chorea he first described over a century ago.

There are other, inborn errors in the formation of the nervous system beyond spina bifida, anencephaly, hydrocephalus, trisomy-21, and Huntington's chorea: for example, phenylketonuria, a form of intellectual deterioration that occurs once in every 6,000 births. Fortunately, a kind of treatment has been found for it: feed the child a diet low in phenylalanine and the amino-acid disorder is kept in check, permitting that infant to grow normally intelligent. Whether the nervous system is the 'most striking, subtle and highly developed' of them all, a sentiment expressed at the start of this chapter, or whether it equates with less exciting organs such as the liver or the skin is a matter for debate, but the nervous system is undeniably bewildering. Small wonder, therefore, that errors do occur in its creation and the aim of this chapter has been to give a flavour of them rather than a list. And a taste of the moral and ethical dilemmas with which they are enmeshed.

14. Damage

Definition / Cerebral palsy / Paraplegia / Head injury / Phineas Gage and Co. / War wounds / Lyova Zasetsky / Boxing / Other sports / Headache / Migraine / Self-damage / Depression / Schizophrenia / Parkinsonism / Stroke / Tumour

To study the phenomena of disease without books is to sail an uncharted sea, while to study books without patients is not to go to sea at all

– Sir William Osler

The man who had received a crowbar through his head walked away from the hospital yesterday with a slight limp
– Boston newspaper

There's a lecture on schizophrenia tonight. I've half a mind to go

– Anon.

Definition The anonymous expert in the *Lancet*, who provides answers for the regular column of questions, once wrote: 'I never use the term "brain damage" unless a child has suffered postnatal injury in an accident.' To use the term – and it is frequently used – is to suggest fault in the medical profession, and among obstetricians in particular; hence the reaction by the profession. The expert continued: 'The term causes great distress to parents, and it implies totally unjustifiable blame on the doctor or midwife who delivered the child: furthermore, it is harmful for the child, for it puts a label on him that is unjustified.' Once upon a time mothers were the ones to be delivered (of their children) but, whether deliveries are of mothers or babies, it plainly is possible for a doctor or midwife to damage a baby and its brain, particularly during childbirth. However, the medical viewpoint and attitude are easily understood for the term 'brain damage' is used excessively. In the United States, 'minimal brain dysfunction' and 'minimal brain damage' are jointly said to include 40 per cent of all children. As a result amphetamines and other drugs are frequently prescribed to combat the alleged damage. If the term were to go, or was used less widely, it is possible that less attention might be paid to the normal

vagaries of children, such as hyperactivity and downright unpleasantness.

This subject was mentioned in the chapter on Growth but it must
be reintroduced in this section on damage. Of course there can be
injury, as the expert said, postnatally. The problem he was high-
lighting is the suggestion of damage done to a baby never seen
before, never assessed until that moment, and of unknown quality.
He was not denying that some babies are wrongly made, as with the
groups discussed in Chapter 13, or that some babies do have a
difficult birth and may be damaged in the process, even dying on
occasion. Instead, he was resenting the frequent presumption that
a baby was whole beforehand but was then injured with lasting
results. Plainly, to imply that kind of injury is also to suggest that
someone had been at fault, turning something previously perfect
into something permanently imperfect.

Dr Richmond S. Paine, of Washington, DC, has defined 'brain
damage' as 'a persistent but relatively non-progressive chronic
abnormality of the brain, manifest by impairment of one of its
cardinal functions'. These are: cerebral palsy in the motor (muscular) sphere; mental retardation in the intellectual sphere; and
cortical blindness or deafness in the sensory sphere. The three
categories sometimes overlap. Many, but certainly not all, victims
of palsy show mental retardation. There can also be faulty diagnosis: someone who cannot speak or who speaks stupidly can be presumed as intellectually sub-normal. Even the word mental can, in
this difficult area, lead to misunderstanding because a palsied patient
is mentally deficient, in that his brain is damaged, but not necessarily mentally sub-normal in that his intellect may be unimpaired.
Mentality is one area of misunderstanding. Damage is another.

Some initial, and general, facts are that the incidence of cerebral
palsy, whatever its cause, is about 0.2 per cent of the live-born
population (which means about eight million in the world). Mental
retardation, in terms of an IQ below seventy, is about fifteen times
higher (or over one hundred million in the world). By comparison,
a treatable deficiency such as phenylketonuria, caused by faulty
amino-acid metabolism (and also mentioned in Chapter 13),
affects 1 in 20,000. Now that the PKU victims need no longer suffer
brain damage, if detected and treated when babies, there is a
growing number of healthy survivors. Britain expects to have 500
soon of child-bearing age (of interest because 1 in 4 of their
children will also have PKU) but such brain damage and potential
damage are microscopic when set beside the 3 per cent of the
population as a whole said to be mentally retarded, 30,000 of every
million people.

In assessing the subject Dr Paine, professor of paediatric neurology at Washington, thought the total figure of cerebral error was very much higher: 'It seems a reasonable estimate that 5 to 8 per cent of the entire population may have some reflection or suggestion of cerebral damage.' That, in the United States for example, means – with the higher percentage – a total of over eighteen million people. His concept of damage is broadened to include 'adverse prenatal influences on the maturation of the central nervous system as well as peri- and post-natal influences on maturation and function'. In other words, the car is at fault whether it was wrongly made or was damaged either on delivery day or subsequently. From the driver's point of view it is a faulty car whatsoever caused the damage and whenever it occurred.

Professor R. S. Illingworth, of Sheffield, has compiled a list of the pre- and peri-natal factors. All can do harm and each is unlikely to operate on its own, but damage is the outcome, whatever the cause or multiplicity of causes. They include: genetic factors (such as those linked with congenital abnormalities, prematurity, multiple pregnancy); kernicterus and haemolytic disease of the newborn (associated with toxic degeneration of nerve cells); social factors, poverty, type of food, age of mother, smoking; low birth-weight and prematurity (generally inconsequential, but have a higher than average association with e.g. mental retardation); irradiation, never welcomed by the foetus; pregnancy abnormalities, such as antepartum haemorrhage, maternal toxaemia; multiple pregnancies (like prematurity are usually normal, but are linked with above-average retardation, palsy, etc.); and asphyxia at birth-time (also usually unimportant).

Even with factors thought to be primarily genetic there are few hard and fast rules. Parents of superior intelligence are likely to have children of superior intelligence, but there is no certainty. Children of a mentally defective parent are likely to come within the normal range (IQ 70 to 130). Asphyxia at birth can be prolonged, and alarming, and lead to cyanosis (a morbid blue), but the majority who suffer it will grow to be normal. However, as Illingworth states: 'It is interesting to speculate how much the intelligence and performance of children . . . could be raised by improved obstetrical care, by the prevention of anoxia, and by improved paediatric care in the newborn period.' If there is mental retardation and possible brain damage in a child, how much was this due to genetic causes, a poor uterus, bad nourishment, smoke, a waning placenta, a difficult birth, a shortage of oxygen, an impoverished upbringing, or some other factor, as yet unsuspected? The car appears faulty, but which mechanic at what stage along the line is to blame? It is easiest to blame the last one, he or she who makes the delivery, which is why obstetricians become so upset quite so speedily.

In one important study L. S. Penrose examined 1,280 mentally defective people, studied their medical history and concluded that eleven of them suffered injuries at birth which were the main cause of their disability. M. Perlstein, less sanguine after a lengthy review of the prevailing opinion, wrote that 'faulty obstetric practice' accounted for 'three to five per cent' of defectives. Sir Dugald Baird, of Aberdeen (and largely responsible for an outpouring of obstetric information from that city), once investigated sixty-four handicapped children. Only seven of them had experienced either an abnormal pregnancy or labour, and in only one of them could a 'causal relation' be found between the handicap and the earlier experience. But, as Ronald Illingworth concluded, 'It would be absurd to suggest that birth injury does not occur.' It would seem, therefore, as if it occurs less frequently than it used to do, and less frequently than many think, particularly those who learn that they have just acquired a deficient offspring. There is often a feeling of guilt at such a mishap, and it is convenient to attribute some of it elsewhere.

Cerebral palsy   Nevertheless, for whatever reason, cerebral palsy does occur and paralysis does result. (Palsy is from the Greek for 'I am disabled'; paralysis from 'I relax'.) Medical palsy means a loss of muscular power due to interference with the nervous system. The cerebral palsies – they form a group – all show themselves before the age of three. The risk is six to seven times greater in multiple pregnancies, but that fact is complex as such pregnancies are associated with older mothers, lower social classes, shorter women, first-born offspring, offspring at the end of large (more than five) families, and birth problems, such as breech presentation, and prolapse (slipping down) of the cord. Also the twins, or triplets, themselves are smaller than normal, and have more congenital deformities, while their placentas are more likely to have problems. You can take your pick, it would seem, as to which abnormality contributes most to the greater number of palsied individuals among multiple births.

A third of all singleton children with cerebral palsy have been born prematurely. There is already the link between twins and prematurity, and this further fact emphasises the virtue of staying in the uterus for the proper time. Or perhaps the premature are already at fault, their prematurity linked to their cerebral palsy, with the palsy helping to cause the prematurity rather than the other way about. It is so easy to blame birth and all its hazards for causing error, but in most cases of physical or mental handicap (or both) there is no accompanying evidence of birth trauma.

Nevertheless, anoxia, a deprivation of oxygen, is almost certainly the most important factor in cerebral palsy. Babies at birth are extraordinarily tolerant of oxygen lack, surviving for many minutes without this vital element, but even for them there can be insufficiency, caused perhaps by obstruction of the cord, or an awkward labour, or early separation of the placenta. It has been argued that prolonged uterine contractions are more relevant to oxygen lack than the amplitude or frequency of the contractions. A perennial difficulty in assessing the cause of palsy is that the degree of anoxia is not measured in the babies, and time apparently without oxygen is not always recorded. Such facts, then, have to be correlated with the degree of palsy when that becomes measurable.

Despite the obvious importance of anoxia during birth most infants that do experience it severely show no sign subsequently of cerebral palsy. Similarly most infants that do show cerebral palsy did not experience anoxia at birth. In one series of thirty-three children, in whom respiration was not established at birth for twenty minutes or more, the follow-up study discovered that twenty-seven were normal, and six had cerebral palsy, but of this damaged number four had suffered 'prolonged oxygen deficiency' even before labour. Plainly, a good supply of oxygen at all times is preferable, and not too lengthy a hiatus between the closure of the umbilical supply and the start of aerial respiration; but, amazingly, a gap like twenty minutes is not as devastating as might be expected by, among others, the anxious mother. The greater oddness is that reactions to anoxia are so different. For one child it causes a wheelchair life, an inability often even to speak, an intelligence locked within a body incapable of responding to its wishes. For another child – in fact, for the majority – it leads to a normal life. As R. W. Beard and R. P. A. Rivers, of London, wrote: 'Such a striking difference in outcome is curious and almost unbiological. With all other forms of injury one would expect the outcome to reflect the severity of the initial insult. Perhaps the brain is different from other organs . . .' It certainly seems so, with foetal anoxia.

Paraplegia Although palsy and paralysis are adequate and general terms for loss of muscular power there are others, more specific and frequently encountered. Hemiplegia is paralysis only on one side, possibly the face and arm and leg. Diplegia affects both sides and is, therefore, more or less total. If only one limb is affected the condition is monoplegia. Paraplegics, so often encountered striking out for independence in their wheelchairs, have paralysis on both sides but only below a certain level. Hemiplegics have their injury or disease located in the brain, but paraplegics have suffered their insult in the spinal cord; hence a loss of power in the region controlled below the injury. If the spinal column is to be damaged, the lower the better. Tetraplegics and quadriplegics have all four limbs paralysed. Their spinal injuries are, therefore, high up the cord and in the cervical portion. (Plegia comes from the Greek for a blow. Therefore, tetraplegia – four blow – is the better name for being all Greek.) The less medical terms of creeping paralysis, shaking paralysis, and wasting paralysis generally refer to (in the same order) ataxia, where strong but not delicate movement is possible, to Parkinson's, and to the progressive atrophy of muscles.

Wheelchairs are a commoner sight these days, notably in the United States. There are many reasons: the steady toll of accidents (notably on the roads); better treatment of other consequences of the plegias (mainly pressure sores and urinary infections); and a general awareness, among doctors and patients, that more mobility is possible and preferable. Architects are being increasingly bullied to make their buildings suitable for four wheels and not just two feet. (In time perhaps, and at a different level, they will make houses more convenient for both young and old people, an even larger proportion of the population, also incapable in their fashion.)

The outlook for those whose severe brain or spine damage has caused loss of muscular control is not good. There can be modest return of sensation and control, but it is only modest. Considerable publicity has been given to a Russian claim, principally from Leningrad's Polenov Neurological Institute, that a combination of enzymes, hyperbaric (or pressurised) oxygen and exercise can help repair spinal damage. It is generally felt in the West that the exercises are the only rewarding part of the programme. A more intriguing advance has been pioneered at the Tufts–New England Medical Center. Just as guide-dogs have revolutionised blind lives so are some capuchin monkeys being trained to aid the paralysed. Even a moderate degree of muscular ability can be sufficient to give instructions – fetch, carry, push, pull – and thereby achieve a greater degree of independence for the wheelchair passenger. Constantly asking another human to do this thing, that thing is a psychological drain, said a quadriplegic from Connecticut. 'And that's where these monkeys help,' she added, 'in doing the little things so you have the strength to carry on.'

Head injury   One price of an increasingly mechanised society is the rising incidence of damage to the head. Whether such an injury does affect the brain or not there is, naturally, awareness that it might have done so or even, if proper care is not taken, will do so. Accident and emergency units in the United Kingdom encounter about one million new head injuries a year (or 2 per cent of the population). The figure is large but represents only 10 per cent of the total accident and emergency cases. This proportion is more acute for road accidents. Figures from the United States, where such accidents are the greatest cause of death and injury to people under thirty-five, suggest that three-quarters of these accidents involve injuries to the head. The World Health Organisation states that the head injury proportion varies between 50 per cent and 80 per cent in different countries (as against 10–40 per cent for chest injuries). What is not known is how much the brain has suffered in all this injury.

Nothing can be done about brain damage sustained during the actual accident. That, so to speak, is spilt milk. What is almost more grievous is the death and injury due to secondary brain damage. This occurs as a consequence of the impact and is, therefore, to some degree preventable. One report from Virginia stated that, of patients 'with non-missile head injuries' who were neither speaking nor obeying commands after their initial resuscitation, 44 per cent also had serious systemic (bodily) disorders capable of damaging their brains. The most frequent was hypoxia, or a reduced oxygen supply. Most people with head injuries become unconscious immediately. This is not as serious as it sounds, or looks, because most people with head injuries recover completely. However, unconsciousness can be partnered by a cessation of breathing, and the brain will be irreparably damaged if respiration stops for six to ten minutes. It is not being denied oxygen the moment that breathing stops because circulation – probably – continues. Nevertheless, every effort should be made to restart breathing (best by mouth to mouth, or mouth to nose), to stop bleeding (by direct pressure on the site, with a clean cloth or just the hand), and to reduce shock (by placing the victim's head lower than his feet).

The hospitals are, in general, extremely undecided about X-rays for head injuries. To irradiate every head injury, just in case there is fracture, is expensive, time-consuming, and fairly unrewarding. In a survey carried out by the Royal College of Radiologists at nine British hospitals all 'uncomplicated head injuries' were assessed. (Plainly the complicated ones formed a different category.) During the survey's ten weeks there were 4,829 such patients. All were routinely X-rayed and 67 fractures were detected, 2 basal, 1 frontal, and 64 vault. In four of these fractured individuals 'intra-cranial haematomas' (blood swellings on the brain) developed, of which three would have been suspected without the benefit of X-ray. Therefore, the incidence of unsuspected blood swelling and fracture in uncomplicated head injuries was 4,828 to 1. As the cost of each X-ray was just under nine pounds the cost of finding that single individual was £43,200.

Currently Britain spends about six million pounds a year on routine skull radiography, and criticism is mounting at this cost and time. Also, all radiation being harmful, no one knows how much damage it is causing. It is, therefore, being suggested, and increasingly loudly, that radiography should be restricted to the more severe cases, such as those with a detectable fracture, with alterations in the level of consciousness (never a good sign), and with neurological indications of damage being done. The saving of money would cause some patients to be sent home wrongly, but responsible relatives could be warned about any signs of deterioration. The wrongful dismissal could then be put right without delay.

A letter to the *Lancet* (by G. T. Watts, of the General Hospital, Birmingham, on 7 November 1981) succinctly raised an issue, quite independent of whether or not X-rays are valuable to the patient.

No one would assume responsibility should the staff find themselves, rightly or wrongly, accused in court of negligence for failing to X-ray . . . If the Department of Health wishes to economise in this way it must, like most other employers, accept liability for its staff when they follow its directives; otherwise it is a foolish casualty officer who does not ask for an X-ray of a head injury . . . Either the lawyers must desist or the hospitals (and ultimately the patient) must pay or protect.

The taking of an X-ray is not the only course of action on behalf of head-injured patients. However, the adage 'Don't just do something; stand there' is pertinent to the general management of severe head injury, at least judging by a report (from B. Jennett and others). They collected information from Glasgow, Rotterdam, Groningen, and Los Angeles. A total of 1,000 cases of severe head damage, all aged under 20, were compared, for admission, for treatment (such as steroids, removal of bone flap at craniotomy, and tracheotomy), and for eventual outcome. There were wide differences in the manner of treatment (Los Angeles giving steroids to 99 per cent, for example, as against Glasgow's 24 per cent) but interestingly no obvious blessing for those who received more attention. In fact 'where there was a difference (in outcome) the treated group had a higher mortality'. Jennett and his co-workers, stated the *Lancet*, 'are to be congratulated for attempting to make us think the unthinkable – namely, that some of our accepted lines of management may make head-injured patients worse rather than better'. Ordinary people, aware of what are known in the automobile industry as 'garage-induced faults', might have been even quicker in thinking the unthinkable, having been thinking it for years.

What the injured brain cannot do, with or without harmful treatment, is recover. Cells in the peripheral nervous system can recover, and often do. They regenerate, and grow back to their original point of contact, recreating abilities that have been lost since the damage first occurred. If cells of the central nervous system are damaged, usually by injury to their axons, they die speedily. Current research suggests that this may not always be the case but it is for all practical purposes; the damaged brain or spinal cord stays damaged. Whatever was done is done, and remains that way for life.

No description of brain damage should miss the opportunity of telling, yet again, the story of the tamping iron. On a show-cased ram-rod in Massachusetts is inscribed: 'This is the bar that was shot through the head of Mr Phinelius P. Gage at Cavendish, Vermont, Sept 14, 1848. He fully recovered from the injure & deposited this bar in the Museum of the Medical College, Harvard University.' In those days the majority of injuries, particularly if received on the operating table or in battle, proved fatal as sepsis took its toll, but Phineas P. Gage (the customary spelling) was not just severely wounded. In fact, he was not wounded in any normal sense because the famous bar went through his skull, from beneath his left eye to the top of his head. Incredibly he survived, but the genial fellow of former days turned into a capricious, obstinate ne'er-do-well. However, that change in personality is almost trivial when set beside the astonishing fact that he recovered, not fully, but well enough to tell the tale for twelve years thereafter. Some thirteen and a half pounds of iron, with the diameter of an old English penny, had gone through a man's brain, leaving him not only alive but with the wit to sell his skeleton, cash in advance, to several medical schools.

For over a century the Gage happening was said to be unique, and indeed it was. Recently others have followed his extraordinary example, not with tamping irons but in similar fashion. Early in 1981 Michael Melnick, aged twenty-four, fell ten feet through the floor of a house under construction in California before impaling his head on a five-eighths-of-an-inch steel reinforcing bar. It entered the back of his head, and six inches of it protruded between his eyes. In the same year John Thompson, aged thirty-nine, was driving near Boston, Massachusetts, when he was involved in an accident. A seven-foot crowbar, loose in his vehicle, went through his head during the impact. The two accidents themselves are not outstanding, at least no more so than Gage's mishap as he tamped down the explosive. What is remarkable is not only that both Melnick and Thompson are alive, but they can tell the tale, and walk, and generally thrive. Thompson was said to have left the Boston hospital with a minor paralysis in his left arm. Melnick also walked from hospital but had injuries to his back (caused by a second steel rod), a shattered nose and tear ducts, and certain psychological complications (such as a persistent – and most reasonable – nightmare of falling through space). It is plainly wrong to label Melnick's injuries as minor, but he looks well enough in recent photographs with his family, and his mind still seems in fair shape. When the *National Enquirer* made offers for his story, 'No way – never' was his reply. One suspects that Gage would have accepted the money, and from a dozen other publications simultaneously. So there are differences between Gage, Melnick and Thompson, but one overwhelming similarity. A huge bar of metal went through their heads – and they lived. A small nick in the spinal cord can put a man in a wheelchair for the rest of his days. A crowbar through the skull can have him walking to his home.

War wounds   Wartime is, of course, a busy time for pieces of iron to be hitting men's heads. And spines. And anywhere they choose, with dramatically different effects. A centimetre to the right, and the soldier would have been a vegetable. As it is he has a modest scar, a thing to laugh about, a sign of those times. A semi-paraplegic friend once described the hospital ship that brought him home. Every bed in his ward contained a spinal injury, some high up and some low down the spine. Those with the highest wounds, and with the greatest degree of bodily paralysis, were those that died most frequently; but not, he observed, directly from their wounds. They would harbour their nightly sleeping pills, and then finish a situation too much for them to contemplate. For a fit young man, with all of living ahead of him, to be turned by a single piece of shrapnel into a supine, useless, incontinent, bed-sored cripple, doomed to stay that way – the change is more than many a man can tolerate. He summons up a final act of courage, and kills himself.

For many the most horrific, astonishing, enlightening and stimulating story of head injury to emerge from any war is that told by A. R. Luria in *The Man with a Shattered World*. The book is part comment by Luria and part the journal, and thoughts, and self-investigation of the shattered man himself, Lyova Zasetsky.

From being a fourth-year student he was called up following the German invasion of the Soviet Union in World War Two. Early in 1943 he was a sub-lieutenant in charge of a platoon of flame-throwers (never popular with the enemy) during the battle of Smolensk. In an attack across a frozen river all went well for a while, but the German machine-guns then opened up and a bullet hit him. As he subsequently wrote in his journal: 'I was killed March 2, 1943.'

The official report of case history No. 3712 phrased it differently:

Sub-Lieutenant Zasetsky, aged 23, suffered a head injury 2 March 1943 that penetrated the left parieto-occipital area of the cranium. The injury was followed by a prolonged coma and, despite prompt treatment in a field hospital, was further complicated by inflammation that resulted in adhesions of the brain to the meninges and marked changes in the adjacent tissues. The formation of scar tissue altered the configurations of the lateral ventricles by pulling the left lateral ventricle upward and producing an incipient atrophy of the medulla of this area.

Luria phrased it differently yet again: 'He suffered intensely, and although his world had been devastated, in the deepest sense he remained a man, struggling to regain what he had lost, to reconstitute his life, and use the powers he used to have.'

For most practical purposes Zasetsky's remark that he had died was correct. He could remember nothing, recognise no one, neither read nor write, and had no idea of his name. Much later he was able to describe this early period: 'I seemed to be some sort of newborn creature that just looked, listened, observed, repeated, but still had no mind of its own.' It was not until the end of the second month after his injury that he could remember his three names, who Lenin was, and words like sun, moon, cloud and rain. He would also fantasise, or so he reported later, imagining he would get over his disability, remember all he had learned, recover proper vision and hearing, become whole again. Simultaneously he was learning even more about his defects: 'Just then I happened to look down, at the floor and at my feet, and I shuddered. I couldn't see the right side of my body, and my hands and feet had disappeared.' Later he realised that he was not able to see out of the right side of either eye. The bullet had destroyed the relevant visual cortex of his brain.

It is easy to imagine that many such victims would have crumpled beneath the weight of their injuries, resigning themselves to a vegetative state. Zasetsky behaved differently. He wanted to be better. He became intrigued by his drawbacks, wondering inquisitively whether his forearm was located near his neck or hands. Increasing knowledge was both good and bad. Aware of a pain in his abdomen he suddenly realised that a lavatory was what he needed. He knew that his penis got rid of urine 'but this pressure was on a different orifice, except that I had forgotten what it was for'. He attempted walking but even this was difficult. '. . . I turned in the other direction and fell because I got confused again, and didn't know which way to walk. Suddenly the words right, left, back, forward, up and down occurred to me, but they weren't any help since I didn't really understand what they meant.' Or, as the psychiatrist Luria put it: 'He no longer had any sense of space, could not judge relationships between things, and perceived the world as broken into thousands of separate parts. Space made no sense for him; he feared it for it lacked stability.'

Nevertheless, the man – both men – persevered. He was assigned a teacher and within a few months was able to remember the entire alphabet, but progress was still painfully slow. 'As the years passed,' wrote Luria, 'he continued to read, trying to recognise the letters, to link one letter to the next, and not forget them.' Writing was even more difficult. When he did learn to write he could not read his own writing, a seeming contradiction that only makes sense in his shattered world. A further spurt of training in a different place, coupled with the casual remark of a doctor that he should try writing automatically – without lifting his hands from the paper – led to further progress. He then began upon his journal.

Initially he called it 'The Story of a Terrible Brain Injury' but he changed this later to 'I'll Fight On'. On some days he wrote ten lines, occasionally more, often less.

Sometimes I'll sit over a page for a week or two. I have to think about it for a long time, slowly considering what I want to say and then comparing various kinds of writing so that I can figure out how to express myself . . . My memory came back to me from the wrong end – that is it became easier for me to remember things that go far back . . . What's happened in my life is simply terrible. This strange illness I have is like living without a brain.

He now lives with his family at Kimovsk but in his own world. He sits at his desk each morning, working on his story, trying to express himself, describing both hope and despair. 'This writing is my only way of thinking. If I shut these notebooks, give it up, I'll be right back in the desert, in that "know-nothing" world of amnesia and emptiness . . . I was killed March 2, 1943.'

Boxing Boxers do die regularly. They have always done so, and the international figure now is about ten a year. Deaths occur in both professional and amateur fights, and in one series of 127 collected by the Welsh National School of Medicine the proportion was 75 to 52. Although damage to the retina is the most frequent severe boxing injury the deaths almost always occur because of damage to the brain. (There has to be qualification because not all dead boxers are given autopsies.) Skull fractures are uncommon, it being difficult to break bones with a gloved fist, and immediate deaths are also very rare, the boxers usually dying later from the injuries they received in the ring. Blood clots are frequent, 'subdural haemorrhage' being the 'outstanding cause of death' in one series of forty-three fatalities examined thoroughly afterwards.

Technically what happens, according to Dr Milton Helpern (then New York City's chief medical examiner), is that

the resulting traumatic cerebral edema from repeated blows to the head can produce irreversible concussion injury, especially of the cerebral vascular system, swelling, and secondary hemorrhagic or ischemic necroses, ending fatally even after evacuation of any subdural hemorrhage.

Essentially this means that blood vessels can leak, or swell or cease supplying areas with blood even after the main clot has been removed. However, there is no difficulty in understanding another part of this report on four dead men. 'When bur holes were made in the heads of the unconscious boxers, brain tissue oozed out like toothpaste from a tube.' The four had all stayed unconscious and then died from fifty-five hours to nine days after their knock-outs.

The reason that a bullet, or even a tamping iron, can go through a skull without even causing unconsciousness (Gage was out only momentarily) and a soft boxing glove can lead to death is that the brain is highly susceptible to sudden acceleration or sudden deceleration when encountering the glove, floor or brick wall. Unconsciousness is likely if the acceleration is equivalent to a change of twenty-eight feet per second. A rabbit punch on the neck or a straight left to the jaw are both good ways of producing acceleration. The resulting unconsciousness is not harmful in itself. It is just a sign that damage may have occurred, either to the brain itself in the tearing of nerve tissue or to blood vessels which will then cause secondary damage. What is unlikely to happen, although it appears in virtually every movie ever made, is that the victim picks himself up, shakes his head, takes in the situation at a glance, and hurries off to catch his assailant. What should happen, at the very least, is that he has a splitting headache or feels sick or is quite unaware of where he is (plus the reason why) and is, therefore, incapable of moving anywhere at more than a self-pitying snail's-pace.

Boxers not only die; they suffer from chronic encephalopathy, alias punch-drunkenness, or being slug happy, slug nutty, or plain goofy. This all means dementia, memory loss, speech-slurring, tremor, and shuffling or other awkward gaits. The brain, in short, does not like being treated as a punch-bag. And neurologists, in general, do not like – as Macdonald Critchley phrased it – 'the deliberate and violent production of a state of motor hypotonus and helplessness'. Or, as Charles Sherrington said much earlier, the reduction of 'a vigorous athlete to an unstrung bulk of flesh'.

Some countries dislike boxing so much that they have banned the professional side of the sport. Sweden was the first to do so, and Norway followed (in 1981). Efforts have frequently been made in Britain, and were stepped up when Johnny Owen, the British and European bantam-weight champion, went to fight Lupe Pintor, of Mexico, in 1980. The press mocked his size, calling him 'skeleton' and the 'world's biggest pipe-cleaner with ears'. In fact, the two men barely differed in weight, both being just under the regulation (for bantams) of 119 pounds/54 kilos, but Owen was taller by 3 inches/7.6 centimetres and, therefore, looked skinnier and weaker. At all events he was knocked out in the twelfth round, stayed unconscious for forty-five days, and died. The following year a private Bill in the House of Lords to ban professional boxing failed as all other such bills have failed. 'Individuals enter boxing from their own interest in the sport, but, having elected to do so, they are subject to the most stringent medical discipline . . .' reported the Earl of Avon, helping the vote to become seventy-seven to forty-seven against.

It would seem, if boxing is the guide, that mankind judges his testicles to be more important than his brain. Life in general makes the same point because 'to hit below the belt' is symbolic of all dastardly behaviour. Certainly such hitting is not allowed either in boxing, in brawls, or in Western punch-ups where shooting a man is less of a crime. Curiosity about this restraint prompted a reading of the Queensberry Rules, first drawn up in 1866 and frequently mentioned ever since. These discuss ring size, hugging, the count of ten, three-minute rounds, one-minute intervals, gloves, boots, the necessary absence of 'seconds' from the ring while the fight is in progress, and nothing whatsoever about where or where not to hit a man. However, Queensberry Rule 10 does say 'that in all other respects' the contest shall be governed by the London Prize Ring's rules.

Curiosity persisted. These rules were initiated in 1838 by the British Pugilists Protective Association, revised in 1853, and revised again in 1861, but were chiefly concerned with alleged fouls and did not themselves initiate the idea that hitting below the belt was particularly distasteful. For that it is necessary to go back to John Broughton, a Bristol fighter and 'Father of Boxing'. In April 1741 he beat an opponent with a blow under the heart. The loser died within a month and Broughton, either in remorse or with anxiety that he too might receive such a blow, helped to frame a set of rules 'agreed by several gentlemen in Broughton's Amphitheatre 16 August 1743'. There were seven, with the seventh stating that 'No person is to hit his adversary when he is down or seize him by the ham, the breeches or any parts below the waist.' It would seem, therefore, that the spur for this ruling came from a wish to prevent death in the ring and to maintain the head-hitting side of the sport. Since then boxers have been content to batter each other's brains rather than their hearts, their abdomens or any other parts below the waist.

The United States has had occasional flurries of attempting to ban the sport, notably when some popular boxer has paid the price; but to no avail. There was furore, for example in 1965, when Lucian ('Sonny') Banks, of Detroit, died of a blood clot on the brain three days after being knocked out by Leotis Martin. Banks had achieved fame in 1962 when he managed to knock down Cassius Clay, only for Clay to knock him out four rounds later. As *Time* magazine laconically recorded, 'Banks was the 64th fighter to die of ring injuries in the last five years.' The latest move to make boxing safer is the creation of a foamier, thumbless glove that cuts down punching power by up to 50 per cent. It was designed to prevent detached retinas, the most common severe injury, and has been mandatory in all New York State bouts, for example, since January 1982. Apparently those who love knock-outs are against it, and even the medical profession is none too happy. Is a one-punch despatch easier on the brain than, as *Medical World News* put it, a 'long drubbing on a groggy but upright gladiator'? Nobody knows 'just which is more dangerous', commented Dr

Vincent D. Campbell, medical director for NY State's athletic commission.

Other sports Of course, what upsets many about boxing is its purpose to inflict damage, particularly to the head. That fact should not detract from the knowledge that many other sports do far more damage in numbers killed and injured, although not in proportion to the contestants involved. There are, on average, twenty-seven deaths a year on the squash courts of the United Kingdom, attributable to the heart rather than the head. Brawling in the British Army is well documented, and comes nearer to boxing. From 1968 to 1977 there were thirty deaths associated with this sport. Some of the soldiers died from sub-arachnoid haemorrhage, a common cause of sudden death as an artery ruptures in the brain's sub-arachnoid space. Although brawling was its main cause in the army, there were others, such as sport itself, pushing and loading vehicles, carrying a friend, making love, and electrocution. 'It would seem,' wrote the doctor who had investigated this series and then reported the facts in the *British Medical Journal*, 'that soldiers spend more time making war – not love.' Not necessarily; it may just mean that their punch-up partners are less well matched.

Golf in Britain is at the top of the league for head injuries, not so much from the ball but from standing too near the swinging club. Horse riding comes second (or first in some areas) and the Jockey Club, well aware of this fact, has strict rules that concussed riders should take compulsory time off to recover properly. Third is football, largely because so many people play it and partly because of heading the ball. There is undoubtedly a correct way to head it, but that does not take into account the jostling activities of other players. A ball, wrongfully received, is a boxing glove in its own fashion. Rugby players also suffer head injuries, notably in the scrum and during tackles. One survey in the north of England discovered that a third of players had had more than one concussion in the previous five years. Most of them had not reported the fact to a doctor. The Senior Medical Officer of the Amateur Boxing Association reported to the *BMJ* in 1965 that he had seen 'a number of Rugby League football players who were much more "groggy" than the average boxer'. The comparison may be unjust, severe cases against average, but the point stays valid. Head injuries receive most publicity with boxers and less in other sports.

American football is, as they say, something else. It has much of boxing to it, in principle if not with fists. There is an express intent to put out of action members of the other side who might tackle the man with the ball. One school coach counted forty-nine football injuries in a year, including seven to the knee, six broken bones and five concussions. Nationwide over a five-year period there were forty-one spinal injuries with paralysis. A schoolboy was made a quadriplegic in 1975. Denied football he entered America's second-favourite sport, and sued. From the helmet manufacturer he received $98,000, and from the school district $6.3 million. (His principal argument lay in not being taught by his school coaches to avoid running with his head down.) Helmet manufacturers have paid out $25 million in damages for similar suits in the past few years, and many school districts feel, understandably, that they should encourage other sports than football. The cost of the necessary protective equipment is becoming prohibitive.

The sport or pastime of motorcycling is particularly prone to head injuries. According to a leader in the *Lancet* 'those who do not wear helmets have head injury rates three to nine times greater than those who do'. The United States, in its shifting legislation, has helped to make this point. In 1967 the government made certain grants to states conditional upon state laws enforcing helmets. Most states obeyed, and the motorcyclist death-rate fell from 10 per 10,000 annually to 7. Congress then cut the strings attached to those grants, permitting states to repeal their helmet laws should they so wish. A total of twenty-eight states wished to do so (or softened their laws so that, for instance, helmets were only compulsory for the under-eighteens). The result: helmet wearers dropped from 100 per cent to 50 per cent, and the motor cycle death-rate went up 40 per cent.

'Boxing,' said Dr Max M. Novich, ex-boxer and medical consultant to the World Boxing Association, 'is one of the least dangerous sports. And it is time we stopped listening to the cries of hysterical old women on boxing safety.' Not everyone would immediately applaud the remark, but, undoubtedly, other sports are also dangerous. And, because so many play them, they can cause more injuries. Boxing should not receive all the limelight for head injuries and damaged brains.

Headache is a series of contradictions. It is mankind's most widespread complaint, and yet some heads have never ached. It is mildly disturbing or puts paid to that day (or week). It may be accompanied by nausea, diarrhoea, constipation, or it may not. It can be felt at the front, top, back, side or sides of the head. It can be related to a high metabolism or a low one. There may be an obvious cause – hangover, accidental whiplash, a knock on the skull, anxiety, or there may not. The pain may be unimportant or the first indication of a lethal condition.

The headache itself is not a disease but a symptom. It has been the subject of considerable study for over two thousand years and yet today the reason why so many bodily conditions result in headache is 'not entirely known', 'poorly understood', 'difficult' (to quote from different authors). Even the term 'migraine' has its origins in the second century AD. Galen coined 'hemicrania' to describe this frequently one-sided, half-headed condition, and yet migraine still assaults its victims much as it always did. The most contradictory point of all is that the brain itself is incapable of pain (it can be cut or burned without sensation); so too is the bone surrounding it. The person with a splitting headache will be the first to deny this statement, so encased is the pain within his head.

Attempts have been made to classify headaches. Some of the groupings are very extensive, but herewith a simpler list (compiled by Dr Joseph D. Wassersug):

1. Migraine-type headaches (about which more later).
2. Cluster-type headaches (also known as histamine headaches). Related to migraine, but different and more frequent in men. Pain is at front of head or around one eye. Ache rapidly increases, but starts to subside after perhaps twenty minutes. May be three or more attacks a day, often at night, for a month or so (the cluster). Then freedom from headache for a few years.)
3. Muscle-contraction or tension headaches (often due to contraction of neck and scalp muscles which then affect blood vessels in the area. Blood vessels, whether dilated or contracted, can be the cause of pain, and provide most reason for most headaches).
4. Nasal and sinus conditions. (All sinuses, such as those in the nose, above the eyebrows and in the cheeks, are lined with nerves. Inflammation or pressure change affecting these sinus nerves will lead to head pain.)
5. Nervous and emotional (which may act in association with raised blood pressure).
6. Fever and systemic infections (probably resulting, as with so many other headaches, from distension of the cerebral and pial arteries. Those that accompany typhoid, typhus and influenza are most intense, and are dull, deep, aching and generalised).
7. Poisons and intoxications. (Similar to fever headaches.)
8. Brain tumours and abscesses (partly cause increased pressure and partly distort nerves and blood vessels, both leading to

pain. A general difference is that tumour headaches become worse with time whereas migraine becomes bad quickly and stays that way until it goes. Usually tumour headache is of a deep, aching, steady, dull nature, not rhythmic or throbbing. Overlies tumour in a third of cases.)

9. Brain inflammation, as in meningitis (often accompanied by a stiff neck. The meninges, which become inflamed, lie between brain and inside of skull; they are extremely pain sensitive. Cerebro-spinal fluid, extracted by lumbar puncture, is no longer clear and colourless owing to presence of dead white cells, or pus.)

10. Blood pressure. (Sometimes there is association between BP and headache, but more often not. Even if high blood pressure exists at same time as headache not necessarily related. Persistent pressure headache may be warning that brain blood vessel has ruptured or clot is forming but, once again, not necessarily.)

11. Eyestrain, and disorders of ears and teeth. (Eyestrain often said to cause most headaches, but not true. If eyestrain is suspected a good eye specialist, writes Wassersug, 'is about as good a place as any to begin'. Once the eyestrain has been eliminated as a possible cause, and if headaches persist, other possible causes can be checked. The ear is uniquely innervated. No other structure is supplied by sensory nerves from so many neural segments. Teeth are also well innervated. Inflammation anywhere in these systems can lead to headache.)

12. Neuritis or neuralgia (less specific than the others, but inflammation or pain along the course of a nerve can, directly or indirectly, lead to headache).

This lengthy list can also lead to wonder that we do not suffer from headache at all times. There is inevitably curiosity about the location of all this undoubted throbbing and unpleasantness. If both the bone and the brain are so insensitive why should the head's top half, almost entirely bone and brain, be the site of so much pain? Why not the right foot, also well supplied with nerves and arteries, or the abdomen where so much occurs? There are three main answers. Firstly, the head is at the top of the body (and, therefore, its blood circulation is more problematical than elsewhere). Secondly, the head is balanced on its seven cervical vertebrae (therefore muscles and ligaments must be constantly holding it in balance). Thirdly, the head is a rigid container (and, therefore, any swelling, as of a blood vessel, immediately raises the internal pressure. A minute tumour in the head can cause great pain. A huge abdominal tumour may not even be noticed).

Headache, according to the US National Ambulatory Medical Care Survey, was the cause of 18 million visits to the doctor during a recent year (1977–78). It, therefore, ranked seventh among symptoms sending people to waiting rooms, but caused only 2 per cent of the doctor-visit total (although 18 per cent of visits to neurologists). Most headaches are dealt with individually, by lying down, taking it easy, or swallowing aspirins (first introduced in 1899). The Survey also reported that twice as many women as men visited doctors because of headaches, but slightly more of the men were found to have 'serious or very serious' causes for them.

The most authoritative work on the subject has for a long time been *Headache and other Head Pain* by Harold G. Wolff, who constantly updated it until his death in 1962. It abounds with information: 'the mean threshold value of jolt headache in normal subjects was approximately 6 g . . . even in the same individual this varied from day to day with a range as broad as ±2.7 g.' . . . 'Much experimental work has been done by inducing headaches, e.g. by draining 20 ccs of cerebrospinal fluid from the brain' . . . 'When a meal is missed or postponed the subsequent hypoglycaemia (sugar lack) in persons who are subject to vascular headache may induce headache' . . . 'There is no evidence that relations between the headache and constipation is that of cause and effect' . . . 'Of 36 persons subject to migraine headache attacks, nine had inverted nipples' . . . 'Vascular headaches of moderate intensity were completely eliminated by centrifuge' . . . three women suffered headache 'which started without warning at the beginning of orgasm and lasted from several minutes to several days'.

Dr Wolff's life-work is impressive and completely contradicts any doubts that the subject of headache might not possess sufficient information to warrant a whole book. He was particularly intrigued by the enigma of headache; its nothingness as a symptom or its awful implications. As he phrased it: 'There are few instances in human experience when so much pain may mean so little in terms of tissue injury, but failure to separate the ominous from the trivial may cost life or create paralysing fear.'

Migraine Needless to say, Wolff had a major section on Galen's hemicrania, and so does every work on head pain. There are, according to one survey, over two million in Britain who suffer from it to some degree (or 4 per cent of any similar population). Another states that there are 5–6½ million (10–13 per cent), with 4 million having more than seven attacks each year. Still other reports state that half the migraine sufferers never tell their doctors about it and, therefore, do not figure in the totals. The number of sufferers is undoubtedly huge, whichever number is taken.

And, so one suspects, it always has been. Events alleged to trigger off attacks are not necessarily modern, for they include: sleep; menstruation; heat, light, noise, travelling; diet, such as cheese, chocolate, alcohol (red wine in particular), absent meals; and psychological. Businessmen are said to get them more on Saturdays, curates on Mondays. As Galen's hemicrania became (according to Wolff) hemigranea, then emigranea, and migranea, and megrim and finally migraine (my *Chambers* and *Oxford* dictionaries both define migraine as 'same as megrim'), the number of sufferers throughout the millennia has not led to a simple remedy. A doctor reported recently that thirty years ago everything known about migraine could be written on a postcard. Today, he said, it is two postcards.

What has always been known is how these headaches manifest themselves. Pain over the temple is (usually) the first sign. This spreads to one or both sides of the head. The pain is due to enlargement of the head's blood vessels and persists (commonly) for some six to eight hours or (occasionally) for the whole twenty-four of a very miserable day. It can be accompanied by nausea, vomiting, constipation or diarrhoea, and – very commonly – photophobia, in that darkness is preferable. The most characteristic visual event is an inability to see with part of the visual field, but there can also be dazzling lines, fragmentation, and distortions of colour and size. (Variations in blood flow to the parietal lobes are thought to be responsible.) The victim does look ill, with pale skin (although the face may be red) that is sweaty and may even smell. Despite all this only very rarely is permanent damage done to the brain. If this were not the case, bearing in mind the frequency of migraine in such a sizeable proportion of the population, there would be very many brain-damaged people. And, because women are the greater sufferers from migraine, there would be even more brain-injured women.

Today's second migraine postcard would contain quite a bit of information about the biochemical changes during an attack. Typically there is a rise in plasma noradrenaline which leads to the greater aggregation of blood platelets. Simultaneously or subsequently there is a release of other substances, such as serotonin (involved in the sleep/wakefulness cycle) and these provoke further aggregation, or clumping, of the blood platelets. Serotonin is also thought to influence the permeability of the blood-brain barrier, thus encouraging its own entry into the brain. As a result of all this, and much more (with the liberation of every chemical affecting the liberation of others), there is constriction of the arteries coupled with neurological disturbance. Many amines in food (its nitrogen components) are influential in releasing serotonin from the platelets, which is possibly why certain foods can trigger migraine; but, in such a complex community of cause, effect, counter-effect and so on, there is – as yet – no straightforward answer. It is even thought that the pre-migraine phase (which sufferers can recognise as the quiet before the storm) may be the greater villain, being a decrease in cerebral blood-flow, which then leads to a compensatory increase that creates the build-up in pressure, the headache, platelet aggregation, and the rest of the cycle.

As for treatment a third postcard would probably have much of its space left blank. Once the attack has begun treatment is less effective than in the pre-headache phase. There are compounds which discourage platelet formation, and others which block serotonin. Claims for their effectiveness vary, of course, but it is generally agreed that migraine is best treated before it happens. Once the headache – and its accompanying symptoms – have started 'the aim should be', according to a *Lancet* leader, 'to relieve pain and nausea by standard analgesics and antiemetics'. In discussing a new drug, which had been tried for acute attacks 'with good results', the *Lancet* added and concluded: '. . . there has been no comparison with aspirin, which has a similar mode of action and is much cheaper.'

A final riddle, fundamental to migraine, is why it should so frequently attack just one side. And why it most commonly varies from side to side in alternate attacks. And why right-handed people most frequently have right-sided attacks. After all, its unilateral behaviour gave the thing its name; but, or so it is depressingly easy to suspect, it may have acquired yet another modification of its 1,800-year-old title before there is either an understanding of it or a proper cure.

Self-damage No one knows the true figure for global self-inflicted damage because each country has a different idea over its interpretation. According to the Soviet Union and China, for example, it does not exist, in that it does not appear in their statistics. According to Egypt and much of the Arab world it occurs only very rarely, such damage still having a stigma attached to it. According to most of the world it is particularly prevalent in Sweden, but the Swedish figures have never corroborated this piece of universal folk-lore. The official United States ratio is about twelve per hundred thousand people, but articles on the subject frequently refer to a proportion three times as high. It all depends, in short, what you mean by suicide; but, whatever yardstick is used, it is probable that at least a million people on this planet kill themselves each year.

In one sense there is no place in a book dedicated to the human brain, to its workings and other attributes, for mention of a custom which merely destroys that brain. In another sense the book would not be complete without a description of this ultimate in malfunction. The brain (for no other organ is in control) decides to kill itself, or rather to destroy the body in which it resides. Suicide is also the ultimate in depression, the far end of the spectrum that could be said to start with mere unhappiness. In any sense it is a killer, taking a toll similar to that exacted by the motor car; but it is in a different category from accident. A million or so brains a year can think of nothing better to do than put an end to themselves. No animal carries out such a final act. The apparent self-destruction of, say, the lemmings is not a multiple or individual choice to end it all, but a mass determination to migrate elsewhere. It just so happens that death lies along the path for numbers of them. With suicide mankind is quite unique.

The act appears to be most frequent in the more advanced societies, among men, among the young adult and the elderly, and in times of peace rather than of war. As the philosopher William James said: 'Sufferings and hardships do not, as a rule, abate the love of life; they seem, on the contrary, usually to give it a keener zest.' Northern Ireland, for example, with all its troubles and high unemployment, has the lowest rate of the four portions of the United Kingdom. Or perhaps the British situation should not be used as an example as it is proceeding on a course not being taken by other lands. Firstly, until recently, there was a very substantial drop in suicides – 34 per cent between the early 1960s and 1970s. Secondly, most other countries experienced a rise during the same period: fifteen out of eighteen European nations did so, the exceptions being Greece, Scotland, and England and Wales. (It is tedious that British statistics so rarely tie up with each other. Only occasionally are there official figures for the entire United Kingdom. Those for England and Wales are almost always united, but Scotland is often separate. Simple arithmetic should be possible – by adding together England-and-Wales, Northern Ireland, Scotland – but rarely do these four portions of the United Kingdom produce comparable figures to be neatly totalled.)

The British and Greek fall was not just different; it was completely contrary. Many of the European nations had rises equal to the British fall, Denmark, Hungary, Ireland, Holland and Poland all having increases of more than 30 per cent during the same period. There are, of course, theories for this British difference: the increased number of prescriptions for anti-depressants (from 2.4 to 5.8 million in England and Wales between 1963 and 1970); improved treatment of psychiatric illness (a Medical Research Council team studied 100 suicides between 1966 and 1968, and diagnosed mental illness in 93 of them); better follow-up of attempted suicides (one-third of all suicides have previously made an attempt); better hospital treatment for those who would surely have died without such prompt care; the founding of the Samaritans in 1953 (although it is difficult to prove this good work does in fact do good); and a slight shift in the collection of information (the stigma may have gone, but that is no reason for grouping every possible suicide into the suicide category. In 1979, for example, 2,564 men and 1,631 women are known to have killed themselves in England and Wales, but a further 1,564 people died in circumstances in which suicide could not be ruled out. By the same token this total could not be ruled in, and that must go for many car accidents, drownings, alcohol bouts, etc. (Drive too fast long enough and you will end up dead, just as surely as with a noose, but possibly killing others *en route*.) Finally, Britain is always telling itself, and even being told on occasion, that it has the world's best television service. It is just possible, knowing the time that the suicide-prone elderly spend in front of their sets, that this ultimate in drugs, Aldous Huxley's 'soma' in its way, also acts as a good Samaritan, and keeps down suicides. (Conversely – dread thought – the very awfulness of TV programmes in many countries may be contributing to their higher levels of self-destruction.)

In every country which compiles and publishes figures, women score less than men (although they are catching up. In England and Wales the ratio was 3.1/1 in 1901 and is now 1.6/1). Totals may be suspect, as countries differ in their definitions, but that fact of the sex-ratio seems unassailable. The international suicide table, published by the World Health Organisation, puts Hungary at the top, with 40 deaths a year per 100,000 of the population (and with twice as many male as female victims). Then come East Germany, Finland, Denmark, Austria, Switzerland, West Germany, Czechoslovakia, Sweden (with 20 per 100,000, and with 2.5 times as many men as women), Japan (also alleged to kill themselves frequently, and where the male/female ratio is 1.6/1), Belgium, France, Bulgaria, USA, Canada, Poland, Norway, Australia, Iceland, New Zealand, Netherlands, England and Wales, Scotland, Israel, Northern Ireland, Spain, and Greece (2.8 per

100,000, with its sex ratio 2.1/1). Remembering the activities of Palestinians, Basques and Irish republicans, it is intriguing that these activists have been operating mostly in and around countries at the bottom end of the suicide league. Otherwise, it is difficult to discover associations, say with socialism, wealth, industrialisation, decline in status, climate, gross national product, religion, or any other parameter.

C. P. Miles, in the *Journal of Nervous and Mental Disease* concluded (in 1977) that almost all American suicides could be attributed to: depressive illness (much the largest category, about which more in a moment), alcoholism, schizophrenia (more on pages 265–270), neurosis, and personality disorder. Similar British studies have considered the proportions to be: depressive illness 64 per cent, alcoholism 15 per cent, schizophrenia 3 per cent. As ever, there is difficulty with definition, particularly with neurosis and depression. The *Lancet* considered (in 1979) that there is the 'distinction between pathological depression and non-pathological unhappiness, the relation between neurotic [reactive] and psychotic [endogenous] depression, and separation of unipolar [depression alone] from bipolar illnesses, in which depression and mania occur at different stages of [the] illness'. Or does everything blend into everything else, with only mankind's lust for classification obscuring the real issue, that sick minds form a sort of continuum with healthy minds? Or is it even possible – an unhappy possibility – that many of those who kill themselves are in fact healthier than many others who just carry on, sadly, unhelpfully, even painfully to themselves and others?

Depression, for all its reasons and appearances, has been bluntly defined as: a disease, a posture, a natural state in the social hierarchy, an understandable reaction to loss, and the final common symptom of a variety of disorders. In other words, and according to the last idea, it is tantamount to fever, being a uniform result from a battery of different causes. With depression the many causes all impair the capacity of the central nervous system to adapt to environmental input (just as fevers all result from an inability of the body to maintain *status quo* and temperature following some external assault). It is believed that depression is overreaction to some kinds of sensory stimuli. This common result from multiple causes is now being said to make the depressions analogous not just to the broad range of fevers but, say, to the similarity of the pneumonias. Dr Joseph J. Schildkraut, of Harvard, has even proposed what the depression similarity might be, namely a deficit of catecholamines in the depressed brain. (For more about them see the end of the section on brain death, page

306.) For treatment, as with the pneumonias, it is, therefore, first necessary to discover which kind of depression is the underlying cause, just as the diagnosis of pneumonia is followed by sputum culture in the bacteriology laboratory. However, and currently, that is easier said than done. One type of bacterial pneumonia can be distinguished from another. The same degree of precision is far from possible with the depressions.

In the United States one American in ten allegedly suffers from serious depression at any one time. It is known that over sixty million prescriptions for benzodiazepines are filled in annually. Not every doctor contributes to this deluge, an article in the *New England Journal of Medicine* saying they ranged in their attitudes from 'pharmacologic Calvinism' to 'psychotropic hedonism'. The wide range of individual (medical) opinion suggests a lack of reliable scientific guidelines for diagnosis and prescription. So long as this lack lasts it is the moral stance of the physician that will, in the main, determine therapy.

In the meantime depression will stay as a depressing problem, one difficult to get hold of, as *Medical World News* phrased it, 'semantically and diagnostically – not to mention therapeutically'. At least everyone knew they were talking of the same thing when they could not cure, for example, the Black Death. Depression is so much more than one thing. It is different things to different people, and the world is still desperately short of a cure. The million or so who take the ultimate step in self-destruction are proof enough of that. The countless millions who live with their depressions are yet further proof, if this is necessary, that the human brain does not always run smoothly within itself. Neither does any organ but these others cannot take the final step of choosing to destroy the organism in which they live. That is the brain's unique attribute, or rather the human brain's for such wilful self-damage is our ability and ours alone. Animals may pine to death, or so it is often argued, but they do not kill themselves. That is a happening, entirely human. And so, one suspects, is the wealth of depression lying to one side of it.

Schizophrenia   It was R. D. Laing, once described as a psychiatrist-cum-poet-cum-guru, who created a catch phrase for schizophrenia when he labelled it a sane reaction to an insane world. The epigram, possibly more suitable for suicide, is becoming increasingly less so for schizophrenia as more and more chemical disturbances are being discovered that partner it. What is also unsuitable is the traditional definition of schizophrenia as split-brained, or a brain divided against itself. Schizophrenia may mean divided mind (after two Greek words), but a lot of redefinition has happened since E. Bleuler first introduced the term in 1911. (The illness had certainly been known beforehand but Bleuler singled out those disturbances of psychological origin which Kraepelin had previously grouped together under 'dementia praecox'.)

A major problem, despite there having been (according to various estimates) 100,000 or 200,000 papers on the subject since it began, and therefore more than on any other form of mental illness, is that there is no firm, diagnostic test for schizophrenia. Certainly there is nothing that can be checked in a laboratory. So how is it known whether someone has the disorder or not? One way is to reach for the nearest volume (and the third edition) of the *Diagnostic and Statistical Manual* of the American Psychiatric Association. Entry DSM-111 states:

> The essential feature of this group of disorders are the presence of certain psychotic features during the active phase of the illness, characteristic symptoms involving multiple psychological processes, deterioration from a previous level of functioning, onset before age 45, and a duration of at least six months. The disturbance is not due to an Affective Disorder or Organic Mental Disorder. At some phase of the illness Schizophrenia always involves delusions, hallucinations, or certain disturbances in the form of thought.

This 1980 definition is terse and somewhat difficult, but it meant that some 30–40 per cent of psychiatric patients previously thought of as schizophrenics could no longer be labelled that way. For them the outlook and general prognosis was probably better than for the victims of schizophrenia.

The so-called active phase is a necessary feature, but it may involve any of a number of characteristic symptoms, such as delusions. They can be of persecution, conspiracy, thought broadcasting (the belief that others can hear personal thoughts), thought insertion (more or less the opposite; that others are pushing their thoughts into the victim's head), thought withdrawal (a sucking-out of personal thoughts, making space for thoughts from others), and a general belief in being controlled from the outside. There are also hallucinations. Even though vision is the No. 1 sense system, the prime disturbances are auditory (possibly making Joan of Arc one of the best recorded, early schizophrenics). Less frequent are hallucinations to do with sight, touch, smell and taste.

There is also, generally, a prodromal phase (giving the earliest symptoms). This was well summed up in the *New England Journal of Medicine* (in December 1981). It

> varies greatly in duration and is characterised by social withdrawal, impaired work functioning or self-care, markedly peculiar behaviour (e.g. collecting garbage or hoarding food), a blunted or inappropriate affect, digressive, vague, overelaborate, circumstantial, or metaphorical speech, odd or magical thinking (e.g. clairvoyance, telepathy, or 'sixth sense'), and unusual perceptual experience.

There must be an active phase for schizophrenia to be diagnosed, and there may or may not be a residual phase; but there must be continuous signs of the illness (as per DSM-111) for at least six months.

The active phase is frequently followed by a residual phase, not greatly different in appearance from the prodromal one. Unfortunately (for diagnosis) there are many mental diseases that mimic schizophrenia. Not one of its symptoms is unique to it. However, there are some that are particularly applicable to schizophrenia, and they, according to Dr Theo C. Manschreck, of Boston, are 'thought insertion, broadcasting, withdrawal, delusion of control, and certain types of auditory hallucinations'. Accurate diagnosis is important, not so much because there is clear-cut treatment for schizophrenia but because other psychotic individuals must not be lumped into this category.

All these clinical definitions and pronouncements about schizophrenia may seem detached or even remote from the actual problem. To restore the balance herewith a small story (reported by Dr Tim Crow at a CIBA Foundation symposium on the subject in 1969). An Englishman was standing in a bar in a small town in New York State when his American brother-in-law picked up a long, straight biscuit from the counter, and said, 'Have one of these; they are salty.' Immediately the Englishman/patient 'realised' that his brother-in-law was accusing him of being a homosexual and was organising a gang to spy on him. The essence of the schizophrenia symptom, added Dr Crow, is that the delusion arises *de novo*, and the patient invests a particular event or perception with a significance which cannot be understood either in terms of the event itself or of the patient's previous life history. A second story (included in a letter to the *Lancet* by David E. Hatoff, of the San Diego School of Medicine) may help to make the point that no two cases are the same.

A twenty-four-year-old schizophrenic, who had swallowed a razor blade padded with bread refused endoscopy (inspection of his stomach) and spent an uneventful week in hospital. By court order, fibreoptic endoscopy was done under general anaesthesia on the eighth day. Corroded fragments of the blade were found in the stomach, but these crumbled when grasped. He recovered – and subsequently ate fluorescent bulbs.

Full recovery from schizophrenia is rare, and rarer still if it has not occurred within the first two years. Its social effects, to use Manschreck's description, are 'devastating', while its use of social and health services is 'monumental'. It has been estimated, for the US alone, that the illness causes a $14 billion loss in individual productivity. The cause of it is still not known and its prognosis is extremely depressing. The current treatment is mainly a matter of sending the patients home (if possible, in that they are not violent or just too ill), of preventing a relapse (frequent if the medication is no longer taken) and maintaining adjustment to the new situation. Notwithstanding this assistance, death occurs earlier for the schizophrenic.

The two brightest recent events for Bleuler's illness have been this increased home treatment and the introduction of neuroleptic drugs. Until 1950 the main task of a mental hospital was to provide asylum for long-term patients, most of whom suffered from schizophrenia; but then came the two advances. More correctly, the two were only one as the new drugs, first used in the late 1950s, made home care feasible. Ever since the first – chlorpromazine – was introduced it has been known they were not a cure but merely a banisher of symptoms. For many sufferers these neuroleptics, sometimes unhelpfully called major tranquillisers, can provide almost complete relief from the disease's symptoms. More intriguing, they apparently have an entirely specific effect – good for schizophrenia but not for other forms of psychiatric disability. It would seem, therefore, that these phenothiazines, the drugs in question, might be plugging a gap, much as insulin does for the diabetics.

Unfortunately schizophrenia is more complex than that, and less easily treated. What appears to be happening is that the drugs affect the working of dopamine, a neurotransmitter or passer of messages from one nerve cell to the next. In some sort of way the drugs affect the action of dopamine, a fact which, in its turn, implies that schizophrenia is caused by a chemical lesion rather than some external psychiatric happening. Further evidence on this score has come from the amphetamines, the powerful drugs so casually called and used as pep pills, notably in the swinging 1960s. Abusers of these drugs, who then became addicts, frequently also became not just psychotic but indistinguishable from acute paranoid schizophrenics. The blessing, in their case, was that they reverted to normal as the pep pill lost its effects. And the blessing for the experimental scientists was that someone could be given amphetamines, show all the signs of schizophrenia, then be given chlorpromazine, and soon return to normal. Animal experiments completed this picture by proving that amphetamine increased the concentrations of dopamine in some parts of the brain (such as the basal ganglia).

It would seem, therefore (riding rough-shod over all manner of other facts, complicating neural chemistry, different neurotransmitters, and varying forms and phases of schizophrenia), that an excess of dopamine action is somehow linked to the cause of the disease. By contrast, a deficiency of dopamine seems to be linked to the cause of Parkinson's disease. There is, consequently, an excitement akin to one completed part of a jigsaw suddenly linking up with quite another part.

Other schizophrenic facts are: abnormally high concentrations of dopamine have been found in the brains of some dead victims of the disease; this discovery became even more specific when it was realised that it was always found excessively among those whose schizophrenia had begun before they were twenty-four (which means about half the cases); and care is necessary in interpreting this information because virtually all schizophrenics have been liberally dosed with drugs (particularly the most long-suffering individuals). The early onset cases (pre-twenty-four) seem to have a greater genetic basis – it runs more in families – but, overall, an identical twin experiences a 60 per cent chance of acquiring the illness if it has already attacked his/her other half. More schizophrenics are born at certain seasons, such as the year's second quarter in Ireland, and its first quarter in Switzerland, and the majority (whenever they are born) have an unusually long fifth (little) finger plus a greater preponderance than normal of all manner of other hand features, such as equal length of fingers three and four, square fingertips, and a Simian crease (as in Down's individuals). One of the latest, and oddest, discoveries is that dialysis seems, on occasion, to help. Quite what is being extracted from the blood, and why this should help, are still unknown; but the debate continues, and so does dialysis.

All such extra peculiarities make it harder and harder to see the illness as a reaction of sanity to insanity, since they make it consistently harder to see schizophrenia as anything simple. At least that was achieved in the old days, when all its sufferers were bluntly, simply, swiftly named as mad.

Parkinsonism is increasingly common with advancing years, affecting 1 in 100 over the age of fifty (as against 1 in 1,000 of the general population). There is a genetic factor, with 5–10 per cent of affected individuals having a family history of it. It shortens life, although less than it used to. More victims of it die from, for example, accidental falls these days rather than the Parkinsonism itself. The prime cause of it is still unknown.

The characteristics which manifest themselves as the Parkinsonian syndrome have a wide variety of causes. Commonest are idiopathic paralysis agitans, encephalitis, and drugs. The first, which merely defines the disease (idiopathic meaning an illness of unknown cause), is the most frequent of the three. The second used to be more so, particularly when it was one delayed result of the encephalitis (lethargica) epidemic of 1918–26. The third – drugs – has already been mentioned (in the previous section). Other events to cause the syndrome are tumour, carbon monoxide or manganese poisoning, brain atrophy (wasting) and brain injury. Parkinson brains have frequently been examined after death, the most regular discovery from this work being, to quote from a review article in the *British Medical Journal* (of December 1978), 'a loss of pigmented neurones in the pars compacta of the substantia nigra'. This is a dopamine-producing portion of the brain, and dopamine deficiency is the most important biochemical error in Parkinson's disease. The sufferers even pass less of it in their urine. Treatment, therefore, involves boosting the dopamine supply, and levadopa is the standard drug, it being a precursor of dopamine. In other words, give levadopa, wait for the body to convert it to dopamine, and then watch as the symptoms diminish or disappear. (Unfortunately levadopa does not work for every patient, and can also become steadily less effective in others. Plainly the disease is more complex, probably involving other neurotransmitters, and leading on to cerebral atrophy with changes much like those in Alzheimer's and other forms of senile dementia.)

'It takes me longer to get going and longer to do things,' is the sort of remark made (almost daily) by many normal humans, particularly those aware that more days lie behind them than ahead. The statement can also be the first suggestion of Parkinson's, particularly if it is allied to poor manual ability and impaired gait and posture. Handwriting often becomes cramped and spiderish. Shoelaces can become, once again, the problem they used to be in very much earlier days. Diagnosis of Parkinson's (named by

James Parkinson, in London, in 1817) necessitates that two of its three cardinal signs must be present – tremor, bradykinesia (very slow movement) and rigidity.

The average age of onset is fifty-five. In the years before levadopa (until the late 1960s) the length of life after this definite onset was about a decade. Longevity has now improved but is still not as good as with ordinary members of the population, with women faring worse than men. However, quality of life has shown a very marked advance, thanks to the dopa drugs. The old bed-ridden Parkinson problems of bed-sores, pneumonia and blood clots are no longer common. Fractures that lead to death are more frequent, an impossibility during the chair-bound, bed-bound days. To die from a fall rather than a bed-sore may seem a slender advance, but this indicates mobility, a better kind of life, a less demanding disease. Besides, Parkinson's victims are also dying more frequently these days of strokes, cancer, and heart attacks, further signs that they are joining the ranks of ordinary people. The fact that 'the prime cause of the disease remains unknown', to quote again from the *BMJ*, may interest medical practitioners rather more than those on whom they practise. Relief from oppressive symptoms is what patients want, and the dopa drugs have undoubtedly prolonged the period of social independence. Parkinson's is still a killer in its way, but less speedily and with greater dignity *en route*.

Stroke A family doctor in the average European community will encounter about six a year. Overall there are 100–150 new cases per 100,000 population or, for the United Kingdom, 55,000 annually. Roughly half the cases – this proportion varies widely – are admitted to hospital, and of this number between a third and a half die within the first three weeks. Of those that do not die, but were admitted (and according to a report from the Greenwich Hospital, London) a quarter will become independent again, one half will be able to walk independently 'with an aid' and have 'limited' personal independence, while the remaining quarter will be confined to 'bed or chair'. What was known to Hippocrates as apoplexy, but is now more commonly known as stroke, is the commonest cause of severe or permanent physical disability in all advanced countries. Currently about one in five hundred of their number are victims of this particular form of damage, an injury most apparent in the body yet caused by damage to the brain.

In essence it is caused either (less commonly) by a clot preventing blood supply to part of the brain or (much more frequently) by haemorrhage of cerebral blood vessels. The resulting damage to energy-hungry nerve cells means that muscular control is thenceforth limited. Typically the damage occurs only in one half of the brain, resulting in hemiplegia to a greater or lesser degree. As one textbook phrased it, most comprehensively but almost tending to bring on the condition:

> Loss of function of the upper motor neurones, anywhere in their course from the precentral gyrus at the posterior end of the frontal lobe to the decussation of the corticospinal tracts in the medulla, causes a disorder of voluntary movement on the opposite side of the body.

In short, it is injury to the most oxygen-demanding and unforgiving part of the body, the one least able to cope with insult. Damage to the brain, particularly where its fibres gather together as tracts, can be dramatic in its effects upon the body as a whole. A normal human can become a hemiplegic, incapable of movement on the opposing side, unable (perhaps) to speak, unable even to prevent that half of the face from sagging wretchedly. And all because of a hiccup in the blood supply, a clot or a haemorrhage whose effect elsewhere might not even have been noticed.

The stroke of apoplexy (all sudden illnesses with permanent effects can be called strokes) varies from mild to severe. The severest cases probably result from damage to the cerebral artery itself, rather than one of its branches. Subsequent unconsciousness is rare, but the limbs are limp, speech is indistinct, swallowing is difficult, and the mouth's corner hangs down on the affected side. The tongue, if extended, turns towards the paralysed side while the eyes look away from it. The plantar reflex is extensor, namely stroking the sole's outer side does not lead to a normal bending of the toes but a stretching and fanning of them. The severest strokes are, not unreasonably, most likely to lead to death. So are those where consciousness declines after the attack, where deep, rapid breathing is maintained, and which follow some earlier infarction (damage due to blood disruption).

Hemiplegia does not have to be either so severe or so total. There can be face and speech paralysis but with unaffected limbs, or just one limb may be involved, or there may be no more than weakness in the various parts rather than complete loss of muscular power. Generally the patient's condition improves after the stroke. This is a bit of an enigma, bearing in mind that destroyed neurons do not live or work again. Perhaps other, undamaged neurons are (cleverly) taking care of the destroyed functions? Or some of the damaged neurons may be paralysed (perhaps by oedema which then diminishes), and inhibited from normal action, rather than destroyed? At all events some recovery occurs, generally starting with the proximal limb muscles (those near the trunk), then with the leg's distal muscles (furthest from the trunk). Walking then follows, along with movement at the shoulder and elbow, but the hand and fingers are the last to recover, that is if they recover at all. The difficulty in swallowing (dysphagia) is usually back to normal after a few days, whereas improvement elsewhere can take weeks or months. Or, turning this paragraph on its head, there may be no worthwhile improvement, however long the interval after the attack. Even if functional recovery is good or excellent there are always detectable differences, notably in the reflexes and in the finest finger movements.

Hippocrates said, 'It is impossible to remove a strong attack of apoplexy.' Some 2,400 years later the *British Medical Journal* reported that 'we still cannot offer any effective specific treatment for acute stroke.' Two doctors from Exeter, Devon, writing in the *Lancet* (in 1980), stated that 'None of the acute medical measures which have been tried in strokes, apart from anticoagulants in cerebral embolism, has proved to be of any real curative value.' In other words, much like leg amputation or blindness, treatment is a matter of rehabilitation. The other leg, the other senses or, for strokes, the remaining musculature must learn how to manage a reduced situation.

As a result there is considerable debate whether home or hospital can provide the best environment for the rehabilitating stroke patient. If the individual is away from home when the attack starts he or she (males are more prone) is inevitably taken to a hospital. The family may demand hospital admission, and bring pressure to bear, even if the attack is at home. Or the individual may have no one at home to help, making hospital necessary for ordinary practical reasons. Or there may be actual medical causes for admission, such as breathing or circulation problems. The two Exeter doctors suggested that moves to hospital were themselves 'a hazard' due to the demands of 'manhandling a patient on and off a stretcher, a journey through traffic, and the various hurdles of lifts, swing doors and portering'. If the patient is old and severely ill, they added, 'the doctor's clear duty is to relieve symptoms and reassure the family that nothing more can be done'.

Reaction was swift to their *Lancet* letter. A correspondent from the United States stated that 'second-class medical citizenship' for stroke victims is neither appropriate nor acceptable. Many reasons existed for hospital admission, such as: the need for correct diagnosis (one Canadian survey reported that, among 821 consecutive 'stroke' patients, 13 per cent were wrongly identified); the correct management of other conditions, not necessarily related to the stroke, but whose mismanagement could hinder recovery; and speedy relocation to suitable rehabilitation units. The fact that no curative treatment is available for the stroke itself has caused, according to another *Lancet* letter, 'over-reaction'. In its turn this has created either 'the denial of hospital facilities' or the setting up of stroke units, 'another form of rejection'. Stroke patients, according to one rehabilitation centre, must be 'first-class medical patients, recipients of first-class medical care . . . following on to equally first-class rehabilitation for their restoration . . . back [to] a family which has not suffered . . . rejection of their member at the time of the original catastrophe.' Even so, many stroke patients never do see the inside of a hospital, at least not initially. According to recent British surveys the proportion in Manchester was 29 per cent, in Surrey 31 per cent, and in South Wales 50 per cent.

There is plainly disagreement about the earliest days, but more unanimity later on. 'Where possible,' stated the *Lancet* in 1981, 'stroke patients should be rehabilitated at home.' It considered the 'sheltering function of the hospital' an essential ingredient but, from the very beginning, therapists 'should be formulating plans for full home care, advising patients, family and friends on how to cope in the home itself'. Unfortunately, as the *British Medical Journal* pointed out, 'once the acute phase is over, many doctors tend to lose interest.' Unfortunately, also, in Britain a third of those aged over sixty-five, and likely contenders for strokes, live on their own. Even in family houses, and when the doctor does not lose interest, there can be problems. In theory a practitioner can solicit the assistance, as one British registrar has pointed out, of a 'district nurse, a physiotherapist, perhaps a speech therapist, a health visitor, an occupational therapist, and a social worker'. Plainly good intentions of this kind can pave a hellish path and, added the registrar, 'such an army of people may well confuse and irritate the family.' It may indeed, quite apart from what it does to the patient at the end of the line. Stroke is the most common cause of severe physical disability but, as the Nottingham registrar concluded, 'we have very little information about the best way to manage individual patients.' In short, stroke cannot be cured, and it is not known if home or hospital is best (although home is generally preferred) or how the malady should be managed. The 1 in 500 of Western populations who have been struck by apoplexy might as well, or so it would seem, be back at the time of Hippocrates who both coined the word and knew the ailment well.

In addition: neurosurgeons are now performing bypass operations (about twelve hundred a year in the US) to rearrange certain blood vessels over the brains of those who have suffered ischaemic attacks (deficiency of blood) and, owing to this earlier circulatory damage, are believed more prone to strokes; not everyone welcomes this new tendency, profitable to neurosurgeons and of doubtful benefit, but growing apace; a system of 'biofeedback' is being used, apparently successfully, to help with rehabilitation, the patient learning how to tense and relax muscles purposefully; and depression after the event is more likely among those with left-hemisphere damage (and, therefore, right-sided paralysis). Strokes are a debilitating feature of Western societies, where people live long enough to be at risk from them, and they look like staying that way for decades to come, despite greater understanding of the event itself. Along with heart disease and cancer it is a killer of our times. Socially it is disturbing, frequently rendering a loved one as a partial human being, good on one side, powerless on the other. Nationally it is a considerable drain upon resources, killing a proportion speedily but turning a greater number into needy invalids. Medically – and to quote a final definition – it is the 'abrupt onset of a focal neurological deficit followed by its gradual resolution [which] usually indicates an acute cerebrovascular lesion, especially in the elderly'. Currently there are more elderly than ever before, and this proportion is still increasing. The neurological deficits will surely rise as well.

Tumour   It was all very well for Galen to classify tumours (after the Latin for swelling) into benign and malignant, the Latin for good and evil respectively. A better nomenclature for malignant and benign brain tumours would be evil and slightly less evil. Neither is to be welcomed. Most cerebral tumours are malignant and inoperable, but even the benign are potentially fatal merely because they create pressure. Tumours within the cranium are relatively common and, for children, create the most prevalent cancer after leukaemia. A brain tumour is also no one thing, varying in virtually every possible variable, such as its place of origin (glial cells are commonest for primary tumours), the kinds of symptom partnering the growth (headache is frequent, for instance, but not the rule), the presence or absence of vomiting, the degree of intracranial pressure, the age of onset, the speed of death.

Most cerebral tumours begin elsewhere, notably within the breast and bronchi, and are carried to the brain as metastases to form secondary deposits. (Many a surgeon, expecting and even hoping to find a primary growth, encounters secondaries and therefore learns of cancer elsewhere.) A prevailing extra hazard of brain tumours is their depth within the brain, and the consequent need to destroy other tissue to reach them. As a general cancer specialist once said: 'If we weren't concerned with ending up with live patients, we could cure all cancers.' His quip is even truer for brain cancers. Much skin or liver or lung tissue can be removed in surgical efforts to excise a growth without killing the patient simultaneously. Not so with brain tissue – or rather very rarely so.

Nevertheless, some cerebral tumours are successfully removed, and such neurological surgery began in London. Lord Lister's nephew and biographer, Sir Rickman Godlee, was first to achieve this feat, the date being 25 November 1884. (It is excellent to note that the medical historian Douglas Guthrie, in reporting this fact, added that the patient's name was 'Henderson . . . and he was a native of Dumfries'. Great surgeons often get their due. Great patients, if that is a suitable term, hardly ever do so.) In the same decade, now a century ago, brain surgery was generally advancing. Arthur Barker achieved in 1886 the first successful draining of a brain abscess, and Sir Victor Horsley the following year was the first to remove a tumour successfully from the spinal cord. In the United States the first brain tumour was removed just one year later, by William Williams Keen of Philadelphia, and then came Harvey Cushing. Generally hailed as America's greatest neurological surgeon he spanned the gap between those Listerian days and (reasonably) modern times, living as he did from 1869 to 1939.

A brain tumour may start by damaging tissue without raising the internal pressure. As the damage proceeds it is more likely to manifest itself in signs or symptoms (signs are what a doctor sees, symptoms are what a patient has) and the intracranial pressure is more likely to increase. As soon as that pressure does rise the tumour's secondary effects become considerable and always detrimental. Venous blood is displaced, capillary pressure rises, and the continuous secretion of cerebro-spinal fluid has to take place against increasing resistance. The normal pressure within the ventricles, where this fluid exists, may rise five-fold. Retinal haemorrhages may be one externally detectable sign of this disturbing internal trend. A symptom is that vomiting often partners the raised pressure; so too early-morning headache. For adults possessing sealed craniums – the sutures have fused by age twenty-five or so – a growth is bound to lead to increased pressure. For children the skull may expand, permitting skilled individuals to detect by tapping what is vividly known as a cracked-pot condition.

Diagnosis of a brain tumour can be fairly simple or extremely difficult. On the simple side, and according to W. B. Matthews and

Henry Miller in their *Diseases of the Nervous System*, 'any patient
with progressive signs suggesting a single lesion in the brain will
naturally be suspected of having a cerebral tumour'. The signs and
symptoms will have much to say about the tumour's location, and
its type may be suspected from its site, rate of development and the
patient's age. Diagnosis becomes difficult when the individual
suffers also from dementia, or depression, or merely has
headaches (along, of course, with practically every member of the
population). X-ray pictures of the skull can help in diagnosis, and
so too of the chest to discover if there are tumours elsewhere that
may be distributing secondaries. The electroencephalogram can
also help, wave patterns being different in the presence of a
tumour. However, and again with the words of Matthews and
Miller, 'the invention of computerized axial tomography (CT
scanning) has revolutionized investigation' of brain tumour suspects. Either with the use of radioactive iodine (which has a short
half-life) or even without it a picture can be acquired of the
different radio-densities in the brain, and therefore of the presence
of abnormalities, such as tumours. The CT scan has, it has been
said, rendered all other techniques obsolete for investigating brain
tumours. (Unfortunately scanners are not yet universally available. At the end of 1981 there were 4,000 in the world, a third being
in the US.)

This happy ability to diagnose brain cancers is not yet partnered
by a similar ability to deal with them. Leaning again on Matthews
and Miller, and performing a visual scan of their section on
treatment, the phrases make disappointing reading.

> Any operation on the brain carries some risk of unexpected
> complications . . . In general the more the brain has to be
> disturbed to reach the tumour the greater the risk of vascular
> damage . . . Some meningiomas are so applied to the base of the
> skull that their removal would carry unacceptable risks . . .
> Malignant tumours can seldom be excised but this does not mean
> that none are operable . . . multiple secondary deposits are best
> left alone . . . Radiotherapy for cerebral tumours is disappoint-
> ing and seldom achieves anything. There is a better theoretical
> case for radiotherapy after successful partial removal of a malig-
> nant tumour but its value is uncertain . . . an apparently single
> metastasis can often be removed with great relief of suffering
> although seldom much prolongation of life.

The operation of a CT scan also clarifies the situation and can bring
little comfort in its wake.

Cancers in general are known as a distinguishing feature of richer communities, but they are not overwhelmingly so. In Europe, according to a recent report (from Sweden), malignant neoplasms cause 200 deaths a year per 100,000 population. In countries with 'moderate' living standards the proportion drops to 150 deaths a year, and in the developing countries of Latin America and Africa it is often below 100. Extreme lows, according to the same report, are Guatemala (with 27.3) and Mexico (with 35.5). What there does not seem to be is any notable difference in the proportion of brain tumours to the total number of neoplasms experienced by different kinds of country. If there are more cancers in general there seem also to be more brain tumours. The only communities which experience relatively fewer cancers wherever they live are the mentally ill, such as the schizophrenics.

Two recent advances have been heralded. The first concerns hyperthermia and 'turning the skull into an oven'. Minute rods are inserted into the tumour and, via a microwave generator, extremely short waves heat up the offending tissue. A bonus is that tumours have (generally and already) damaged blood supply in the area, making it harder for that region to dissipate the heat which then destroys the tumour tissue. The second advance, known as gamma-thalatomy, uses gamma radiation to destroy an appropriate sensory-relay portion of the thalamus. This does nothing for the cancer, but can do much for the patient by eliminating previously intractable pain. Most cerebral tumours, as already pointed out, are both malignant and inoperable. Therefore any procedures permitting tumour cell destruction by other means than the surgeon's knife are to be welcomed. So too any that lessen the fearful pain which can partner the malignancy.

This chapter, as explained at its outset, has given a flavour of damage to the brain rather than a list of all possible kinds. To be so exhaustive would have been exhausting – to both writer and reader. Of course, there are countless other forms of injury, ranging from cerebral malaria (where the parasite lodges in the brain's blood vessels) to the effects of inhaling lead, from irradiation to electrocution, but this chapter's flavour will have to serve for the entire meal.

A fitting, final point is that injury to the brain emphatically incurs the greatest payments as assessed by courts of law. Many may feel the sums are still inadequate, however large by comparison with those given for other injuries. One recent case (Connolly v. Camden and Islington Area Health Authority, 1981) involved a baby, born normal and healthy. When aged seventeen days he received a serious overdose of anaesthetic while being prepared for an operation to cure persistent vomiting. When aged five years he had the mental age of a one-and-a-half-year-old, was subject to epilepsy, was bandy-legged, incontinent, and short on speech. He possessed a squint and could not feed himself. He was hyperactive, obstructive, destructive. His life span, it was estimated, had been shortened to twenty-seven and a half years. Liability for negligence was admitted by the Area Health Authority, and damages were assessed (after considerable wrangling and without much detectable logic to outsiders) as:

Pain and suffering and loss of amenities	£50,000
Cost of future care and attention	£156,000
Loss of earnings	£7,500
Agreed special damages	£5,667
Loss of earnings during lost years	nil
	£219,167 + interest

In America the state of Florida recently up-staged the traditional pace-setters of California and New York. One of its juries awarded (in 1982) $12 million to a young woman allegedly brain-damaged. The award is being contested; but the very thought of such a sum being paid has caused premiums to leap. A general surgeon in Miami may have to pay $66,000 in insurance a year, partly for his own basic coverage and partly to make Florida's Patient Compensation Fund solvent once again (it owed $50 million in mid-1982). Neurosurgeons in the same expensive city may have to pay up to $80,000 a year, the brain being so susceptible not so much to damage (and that is bad enough) as to damages. It may be our most prized possession. It certainly wins the prize, in legal handouts, in juries' estimates, in compensation paid. Of course, it can also be damaged naturally. In which case the person concerned receives absolutely nothing. It is always better, it would seem, to have someone who can be blamed rather than chance, bad luck, or an ordinary ill, such as some of those described in the section now concluded.

PART FIVE

Dilemmas have already been encountered, mental health – or mental sickness – being one example, but various modern techniques can appear to bring more problems than they solve. The time of death used to be simple; it no longer is. Operations upon the mind rather than the brain can lead to controversy as well as cure. So too the convulsive therapies or the relaxing drugs. And so, too, although in different fashion, the super brains of intelligent computers. Part Five encounters these issues, and concludes the book.

15. The Old Brain

Deterioration / Senility / Senile dementia / Other ageing illness /
Brain death / The new criteria / Transplantation needs / Lawful
death / Future ruling

> The greatest problem about old age is the fear that it may go
> on too long
>
> – A. J. P. Taylor

> I'm growing old. I'm falling apart. And it's very interesting
> – William Saroyan

> When people are well in old age, they're agreeably sur-
> prised to find that they are not unemployable, demented,
> asexual, sickly, and generally in a state of increasing decre-
> pitude
>
> – Alex Comfort

> As we grow old, we become both sillier and wiser
> – La Rochefoucauld

> President Coolidge dead! – How did they know?
> – Dorothy Parker

Middle age, so says one dictionary, lies between youth and old age,
'variously reckoned to suit the reckoner'. Objective science, less
obliging, is more likely to forget middle age completely and define
old age as the process which begins during youth. Think of
wound-repair and skin-healing, never so satisfactory as during the
earliest years of life. Think of language learning, an impossibility
(if pronunciation is to be perfect) after adolescence. And a surgeon
knows well enough, via texture, appearance, and a dozen other
signs, if he is cutting into the very young, the less young, or the old.
We are seventy years *old* when we die, and we have been ageing all
that time.

Neurologically we have our full complement of nerve cells at
birth, however early we are born. We are certainly not most
intelligent then, but no one knows when that day comes, intelligence being a compromise between youth (maximum of brain

cells, sound circulation, good respiration) and age (experience, neural network, cunning). Mathematicians, scientists, pilots are said to be at their most skilful in their twenties, but many do better later. The astronauts and cosmonauts are all quite aged, and certainly older than the fighter pilots of World War Two. John F. Kennedy was thought (by many) to be too young – at forty-three – to rule a country, and few countries make a point of retiring politicians early, even if the politicians make laws to retire everyone else at sixty-five or so. (The Soviet Union, in particular, is perpetuating a gerontocracy.)

It is arguable that politics is the most important job, and retirement should therefore be compulsory for politicians above all others, but society is confused about ability and age. Motorbicycles are trickier to control safely than cars; but, in general, motorcyclists can start younger than motorists. Pilots need swift reactions but the airlines make it difficult or impossible for anyone to captain an aircraft until those more senior have died/retired/resigned. Depression, paranoia, hypochondria are all more common among the elderly, and reach a peak at sixty to sixty-five in both sexes, but top posts are generally given to the old, with the chairman of the board being the oldest person present. 'Life begins at forty,' wrote Walter B. Pitkin, whose book of that title sold millions in the 1930s. Biologically, reproductive life is absolutely finished for most of our child-bearers by the age of forty. Evolutionists argue that we live so long because reproduction is finished, more or less, half-way through our lives and natural selection cannot, therefore, exert pressure upon the elderly who, biologically, are as good as dead.

There are three components in any mammal. First, the cells which multiply throughout life. Second, those cells which do not. Third, non-cellular materials. Neurons come into the second category since there is no replacement during life, and there is probably a great deal of loss. How much loss is unknown, it being impractical to count the total at death and impossible to compare that figure with its earlier counterpart. Nevertheless the brain does diminish in weight, being about 25 per cent less in the very old. That does not, in itself, mean fewer cells because the foetal brain, having acquired its adult total at about the mid-term of pregnancy, then increases its bulk and weight several-fold by adulthood. However, it is believed that neuron loss does occur, and a figure of 100,000 cells a day, from age twenty-five onwards, is frequently quoted. (It originated from an American scientist, C. F. Hodge, working on dead brains at the end of the nineteenth century, and it is not generally believed or denied but is, as stated, often mentioned as if gospel). If true, a decay rate of 36 million a year, or 1,000 million in forty years, still only means a 10–15 per cent loss of the considerable total with which we are born.

Many an old person, aware of a failing memory and of a less agile cerebrum, can suspect rather more than 15 per cent of the cells have perished. In fact other attributes than a slumping cell count are probably more relevant. As Sir Derrick Dunlop once wrote: 'If you have 4 good tubes going to the brain – 2 carotid arteries and 2 vertebrals, 2 good tubes going to the kidneys and some good coronary ones, you can be an active, intelligent, aggressive man at the age of 80, whereas if they are defective you can be an enfeebled old dotard at the age of 50.' Life may not begin at forty: it can certainly end there.

One of the first to write a recipe for longevity was the Venetian architect Ludovico Cornaro who stretched his life to its hundredth year. His discourse on a sober life, published in 1558, achieved fame but also a rebuke in the following century. Cornaro, said a dramatist, had lived all his life as an invalid in order to die healthy. (James Thurber made a similar point with his 'Early to rise, and early to bed, makes a man healthy and wealthy and dead.') Coupled with the oft-quoted assertion of 100,000 cell deaths a day is the addendum that one dry martini will kill a further 10,000. Some time you realise, said Jeanne Moreau, that 'you're born with a fatal disease which is called Life'. A waning brain, we quickly realise, is just one symptom of that disease.

Hodge not only pioneered work on human neuron loss with age but he then turned his attention, with a great leap across the phyla, to the honey bee. He discovered that neuron loss in an old worker bee was about 75 per cent. As the queen lives for years, whereas a worker survives only for weeks, interest grew in royal jelly, the queen's special food. Certain humans thought it might similarly benefit them and reduce neuron loss; but, as Alex Comfort phrased it, the substance has only proved 'effective in prolonging the life of pharmaceutical firms'. Should the bees be diseased, and therefore inactive, the loss is less than among the healthy workers. The postulation therefore grew that wear and tear (and loss) was due to use, and that this deterioration was linked with a change in behaviour. In fact this alteration in habit can be so marked that it renders the insect more conspicuous to predators. Some lepidoptera become overactive with age, and are therefore more likely to be noticed and consumed.

Perhaps the middle-aged mental behaviour of the average human did, in the true old days, lead to increased predation. Modern times are a poor indicator of past realities and, as Anon. phrased it:

'A robin redbreast in a cage lives to a tremendous age.' Human beings also do better in their current kinds of home. Not only are many more than ever before reaching the psalmist's (90:10) three score and ten, but more are becoming senile, physically and mentally. We should perhaps not forget that the psalmist continued: 'And if by reason of strength they be fourscore years, yet is their strength labour and sorrow.' One definition of labour and sorrow could be a 10–15 per cent loss of neurons up to the age of sixty-five, and more thereafter.

Deterioration There is no scientific method to assess if a person is younger or older than his or her chronological age. We can all tell, remarkably accurately, even from photographs and despite the attentions of cosmetic surgeons/beauticians/unguents, just how long ago a particular birth happened. People of equal age do not behave equally youthfully, and one person may die – in effect of old age – long before another, but there are all sorts of physical signs that help us guess the number of their years. Nevertheless there is no scientific yardstick. The arcus senilis, or white ring round the eye's cornea, occurs after age fifty but at no fixed time. Hair whitens, due to numerous air spaces throughout its cells, but in its own good time. Good teeth fall out, and when they choose to do so. We know that he or she is sixty-five, and looks it, but science cannot tell us yet.

All of this is equally true for mental ageing, save that the link between outward signs of an elderly brain and its precise age is nothing like so strong as the connection between physical appearance and life span. Also, as La Rochefoucauld put it, we do grow both wiser and sillier with the same ageing brain. Sir Francis Galton, pioneer in so much, was the first to demonstrate (in the nineteenth century) a difference in response speeds between young and old, namely a 13 per cent loss between age twenty and sixty. This work was recently repeated and the change in reaction time between young and old was found to be 20 per cent. Conversely one recent study found no age difference in the patellar (knee-jerk) reflex. Other researchers have reported a general decline in intellectual function beginning as early as adolescence and continuing in a linear fashion across the life span. Also, along with this normal mental decline with age, is an increased incidence of abnormal brain conditions. It becomes more normal to be abnormal.

The electroencephalogram is able to register age – to a degree. There are considerable brain-wave changes during childhood, but the patterns stabilise before adulthood is reached. This stability is generally absent in the senescent brain as the waves revert to a childhood pattern. Specifically the dominant alpha rhythm slows down its frequency, a fact first discovered in 1941, but the slower theta and delta waves speed up. However (as we might expect from our personal observations of others) some EEG tracings from elderly heads resemble those of youngsters while those from the merely middle-aged can show signs of age. The faster the slowing down of alpha waves the more likely are those brains to die than are brains with less declining rhythms. This may be just one more confirmation of the adage that people are as old as their arteries. A significant correlation has been found (albeit in certain sick people) between EEG frequency and both cerebral blood-flow and the cerebral metabolic rate for oxygen.

The decay of memory is one universally accepted mental drawback of old age, but the prevailing viewpoint is not strictly accurate. First, it does not appear to be true that the elderly are excellent at recall about years long passed: they remember, it seems, less than youngsters do for all decades in the past. Secondly, and contrarily, old people score less well in laboratory situations, but get there on time, bring the facts for which they were asked, and learn the tasks speedily. Youngsters are not always so reliable. A third point is that we all forget names and faces at every age but can at least blame old age when we do so later on.

Some further generalities are: there is no indication that wear and tear (i.e. use) have any detrimental effect upon neurons; actual age is much less important an effect up to the early seventies than social/work status, health, and education; entry to a nursing home can contribute to senile deterioration; and we live much longer than is to be expected from our body size. All mammals experience a similar number of breaths and heart beats in their lifetimes, frequency per minute being proportional to body weight. Big creatures live longest and small ones shortest. The two species which deviate most from the standard curve are the bottle-nosed dolphins and man, both big-brained.

Somerset Maugham, at a dinner to celebrate his eightieth birthday, said there were many advantages in growing old. He then paused, and searched his memory before, with exquisite timing, adding: 'For the moment I can't think of one of them.' It sounds therefore as if his mental agility was still in first-class condition. Perhaps he was one of the small but significant proportion of elderly people who show no mental deterioration with age. According to work done at Cambridge, 10–15 per cent of old people do as well as students in learning ability, memory, reaction time, verbal fluency and concentration. As for the bad news, doctors are less interested in the old. Not only do they give them less time – 13.7 minutes per visit against 15.3 minutes for the middle-aged, according to one California enquiry – but the effective time is even less as the old take longer to describe their state. Much like mechanics, doctors prefer working on the newer models. According to *Mind*, publication of the (British) National Association of Mental Health, the old suffer more than they should because some doctors overprescribe drugs for them, most students are not interested in geriatric work, and the bulk of it is done by untrained social workers. 'We have many doctors who regard the ailments of age as chronic and eventually fatal,' said one American report (by the Gray Panthers), 'so they think treatment is largely a waste of time.' British doctors can be equally curt. '*Anno domini,*' they sometimes say, nodding sympathetically while reaching for the door, 'and the next, please.'

We have two strong and conflicting prejudices about old age. The first states that certain places, perhaps Georgia, or Sikkim, or Ulan Bator, contain people of incredible age and of undiminished vigour, physical, sexual, mental. Alas, but there is a relationship (as pointed out in the *Guinness Book of Records*) between the national illiteracy rate and alleged longevity, the correlation being 0.83. If people can count and can write down their birth date they do not live so long. In literate communities no one has exceeded 115 years, and only 1 in 10,000 achieves a century. The second and contradictory prejudice is that old age is inevitably partnered by stupidity. The word senility is merely from the Latin for old age, but the first two dictionaries I approached gave 'Senility, old age: the imbecility of old age' and 'Senility; atrophy, apathy, garrulity, dementia, &c.' Old people these days are said to be senile, implying atrophy, dementia, etc. In most cases this should not be so. They are just old people.

Senile dementia   Nevertheless a relationship does exist between advancing years and psychiatric illness. The commonest of all forms of mental illness, depression and its colleagues, frequently arises in middle age, reaches a peak at sixty to sixty-five, and thereafter lessens. People over sixty-five account (in the UK) for 21 per cent of all admissions to psychiatric hospitals but are only 15 per cent of the total population. Despite this high proportion most old, mentally sick people are at home rather than in an institution. Their symptoms may be mental/psychiatric but their cause, if it is appearing for the first time in middle age, is probably organic disease or internal fault. The depressive symptoms may so cloud the scene, and then respond to anti-depressive treatment, that the underlying organic trouble may be missed and neglected. The commonest psychiatric disorders for the elderly, whatever the cause, are: 1. Depression. 2. Hypochondria. 3. Paranoia (both hard on the heels of depression), and 4. Adjustment to Age.

All such symptoms can be exhibited by normal, stable, healthy people, for there must be few who have not been depressed, morbid, overanxious (about some novel pain), suspicious (of office politics/home relationships), jealous (of the young), or fearful (of – to use a *Goon Show* phrase – the 'dreaded deadeds'). To help us decide individually whether anxieties are normal or excessive there are 'evaluation schedules' (which may inadvertently transform normal worry into considerable fright). Nevertheless, here is one such self-administering questionnaire (devised by E. Pfeiffer of the University of South Florida and published in *Brain Function in Old Age* edited by F. Hoffmeister and C. Müller):

Do you wake up fresh and rested most mornings?	yes	NO
Is your daily life full of things that keep you interested?	yes	NO
Have you, at times, very much wanted to leave home?	YES	no
Does it seem that no one understands you?	YES	no
Have you had periods of days, weeks, months when you could not take care of things because you could not 'get going'?	YES	no
Is your sleep fitful and disturbed?	YES	no
Are you happy most of the time?	yes	NO
Are you being plotted against?	YES	no
Do you certainly feel useless at times?	YES	no
During the past few years, have you been well most of the time?	yes	NO
Do you feel weak all over much of the time?	YES	no
Are you troubled by headaches?	YES	no
Have you had difficulty in keeping your balance in walking?	YES	no
Are you troubled by your heart pounding and by a shortness of breath?	YES	no
Even when you are with people, do you feel lonely much of the time?	YES	no

In this questionnaire it is not the yes or no answers that count, but whether the answer is in capital letters or not; YES or NO count as 1, yes or no score nil (but of course both Yes and No must be printed equally on the patient's copy). According to Pfeiffer a total of 0–4 indicates normality, but higher numbers suggest psycho-pathology. Plainly a degree of moderation is required if the healthy and normal are not to identify themselves as mentally sick. Everyone feels unfresh, useless, weak, puffed, unhappy, misunderstood, restless, unexcited, and lacking zest at times, thus scoring more than 4; but each is no more sick than the next (unfresh, weak, zestless) individual. All of us are likely to score higher as the years progress, and a certain number of us will be classified, by others if not by us, as psychopathological.

Just as there are many sets of questions there are also many groupings of mental illness affecting the elderly. One batch (of sixteen) includes: depression, anxiety, hypomania (mildly manic), obsessions, depersonalisation, paranoid delusions, subjective thought disorder, somatic (body) concern, impaired memory, disorientation, cortical dysfunction, lack of insight, incomprehensibility, retarded speech, belligerence, and visual hallucinations. Coupled with all age-related mental illnesses are many others, such as alcoholism and schizophrenia, that are acquired earlier in life and then carried through into senescence.

Both kinds swell the numbers of old patients in mental institutions. In the 1960s these reached a peak. Almost 30 per cent of old (over sixty-five) people in any kind of American institution were then in psychiatric hospitals. The equivalent British figure is now 21 per cent but the British high point (arguably its low point) occurred in 1969 when 385 in every 100,000 old people were in such a hospital. Both countries, and many others in the world, considered these high numbers unsatisfactory. The Americans began to move their dementia cases into profit-making nursing homes, away from hospitals, while the British, and others, favoured returning them home. The proportion of old people in British psychiatric hospitals fell to 242 per 100,000 by 1974. As there has been no proper cure for senile dementia the fall can only be attributed to home-care (or nursing-home care) replacing institutional existence.

What is not true is that dementia (out of mind) and old age inevitably go together. It is also not true that extreme old age and dementia are necessary partners. What is true is that the bundle of mental disabilities generally summed up as dementia, or senile dementia, or multi-infarct dementia, do affect about 7 per cent of those over sixty-five. The prevalence rises from 2 per cent in the sixty-five to seventy-five decade to 20 per cent in those over eighty. It is also true there are more old people today than ever before, and not only are their numbers increasing but their proportion in the population (of Western countries) is rising. This trend will con-

tinue until the end of the century. In Britain the projected increase
for the very old is greater than for the normal old (over sixty-five),
being a rise of 37 per cent for the over-seventy-fives and 42 per cent
for the over-eighty-fives. Already the proportion of old people in
Britain is 15 per cent, or about eight million. In the United States
the proportion is less (more immigration, a higher post-World War
Two birth-rate), but the total is already 25 million. Therefore, if 7
per cent of those two totals are demented (some say the percentage
is higher), the number of demented old is 2.3 million in just two
countries. And the numbers are rising. And there is no real sign of
a cure.

Dementia is not normal deterioration, akin to running less and
less fast for the bus, then not running, and finally hobbling towards
it. The Geriatrics Committee of the Royal College of Physicians of
London, reporting recently (1981) on old age and mental impairment, felt it necessary to define the word.

> Dementia is the global impairment of higher cortical function
> including memory, the capacity to solve the problems of day-to-
> day living, the performance of learned perceptuo-motor skills,
> the correct use of social skills and control of emotional reactions,
> in the absence of gross clouding of consciousness. The condition
> is often irreversible and progressive.

In more human phraseology, and to quote Professor Thomas Arie,
it is the

> poor ability to think, understand, perhaps to dress, to toilet, to
> cook, to put oneself to bed, to differentiate between night and
> day, to want to go to school (aged 80), to want mother, to go
> naked, to put paraffin on the electric fire.

Victims of dementia, he added, are 'extremely disabled people'.
Making the definition yet more human, and stating more precisely
just what happens, a recent 'Occasional Note' in the *New England
Journal of Medicine* gave a telling summary:

> When a demented person is living with his family, especially with
> his wife, he can stay at home longer. In fact, adaptation to the
> first subtle changes of dementia is often automatic and un-
> noticed. The keeping of the chequebook changes hands. Groom-
> ing is inspected by another person. Food preparation is gradu-
> ally modified so that the items are easier to eat, chew, and
> swallow. Sandwiches may take the place of food requiring knife,

fork and spoon. In this way the spouse of a demented person may preserve that person's appearance of mental integrity long after it is gone. There may be a gradual shift in roles. A daughter may treat her demented mother more like her child. A formerly dependent wife may become the family manager and factotum. The breadwinner may also become cook, housecleaner and launderer.

The average life expectancy after diagnosis of dementia is seven years. Five in every six patients are (in Britain) cared for at home. A survey, conducted in Edinburgh, discovered that 80 per cent of demented patients identified were not known to their family doctor. The feeling is therefore widespread that the disease is incurable. 'We are now,' reported one authority, 'at about the same stage in understanding dementia as doctors were 100 years before knowledge of bacteria explained infectious diseases.' For people over eighty, where a fifth of the population suffers from it, the disease is of epidemic proportions, equivalent in its virulence to many of the old infectious diseases in the old days.

It also affects 1 person in every 10,000 under the age of sixty-five, when it is labelled as pre-senile dementia. This fact should further emphasise the point already made that feeble-mindedness and old age are not necessary bedfellows. Most people grow old, and even very old, without suffering from dementia. A few suffer from it without growing old, forty-four being the mean age of onset for pre-senile dementia.

The sexes are equally subject to dementia when under seventy-five, according to a report from the Hollymoor Hospital Dementia Service, Birmingham. In older age groups women greatly outnumber men (but women greatly outnumber men in virtually everything then owing to their greater numbers). For the older patients, added the report, more men than women were in need of institutional care, and more men died. Aggressive behaviour was commoner among men, and 'paraphrenia-like symptoms' (where one particular idea becomes an obsession) were commoner among women. This dementia service has received more and more referrals each year since it started in 1976, and the trend will probably continue. By the end of the century Britain can expect another 120,000 demented old people (on top of the current total of over half a million).

So what is dementia, beyond being a firm title for somewhat vague connotations? Firstly, it is, as the word says, a mindlessness. Secondly, the mental rate of decay is much faster than in ordinary ageing. Thirdly, the kinds of loss, such as memory, are more total:

the demented cannot even remember childhood. Most definitions, such as a 'global deterioration of mental functioning', refer to an advanced stage of the disease, but someone can be a victim of dementia when it is not advanced but merely advancing. The word irreversible should never be part of any dementia definition, even though the disease is customarily permanent. Current thinking is that 15–20 per cent of the victims can be treated/cured/improved, provided that the examining practitioner does not dismiss them as anno domini, dying people not yet dead with atrophied brains like their hardened arteries.

So why dementia? To ask for its causes is like asking about ageing itself, but there are theories. There may be some toxic process affecting the brain (and killing off the neurons far faster than their normal decay rate). There may be some infective agent that is equally destructive (although few believe this view). There may be a fundamental cause, like an error in immune reaction or even in metabolism. Dementia is not, despite traditional belief, due to a hardening of the cerebral arteries. Some of the demented do have a reduced blood-flow to their brains, but this is probably a result of the cerebral decay rather than its cause. When there is blood-vessel damage plus dementia at least fifty millilitres of the brain (about 4 per cent) are lost before the symptoms of dementia occur. (This kind of loss is damage. It is different from the ordinary wasting and atrophy of the ageing brain.) One reversible cause of dementia is a lack of vitamin B_{12} and folic acid. Destroyed neurons can never regenerate, but some degree of recuperation is possible once the degeneration has been stopped. Drugs are on the market (over twenty in Britain) which are said to arrest or reverse brain failure in old age, and some do improve cerebral blood flow, but there is no correlation in the published results between improved blood-flow and clinical improvement. Unfortunately for most cases of dementia, there is not only no cure but no sign of one. There is still no comprehension of the cause.

The irreversible dementias are under four main headings, all named after doctors who first properly described them. They are:

Alzheimer's disease. By far the commonest dementia. First description in 1907. Alois Alzheimer was a German neurologist.

Pick's disease. Second most common. Very similar to Alzheimer's. Arnold Pick was a Czech psychiatrist.

Creuzfeldt–Jakob's disease. Rare. Identified by two doctors in the 1920s.

Huntington's chorea. First described by an American doctor in

1872. Only one with clear genetical history (although others sometimes run, to varying degrees, in families).

All four are partnered by atrophy of the brain, and are therefore quite distinct from psychiatric disorders (depression, schizophrenia) or epilepsy or Parkinson's. The greatest shrinkage is to the frontal lobes, the least to the rear of the brain. After degeneration the neurons have a characteristic appearance, picturesquely called the neurofibrillary tangle. Another sign is the presence of many plaques, assumed to mark the location of dead nerve cells. (Such plaques can be found in the very young, and more so in the aged, but most of all in brains of the demented.) Unnervingly, the first sign of Alzheimer's disease is a deterioration of memory, unnerving because 100 per cent of the population is so afflicted. However, Alzheimer's is no ordinary failure or diminution. Before the end of a year, in most cases, it is rampant. Absentmindedness becomes gross, reasoning becomes a thing of the past, and speechlessness can occur, coupled with an incomprehension of surroundings. Both relatives and patient can combine to conceal the disease, with them covering up for mistakes (in hygiene and forgetfulness) and the patient producing platitudes and commonplaceisms in lieu of original speech. An interest in television is often maintained, providing a veneer of normality and relief for all.

Unfortunately the disease marches on – Alzheimer's and the other three are all progressive and incurable. The family-plus-patient pretence breaks down as the brain does so. Differences between the four kinds are of interest to neurologists, but less so to others because the general Alzheimer progress of first signs followed by first deceptions, of grosser changes following inevitably in their wake, and of death within half-a-dozen years or so, is a picture that covers all of them. Huntington's chorea is particular, in that its gene has usually been passed to the next generation before the sufferer knows he has been harbouring it for all his life (there is more on Huntington's under congenital malformations on p. 237). It is sometimes called the vilest disease on earth.

What seems to be at fault in Alzheimer's disease is a lack of acetylcholine. This nerve transmitter agent is vital in the conduction of some impulses from one neuron to the next. More specifically, and possibly more fundamentally, a deficiency of the enzyme choline acetyltransferase has been noted in the brain tissue of Alzheimer victims. Also the synapses lying between nerve endings look abnormal under the electron microscope. Attempts have been made to give choline, acetylcholine's precursor, to demented patients to maintain their supply of the transmitter agent, but the benefits are currently matched by the difficulties. In short, despite the many thousands of Alzheimer deaths each year in Britain alone, the hundreds of thousands in the world, and the mindless cruelty of this form of departure, there is no real understanding of it and no effective treatment.

As to the cause, or causes, accusing fingers have pointed of late towards aluminium (animals given large doses of the metal suffer brain degeneration, and human victims of dementia have larger than average quantities in their brains) and towards zinc (a lack of it is damaging to the production of correct enzymes for the brain). Therefore efforts are being made to remove aluminium from the body, and to boost zinc, but these are early days in this research. The most rewarding work, in cutting down the numbers of the demented, is to make certain that the alleged (and diagnosed) demented are correctly so. Many drugs, wrongly prescribed and wrongly taken, can make them seem that way. So can psychiatric illness, or a tumour, or injury. Plainly any condition that is treatable should never be categorised with the irreversibility and downhill path of true dementia.

Two final points may serve, in different fashion, to draw this section to its close. The first concerns drawings penned by a group of demented people. They had all been asked to put a clock-face on paper, and make its time 3.30. The first person drew a circle with three smaller circles inside it, the second a circle with 'clok' inside, the third put the numbers 123456789 in a row (just like that), and the fourth drew four lines all intersecting at a central point, and then inserted the numbers 1 to 8 in an anti-clockwise fashion in the eight angles formed by the four straight lines. All four, and the others in the group, had been just like us, doing jobs, raising families, and certainly telling the time. Dementia then assaulted them.

The second postcript comes from a senior physician at London's National Hospital for Nervous Diseases. In our work, he once wrote, we see the demented, the mentally defective, the psychotic, the depressed, the addict, the hallucinated, the hemiplegic, or those with space-time disorientation.

It is difficult to know into which or how many of these diagnostic groups we should classify the politician who regularly shows defective judgment, heart failure, stroke, alcoholism, psychopathy; the religious or political fanatic, who may also be a head of state; the public figure who has furthered his ends by corruption; or the maintainers of outmoded dogmas who have the power to inflict misery on countless millions of life hours.

Inevitably, various statesmen come to mind, both past and present, and Dr William Gooddy then further underlined his point.

> Men and women become more powerful in human affairs as they grow older. Though they may grow wiser with experience up to a great age, powers of intellect, and especially of insight, eventually fail. The people are positively dangerous in proportion to the powers they wield and to the rate of progression and degree of damage before the problem is detected. The most frightening state occurs when brain failure is detected but concealed for reasons of policy and power.

Dementia, in short, may not just be the end of an individual but the ending of the world.

Brain death   It is so easy in films. A man slumps. Another, medically inexpert, certainly harassed and possibly out of breath, either puts his head momentarily on the slumped one's chest or feels, equally briefly, for a pulse before gravely pronouncing 'He's dead'. It also used to be fairly easy in ordinary times gone by. If the tumbler of water on the chest no longer told of movement, if a feather failed to indicate signs of breathing, or if the doctor himself said so, having heard not the faintest lip-dup through his stethoscope/trumpet/naked ear, the patient was dead. The momentous event had occurred at that moment. The person was a corpse.

Simplicity is no longer with us (however much it persists in the movies) because technology has permitted a step forward that possesses a considerable backwards component. (Nuclear fission or supersonic travel evoke similar reaction.) Whereas it is still true that cessation of breathing or of circulation can cause death as effectively as in the old days, it is also true that such mechanical happenings can now be boosted artificially. Conversely, a patient may now be dead to the world and permanently unconscious, but still breathing without outside assistance and therefore, if properly nursed, still eating and maintaining a state of being. (The recent American case of Karen Ann Quinlan was an example of this condition, made famous by the parental wish to terminate a hopeless situation and medical reluctance to do so.)

The fundamental problem is that consciousness resides in a different region of the brain from that of the mechanisms for heart beat and respiration. These two are controlled from the brain stem whereas consciousness resides (and see the chapter on this subject for elaboration on its residence) in the higher centres of the fore-brain. Karen Quinlan had a sound brain stem but was otherwise, in the words of a terse neurologist, 'as dead as a corpse'. Her vital functions were still functioning, despite the total (and judged to be permanent) loss of consciousness. To regard this state of affairs as death would clearly be 'unacceptable', said Professor Ian Kennedy, legal gadfly of the medical profession, in his BBC Reith lectures. The argument, he affirmed, has to debate not just brain-stem death or higher brain death but the demise of both, or total brain death. That may be the philosophy but there has to be the practical component as well. Just how is a brain, or a portion of it, said to be dead?

For most of us there will be no such query. A mortal disease or injury will, either speedily or at its leisure, cause our lives to end. There is no need for medical say-so on the fact. We will be dead for all to see, sans pulse, sans respiration, sans every show of life. However, in a minute minority of cases, there is less simplicity. A heart-lung machine can serve as adjunct to proper hearts and lungs. Drugs can confuse the picture, creating apparent death. Extreme cold can do likewise, and human beings have recovered from body temperatures as low as 65°F (18.5°C) or 33.5°F below normal. At that kind of heat the heart beat is paltry and conscious-ness non-existent.

The current spate of litigation, notably in the US, also exacer-bates the situation. Relatives sue doctors for 'pulling out the plug'. Doctors sue the patient's nearest/dearest for countermanding their commands. The urgencies of transplantation are also critical: organs for grafting should be removed speedily from the dead, preferably within the hour. Who died first can be yet another issue: is it his will and testament that applies, or hers, when a couple have died (almost) simultaneously? In a recent American accident it was judged that one victim had survived longer than the other because blood, according to a witness, was still spurting from one decapi-tated neck immediately afterwards, while the other body was showing no such extravagance of life, in fact no life at all.

The existence of electroencephalograms has also permitted new problems to arise. (For a full account of the brain-wave story see pages 102 to 106.) Today's EEGs are able to detect a great variety of different wave forms – as well as the silence of death. They can also pick up much in the neighbourhood which often resembles – to an inexperienced encephalographer – signs of life. Apparent-ly, according to a letter in the *Lancet*, these include 'sweats, microreflexes, intravenous drips, ventilators, people walking around, public paging systems, and monitors'. The letter also said that waves were once obtained from a 'slab of jelly'. There is some comfort in these wrongful attributions: if jelly seems alive, or if the complex clamour of a hospital makes us seem so, there is less likelihood of being pronounced dead before our time.

This is the nub of the matter. Are we dead when they say so? And are we brain dead, that organ being a more central part of our welfare than an ailing (or ailed) respiration? In one sense, as we talk of brain death rather than heart death, nothing has shifted. Whether it is the heart itself that has stopped or the heart control centre (in the brain stem) the difference is not particularly significant. As Ian Kennedy phrased it, the law will follow medical opinion 'once it is understood that brain-stem death is not a new kind of death but the same state as always, although identified by reference to more appropriate criteria'. Furthermore, death of the brain stem is not something that can be disregarded for long, however skilful the mechanism of keeping a body going without its control centre. For example, a heart connected to a dead brain stem will stop beating within a few days even if the plug is not pulled out and the machine continues, but timing is always important. Was it a living patient from whom organs were removed or not? Just when did that person die? In despair a *Lancet* editor recently wrote that 'Death is the time at which the brain-death forms are completed.'

The new criteria   So when is someone dead? Or rather, when is someone dead today if some parts of that body are kept going artificially? In the 1960s countries and committees began to question and redefine the occurrence of death. (Or perhaps to define it for the first time, most countries having gone along with the concept that a person is dead when a medical practitioner says so.) In 1966 the French National Academy of Medicine stated that someone could be ruled dead if it could be proved that the brain would never be able to resume control of the body's vital functions. The driving force of that edict was not so much for clarification, or to improve doctor/relative trust and harmony, but to permit organ transplantation. Other countries also set out to establish how brain death could be defined, partly to give doctors a set of rules, partly to allay suspicions (notably among kidney-donor card-holders whose deaths are not wholly unwelcome), but also to cover all possibilities so that the seemingly dead are not written off, medically and therefore legally, before their time. This is not a new anxiety. Edgar Allan Poe was much exercised by this thought, a fact reflected in many of his stories. Similarly we are all troubled whenever it is reported that some observant mortuary attendant has recorded the premature arrival of one of his charges. A new set of rules should be able to take advantage of new techniques (such as the EEG) instead of being inconvenienced by them, and creating confusion where straightforwardness used to lie.

Finland became the first country in which brain death was legally accepted. Its National Board of Health published firm criteria in March 1971. Other countries had established guidelines, such as France, but the Finnish priority lies in the lawfulness of its proposals. The most important American statement in those early days was the so-called 'Harvard criteria', published in 1968 by the Committee of Harvard Medical School. (Lesser or different strictures are sometimes called Yale criteria, notably by Harvard men who like the joke.) Britain's similar recommendations were published by the Conference of Medical Royal Colleges and their Faculties in the United Kingdom in 1976. In a statement made in 1979 by a Finnish hospital, in which various sets of criteria were reviewed, it was considered that the procedure put forward by the Swedish Medical Society was 'the most complete' and 'the most accurate' but 'technical limitations' might prevent it from being widely used. In this context, as EEGs are sometimes considered mandatory, it is relevant that only 10 per cent of British hospitals possess suitable machines.

In the United States, and by 1980, about half the states had incorporated some sort of brain-death criteria in their statutes, but their law-makers were not equal, either in what they intended or in convincing others of their intention. There is prevailing doubt, for example, whether brain death or brain-stem death is meant, and in a Maryland case (of April 1980) the testifying medical experts could not agree on an interpretation of 'spontaneous brain function'. Presumably these are still early days, both in this new idea of brain death and in our general comprehension of it. The fact that over thirty sets of brain-death criteria were published by 1978 indicates that there was no firm agreement even within the medical profession (let alone among the rest of us) and probably there will be many more published before this way of dying becomes, as it were, a normal part of life.

With many sets of criteria to choose from it is invidious to select just one, and difficult to pool their various recommendations. However, there are some basic guidelines. There must be an absence of brain-stem reflexes; the eyes' pupils, for example, must be central and not respond to light. Eyes themselves must remain stationary even when the head is moved rapidly or when ice-cold water is squirted into the ear. There must be no response if either the cornea or the windpipe is stroked/tickled. The arms or legs must not adopt stretched-out or bent positions in response to stimuli. There must be no natural respiration even in the presence of high carbon dioxide levels (which normally stimulate the lungs into intense activity). And an EEG should not be able to detect anything (once all those vacuum cleaners etc. have been eliminated). There may be reflexes – such as the knee-jerk variety – but these do not indicate a living brain stem and are only a reminder that reflex mechanisms do not travel through the brain. All these tests should be repeated after a few hours so that equally negative results can be obtained. (One remembers again our movie hero, so swift in diagnosis, so adept, so all-convincing.)

The tests are designed to ensure that a patient is truly dead, will not recover, is not drugged or cold, and there is nothing about him/her, such as metabolic or endocrine error, simulating death. Anyone on whom such an enquiry is being made is inevitably on a respirator (and seven minutes' absence from the machine would have the patient dead without further argument) and equally inevitably in a deep coma. The criteria have not been established as rules for normal death but for determining whether a patient in deep coma, so deep that self-maintained breathing is impossible, will ever surface again even if everything is done to aid that recovery.

It is always important, therefore, to know the reason for the coma. The Finnish code, in particular, is strict on this. If the brain damage is caused by increased pressure (tumour, haemorrhage, bruising) the sort of tests already outlined must be carried out. If the damage is not understood, or if there is any doubt, both an EEG and angiography (observing blood vessels by making them visible/opaque to X-rays) must be performed. These last two procedures are not on everyone's list, partly because deaths may occur where the equipment does not exist but also because the EEG is not foolproof. A totally flat tracing, for instance, is possible from some children, from the severely poisoned and the extremely cold. Such individuals may or may not survive their predicament, but the flat EEG is only one more guide to their condition. It is not a perfect indicator of non-recovery. Even if the equipment becomes more reliable machines can never dictate conclusions: only humans do that. As the transplanter Christiaan Barnard said: it is still a fact that 'you're dead when a doctor says you're dead'.

The British set of criteria received a considerable battering from interested parties after its official publication, despite that date being ten years after the French had first made a stab at the subject and five after the Finns had made their criteria legal. Even though, for example, the needs of the transplanters formed a prime motive for redefining death, the 1976 British statement made no reference to organ transplantation. In 1979 the same Conference of Medical Royal Colleges and their Faculties in the United Kingdom saw fit to produce an addendum. This made eight points and a conclusion, all of it as confident in tone as the earlier statement.

Briefly, it stated:

1. The 1976 report that brain death (when it had occurred) 'could be diagnosed with certainty' had been 'widely accepted'.
2. Death, in most cases, is 'not an event, it is a process'.
3. Because the moment that a heart stops beating is (usually) detectable that has been accepted as the time of death 'without any serious attempt being made to assess the validity of this assumption'.
4. It is no longer possible to equate death with the lack of a heart beat. The only aspect of death 'beyond debate is its irreversibility'.
5. When organs are failing a point is reached 'at which brain death occurs and this is the point of no return'.
6. Sometimes the reverse of 5 can happen. The brain can fail and gradually the other organs will do so.
7. Brain death 'represents the state at which a person becomes truly dead' and this can be equated 'with the concept in many religions' of the spirit's departure.
8. Usually there is no need for a doctor to identify brain death. The fact that other systems can be artificially maintained if the brain does die means that a diagnostic routine should be established 'which will identify with certainty the existence of brain death'.

A final statement affirmed that 'the identification of brain death means that the patient is dead, whether or not the function of some organs, such as a heartbeat, is still maintained by artificial means.'

The explanations still did not fully satisfy others. The repeated assertion of infallibility frequently lay at the root of subsequent criticism. If brain death could be 'diagnosed with certainty' (1) and identified 'with certainty' (8) why was there fuss? And doubt? And the existence of so many sets of criteria?

In Britain, for the public at large, such doubts were expressed in the famous *Panorama* television programme of October 1980. Its title was 'Transplants. Are the donors really dead?' The implication, inevitable with such a heading, was that some donors were still alive when providing their donations, and the transplant operations therefore caused their deaths. Four Americans, who had been near to the grave and had then recovered, were cited as evidence that brain-death diagnoses were sometimes premature. These four patients had been severely comatose owing to: drug overdose; a congenital enzyme deficiency; the administering of a neuro-muscular blocking agent; and temporary hypoxia encephalopathy, itself due to a heart attack. All four individuals said – in so many words – they were happy that some enthusiastic surgeon had not pounced upon their kidneys prematurely to keep someone else alive. As American hospitals possess more EEG machines than do British establishments, and therefore use them more to check on the brain-dead (machines being used in direct proportion to their availability, as C. Northcote Parkinson might have said), the further implication was that these four would have been pronounced dead in Britain. And would have had their kidneys removed. And been killed in the process; with no one, least of all the victims, wise to the misadventures.

Many television programmes make awesome and awful statements – which lead to nothing. This one stirred up hornets. The public, apparently, destroyed its kidney-donor cards in large measure or vowed to die without, as it is said, medical aid. The healing profession was, by and large, indignant. An editorial in the *British Medical Journal* concluded: 'When, as is inevitable, patients die [from a lack of kidneys for transplantation], the BBC will have those deaths on its conscience.' The debate then moved from doctors against the media to doctors against doctors. 'Such unprofessional phraseology' as in that *BMJ* leader, wrote one, 'will not reassure either members of the British Medical Association or the general public'. 'In this battle between medics and the media,' wrote the *New Scientist*, 'it is the medical profession that has come out worst.' Many members of that profession were inclined to agree.

The battle continued to rage. The BBC, made aware of considerable fault in the programme (produced by a political department without reference to the science unit), offered a second slot on the same subject. The BMA accepted, with the proviso (more or less) that it controlled all content. The BBC was no more willing to accept such dictation than the BMA would have tolerated medical intervention by a set of broadcasters on a medical question. The projected second programme was therefore cancelled for lack of participants.

Although the viewing public was outraged by a hundred other issues in the weeks after the Brain-Death transmission, and therefore diverted from this topic of how and when we die, the letters columns of the *BMJ* and *Lancet* still reverberated. 'Your [comment] was in some respects as misleading as the television production itself.' 'Many problems remain, but they are not in the areas you mention.' 'The fault may lie with newspapers . . . even with the *Lancet* and *BMJ* for not pointing up the subject earlier.' 'The impasse which has led to the cancellation [of the second programme] has wide-ranging implications in relation to the external censorship of the media . . .' 'You've been watching Panorama without a prescription' drew a cartoonist, as a doctor haughtily humbled his patient. Plainly Panorama had done part of its job well which, as in all journalism, is to bring a controversial subject to the surface.

But what about the medical conclusions? It was generally agreed that the four Americans, whose various comas formed the programme's kernel, were irrelevant. They would not have been pronounced dead in Britain any more than they were in the United States. The use of an EEG, not considered crucial under the British code, was thought useful in certain cases, but not if the heart had stopped beating or rigor mortis had set in. If it was suspected that cerebral function might return, and if resuscitation procedures had been carried out, an EEG could be valuable. It might even be a life-saver on very rare occasions if it detected flickering signs of life. Dr R. Paul of Coventry stated, with vehemence, that he knew of two patients who had survived after fulfilling the British criteria for brain death. This unique statement was then questioned, no less vigorously. Eventually, in view of further 'information received', he withdrew 'unreservedly' his broadcast statement 'at the request of the neurosurgeons involved'.

His particular retreat, although important, did not mean a withdrawal on all fronts. What continued to stick in many medical gullets was that the statement 'properly tested and found virtually certain to die within a few days' could be equated with 'dead'. The 1979 Conference had made this leap which represented, according to one correspondent, such a 'major change of professional attitude' that considerable argument should have been put forward to justify it. The same writer also doubted whether the Conference still considered, so unanimously, that 'brain death, when it occurred, could be diagnosed with certainty'. The TV programme had done much to publicise this and other doubts. It is these which now exist 'with certainty'.

Transplantation needs Two points need to follow which shed their own kind of light on the brain-death controversy. The first concerns kidney donation, the second the law. Although the new definitions of death were not 'invented for the benefit of harvesting organs', as a *Lancet* correspondent took pains to point out, the necessity of finding organs was midwife if not mother to their invention. The need for transplants was a goad, a spur, a definite instigation.

Some numbers help to make this point. Kidney transplantation needs about two thousand kidneys a year solely in the United Kingdom. Only 700 are actually transplanted and, of this number, about a fifth fail to function. Consequently, one-quarter of the need is fulfilled; the remaining three-quarters is unfulfilled owing to a lack in the supply of kidneys. On the donor side of this coin some six thousand people under sixty-five die annually from head injury or spontaneous subarachnoid haemorrhage, both kinds of death providing the bulk of suitable candidates for kidney donations. However, other kinds of brain-dead patients could, or should, be regarded as potential donors, such as those dying from cerebral tumour, from resuscitated cardiac arrest (with subsequent brain death, the attack having been too severe) and poisoning (provided, of course, that the toxin which killed the patient is no longer doing harm).

In other words there are more possible donors than potential recipients. A clarification of the brain-death state, and greater awareness of this new-found circumstance, would improve the existing shortfall. More donors could be discovered and more donations could be made. If the failure rate of 20 per cent continues (which is largely caused by poor terminal care of the donor and therefore of his/her kidneys) it will be necessary to find about two thousand four hundred good kidneys a year. The present supply needs to be increased some three- to fourfold, a not impossible feat.

It is unethical, to say the least, to kill a patient. Therefore, it is unethical to switch off a respirator, wait until its lack has killed the patient, and then remove his kidneys. To do so would also border on malpractice. Somehow, without breaking the Hippocratic oath (Rule 1: Above all do no harm), the medical profession has to switch its loyalties from Patient 1 to Patient 2 without killing or harming either in the process. As such an emotive leap is difficult for one doctor, if not impossible, the accepted code demands that the transplanter is not also the one to determine death.

Lawful death Legality is yet another spur to define brain death correctly. The procedure of having two doctors, each with independent interests, is partly to offset any subsequent claims of civil or even criminal irregularity. It may be difficult emotionally for one man to do all jobs, recognise brain death, switch off the machine, confirm death and then extract the kidney. It is almost certainly unlawful. Not only is there murder – of a kind – but there is also motive – of a kind. However, the law also has to deal with cases that would probably never arise unless lawyers existed to instigate them. The brain-death issue opened up fresh areas for debate, and litigation, for conviction and appeal. It is all legal grist, and the following four cases will show the sort of petitions now heard, now that death is without its ancient simplicity.

Cases 1 and 2 both involved British murderers. In the first a man stabbed his wife. She was treated for the wound, and initially was recovering, but later collapsed, her blood circulation being poor or non-existent for thirty minutes. For four days she was attached to a respirator but was finally certified as dead, and her husband was convicted of her murder. With Case 2 the preliminaries were similar. A man hit a woman with a stone (of fifty pounds), causing multiple skull fractures and brain damage. After two days on a life support system it was considered that the machine was working on a lifeless body. The electricity was therefore disconnected.

Case 1 appealed (Regina v. Malcherek) and Case 2 sought leave to do so (Regina v. Steel). The judge did not think it right to discuss (in that context) what constituted death but affirmed that the chain of events – attack leading to death – had not been altered by medical efforts to prevent that death. The suggestion was thought bizarre that doctors, who did their best to heal a patient and, having failed, discontinued treatment, should then be accused of the death of that patient. Both the appeal and the application were therefore dismissed. Nevertheless it is interesting that a couple of murderers, who did not quite finish off their victims at the time, should be thought to have a case. They had undoubtedly damaged people but the doctors had done the actual killing – or so some lawyers were prepared to argue.

American law is not the same as British law. Similarly the American enthusiasm for litigation is not equalled in the British Isles (which therefore pulsate with British doctors heaving sighs of relief). Brain-death cases are becoming increasingly frequent in the United States, but these are becoming more concerned with the right to die than with the opposing issue of a right to live. It is more frequently a matter of doctors allegedly keeping patients on machines painfully, needlessly and expensively rather than taking them off machines prematurely, cruelly, lethally. Brain death hits both ends of this particular spectrum, but unnecessary prolongation has more often reached the courts.

For example, as Case No. 3, there was the Brother Fox story or, as the Court of Appeals referred to it, 'In the Matter of Father

Eichner'. At the age of eighty-three this man suffered a heart attack and, as a result, considerable brain damage. The New York hospital put him on a respirator and there he remained, despite the fact that in his conscious lifetime he had expressly wished not to be preserved in this fashion. Apparently, at the time of the Karen Quinlan case, he and some others of his religious group had discussed the matter, and had decided it was not amoral to have a respirator switched off. Such brain-dead people should be allowed to die. He then became one of those people and was kept alive against a will he was no longer able to express. So far as New York's highest court was concerned, his earlier, considered, authenticated and definite wish clinched the matter. The hospital was told to let the father die.

'In the Matter of John Storar' was also judged by the same court. He was fifty-two, being treated for terminal bladder cancer, profoundly retarded and a lifelong inmate of a mental hospital. He had only one close relative, his seventy-seven-year-old mother. She was officially named as his guardian when permission was needed to start radiation therapy, and she gave it.' There was some remission, but the mother grew discouraged at this prolongation of life for her dying son. So she then withdrew her consent. This caused the hospital to bring a suit so that it might be authorised to continue treatment. Without that care he would die 'within weeks': with it he was expected to live longer.

Unlike many other famous American cases where the courts have permitted or aided the right to die – Quinlan, Saikewicz, Perlmutter, Spring, Severns, and Eichner – the New York Court of Appeals behaved contrarily over John Storar. It overruled the mother's wish that further treatment should be withheld from her retarded, cancerous, dying son. There was no rational, considered opinion from the man – indeed none was possible – and the court did not like the idea of postulating what opinion such a man might hold, were he able to reach any such conclusion and then express it. It also did not like the idea that a guardian, even a mother, should be able to cut short the life of another, however despairing and valueless that life. It therefore gave consent for further treatment.

This judgment may reverse the current trend – of pulling out plugs and refraining from valueless prolongation – or it may merely emphasise the difference between hopeless brain failure and hopeless body failure. Brother Fox's normal brain had died; the rest of him was then allowed to do so. John Storar's malfunctioning brain had not died; therefore his body had to be kept alive as long as medical science could do so. The brain and not the body is what matters now – or so it would seem. Even an idiot's brain is sufficient, or so John Storar proved.

A dozen years ago H. K. Beecher wondered (in the *New England Journal of Medicine*) whether doctors had 'as yet achieved enough emotional and sociological maturity' to handle brain death compassionately, boldly and with intelligence. Judging by some of the professional outpourings following the British television programme Dr Beecher may still be wondering. What hope therefore for calm and good sense among the rest of us? That same journal once listed strange causes of death discovered among nineteenth-century death certificates. It particularly liked: 'Don't know. Had never been fatally ill before.' These days, with all the confusion about brain death, an honest doctor could well write: 'Don't know. Had never been fatally ill before in this way.'

Future ruling So what of the years ahead, of notable concern to those whose deaths are yet to come? EEGs will probably become more routine, not because doctors prefer their tracings to good clinical judgment, but because the machines exist, will do so much more in the future, will help to placate some fears and may even contribute to legal outcomes. There is positive uncertainty today, among the profession, among relatives and patients who, before becoming comatose, may have torn up or hidden their kidney-donor cards. If the EEG is no more than a palliative, restoring public confidence, the kidney recipients may well have cause to cheer at its greater use.

A kind of unpalliative, exposed in a letter (of July 1980) to the *Lancet*, is that 'no medical school in Britain gives students any instruction in the diagnosis of brain death.' Maybe the future will produce better diagnostic devices than a squirt of cold water into the ear or EEGs that produce both flat tracings from the recuperable patients or signs of life from others whose brain stems are already dead. Instead of the water test there should be electrical stimulation of the patient's mastoid bones, say researchers at Philadelphia's Temple University. Equally preferable would be the discovery of specific biochemical markers of brain death. Neurologists at Rochester, searching for such indicators, found that catecholamines in both blood and urine fell to a tenth of their normal level 'as soon as clinical brain death became evident'.

This is all a far cry from the old days, when tumblers on the chest became motionless, feathers fluttered to a standstill, and an ear to the heart no longer heard a sound. 'I must inform you that her catecholamines are dropping rapidly,' has less of the age-old dignity to it, however accurate. At least the movies will persist, despite alleged realism, with their vintage images. 'Make way, make way. Unbutton his coat . . . My God, he's dead.' There is much to be said for dying in this way.

16. Postscript

Neurology in general / Early lobotomy / Modern psychosurgery /
Electroconvulsive therapy / Alcohol / Drugs / Computers / Finale

> By 1984 . . . we should understand what the brain does
> when we think
> — Lord Brain (writing in 1964)

> I don't know if the French revolution was a good thing; it's
> too early to say
> — a Chinese spokesman (in 1981)

The journey is nearly over. The three pounds of human tissue
known as the brain have been examined from all manner of
angles – evolution, animal comparison, anatomical, physiological, medical, musical, endocrinological, legal, plus scores of
others – and have therefore encompassed more width and breadth
than would have occurred with other lumps of tissue, such as liver
or pancreas. In one sense there has always been too much information from which to select. 'Picking out the news,' someone said in
another context, 'is like trying to get a drink from a fire hydrant.' In
a different sense there has never been enough. Activities such as
thought, memory, reasoning or even smell are still so poorly
understood that, from the outside, there is frustration at so little
positive fact. Just what is intelligence? And how does the brain first
absorb, store and then recall the sensations it has learned along the
way? Some of the hydrants do gush plentifully, but often are more
like soda-siphons, producing gas along with the flow. The information is still short, despite the torrent of words.

Some of the advance, notably in physiology, can erode original
curiosity. Wonder at mental processes is replaced by biochemical
events of such complexity that only neuro-physiologists particularly
skilled in this area know what is happening. 'It is the business of
scientists to explain away the magic in the world,' said William G.
Quinn. It is the business of the scientific writer, I suppose, both to
explain scientific advance and yet retain that magic.

There are, presumably, as many approaches to this problem as
there are individuals solving it. For example, to quote from one

style encountered when reading for *The Mind*, 'The actual storage capacity of the human brain has never been measured, although it has been estimated that during our lifetime we store about ten times more information than is contained in all the books in the Library of Congress.' Other writers have exposed more of the arithmetic in reaching conclusions whose laudable purpose is to astonish. If a computer were to be constructed like a human brain, wrote one of them in the pre-chip age, there would have to be 'ten thousand million of the most minute transistor valves' which; at a few pence each, would cost '£375 million for a start'. All the connections 'at 2 cents each' would cost far more and 'the whole contraption' would need 'an aircraft-hangar'. The human brain, this writer concluded by way of comparison, 'is about 8 inches in length, 4 inches in height, and weighs 3 lbs'. The point he made was undoubtedly impressive but a final method is to let facts speak for themselves without undue embellishment.

There have undoubtedly been many in the preceding pages. This *is* the decade of neurology, and even the hydrants are difficult to count. It is also the occasion for non-neurologists to learn about the brain, partly because the new facts are exciting but also because the subject is entering the market place. There are questions such as those involving drugs, the ethics surrounding mental health, electroconvulsive therapy and depression, or psychosurgery and operations to cure the mind rather than the brain which should no longer be answered just by the experts. The computer is a revolution entirely on its own, threatening to become intelligent or, possibly, permitting our salvation. The brain, as outlined principally in Chapter 1, created *sapiens*. It is high time for Man to take more than casual interest in this brain that made him, and which might – as also stated – be the death of him.

Much earlier in this book it was written that we are in general about as knowledgeable of our central nervous systems as we are of Antarctica or the mountains on the moon. It is strange that this is so. For the one person who has heard of the fissure of Sylvius there are a dozen (or a hundred) who know of the tendon of Achilles, cervical vertebrae, or the duodenum. The brain's parts are very poorly known, even by those who should be better trained in them. The book *Foundations of Anatomy and Physiology*, written for nurses most competently, contains scant reference to the brain. There are thirty-one index references to Hormones, eleven to Kidney, over a column to Muscles, almost a column for Bones, but just four entries for the Brain. It is writing of lions with modest reference to their strength, or of elephants to their bulk. We are the cleverest species on the planet, but all of us, nurses or the common lot, can probably name more bones than bits and pieces of the brain. This book is an attempt to rectify that wrong.

As for the future, and its market-place debate, the innumerable issues will be better discussed if more knowledge is in circulation. (Uninformed debate can be more fun, or of the inattentive kind as in politics, but there is nothing quite like fact for bringing discussion to conclusion.) The brain, after all, is not some casual organ, some extra thing without much purpose, akin perhaps to the spleen whose removal occasions nothing save some minor changes to the blood. The brain is what we are, most fundamentally. Hippocrates, still to be relied upon for invading opening paragraphs in medicine, said it rather better.

Men ought to know that from nothing else but the brain come joys, delights, laughter and sports, and sorrows, griefs, despondency and lamentations. And by this, in an especial manner, we acquire wisdom and knowledge, and see and hear, and know what are foul and what are fair, what are bad and what good, what are sweet and what unsavoury . . . and by the same organ we become mad and delirious, and fears and terrors assail us, some by night and some by day, and dreams and untimely wanderings . . .

Early lobotomy   For all his Greek breadth of vision he did not dream of the problems assaulting us today, such as psychosurgery. This began in 1935 when Egon Moniz, Portuguese neurologist, severed the frontal lobes of four depressed, paranoid schizophrenics. Their original symptoms were relieved, but replaced by nausea and disorientation. Moniz himself also suffered – from colleagues, poor health, and even one attempted assassination – but he persevered and received the accolade of a Nobel prize in 1949 (when aged seventy-four). Others took up the scalpel where he had pioneered, and by 1951 over eighteen thousand Americans – the depressed, violent, schizophrenic and alcoholic – had been lobotomised. Principal exponent was Walter Freeman, who allegedly cut into more human brains (3,500) than anyone else in peacetime medicine. He once operated on twenty-five women in a single day, and even cut into children, convinced that lobotomy 'made good American citizens' out of society's misfits, 'schizophrenics, homosexuals, radicals . . .'

'There is only one rule of practice,' said Lord Lister, 'put yourself in the patient's place.' Freeman, who died in 1972, did keep considerable follow-up records, but these were principally his opinions about the patients rather than each patient's opinion either about the operation or of progress afterwards. Besides – which is the nub of the matter – it is difficult for anyone, disturbed citizen or not, to state if he or she is better after tamperings to their mind, perhaps forcibly, certainly irreversibly. In the fifteen years after Moniz had first cut the human brain a further 1,300 were equally severed each year. Freeman simplified the technique, giving up the old-style boring through the side of the skull and preferring to gain access with a sharp instrument over the eye and through the orbit. By 1965 the operation, using either method, was still being performed frequently, with an alleged 1,000 a year in Britain alone.

The tide then began to turn. Critics became more vociferous, claiming the procedure 'partially killed' the patient, that it was a 'blunting mutilation'. The proponents fuelled the flames by attacking the critics, calling them 'ideologically motivated cranks'. Anyway, the operation numbers dropped, from 178 throughout 1974 (in Britain), to 119 in 1976, and 71 in 1980. There has been a similar trend in the United States, falling from 400 operations a year in 1971 to less than 200 before the end of the decade, but the trend was given more than a nudge in 1979 by the case of Geis v. Mark and Ervin. Dr Vernon H. Mark, neurosurgeon, and Dr Frank R. Ervin, psychiatrist, were sued for $2,000,000 by Helen J. Geis, the mother of Leonard Kille. He had been given treatment back in 1967 (when aged thirty-four) which had led, she claimed, to his 'total incapacitation'. Moreover, as he had been a sick man beforehand, it was doubted if he could have given the proper informed consent; therefore the doctors, according to this argument, had acted improperly. The medical case was that they had performed a bilateral amygdalatomy (cutting out both amygdala, clumps of cells in the temporal lobe thought to control emotional states) and argued that this was not psychosurgery. Kille was in his present condition owing to an 'inexorable, underlying progressive brain disease'.

The trail started with national headlines but ended with a whimper seven weeks later when the superior-court jury found in favour of the two doctors, that they had obtained the patient's consent and were not negligent in either diagnosis or treatment. It had earlier been hailed as the first US psychosurgery case to come to trial; and so it was, in a way. The dissection involved proved to be neurosurgery rather than psychosurgery – on the brain rather than the mind, but the case gave more than a hint of what might happen should some psychosurgeon ever be tried in similar fashion. It was a *cause célèbre*, but only indirectly, of surgery upon the mind.

The Soviet Union bluntly banned such operations in the 1950s. A prominent Soviet psychiatrist of the time condemned them as 'an antiphysiological method that violates the principles of humanity and makes the patient an intellectual invalid . . . an insane person is changed into an idiot.' Simultaneously Freeman was saying it was better for patients to have simplified intellects capable of elementary acts than intellects where there reigned the disorder of subtle synthesis. 'Society can accommodate itself,' he added, 'to the most humble labourer but justifiably distrusts the mad thinker . . . lobotomised patients make rather good citizens.' Whether or not society has influenced the outcome, accommodating itself to humbler surgeons while still distrusting mad thinkers, 'functional neurosurgery' has diminished markedly in recent years. This term is preferred these days by the Society of British Neurological Surgeons to 'leucotomy' or 'psychosurgery', another indication thah the old ways are out of favour. Not only has a tide turned, but other methods for attacking mental illness have steadily been surfacing.

Electroconvulsive therapy is one of them. First introduced in 1934 it therefore just preceded lobotomy, but has since bobbed in and out of favour. In the United States, in particular, it was seen as a 'barbaric anachronism', to use one disparaging term, but is currently on the ascendant. It certainly has a flavour of barbarism about it, as electric current is jolted through a brain, and is also anachronistic in that no one knows what precise effect it is having; but it is therapeutic and can (often) clear depression when all other methods have failed.

The electric shock is delivered either unilaterally or bilaterally (about which more in a moment), is of extremely short duration, is strong enough to produce unconsciousness, often causes a degree of amnesia, and can be a boon for other mental disorders as well as depression. Patients these days tend to be given an anaesthetic and muscle relaxants before the shock, so there is less of the muscular convulsion that used, most dramatically, to partner the treatment. (Because convulsive is an awesome word, even for the courageous, there is a move to change this treatment's name, perhaps to electroplexy. However, the old name is well engrained and its initials are euphemistically acceptable; so ECT is probably here to stay.)

By the mid-1970s, when ECT had been performed on patients for four decades, medical editorials began to wonder – and with reason – why the treatment had never been subjected to proper testing. The US National Institute of Mental Health stated in 1974 that, of the $10 million granted for 'somatic-therapy research' in the previous financial year, less than $5,000 had been spent on ECT. There were many testimonies to its value but, as the *Lancet* phrased it, a 'dearth of scientific inquiries into efficacy'. In 1981 the same journal was able to report that the Royal College of Psychiatrists had published 'what must be the most complete and thorough medical audit of a particular form of treament . . . ever undertaken'. However, the journal then added that every British psychiatrist 'should read this report and feel ashamed . . . If ECT is ever legislated against or falls into disuse it will not be because it is an ineffective or dangerous treatment; it will be because psychiatrists have failed to supervise and monitor its use adequately.'

The report was undeniably comprehensive. It learned that 200,000 individual treatments were given in Britain during 1979, each course for any patient usually consisting of four to eight treatments. It also discovered (from the 86 per cent of psychiatrists who answered the questionnaire helpfully) that only 1 per cent were wholly opposed to the use of ECT, that 87 per cent thought it occasionally useful, that they rarely used it on children (and then mainly on adolescents), that 5 per cent would use it without anaesthetic and relaxants if need be (if, for example, the patients did not welcome drugs), that 59 per cent would inform the next of kin and give it when the patients themselves were unwilling to receive it, and 16 per cent would give it even if both next of kin and patients objected. According to the survey most ECT is administered by junior medical staff who have received little training in it, and whose technique is often faulty. Only in 43 per cent of the clinics would the official observer (one of the team compiling the report) have accepted treatment with few qualms, and 27 per cent of clinics had serious deficiencies, such as unsuitable conditions, lack of respect for the patients, and poorly trained staff who even failed on occasion to induce the seizure, generally considered an essential part of the treatment. Finally, in this battery of criticism – and percentages – more than half the machines in some parts of the country 'were obsolete'.

The report, and the editorial commenting on it, stirred up hornets, some for and some against. The article was 'trenchant' and 'salutary' but 'unfair' in its picture of 'bored and callous staff' using ancient machines. Equipment is not obsolete just because a particular model is no longer made; and what purpose was the *Lancet* serving in 'reacting so extremely to a perhaps exaggeratedly honest and pioneering piece of self-audit'? The suggestion that psychiatrists should be ashamed of themselves bordered 'on impertinence', wrote one correspondent, whereas another applauded the 'forthright indictment' of the 'ignorant, inexperienced and inhumane clinicians who have brought a valuable treatment into disrepute'.

The question of one-sided or two-sided ECT, through one or both halves of the cerebrum, seems to be in particular need of examination. In its indictment, the *Lancet* wrote that American practice had 'slowly shifted' to the use of 'unilateral electrode placement'. A correspondent disagreed, pointing out that, according to the American Psychiatric Association Task Force on ECT, '75 per cent of practitioners' used 'bilateral ECT exclusively'. There is agreement that the double-sided treatment is more disruptive – it induces 'more cognitive dysfunction' – but no similar certainty that it treats depressives more effectively. Only research, as another correspondent added, will clarify the 'important but unclear relations' between the kind of stimulus, the degree of seizure, and the therapeutic outcome. The fact that these three are still so unclear is possibly the most disturbing feature of a treatment jolted through the human brain 200,000 times a year in Britain alone.

Any potential ECT patient, sitting in the waiting room, might become further depressed by reading through medical journals inadvertently lying there. The level of disagreement could be disturbing until he or she realises that unanimity of opinion is rare in any sphere. Nevertheless the language is shrill. 'The crescendo of demands for proof of efficiency of ECT is uninformed and emotional.' 'This line of thinking is being forced upon contemporary psychiatry . . . [causing] elaborate and suffocating legal restraints, which leave patients the "freedom" to suffer their psychotic illnesses untreated, as seems to be the disturbing trend in the U.S.A.' Patients might rush from the waiting room, shocked into flight before more current is switched through their brains. They too might react in an uninformed and emotional manner, preferring the freedom of their illnesses. Or, with reason, they might prefer ignorance and merely hope, as we all do, that every treatment offered might do some good.

One definition of the human species is its uniqueness in both wanting and taking medication. As individuals we are dissimilar in this respect, ranging from a near-permanence under some influence or other to the kind of self-denial which forswears virtually every sort of proven aid. The drugs that work upon the brain are numerous, popular, frequently effective – and often damaging. Some facts may help to clarify the powerful role they play, and Number One on any list is alcohol.

Alcohol Buy cigarettes in many countries, and there is printed warning of the damage they can cause. Buy soft drinks, and there may be warning of the saccharin they contain. Buy alcohol, whether in beer and wine or in greater concentrations as in spirits, and there is no warning whatsoever. But it can kill, as everyone knows, and can kill others, as it does so regularly. Figures from the United States affirm alcohol's involvement in 60 per cent of homicides, 40 per cent of rapes, 33 per cent of suicides, 50 per cent of motor-vehicle fatalities, and 10–30 per cent of all motor injuries. With saccharin there is a faint possibility that it can be carcinogenic; with alcohol there is dead certainty that it can kill. Some countries find it difficult estimating their consumption of alcohol per head of population, but it is easy calculating that quantity by counting the dead from cirrhosis of the liver. The more alcohol is consumed the greater incidence of cirrhosis. Without doubt alcohol can damage health, and cars, and marriages, and children, and productivity, but it never says so on the bottles. According to the World Health Organisation, in 'virtually all countries' liver cirrhosis 'now ranks among the five leading causes of death among males aged 25 to 64'. It is an epidemic.

It has been one for a long time. Alcohol is fun to drink, a (temporary) pick-me-up, a social lubricant, an accepted habit, and very big business. Its effect upon the brain is presumably the dominant reason for its popularity – and for most of its catalogue of drawbacks. *Homo sapiens*, in discovering what things were good to eat and what were toxic and which had medical properties or could induce mental states if smoked, chewed, or merely swallowed, has been (almost) universally partial to ethanol, alias ethyl alcohol, alias booze or tens of thousands of other names around the world. Practically anything that grows can be brewed, fermented, distilled, or so it would seem, to create the all-important potion.

Nevertheless it also creates problems and can be, if abused sufficiently, a disease. Thomas Trotter, British naval surgeon during the Napoleonic wars (he retired in 1802), is generally credited as the first to promote the notion of disease for alcoholism. He also recommended uniforms (not implemented until 1857) and vaccination for sailors (not performed until 1858), but his ideas on drink were accepted even less speedily. In 1948 the WHO included alcoholism (as distinct from alcohol poisoning and alcohol psychoses) in its International Classification of Disease. In 1956 the American Medical Association also formally declared that alcoholism was a disease, just 124 years after Trotter's death. For the past twenty years, as the *British Medical Journal* phrased it in 1979, 'the "disease concept" has been everyone's official dogma', urging governments and employers 'to accept and act on its implications'.

These are formidable, even in a country such as Britain where the annual consumption per head of absolute alcohol is seven litres. Countries with higher rates are, for example, and in ascending order, Belgium, Canada, Czechoslovakia, Australia, West Germany, Austria, Portugal, Italy and France (whose consumption is over three times higher than Britain's). In 1957 Britain had 490,000 alcoholics (almost 1 per cent of the country). By 1967 there were 540,000 (1 per cent) and in 1977 there were 740,000 (1.3 per cent). (Countries with higher levels of alcohol consumption have higher levels of alcoholism.) The annual deaths from cirrhosis of the liver for England and Wales are 1,800, from alcoholism and alcoholic psychosis 180, and admissions to mental health hospitals from these two causes are 14,000 a year.

Alcoholism in Scotland has always been a special case, with wee drams being outrageously misnamed; but even there, and despite a national characteristic of excessive drinking, it has been rising. In 1956 there were 732 hospital admissions for 'alcoholism and alcoholic psychoses'. Within ten years the same total was 2,755, and by 1976 it was 4,388. Twice as many men are currently admitted to Scottish mental hospitals for alcoholism than for any other single diagnosis. Public drunkenness has also gone up, so too consumption – they traditionally partner each other. Inverness (in eastern Scotland) drinks most and has most alcohol-related offences. Ayr (in western Scotland) drinks least and has least. Alcohol is a drug of dependence, like heroin or amylobarbitone, and differs only in the quantity that must first be consumed. Twenty to thirty milligrams of heroin a day for a few weeks will create dependence; 120 grams of alcohol (about five thousand times as much) per day for several months – eight pints/4.5 litres of beer or half a bottle of spirits – will lead to a similar condition. What makes a person start drinking may be his/her attitude to life; but, as Professor R. E. Kendell, of Edinburgh, put it, 'What determines whether a person becomes dependent upon alcohol is how much he drinks and for how long, rather than his personality, psychodynamics, or biochemistry.'

One of the amazing stories about the United States – if not the most amazing – is that it prohibited the manufacture, marketing and drinking of alcohol from 1919 to 1933. The cost, in crime, corruption and law enforcement eventually became too great to bear, but the cost of renewed drinking has also been considerable. In 1971 Congress established the National Institute on Alcoholism and Alcohol Abuse, and its 1978 report to Congress estimated that: 13 million Americans misused alcohol; this abuse cost $42,900 million (in 1975) for accidents, crime, fire, health care etc; 50,000 to 200,000 deaths (according to different estimates) were related to alcohol abuse; and a wide variety of disease, from liver cirrhosis to mentally deranged children of alcoholic women, were also linked with this mismanagement. Prohibition, for all its crime and abuse of the system, can suddenly appear in a better light. A regulation requiring 'ingredient labelling' on alcoholic drinks was issued in President Carter's time, but was never implemented. In 1981, and during Reagan's era, it was rescinded. Because of alcohol's involvement in half the US car accidents, 60 per cent of its drownings, 70–80 per cent of the deaths in fires, and 85 per cent of the annual 11,000 liver-disease deaths, it is a major killer of American people, and the leading killer for those aged fifteen to forty-five.

This indictment reads like some account of the Black Death, with the fourth horseman busily cutting through the population; but alcohol is what we go out and buy, for ourselves, for a good time, 'for the road'. The human brain is undoubtedly a subtle and clever instrument. It then proceeds to imbibe great quantities of alcohol, the better to diminish much of that subtlety and cleverness, like a lion extracting its teeth, or an eagle clipping its wings. The human phenomenon is once again astonishing. It has a lovely brain and then, given almost any opportunity, blunts its edges, lessens its capabilities, and feels all the better for doing so before realising, with a final flicker of insight, that – once again – it has gone too far.

Some final facts can end this homily. Alcohol abuse during pregnancy 'is now the most important preventable cause of mental deficiency in the Western world', according to Glasgow's Royal Hospital for Sick Children. The drink industry is big enough, but even its converse is expensive. 'A single inpatient treatment episode [for alcoholism] can cost up to $10,000', according to a book on the subject published in 1981. It has been estimated (within the *New England Journal of Medicine*) 'that between 13,600 and 22,600 physicians in the United States are alcoholic or will become so.' In the state of Georgia, for example, and according to the same article, 'one of eight physicians . . . has been, is, or will be afflicted with the disease of alcoholism.' An ultimate point is that the world record for alcohol level in the blood, according to a hospital at Gentofte, Denmark, is 1,127 milligrams per decilitre. A 59-year-old, 66-kg/145-lb man, who had drunk 2½ bottles of whisky in a suicide attempt, was found to have this level on admission. The culpable limit for motorists is 80 milligrams per decilitre (in

Britain, anyway), the 50/50 mortality level is 500 milligrams per decilitre and, until that Danish happening, the previous high for blood-ethanol had been 780 milligrams per decilitre. On his discharge one month later there were neither physical signs of damage nor, according to his wife, signs of intellectual malfunction after the most monstrous intoxication ever recorded.

Drugs Alcohol is but one, and has a long history of usage and abusage, but there are thousands of others that also affect the brain. Indeed *Homo pharmaceutiens* has been on the hunt for natural remedies, prophylactics, stimulants and sedatives ever since he had the wit to find, take and enjoy such things. The story of aspirin alone could fill a book, starting as it does with the discovery (known, of course, to Hippocrates) that willow bark and leaves would reduce fever, and moving on to the current fact (perhaps to amaze even the father of medicine) that 35 million pounds of it are produced annually in the United States alone, or almost one tablet of aspirin per American per day. It is the most widely used medicine in the world.

A few pronouncements may serve as pointer to mankind's supreme enthusiasm for chewing, swallowing, breathing, or injecting substances with power to affect the body in general and the brain in particular. Cut out those individuals who neither drink alcohol frequently, nor smoke regularly, nor take pills, tablets, potions or physic of some form on most days, and very few people remain to wonder, as any Martian might do, at all this human medication. The substances sedate, they stimulate; they soothe, they excite; they are an extra, they are vital. In one form or another they are universal.

Medicines do harm along with their good. 'Show me a drug with no side effects, and I'll show you a drug with no actions,' said Sir Derrick Dunlop. Even aspirin and paracetamol (the principal rival to aspirin in, for example, the UK) which are (in Britain) the 'only effective general-purpose antipyretic analgesics available without prescription', as the *Lancet* described them, can both do harm. There are enthusiasts for the relative harmlessness of each, a kind of affirmation that neither is harmless. About four hundred people a year die in Britain from paracetamol overdose, but more children – about seven a year in Britain – die from salicylate poisoning. In fact aspirin (acetylsalicylic acid), again according to the *Lancet*, has 'a much greater potential for toxicity than paracetamol'. In other words, despite the popularity, and history (aspirin was introduced in the nineteenth century), and phenomenal sales of these two drugs (paracetamol selling even more than aspirin in

Britain), they are both capable of harm. They are undoubtedly effective and, therefore, to rephrase Sir Derrick, have effects other than those for which they are taken.

'I love doctors and hate their medicines,' said Walt Whitman. Not everyone would agree, possibly loving medicines even more than doctors. The physicians are often accused of over-prescription, but rarely by patients happy to receive a medicine that just might cure an ill. 'If you want to know whether you need a haircut, don't ask a barber,' runs the adage. In this context it is unfair to doctors, implying they never say no. Perhaps the greater fault is in sitting in the barber's chair, expecting a haircut, and being cross (or going next door) if one is not given. Hence the suspicion that mankind has, and always has had, an enthusiasm for drugs, with or without a pharmaceutical industry or a rubber-stamping medical profession to dish them out.

(As a personal aside, and having been privileged to meet Austra-lian aborigines, Xingú Indians, Eskimos, high-altitude Nepalese, and all manner of up-country Africans, I have never encountered any resistance to the taking of every pill, powder, or other alleged panacea I have had about my person. I do not believe this follows from an unrealistic faith in the pale-faced foreigner's supposed powers, because the locals – to generalise – welcome every-thing – local brew, however foul, or visitor's medicine chest. My contention is that humans have always been addicts, for the latest potion, the oldest old wives' tale, or the newest patent medicine to come their way. It does please if some 'blood purifier' turns urine purple within a minute of its ingestion – I have seen the joy this brings – but there is nothing quite like a drug that acts upon the mind. If knowledge of drug power is what is required then it is necessary to assault, or so it would seem, the seat of knowledge, to attack the human brain. Coca, alcohol, peyote, bhang, morphine, tobacco – it does not really matter, just so long as the effects are made aware within the centre of awareness. It is often said, usually erroneously, that animals know what is best for them, ingesting salt, vitamins, fats as and when need be. Mankind, or so it appears, ingests virtually everything, whether good for him or not, but most happily of all if it acts upon his brain.)

In recent years the drugs industry has been working miracles for us. First (in the 1930s) were the sulphonamides, wonder drugs every one. Then came antibiotics, actually with power to cure dangerous diseases. Then the tricyclics, said by enthusiasts to be penicillins of the mind, and alleged to allay anxiety. Then, yet more wondrous, and in the early 1960s, came benzodiazepines. *World Medicine* has described them as 'one of the world's most avidly gobbled psychoactive drugs', before adding the statistic that 'maybe 10,000 tons' are consumed each year in the United States alone. (If that sort of tonnage makes little sense for something like a pill, it is 333 trucks of 30 tons each, or a five-mile line of trucks). American prescriptions for Valium total 80 million every year, a number equal to over a third of the US population.

If it is possible to generalise about the plethora of drugs, and our steadfast affection for them, it is that drugs are increasing in their usage and the brain-drugs most of all. *Homo pharmaceutiens* is still a legitimate description, but *Homo psychotropiens* is gaining all the time.

Computers Artificial intelligence (AI) has been called the 'most profoundly depressing of all ideas about the future of the human species'. It has also been said that computers, when cleverly made to be clever enough, will 'lead to the eventual subjugation of human beings to machines'. Others, notably researchers in the field of AI have been quick to deny 'such slander'. 'If we assume that we can never build a machine to equal the human mind, we must conclude that the human mind is unequal to the task of understanding the human body,' wrote David S. Touretzky. Outsiders have expressed concern about the work, or have reacted flippantly – 'Why don't they start with artificial stupidity, and then work their way up?'

Pocket calculators were introduced in 1972. (Was it only that long ago? we all say.) They, and their bigger brethren in offices and government, have created a revolution almost as speedily as they do their sums. And print payrolls. And check lists. And discover if Flight 234 is fully booked. Most of the research effort linked to them has been limited to their speed and storage capabilities, permitting these 'high-speed idiots' (there are many derogatory names) to stay emphatically as servants to our whims. We – the great bulk of us – are no more alarmed by their restricted efficiency than we are by the clever humans who treat complex mental arithmetic as if reciting two times two. The machines are in straitjackets, and we have put them there.

Machine intelligence is another matter. Will the swift idiots of today become high-speed geniuses of the future? And, if so, will they outthink us? And if yes to that, who will be master, them or us? Donald Michie, fervent member of the machine intelligentsia, has replied: 'not as servant nor as master, but as tutor, as secretary, as playmate, as research assistant'. Some playmate examples are already in the shops, notably the computer chess sets. It is intriguing, depressing, exciting and also instructive to be beaten so straightforwardly by such little gadgets – particularly by grade one of eight grades of skill. Their play has been described as 'clumsy, inefficient, diffuse and just plain ugly, but this does not mean they do not win'.

They do, and David Levy has the two-edged distinction of being the very first grandmaster to lose to a computer. The year 1977 was a significantly early one in the rivalry between man-made chess-players and the human kind. The 84th Minnesota Open was won by a computer even though the opposition was just under the master level. By 1980 a Bell Laboratories computer was winning frequently against masters, and no wonder because it could calculate possible scores (relative advantages) for about 100,000 positions a second. By the end of 1982 there were five computer programmes playing around the master level, two at it and three just below. The computer ability is, therefore, considerable (and the 700 United States masters have to concede that fact) but the style of play is still as crude as ever, just faster and faster calculations of what might happen to every piece if every move were followed by every other possible move, and each of these were followed by every other variable, and so on. That technique may win the game, but is hardly clever. The machines are still just speedy idiots.

The alarm, and the argument, concerns computers of the HAL kind on Arthur Clarke's spaceship of 2001. This mastermind of the Jupiter mission not only resented its planned destruction but took steps to prevent it. Is consciousness, therefore, an integral part of a silicon network, just as it is of a nervous one? And, if so, what does that possibility hold in store for us? HAL started as playmate and research assistant, but became murderer along the way. Perhaps all man-made computers will be no better than man has been. As Toretzky phrased it: 'If it were possible to describe the body in unambiguous terms, one could build a machine to interpret this description, and its mind would by definition be human.' The conclusion is modest comfort for those who know a thing or two about humans. The species may have the best brain so far discovered in the universe. It also possesses the only brain known to be capable of destroying the very planet that gave it birth.

Finale That is too depressing a note on which to end. The human brain is not only capable of the greatest evil but of the greatest good. It has created saints along with all the sinners, and will presumably do so in the future for there is no sign it is evolving in any particular direction. Such evolution as is occurring is cultural, being independent of the brain creating it. The odd fact, already expressed in earlier pages, of modern man's cerebral hemispheres being developed for a hunter-gatherer's style of life will remain just as true and odd for centuries to come. The living customs of future man will presumably be yet more distanced from the simple, palaeolithic manner of existence, but future man will still be equipped with that ancient form of brain. Natural selection for bigger, better brains is just not happening any more; so no change is likely for that cause. Besides, as Alfred Russel Wallace said (and was quoted at the very outset of this book), 'An instrument has been developed in advance of the needs of its possessor.' The brain of modern man, whatever its origins, is better than it need be, and rarely tapped for its true potential. The brain of future man will also, for quite a while, be ahead of its requirements. This fact will only change when some future generation learns how to use the instrument, to the full, to the best of its extraordinary abilities.

Much earlier in this volume, at the start of the introductory chapter, were various statements that might bear a second reading in view of all the words bridging the gap between them and this final paragraph. 'It is, say humans, the most important thing in the world, but it looks as interesting as intestines, and indeed was frequently drawn formerly as if intestinal, a tube from start to finish. Our forefathers were more intrigued by the pulsing heart, the moody spleen, the colour-changing liver, the wandering and peristaltic gut. Even urine, in their opinion, held more excitement than the brain . . . We, who are equipped with this evolutionary miracle, do likewise in our fashion and are, in general, about as good at naming its parts as in pinpointing mountains on the moon. Yet the brain has made us. It is not our guts or our liver that has created *sapiens* . . . It is the human brain.' At long last not only neurologists but the rest of us are realising it *is* the most extraordinary development of all. Liver, spleen, heart and guts are all intriguing, but cannot hold a candle to the brain. It *is* the most important thing on Earth, for good or ill.

INDEX

Index

Entries in bold type refer to major descriptions in the text.

abducent nerve, **75–6**
Aberdeen, 198, 199, 243
aborigines, and evolution, 14–15, 18
accessory nerve, **76–7**
acetylcholine, 88, 239
  and Alzheimer's disease, 239
  and impulse transmission, 100–1
acromegaly (large extremities), 91
active sleep, 135–6
  and dreams, 139
acupuncture, 199–200
Addison, Joseph, 159, 206
Addison, Thomas, 89
adrenal cortex, 88, 89, 90
adrenal glands, **88–90**
adrenal medulla, 88, 89, 90
adrenaline (epinephrine), 88
Aesop, 205
agraphia (writing inability), 157
Aitken, A. C., 3
alcoholism, 315–18
  and suicide, 264
Alcmaeon of Croton, and foundation of neurology, 59, 63
Alexander the Great, 205
alexia (word blindness), 157
alpha-fetoprotein, 226, 227

alpha wave, 103, 107, 286
  and asymmetry, 116–17
Alzheimer, Alois, 292
Alzheimer's disease, 292, 293–4
Amateur Boxing Association, 255
American Journal of Human Genetics, 217
American Journal of Psychiatry, 167
American Medical Association, 315
American Psychiatric Association, 266
Ameslan (sign language), 155
amines, 88
  and impulse transmission, 100–1
amino acids, 101, 198
amnesia, 130, 131, **170–3**
amniocentesis, 226, 235
Ampère, André, 107
amphetamines, 240
amphibia, 12, 135
  brain function of, 26, 27
  in evolution, 6, 7, 82
Amphioxus (marine creature), nervous system of, 25–6
amusia (inability to recognise tunes), 161
anaemia, 89

anaesthesia, 200
analgesics *see under* individual
    headings and drugs–pain
    killing
Anatomy of the Human Body,
    1959 (Lockhart,
    Hamilton, Fyfe), 81
anencephaly (brainlessness),
    222, 223
Angell, Dr Marcia, on pain
    killers, 194–5
animals
    and brain size, 4–5, 8–9
    and colour vision, 180
    and communication, 10, 11,
        152
    and consciousness, xvi, 128
    foetal development of, 30–3,
        34
    fore-limbs of, 12–13
    hearing of, 182, 184
    intelligence of, 3
    music and, 160–1
    nervous system of
        invertebrates, 19–26
        vertebrates, 25–29
    olfaction of, 186
    senses of, 176
Ankara, 166
Anokhin, Pyotr, 173
Annelids (worms with ringed
    segments), 23
anorexia nervosa, 93
anosmia (loss of sense of
    smell), xi, 187, 189
anoxia (deprivation of
    oxygen), 53, 83
    and cerebral palsy, 243,
        244
antibiotics, 319
ants, 24
apes, xvi
    abilities at birth, 42
    and communication, 15

language learning abilities,
    155–6
and consciousness, 129
and evolution, 7
and right-handedness, 123
brain size of, 55
fore-limb arrangement of, 12
aphasia (speech difficulty),
    114, 157
Aplysia (marine snail), nerve
    cells of, 21, 23, 25
arachnoid membrane, 73, 78
Archimedes, 205
Arie, Prof. Thomas, 290
Aristotle, 204, 205
    ideas on intelligence, 2
    and nervous system, xv, xvii
    and senses, 175, 192
Armstrong, D. M., 128
Armstrong, Louis, 146, 148
arthropods (invertebrates with
    jointed limbs), 23, 24
Ascaris (nematode worm), 20,
    23
    nerve cells of, 19, 21
Asimov, Isaac, 93
aspirin, 318–19
asymmetries, 110–17
    and handedness, 124
    and hemispherectomy,
        121–2
    and split-brain, 117–20
Attila, 205
auditory cortex, 183, 184
auditory nerve, **76**
Augustine, St, and Cell
    Doctrine, 59
Aurelia (jellyfish), 22, 23
Aurignacian culture, 14
Australia, 14, 15, 18
    suicide statistics of, 263
Australopithecines, 8, 10
    *Australopithecus gracilis, 9
    robustus, 9*

brain capacity of, 15
  right-handedness and, 123
Austria, suicide statistics, 263
autonomic nervous system, 80,
  85–94
  impulse transmissions of, 99
  see also parasympathetic
    nervous system;
    sympathetic nervous
    system
Avicenna, and foundations of
  neurology, 60
Avon, Earl of, 235
axons, 32, 33
  damage to, 248
  in neurons, 96, 97, 98, 99,
    100

babies *see* neonates
Bach, J. S., 161, 206
Bacon, Francis, 206
Baird, Sir Douglas, 243
Ball, J. M., 60
Baltimore, 199
Banks, Lucian ('Sonny'), 254
Barker, Arthur, 276
Barnard, Dr Christiaan, 299
basal ganglia, 66
  function of, 67
basal nuclei, 28
Bateson, Patrick, 146, 147
bats, hearing of, 182
Beard, R. W., 244
Beecher, Dr H. K., 306
Beethoven, Ludwig van, 161,
  206
Belgium, suicide statistics, 263
Bell, Charles, 58
Bellairs, Ruth, 33
Benda, Prof. Clemens, 235
Bentham, Jeremy, early
  abilities of, 206, 207–8
benzodiazepines, 319
Berger, Hans, 103, 106

Bernard, Claude, 85
Bernard, St, 205
Bible, and right-handedness,
  110, 123
birds, brain construction of,
  27–8
Birmingham General Hospital,
  247
birth
  brain damage during, 241–4
  trauma, 53
Bisected Brain, The
  (Gazzaniga), 119
Blake, William, 205
Blakemore, Colin, on vision,
  176–7, 181
Bleuler, E., 266
blindness, and hearing ability,
  185
blink reflex, **43**
blood-brain barrier, 107–8
blood pressure, 258
blood stream, 72, 73
blood supply to brain, **83–4**
blood vessels, 33
blue whale, 29
body temperature control,
  43–4
Body, The (Anthony Smith),
  xviii
Bohr, Niels, 212
Bonica, J. J., 200
boxing injuries, 252–5, 256
Boyle, Robert, 58, 63, 205
Boynton, Sir John, 220
brachial plexus, 79, **81**
Braid, James, 140
brain, xii
  and abnormality, 219,
    222–39
  damage to, 41–2, 45, **52–4**,
    240–79
    compensation for, 278–9
    identification of, 50

brain – *cont*.
  death, 295–307
  definition of, xv, **2–6**
  diseases of, 67, 91, 93
  distinction from the mind, xviii
  dominant handedness and, 17, 113
  foetal development of, 32–3
    human, 33–8
    and prematurity, 38–42
  growth of, **4–6**
    and dexterity, 15–17
    and speech, 10–11
    in childhood, 45–50
    in evolution, **6–10**
    speed of, 7–10
  impulse transmission in, 97–108
  injury to, xv, 246–56
  of invertebrates, 19–25
  pain killers and, 198–201
  parts of, 63–84
    blood supply of, 83–4
    cells of, 95–102
    nerves of, 73–82
  resilience of, 185
  size and weight of, xv–xvi, 2–3, **54–5**
    and intelligence, 3–4, 5–6, 8, 9, 45, 54–5
  study of, 58–63
  surgery, 118–19, 279; *see also* commissurotomy; lobotomy
  symmetry in, 111–126
  waves, 100, 102–6
    and feedback, 106–7
    and sleep, 135–6
  see also fore-brain; hind-brain, nerve cells; nervous system; split-brain
Brain Function in Old Age (ed. Hoffmeister and Müller), 288
Brain, Lord, 308
British Broadcasting Corporation, and brain-death controversy, 300, 301, 302
British Medical Association, 140, 236
  and brain-death controversy, 301–2
British Medical Journal
  on alcoholism, 315–16
  on alexia, 157
  on analgesics, 198
  on Army brawling injuries, 255
  on brain-death controversy, 301, 302
  on foetal defects, 226
  on mental patients, 216
  on Parkinsonism, 270, 271
  on right-handedness, 125
  on strokes, 273, 274
British Paediatric Association, 236
British Pugilists Protective Association, 254
British Society of Medical Hypnotists, 140
Broca, Paul, 17, 64, 114
  brain size of, 54
Broca's area, 114, 152–3
Broughton, John, 254
Browne, Sir Thomas, 122
Bruce, Robert, 205
Bulgaria, suicide statistics, 263
Bülow, Hans von, 3, 166
Bulwer, John, 15
Bunyan, John, 207
Burke, Edmund, 206
Burnet, Sir Macfarlane, xviii
Burney, Fanny, 208
Burns, D. B., 168

Burns, Robert, 213
Burt, Sir Cyril, 150
Byron, Lord, 205

calcarine fissure, 37
Calder, Ritchie, 103
California, 249
Cambridge, 146
   University, 286
Campbell, Dr Vincent D., 255
Canada, 173
   suicide statistics, 263
cancer, 278
   see also tumours, cerebral
Capute, Ann, 195
cardiac plexus, 87
Carlyle, Thomas, 11
   and left-handedness, 113,
      126
   early genius of, 207
carotid arteries, 83, 84
carp, 26
Carter, C. O., 149
Carter, President Jimmy, 317
Casals, Pablo, 215
Cassell, Dr Eric J., 195
Casserio, Guilo, 61
catalepsy (sudden
   unconsciousness), 138
cataplexy (weakness following
   emotional trigger), 138
Caton, Richard, 103
Catullus, 127
Cavour, Camillo, 206
Cell Doctrine, and early
   theories of neurology,
   59–60
Cellini, Benvenuto, 205
central fissure, 37
central sulcus, 191
cerebellar cortex, function of,
   64–5
cerebellar hemispheres,
   function of, 64–5

cerebellum, 191
   construction of, 27, 28
   foetal development of, 36
   function of, 64–5
   in reptiles, 26–7
cerebral cortex, 37, 38, 50
   and hydrocephalus, 230
   and memory, 170
   function of, 64–5
cerebral decay, 292
cerebral hemispheres, 191
   and music, 160–1
   and speech, 115, 120
   construction of, 27, 28–9
   function of, 64–5, **67–73**
   see also asymmetries;
      handedness; symmetry
cerebral palsy, xii, 50, 243–4
   definition of, **52–3**, 241
   peri-natal factors affecting,
      242
cerebral peduncles, 65
cerebral resuscitation, 133, 134
cerebral ventricles, **71–2**
Cerebri Anatome 1664 (Willis),
   62
cerebrospinal fluid, 59, **72–3**
   and headaches, 258, 259
   and hydrocephalus, 228, 230
cerebrum, 74
   function of, 64–5
Cervantes, Miguel de, 205, 207
cervical nerves, 78, **79–80**
cervical plexus, 79, **81–2**
cervical vertebrae, 78
Chaplin, Charles, 122
Charles V, 205
Chateaubriand, Comte de,
   206
Chatelperonian culture, 14
cheirognomy (palmistry), 15,
   16
cheiromancy (fortune-telling),
   15

childbirth, 53
  brain damage during, 240,
    241–4
  see also prematurity
children
  and active sleep, 139
  and brain damage, 240–3
  and convulsions, 141, 142, 143
  and handedness, 125–6
  and intelligence, 149
    tests, 151
  and learning, 147, 148
    and dyslexia, 158
  and speech development, 11,
    115, 120, 154, 155
  childhood of geniuses,
    208–12
  education of, 212–15
  neural development in,
    46–50
  personality development in,
    51
chimpanzee, brain size and
    dexterity of, 8, 13
China, suicide statistics, 261
cholesterol, 89
chromosone No. 21, 218, 219
  and Down's syndrome, 234,
    235
Churchill, Winston, 19
  childhood of, 208–9
CIBA, 267
Cicero, 18
Clarke, Arthur, 321
Clarke, Prof. C. A., 227–8
Clarke, Edwin, 63
Clay, Cassius, 254
Clinical Research Centre,
    London, 196
Cobbett, William, 207
coccygeal nerve, 78, 79, 80
coccygeal plexus, 79, 82
coccyx, 78
cockroaches, 24

coelenterates (many-celled
    animals with a single body
    cavity), 22, 23, 29
  and memory, 164
Coleridge, S. T., 207
colitis, 42
colour blindness, 180
Coltheart, Max, 157
coma, 130, 132
  and death, 299
  recovery from, 132–4
Comfort, Alex, 282, 284
commissurotomy (bisection of
    the brain), 118–19, 170
communication, role of the
    hand in, 15–16
  see also speech
Compton, Denis, 122
computerised axial
    tomography (CT or CAT)
    scans, 277
computers, 320–1
concussion, 130–4
Conference of Medical
    Colleges, 1979, 298, 300
consciousness and asymmetry,
    116–17
Constable, John, 206
convulsions, **141–5**
  see also epilepsy
Cook, James, 207
Copernicus, Nicolaus, 206, 207
Cornaro, Ludovico, 284
corneal reflex, 132
  and death, 130
corpora pendunculata, 24
corpus callosum (hardbody),
    xvii, 69, 117
  and split-brain, 118–19
corpus striatum, 28
cortex, 26
  and dominance, 116
  in mammals, 28
  in reptiles, 27

study of, 58, 62, 63
cortical blindness, 241
corticoid hormones, 89
cortisone, 89
Cox, Catherine Morris, 207
cranial nerves, **73–7**, 189
Cravettian culture, 14
crayfish, 21
Creuzfeldt-Jakob's disease, 292
crickets, 24
Critchley, Macdonald, 159, 160, 253
crocodiles, 27
Cromwell, Oliver, 54
Cromwell, Thomas, 207
Crow, Dr T. J., 193, 267
cryoanalgesia, 195–6
Cummins, Harold, 16
Cushing, Harvey, 276
Cushing's disease, 91
Cuvier, Baron Georges, 54
Cyclopaedia of the Practice of Medicine 1877 (Kussmaul), 157
cyclostomes, 26
Czechoslovakia, suicide statistics, 263

Damasio, Antonio R., 160
Dante Alighieri, 205
Darwin, Charles, 205, 208
da Vinci, Leonardo, 122, 206
and early studies of anatomy, 60, 61
deafness, 185
Dean, John, 172
death, 104, 105
brain death, 295–307
coma and, 130, 132, 133–4
legal aspects of, 304–6
de la Boë, Franciscus, 62
Delgado, J. M. R., 127
de Luzzi, Mondino, 60

dementia, 104
and hypothalamus, 93
see also senile dementia
Demosthenes, 205
dendrites, 96, 100
Denmark, 317
suicide statistics, 236
Dennett, Daniel C., 127
De partibus animalium (Aristotle), 2
depression, 283
and ECT, 312
and hypothalamus, 93
and suicide, 262, 264–5
see also senile dementia
Descartes, René, xvii, 206
and study of neurology, 62
Detroit, 254
Developmental Medicine and Child Neurology, 230
Devi, Mrs Shakuntala, 212
Dewhurst, Kenneth, 63
dexterity, evolution of, **14–17**
dextrocardia, 110–11
diabetes, 148
insipidus, 91
Diagnostic and Statistical Manual, 266
diaphragm, 81
Dickens, Charles, 206, 208
Dictionary of National Biography, 207
diencephalon, 28, 36, 74
function of, 64, 65
Dilly, Prof. Noel, 233
Diseases of the Nervous System (Matthews and Miller), 277
Dobzhansky, Theodosius, 149
doll's eye (oculocephalic) reflex, **43**, 132
dolphins, and sleep, 135
Donizetti, Gaetano, 205

dopamine, 239
  and Parkinsonism, 270
  and schizophrenia, 268, 269
Down, John Langdon Haydon, 233
Down's syndrome, 52, **233–7**
  and birth statistics, 219
  and X-chromosome, 218
  identification of in palm prints, 16, 17
Drake, Francis, 207
dreams, **138–40**
drugs, 318–20
  and brain, 101
  pain killing, 196
  and phantom pain, 197–8
  see also endorphins; enkephalins; and under individual headings
Dryden, John, 204
Dumas, Alexandre (père), 207
Dunlop, Sir Derrick, 284, 318, 319
dura mater (meninges), 72, 78
Dürer, A., 161
dwarfism, 91
dynorphin, 198
dysgeusia (malfunction of taste system), 188
dyslexia, 111, **157–8**

Early Mental Traits of Three Hundred Geniuses 1926 (Cox), 207
earthworm, 23
  impulse transmission in, 99
Eccles, John C., 151
ectoderm, 31
  and formation of neural tissue, 31–2
Edinburgh, 88
  University, 3, 129, 208
Edison, Thomas A., 168, 208

education, and gifted children, 212–15
Egypt, 59
Einstein, Albert, 52, 212
  brain size of, 55
elasmobranchs, 27
electrocardiographs (ECGs), 102
electro-convulsive therapy (ECT), 171, 312–14
  and handedness, 115
electroencephalograms (EEGs), 100
  and death identification, 296–7, 298–9, 306
  and epilepsy, 143
  and hypnosis, 141
  and old age, 285–6
  and sleep, 137
  development of, 102–4
  uses of, 104–6
electrophysiology, 33
elephants, 5, 29
Elliotson, John, 140
Ellis, Havelock, and *A Study of British Genius*, 206–7
embryology, **30–3**
  development of human embryo, 34–5
encephalitis, 270
encephalopathy, 253
endocrine glands, 90, 93, 94
endoderm, 31
endorphins, xix, 101, **198–201**
enkephalins, xix, *101*, **198–201**
environment, and child development, 51
epilepsy (cerebral dysrythmia), 104, **141–5**, 216
  and sleep deprivation, 137
  and split-brain, 113–14, 117, 118, 119
epithalamus, **65**

Erasistratus of Alexandria, 61
Erasmus, D., 205
Ervin, Dr Frank, 311
Essentials of Neuroanatomy, The, (Mitchell and Mayor), 181
Eustachian tubes, 59
Evans, Chris, dictionary of, 128–9, 147, 148, 167
Evolution, xi, **3–18**
  cultural, 17–18, 130, 163
  of brain, **3–6**
  growth of, **4–6**
  of brain-controlled behaviour, xvi
  of hand, 12–13
  dexterity, 14–16, 17
  of man, 6–10
  of speech, 10–11, 152
Exeter, 273
exophthalmia, 92
Ex-prodigy: My Childhood and Youth (Wiener), 209–12
Eysenck, Prof. Hans, and intelligence testing, 149, 150, 151
eyes, foetal development of, 38

facial nerve, **76**
Faraday, Michael, 207, 213
Fessard, A., 128
Finland and brain-death criteria, 298, 299
  and suicide statistics, 263
fish, 135
  brain development of, 26, 63
  cranial nerves in, 73–4
  formation of neural tissue in, 32
  in evolution, 6, 7, 82
  see also teleosts
Flaubert, Gustave, 206
foetus
  and active sleep, 139

brain of, 283
  evolution and, 7
  growth of, 5, 32–3
  human, 33–8, 71
  size of, 3, 6
  defects of, 225–7
  growth rate of, 24
  prematurity and, 38–9
fontanels, 45, 48
foramen magnum, 83
fore-brain, 18, 26, 64
  and manual dexterity, 13
  cranial nerves in, 74
  evolution of, 6, 7
  foetal development of, 35
  in mammals, 28
  in reptiles, 27
Forel, Auguste, 164
fornix, 66
fossil remains, 14, 15
Foundations of Anatomy and Physiology, 309
France, Anatole, 54, 55
France, suicide statistics, 263
Francis Xavier, St, 205
Franklin, Benjamin, 13
Freeman, Walter, and lobotomy, 310, 311, 312
French National Academy of Medicine, 297
Freud, Sigmund, 138, 140
  and hypnosis, 141
Friesland, 236
Frisby, John P., 179
frogs, 26
frontal lobe, 69
Fuller, Buckminster, 137–8

Gage, Phineas, 171, 248, 252
Galant's reflex, **43**
Galen, xvii
  and description of brain, 59, 60, 61, 67
Galileo, Galilei, 206

Gall, J. F., 17, 55
  and phrenology, 62–3
Galt, John, 206
Galton, Adèle, 204–5
Galton, Francis, 204–5, 285
gammathalatomy, 278
ganglia (nervous bundles),
    86–7
  foetal, 32
  highest, 22, 23
Gardner, Robert and Beatrice,
    155
Gassendi, Pierre, 207
Gazzaniga, Michael S., 119
Geis, Helen J., 311
genetics, 33
  and child development, 51
  and intelligence, 149
Genetic Studies of Genius
    (Terman), 214
Gentofte, Denmark, 317
Georgia, USA, 196
Gerard, R. W., 167
Germany, suicide statistics, 263
Gesell, Arnold, 46
giantism, 91
Gibbon, Edward, 205
Giotto, 205
Glasgow, 247
  University, 207
glial cells (neuroglia), 2, **96**
glossopharyngeal nerve, **76**,
    188–9
Glover, E., 51
Godlee, Sir Rickman, 276
Goethe, Wolfgang von, 207
goitre, 92
Goldschmidt, Richard, 19
Goldsmith, Oliver, 205, 206
Goldstein, A., 199
Gomulick, B. R., 167–8
Gooddy, Dr William, 295
gorillas, 7, 8
  brain size of, 4, 9, 55

Gorky, Maxim, 54, 208
Gould, James L., 33
grand mal, **142–3**
granule cells, 187
grasp (Babinski reflex), **43**
Greece, suicide statistics, 263
Green, J. H., 190–1
Grey, Sir Edward, 208
Groningen, 236, 247
*Growth and Development of
    Children* (Watson and
    Lowrey), 40
Guatemala, cancer statistics,
    278
Guilford, J. P., 213
Guinness Book of Records,
    212, 287
Guthrie, Douglas, 276
gyri, 37, 70
  and blood supply of brain,
    83–4
  and early theories of
    neurology, 61, 63
  angular gyrus and alexia, 17

haemophilia, 147–8
Halici, Mehmed Ali, 166
Haller, Albrecht von, 207
*Hampstead and Highgate
    Express*, 221
hand
  and disease identification,
    16–17
  description of, **12–13**
  in communication, 15–16
  use of by children, 49, 50
handedness, 110–13
Handel, George Frederick,
    161, 206
Harrer, G. and H., 159
Harrison, Rex, 122
Harvard criteria, 298
Harvard University, 29
  Wiener at, 209, 210

Harvey, William, xvii, 61
Hatoff, David E., 267
Hayes, Douglas, 116
headache, 256–9
  see also migraine
Headache and Other Head Pain
  (Wolff), 259
head injury, xii, 246–9
  caused by boxing, 252–5
  caused by other sport, 255–6
  caused by war wounds,
  249–52
hearing, **181–5**
Hearne, Dr Keith, 140
Hebb, Donald, 138, 168
Heckel, Ernst, 11
Hegel, Georg, 204
Helmholtz, Hermann von, 97
Helpern, Dr Milton, 252
hemiplegia, 272–3
hemispherectomy, **121–2**
Hendrickson, Alan, 151
Henson, R. A., 159
Herder, G., 10
Herophilus of Alexandria, 59
herpes, 79
Hess, W. R., 128
Hillaby, John, xvi
hind-brain, 26, 35
  function of, 64–5
hippocampal gyrus, 187
hippocampus, 66, 170
Hippocrates, 67, 140, 142, 310
  and strokes, 273
Hobbes, Thomas, 206
Hodge, C. F., 283, 284
Hodgkin, A. L., 98
Hofmeister, F., 288
Holland, 236
  suicide statistics, 263
Hollingworth, Leta, 213
Hollymoor Hospital Dementia
  Service, Birmingham, 291
Homo erectus, 9, 15

Homo habilis, 9, 13, 125
Homo neanderthalensis, 9, 13
Homo sapiens, 6, 9
  and speech development,
  10–11
honey bee, 19–20
  nerve cells of, 2, 284
hormones, 66, 89
  and sleep, 136
  pituitary, 91
  thyroid, 91, 92
Horsley, Sir Victor, 276
Hubel, David H., 178
Hughes, John, 198
Humboldt, Baron von, 205
Hungary, suicide statistics, 236
Hunter, John, 205
Huntington, George, 237
Huntington's chorea, **237–9**,
  292–3
Huschke, Emil, 63
Huxley, A. F., 98
Huxley, Aldous, 159, 263
Huxley, Julian, 7, 10, 17
hyaline membrane, 42
hydra, 164
hydrocephalus, xix, 45, 222,
  228–33
  and genius, 205
hyperactivity, 52, 241
hyperthermia, 278
hyperthyroidism, 92
hypnosis, **140–1**
hypochondria, 283, 288
hypogastric plexus, 87, 88
hypogeusia, 188, 189
hypoglossal nerve, **77**
hypothalamus, 65–6, **92–4**
  and sympathetic nervous
  system, 87, 88

Iceland, suicide statistics, 263
Idea of a New Anatomy
  (Charles Bell), 58

Illingworth, Prof. R. S., 46, 50, 52
  on childbirth and mental deficiency, 242, 243
impulse transmissions, **97–102**
  see also brain waves
infundibulum, 66, 90
insects, 5, 135
Institute of Neurology, London, 155
insulin, 148
intelligence, **148–152**
  and abnormal ability, 204–15
  and brain size, xvi, 3, 5, 54–5
  and evolution, 8–10
  and mental deficiency, 215–19
  and sleep, 135
  development of in children, 49–52
  and education, 212–15
  inheritance and, 206, 242
  tests, 149–52, 213, 214
  see also education; learning; reading; speech
Intelligence: The Battle for the Mind (Eysenck and Kamin), 150
International Association for the Study of Pain, 195, 200
Interpretation of Dreams, The (Freud), 138
Intractable Pain Society, 195
invertebrates, nervous systems of, 19–26
  see also under individual headings
Ireland, suicide statistics, 263
Isidore of Seville, 159, 161
Israel, suicide statistics, 263–4

Jack the Ripper, 122
Jacksonian fit, **143**
Jahoda, Prof. Marie, 146

James, William, 128
  on memory, 164, 173
  on perception, 175
  on suffering, 262
Japan, 166
  highest IQ in, 151–2
  suicide statistics, 263
Jennett, B., 247, 248
Jerusalem, 236
John, E. R., 128
John Paul II, 236
Johns Hopkins University, 102, 199
Johnson, Samuel, 158, 186
Jones, Wood, 176
Jonson, Ben, 152, 156, 166
Journal of Nervous and Mental Disease, 264
jugular vein, 84
Julius Caesar, 206
Jung, C. G., 129

Kamin, Leon, 150
Kant, Immanuel, 205, 206, 213
Kaye, Danny, 122
Keats, John, 206
Keele, C. A., 193, 194
Keen, William Williams, 276
Keith, Sir Arthur, 13
Keith's Rubicon, 13
Kelvin, Lord, 207
Kendell, Prof. R. E., 316
Kennedy, President John F., 283
Kennedy, Prof. Ian, 296, 297
Kepler, Johann, 207, 213
Kerr, Dr James, 157–8
Keynes, Maynard, 127
kidney, 89, 91
  transplants, 296, 297, 302–3, 304
Kierkegaard, Sören, 127
Kille, Leonard, 311
Kimovsk, 252

Kipling, Rudyard, 204
Klein, William, 212
Kleitman, Nathaniel, 138
Koestler, Arthur, 2, 173
Köhler, Otto, 153
Kosterlitz, Hans, 198
Krause's end bulbs, 190
Krause, Wilhelm, 190
Kuffler, Stephen, W., 30
Kussmaul, A., 157

Laetoli, 8
Laing, R. D., 265
lampreys, 26
Lancaster, Jane, 15
Lancet, the, 267, 269
    on acupuncture, 200–1
    on aspirin, 318
    on brain damage, 240
    on brain-death controversy,
        301, 302, 306
    on depression, 264
    on Down's syndrome, 237
    on dyslexia, 158
    on ECT, 313–14
    on EEG, 104–5
    on head injury, 248, 256
    on hypothalamus, 93
    on low birthweight babies,
        42
    on memory experiments,
        168
    on mental patients, 220
    on mesmerism, 140
    on migraine, 261
    on pain, 195
    on retardation, 217
    on split brain, 114
    on strokes, 273, 274
    on X-rays, 247
Landau, Lev, 212
Landseer, Sir Edwin, 124
La Rochefoucauld, Duc de,
    282, 285

larynx, human, **154–5**
    and speech, 153, 154
Lashley, Karl, 169–70
Laski, Harold, 174
lateral geniculate nuclei, 177,
    178
Lawrence, Ruth, 213–14
Leakey, Louis, 13
Leakey, Mary, 8
Leakey, Richard, 4, 8
learning, **146–8**
left-handedness, 122–6
lepidoptera, 24
levadopa, 271
Levine, Dr John D., 196, 197
Levy, David, 321
Lincoln, Abraham, 208
Linnaeus, 205
Lister, Lord, 276
lizards, 27
lobotomy, 119, 310–12
Locke, John, 128
loligo (visual squid), 25
Lombroso, Cesare, 205, 206
Longfellow, Henry, 207
Lorber, Prof. John, 230, 231
Lorenz, Konrad, 147
Los Angeles, 247
Louis XVI, 140
Lowrey, G. H., 40
Lubs, Herbert, 217, 218
lumbar nerves, 78, 79, **80**
lumbar plexus, 79, 82
lumbar vertebrae, 78
Lumbricus, 23
Luria, Alexander, 166
    and investigation of
        memory, 172–3
    and Zasetsky, 250–2
Luther, Martin, 213
Lynn, Richard, 152

Macaulay, Lord, 146
Machiavelli, Niccolo, 205

machine intelligence, 320–1
Maddock, Sir Ieuan, 174
Madrid, 61
Magdalenian culture, 14
Malpighi, Marcello, 62
*Mammalian Cerebral Cortex,
    The* (Burns), 168
mammals
    abilities at birth, 42
    and evolution, 6, 7
    brain structure of, 28–9
mammillary bodies, 66
Man of Genius, The
    (Lombroso), 205–6
Manschreck, Dr Theo C., 267,
    268
Marcz, Darren, 133–4
Mark, Dr Vernon H., 311
Martin, Leotis, 254
Marx, Groucho, 95
Marx, Harpo, 122
Massachusetts Institute of
    Technology, 209
mastectomy, 116
Matthews, Dr W. B., 188
    and brain tumours, 276–7
    and EEG, 104–5
Maugham, Somerset, 286
Maupassant, Guy de, 54
Mayor, D., 181
Maxwell, James, 208
McCartney, Paul, 122
McGraw, M., 46
McManus, I. C., 112
Meaning of Intelligence, The
    (Stoddard), 148
Meanwood Park Hospital,
    Leeds, 216
Medawar, Sir Peter, 146, 163
median (superior) longitudinal
    fissure, 69, 71
Medical and Surgical Reporter,
    237
Medical News-Tribune, 222

Medical Research Council,
    London, 217, 263
Medical World News, 254, 265
medulla oblongata, 65
    and sympathetic nervous
        system, 87
    cranial nerves and, 76, 77
    foetal development of, 36
    in mammals and reptiles, 27,
        28
Mehemet Ali, 207
Meissner, George, 190
Meissner's corpuscles, 190
Melbourne, Lord, 146
Melnick, Michael, 248–9
membrane chemistry, 33
memory, **164–70**, 173–4
    amnesia, 170–3
    and learning, 147
    of musicians, 3
    of old people, 284, 286, 293
Mendel, George, 238
Mendelian laws, 51
meninges, **72–3**
meningitis, 73, 258
mental deficiency, 53, 215–19
    and thyroid, 91–2
    causes of, 217–19
mesencephalon, 36, 64
Mesmer, Franz, 140, 141
mesoderm, 31
Mesopotamia, 18
metencephalon, 36
Mexico, cancer statistics, 278
Michelangelo, 122, 206
Michie, Donald, 320
microcephalus, 45
microcephaly, 52
mid-brain, 75
    and parasympathetic
        nervous system, 87
    parts of, 65
migraine, xii, 257, 259–61
Miles, C. P., 264

Mill, John Stuart, 207, 208
Miller, Henry, 188, 277
Milton, John, 205, 206
mind, xvii–xviii
  mental ageing, 285
  mental development of
    children, 45–52
  see also brain; intelligence;
    memory
Mind, 287
Mind of a Mnemonist, The
  (Luria), 173
Mirabeau, Comte de, 204
Mitchell, G. A. G., 181
mitral cells, 187
molluscs, 21, 24–5
mongolism *see* Down's
  syndrome
Moniz, Egon, 310, 311
monkeys
  abilities at birth, 42
  and communication, 15
  and consciousness, 129
  dexterity of, 12
  hearing ability of, 184
Moreau, Jeanne, 284
Moro reflex, 40, **43**
morphine, 196
  and enkephalins, 198–9
motorcycle accidents, 256
motor nerves, 74–7, 81
Mountcastle, Vernon B., 175
Mozart, Wolfgang Amadeus, 3
  early ability of, 161, 207
Müller, C., 288
Müller, G. E., 168
Müller, Johannes, 97
Murphy, T. M., 200
music, 158–61
myelinisation (sheathing of
  nerve fibres), 37
myxedema, 92

naloxone, 199, 201

Napier, John, 15, 125
Napoleon, 206
narcolepsy, 138
National Association of Mental
  Health, 220, 286
National Enquirer, 249
National Hospital for Nervous
  Diseases, London, 294
National Institute of Mental
  Health, 312
National Institute on
  Alcoholism and Alcohol
  Abuse (US), 316–17
Nature, 152
Nelson, Horatio, 122, 205
nematodes (round worms), 23
nemertines (marine worms), 23
Nemesius, Bishop of Emesia,
  59
Neminski, Prawdwicz, 103
neonates, human, 34, 38
  and active sleep, 139
  and asymmetry, 115
  and brain damage, 240
  and consciousness, 128
  and learning, 147
  and speech, 153–4
  and split-brain, 120
nerve cells (neurons), 2, 4, 5,
  95–100
  and brain growth, 5–6
  and impulse transmission,
    97–100
  and intelligence, 55
  and vision, 177, 178
  damaged, 272–3
  decayed, 284
  foetal development of, 32–5,
    36, 37, 38
  of invertebrates, 19, 21, 24,
    25
  of vertebrates, 25–9
nervous system
  abnormalities, xii, 222–39

nervous system – *cont.*
  and hypothalamus, 65–6
  autonomic, 85–95
  cerebral and spinal nerves
    of, 73–84
  development of in
    childhood, 46–50
  foetal development of, 30–3
  human, 33–8
    and prematurity, 40–2
  of babies, 42–4
  of invertebrates, 19–26
  see also brain; nerve cells;
    reflexes
neural development, in
    childhood, 46–50
neuralgia, 82, 258
neural plate, 31–2
neural tissue, 32–3
neural tube defects, 222–8
neurocranium, growth and
    development of, 45–6, 49
neuroleptic drugs, 268
neurology, history of, 58–63
neurosurgery, 275, 278, 279
  see also commissurotomy;
    lobotomy
neuro-transmitters, 100–2
neurons *see* nerve cells
Neuron to Brain (Kuffler and
    Nicholls), 30
Nevada, 155
*New England Journal of
    Medicine*
  on alcoholism, 317
  on cause of death, 306
  on Down's syndrome, 218
  on drug prescription, 265
  on epilepsy, 144–5
  on schizophrenia, 267
  on senile dementia, 290–1
  on suffering, 195
New Scientist, 150, 301
New University, Ulster, 152

New York, 235, 254
New York Academy of
    Sciences, 156
Newman, Ernest, 161
Newman, I., 159
Newton, Isaac, 12, 175
  and genius, 205, 206, 208
Nicholls, John G., 30
Nightingale, Florence, 206
Nixon, Richard, 172
nodes of Ranvier, 96
noradrenaline, 88, 100, 260
Northern Ireland, suicide
    statistics, 262, 263–4
Norway, 253
  suicide statistics, 263
Notoplana, 22
Novich, Dr Max M., 256

Oates, Titus, 207
occipital lobe, 69, 177
octopus, 25
oculomotor nerve, **75**
odonata (dragonfly), 24
Ogawa, F., 23
old age, and memory, 173–4
Olduvai Gorge, 8
olfaction, xi, **185–8**
  anosmia, xi, 187, 189
  and fore-brain, 7, 66–7
  in lepidoptera and lampreys,
    24, 26
olfactory bulb, 187
olfactory nerve, **74**, 186
olfactory system, 186, 187
Open University, 150
optic chiasma, 66
optic lobes, 27
  in humans, 66, 177
  in squids and birds, 25, 28
optic nerve, **74–5**, 177
organ transplantation, 299–300
  kidney transplants, 296, 297,
    302–3, 304

Osler, Sir William, 240
Owen, Johnny, 253
Oxford University, and gifted
    children, 213–14

Pacinian corpuscles, 190
Pacini, Filippo, 190
Padua, 61
Paget, Sir Richard, 11
pain, 192–7
    receptor for, 190
    relief, 194–5
    surgical, 196, 197
    see also drugs under
        individual headings;
        endorphins; enkephalins;
        phantom pain
Paine, Dr Richmond S., 241,
    242
palate, 188
Panorama (BBC), and
    brain-death controversy,
    300, 301, 302
paracetamol, 318–19
paralexis, 157
paramecium, 33
paranoia, 283, 288
paraplegia, 244–5
parasympathetic nervous
    system, 85–8, 89
    and hypothalamus, 92
Paré, Ambroise, 197
parietal lobe, 69
parieto-occipital fissure, 37
Parker, Dorothy, 282
Parkinson, C. Northcote, 301
Parkinson, James, 271
Parkinsonism, xii, 67, 124,
    270–1
    and dopamine, 269
parosmia, 187
Pascal, Blaise, 207
Pasteur, Louis, 213
Paul, Dr R., 302

Pavlov, Ivan, xvii, 160
penduncles, 65
Penfield, Wilder, 63
Penrose, Lionel S., 217, 234
peptides, 101
Perlstein, M., 243
personality development, in
    children, 51
petit mal, 143
Petrarch, 205
Pfeiffer, E., 288
phantom limbs, 176, **197–8**
    sensations, 115–16
phantom pain, 193
    treatment of, 197–8
phenobarbitones, 144
phenylketonuria, 239, 241
pheromones, 187
Philosophy of Sciences 1838
    (Ampère), 107
phrenic nerve, 81
phrenology, 55, 62–3
pia mater (meninges), 72, 78
Picasso, P., 161
Piccolomini, Archangelo, 61
Pick, Arnold, 292
Pick's disease, 292
Pilzecker, A., 168
pineal gland, 27, 62, **65**
pinna, 182
Pintor Lupe, 253
Pithecanthropus alalus, 11
Pitkin, Walter B., 283
pituitary fossa, 196
pituitary gland (hypophysis
    cerebri), 66, 88, 89, **90–1**
    and thyroid, 92
pituitrin, 91
placebos, 196, 201
    and acupuncture, 200
Plato, 152, 167
platyhelminthes, 22
Poe, Edgar Allan, 297
Pollak, Shasa, 166

Poland, suicide statistics, 263
Polenov Neurological Institute, Leningrad, 245
pons Variolus, 65
  and parasympathetic nervous system, 87
  cranial nerves and, 75, 76
Pope, Alexander, 205, 206
Popper, Karl, xvi, 151, 154
porifera (sponges), 22
postcentral gyrus, 191
potassium ions, in neurons, 97–9
pregnancy
  and alcohol, 317
  and neural tube defects, 222–3, 226
  diary of a, 34–8
  Down's syndrome and, 235
prematurity, 38–9
  and low birth-weight, 39–40, 40–1
  dangers of, 41–2
  cerebral palsy, 242, 243–4
primates and evolution, 6–7
primitive man
  evolution of, 6–10
  dexterity of, 12–14
  speech of, 10–11
  see also tool-making
Princeton University, 150
proprioception, **175–6,** 190–1
prosencephalon, 64
protozoa (single-celled animals), 21, 164
psychiatric disorders *see under* individual headings
Psychology: A Dictionary of the Mind, Brain and Behaviour (Evans), 128–9, 147, 148
  definition of memory, 167
Psychology News, 150
pulmonary plexus, 87

Punch, 127
pyroteuthis (squid), 25
Pythagoras, 59

Queensberry rules, 254
Quinlan, Karen Ann, 295, 305
Quinn, William G., 33, 308

Raglan, Lord, 17–18
Rampton Special Hospital, 220
Ranvier, Louis, 96
rapid-eye-movement (REM), 135, 140
reading, **156–8**
Reagan, President Ronald, 317
reflexes of newborn babies, **42–4**
reptiles, 135
  and evolution, 6, 7, 82
  brain construction of, 26–7
retina, 74, 177
retrolental fibroplasia, 41, 42
rhinencephalon, 66–7
rhombencephalon, 64
right-handedness, 122–6
Rivers, R. P. A., 244
Rix, Brian, 222
rodents, 42, 182
Rolando fissure, 69
Romer, Alfred S., 29
rooting reflex, **43**
Rose, Prof. Steven, xvi, 150
Rotterdam, 247
Rouse, Dr Robert, 188
Royal College of Physicians, 19, 290
Royal College of Radiologists, 246
Royal Hospital for Sick Children, Glasgow, 317
Royal Society, 62
Rubens, P. P., 207
Ruffini, Angelo, 190
Ruffini's end organ, 190

Russell, W. Richie, 128
Ruysch, Frederick, 62

sacral nerves, 78, 79, **80**
sacral plexus, 79, 82
sacrum, 78
St Joseph's Hospice, London, 196
St Vitus's chorea, 67
Salzburg, 159
San Diego School of Medicine, 267
San Francisco, 196
Samaritans, 263
Saroyan, William, 282
Schildkraut, Dr Joseph J., 264
Schiller, Friedrich von, 207
schizophrenia, xii, 265–70
    and lobotomy, 310
    and suicide, 264
Schwann cells, 96
Schwann, Theodor, 96
Scientific American, 177
sciatic nerve, 82
Scotland, alcoholism in, 316, 317
Scott, Sir Walter, 207, 208
Sears, T. A., 155
Seeing With Two Eyes (Frisby), 179
Seneca, 204
senile dementia, 270, 287–95
senses, 175–201
    see also under individual headings
sensory cortex, 191
sensory fibres, 78, 191
sensory nerves
    cranial, 74–7, 78
    spinal, 79–80, 81
serotonin, 260, 261
Severtsov Institute, Moscow, 135

Shakespeare, William, 70, 146, 206
sharks, 26, 27
Shaw, George Bernard, 41, 139
Sheffield University, 230, 242
Shelley, P. B., 206
Sherrington, Charles, xviii, 253
Shirley, M. M., 51
situs inversus totalis, 110–11, 113
skin
    and pain, 193
    and touch, 190
    as external nervous system, 176
skull, **44–5**
    fracture, 134
sleep, **134–8**
    deprivation, 136–7
smelling, **185–8**
    see also olfaction
Smetana, B., 161
Smith, Adam, 205, 206
Smith Papyrus, 56
Smolensk, 250
snails, 25
Snyder, Solomon, 102
Society for Neuroscience, 197
Society of British Neurological Surgeons, 312
sodium ions, in neurons, 97–9
solar (coeliac) plexus, 87, 88
Soviet Union, and lobotomy, 312
    suicide statistics, 261
Spain, suicide statistics, 263–4
speech, **152–6**
    and brain hemispheres, 115, 120
    and language development, 15, 152–3
        in children, 48, 49
    aphasia, 157
    origin of, **10–11**, 13–14

speech disorders, and left side of brain, 114–15
Sperry, R. W., 130
Sphenodon, 27
spina bifida, 222–4, 227
spinal column, 78
spinal cord, 73
  and nervous system, 87
  as sensory pathway, 191
  nerves of, 77–82
spinal nerves, **77–82**
Spinoza, Benedict, 206
split-brain, 113–4, **117–20**, 145
sport and head injuries, 255–6
  see also boxing injuries
Spurzheim, Johann Caspar, 63
stammering, 125, 205
Stanford, Charles, 3
Stephenson, George, 208
stereopsis, 178–9
Sterne, Laurence, 205, 206
sterno-mastoid muscle, 81
steroids, 89, 247
Steward, William H., 207
Stoddard, Dr George, 148
Storar, John, 305, 306
stroke, xii, 271–5
Study of British Genius, A 1904 (Ellis), 206–7
sub-arachnoid haemorrhage, 255
subthalamus, **65**
suicide, 261–5
  and alcohol, 315
  and war wounds, 249
sulci, 63
  and blood supply to brain, 83–4
  description of, **69–70**
  foetal development of, 37, 38
sulphonamides, 319
surgical pain relief, 196, 197
Sussex University, 169
Sweden, 235

suicide statistics, 263
Swedish Medical Society, 298
Swift, Jonathan, 54, 127, 146
Switzerland, suicide statistics, 263
Sydney, 196
Sylvian fissure, 62, 114
  description of, **69–70**
  foetal development of, 36, 37
symmetry, **110–17**
  and hemispherectomy, 121–2
  and split-brain, 117–20
sympathetic nervous system, 79, **85–8**, 89
  and hypothalamus, 92
synapses (nerve cell connections), 2, 4, 6, **100–2**
  and senile dementia, 293
  and smell, 187
  and vision, 177, 178
  of *Ascaris*, 21

tabes dorsalis, 191
Tanzania, 8
Tasmania, 15, 18
Tasso, Torquato, 205, 207
tasting, **188–9**
Taylor, A. J. P., 282
tectum, 65
tegmentum, 65
telencephalon, 36, 64
  function of, 66–7
teleosts (bony fish), 26, 32
Temple University, Philadelphia, 306
temporal lobe, 69, 70, 74
Terman, L. M., 214
thalamus, **65**, 71
  and sensation location, 191, 192
Themistocles, 166
Thompson, John, 249

thoracic nerves, 78, 79, **80**, 82
thoracic vertebrae, 78
throat, 188
Thurber, James, 284
thyroid, **91–2**
Tiberius, 122
Time magazine, 254
Tolstoy, Leo, 49, 54
Tomoyori, Hideaki, 166
tongue, 188, 189
tonic neck reflex, **43**
tonsils, 188
tool-making, 17
   evolution of, 9, 13, 14
Toscanini, Arturo, 166
touching, **190–2**
Touretzky, David S., 320, 321
trachea, 84
trapezius muscle, 81
Trevarthen, Colwyn, and
   consciousness, 128, 129,
   130
tricyclics, 319
trigeminal nerve, **75**
trisomy 21 *see* Down's
   syndrome
trochlear nerve, **75**
Trotter, Thomas, 315
Truman, President, 208
tuberculosis, 89
Tubipora, 22
Tubularia, 22
Tufts College, 210
Tufts-New England Medical
   Center, 245
Tulane University, 16
tumours, cerebral, 275–8
Turgenev, Ivan, 54, 55
Turin University, 205
Turner, G., 218
turtles, 27
Twain, Mark, 30, 268
twins, 125
tympanum, 182

*Über das Elektrenkephalogram
   des Menschen* (Berger),
   103
unconsciousness, **130–4**
   and brain-death, 296
   and convulsions, 142, 143,
   145
   see also coma
ungulates, 12, 42
United Kingdom
   alcoholism statistics, 316
   lobotomy statistics, 311
   suicide statistics, 262, 263
United States of America, 41
   alcoholism in, 315
   ECT in, 312–13
   lobotomy statistics, 311
   suicides in, 264, 265
   statistics for, 262, 263
University College, London,
   140

vagus nerve, **76**
Valium, 320
Vanderbilt University, 186
Van Leeuwenhoek, Anton, 62
Varolius, 64
Veniaminoff, Solomon, 166,
   172–3
ventricles, theories of function
   of, 59–60, 61, 62
Vernon, Philip, and gifted
   children, 212, 213, 214,
   215
vertebral arteries, 83
vertebrates, 32
   nervous system of, 25–29
Vesalius, Andreas, 60–1
Virgil, 205
vision, **177–81**
   in children, 47, 50
visual cortex, 75, 177, 178
   and reading, 157
   damage to, 251

Voltaire, François, 206, 207

Wallace, Alfred Russel, 322
War of '39, The (Hayes), 116
war wounds, 249–52
Washington, George, 208
Washoe (chimpanzee), and
    language learning, 155,
    156
Wassersug, Dr Joseph D.,
    257–8
Watson, E. H., 40
Watson, J. B., 51
Watts, Geoff, 194
Watts, G. T., 247
Weiner, Dr S., 218
Weiner, J. S., 15
Wellington, Duke of, 208
Welsh National School of
    Medicine, 252
Wernicke, Carl, 17, 114, 153
What Music Can Do (Isidore of
    Seville), 159
Wheatstone, Charles, 179
White, T. H., 188
Whitehead, A. N., 85, 146
Whitman, Walt, 55, 319
Wiener, Norbert, 107
    childhood of, 209–12, 215
Wiesel, Torsten N., 178
Willis, Thomas, xvii, 64
    and study of neurology, 61–2

Wisby, Audrey, 158
Wiseman, Cardinal, 208
Wolff, Charlotte, 15
Wolff, Harold, 259
Wolsey, Cardinal, 207
World Boxing Association, 256
World Congress on Pain, 195
World Health Organisation,
    145, 216, 246
    alcoholism statistics, 315
    suicide statistics, 263
World Medicine, 188
    on benzodiazepines, 319
    on learning disorders, 158
    on Lorber's work, 230
    on pain relief, 194
worms, 23–4
Wren, Sir Christopher, 62, 205
Wright brothers, 208
Wyke, Maria, A., 160

X-chromosome, and mental
    retardation, 217–19
Ximenes, 205
X-rays and head injury, 246–7

Yo-Yo Ma, 215

Zasetsky, Lyova, 172, 250–2

MORE ABOUT PENGUINS, PELICANS, PEREGRINES AND PUFFINS

For further information about books available from Penguins please write to Dept EP, Penguin Books Ltd, Harmondsworth, Middlesex UB7 0DA.

In the U.S.A.: For a complete list of books available from Penguins in the United States write to Dept DG, Penguin Books, 299 Murray Hill Parkway, East Rutherford, New Jersey 07073.

In Canada: For a complete list of books available from Penguins in Canada write to Penguin Books Canada Ltd, 2801 John Street, Markham, Ontario L3R 1B4.

In Australia: For a complete list of books available from Penguins in Australia write to the Marketing Department, Penguin Books Australia Ltd, P.O. Box 257, Ringwood, Victoria 3134.

In New Zealand: For a complete list of books available from Penguins in New Zealand write to the Marketing Department, Penguin Books (N.Z.) Ltd, Private Bag, Takapuna, Auckland 9.

In India: For a complete list of books available from Penguins in India write to Penguin Overseas Ltd, 706 Eros Apartments, 56 Nehru Place, New Delhi 110019.

Also by Anthony Smith in Pelican

THE BODY

'The masterpiece among all those works that tell us how we work and how we don't' – Alistair Cooke

Translated into fourteen languages and later filmed, *The Body* is a stunning achievement.

In it Anthony Smith examines the human body marshalling an amazing array of facts to define its functions, abilities, limits and peculiarities. From sex and reproduction, to digestion, sleep and the senses, his book is an unbeatable reference source supplemented by a variety of information on such topics as inheritance, circumcision, twinning and haemophilia.

'A riot of fact, definitive, informative, curious' – *Economist*

'I love it! The author's quantity of information is enormous' – Isaac Asimov